Also by Constantine C. Menges

Spain: The Struggle for Democracy Today

INSIDE THE NATIONAL SECURITY COUNCIL

THE TRUE STORY OF
THE MAKING AND UNMAKING OF
REAGAN'S FOREIGN POLICY

CONSTANTINE C. MENGES

A TOUCHSTONE BOOK
Published by Simon & Schuster Inc.
NEW YORK   LONDON   TORONTO   SYDNEY   TOKYO

Touchstone
Simon & Schuster Building
Rockefeller Center
1230 Avenue of the Americas
New York, New York 10020

Copyright © 1988 by Constantine C. Menges
First Touchstone Edition, September 1989
TOUCHSTONE and colophon are registered trademarks
of Simon & Schuster Inc.
Designed by Irving Perkins Associates
Manufactured in the United States of America

1 3 5 7 9 10 8 6 4 2

1 3 5 7 9 10 8 6 4 2 Pbk.

Library of Congress Cataloging in Publication Data

Menges, Constantine Christopher.
Inside the National Security Council: the true story of the making
and unmaking of Reagan's foreign policy / Constantine C. Menges.

p. cm.
Bibliography: p.
Includes index.
1. National Security Council (U.S.)—History. 2. United
States—National security—Decision making. 3. United States—
Foreign relations—Decision making. 4. United States—Foreign
relations—1981- 5. Menges, Constantine Christopher. I. Title.
UA23.M465 1988
353.0089—dc19   88-18289
                                                              CIP

ISBN 0-671-64996-5
ISBN 0-671-68734-4 Pbk.

WITH DEEPEST APPRECIATION TO MY PARENTS
FOR THEIR LOVE AND THOUGHTFULNESS:
VALESKA M. MENGES
KARL H. MENGES

CONTENTS

PREFACE

After serving as a foreign policy adviser to candidate Ronald Reagan in 1980, I was pleased to join his administration, working two years for the Director of Central Intelligence and then three years as a special assistant to the president with the National Security Council staff in the White House. Among the officials I saw and worked with during these years are George Bush, William Casey, William Clark, Jeane Kirkpatrick, Robert McFarlane, Oliver North, John Poindexter, George Shultz, Caspar Weinberger and the president.

The good news from my experiences during those five years is that the overwhelming majority of career and political officials working on foreign policy performed their duties properly and with respect for the authority of the president and our laws. Unfortunately, I also encountered a small but influential group of foreign policy officials who believed they knew better than the president what was best for the country and who could and would manipulate events to attain their preferred course of action.

These officials constituted what I came to view as a subculture of manipulation and deception inside the foreign policy institutions of the executive branch. And the persons they were in effect manipulating were the president, the millions of voters who had elected him and those members of his Cabinet and subcabinet who were trying to carry out his decisions. The events I witnessed and describe went far beyond the normal competition and differences of viewpoint among the various policy agencies. Even before I learned about the Iran-contra issues along

11

with everyone else in November 1986, I had felt that there were serious ethical problems in the functioning of the foreign policy institutions, and in August 1985 I wrote President Reagan a letter to warn him about this but was unable to get it to him.

I began writing this book immediately after leaving the Reagan White House in the summer of 1986. My purpose has been to help my fellow citizens and future presidents—whether they are Republicans or Democrats—understand how the manipulative elements of our foreign policy institutions really operate against a president, so that future presidents will have a better chance to exercise their full constitutional authority in foreign policy.

This book describes dramatic and hard-fought inside battles about major foreign policy issues (Central America, the Reagan Doctrine, international terrorism and armed subversion, Grenada) in which I participated. The episodes illustrate how the foreign policy process worked well—and how it failed. There was secret plotting by cabinet-level officials who deliberately kept their peers in the dark hoping to create situations that would assure their policy views would prevail. This included what seemed to me calculated attempts to keep information about major foreign events and plans from President Reagan himself. These stories reveal the inner world of power and competition, how the National Security staff really functions, what it did for the president and what it failed to do. There are cliff-hangers—situations where major setbacks were averted only by last-minute decisions of the president preceded by intense conflict and maneuvering among members of his foreign policy cabinet.

My consistent effort was to assure that President Reagan had full and fair information on major foreign policy issues for which I was responsible, that he made the major decisions and that the executive branch carried these out. This was my understanding of the purpose of the NSC staff. Whether readers agree or disagree with President Reagan's policies and decisions, I believe virtually all will concur that the president we elect—not unelected subordinates in the executive branch—should be in charge of foreign policy. This book tells about the real obstacles and challenges that every modern president confronts in the management of large, complex foreign policy institutions in a fast-moving and dangerous world.

Most Americans instinctively understand that in these times the greatest challenge facing our presidents is to defend our freedom while maintaining peace. At the end of World War II, the United States helped establish the United Nations collective security system to settle disputes and prevent violence among governments. The United States proposed international control of nuclear weapons, quickly demobilized most of its more than ten million strong armed forces, dismantled its intelligence service and emphasized peaceful reconstruction of the defeated and devastated countries. Unfortunately, the Soviet Union maintained an army of millions and broke the solemn commitments it had made at three summit meetings of the Grand Alliance. Instead of permitting genuinely free elections in the newly liberated countries of Eastern Europe as promised at Yalta, it began a decades-long process of military buildup and aggression through armed subversion. The result has been that hundreds of millions of people have been brought under the power of pro-Soviet dictatorships and have then seen their countries harnessed to this continuing indirect aggression against additional free-world countries.

Beginning in 1947, to counter these dangers and to assist in the rebuilding of democracy and economic vitality the United States established entirely new peacetime institutions. These included economic reconstruction, international information institutions, a central intelligence agency and sizeable peacetime armed forces. These new institutions were now direct participants in foreign policy, joining the long-established diplomatic and consular service of the Department of State.

All were under the direct authority of the president as head of the executive branch. But could any one person really lead and manage these foreign policy agencies comprising hundreds of thousands of career employees with many based abroad and conducting secret as well as open activities in hostile and dangerous situations? To help the president effectively lead and control the foreign policy agencies, Congress established the National Security Council in 1947 with this mandate:

> The function of the council shall be to advise the President with respect to the integration of domestic, foreign, and military policies relating to the national security so as to enable the military services and the other departments and agencies of the Government to cooperate more effectively in matters involving the national security.

By law the members of the NSC are the president, vice president, secretary of state and secretary of defense. The president may appoint others, and among the regular participants during my experience were the attorney general, secretary of the treasury, the U.S. ambassador to the United Nations, and director of central intelligence and the chairman of the Joint Chiefs of Staff.

As the Tower Commission concluded in 1987, the National Security adviser and his staff are supposed to provide "advice from the President's viewpoint unalloyed by institutional responsibilities and biases. Unlike the Secretaries of State or Defense, who have substantial organizations for which they are responsible, the President is the National Security Adviser's only constituency."

That was how I understood the function of the NSC staff when I joined it in 1983. As an analyst of and participant in foreign policy issues for more than twenty years, I had seen, read about, and even taught university courses about the competition among government agencies in the making of foreign policy. (There is a significant literature on this usually labeled "bureaucratic politics.") Much of this competition is inevitable because it derives from the understandably different ways the foreign policy agencies will approach issues and from different personal judgments senior officials will have about major issues in the context of uncertainty. These conflicts and differences are a normal part of life and can be very constructive for a president if there is a process which assures that this competition is conducted in an honorable and fair way, providing full information to the president and his senior advisers. It is the NSC staff that is intrinsically responsible for assuring that the president has full information, that he is not manipulated by acts of omission or commission, that he makes the key decisions and that they are obeyed.

As I tried to fulfill this responsibility to the president, I was astonished by the ever more cunning maneuvers of the manipulative elements within the foreign-policy process. On Central America alone there were, I believed, seven attempts to end run clear, written policy decisions of the president. An important reason why I knew that President Reagan really meant what he said in his public speeches and in his top-secret National Security Decision Directives is that when these end runs were made known to him and when he heard the sometimes heated debate at NSC meetings he *always* held to his policy.

There has been virtually no public information about these episodes because I and the members of the foreign policy cabinet who acted to assure that President Reagan remained in charge did not discuss these confrontations with the media at the time. In contrast the manipulative elements of the foreign policy organizations tended to use the media frequently to embarrass, diminish or attack their policy opponents within the administration. Also, they sometimes seemed to use the media to recast these events and to set the stage for the next end run. Besides my hope that public knowledge of these stories will help future presidents and improve the way foreign policy is made, it is important to our understanding of history and to genuine accountability that this side of these events also be presented.

When I entered the Reagan administration I had no explicit intention to write a book. If I had thought about writing something after leaving public service, it most likely would have been a book about the substance of the foreign policy issues, not about the struggles to determine policy. It was the experiences and my concern about the future that impelled me to write this book.

I understand full well that I am describing the events as I lived and perceived them; other participants may well have different perceptions of events. This book represents my honest recollections and judgments based upon my firsthand experiences and reinforced by my practice of maintaining daily records of key events, conversations and actions I was required to do. My reason for keeping these daily notes was simply to enable me to perform my duties and to keep track of the enormous number of events, judgments, surprises and future required actions so that I could correctly and honestly convey the views of the foreign policy leadership to the National Security adviser and the president in my areas of responsibility. If I had a conversation personally or on the telephone with a member of the cabinet or subcabinet, for example, I would tend to note down the comments, often using direct quotations, so that I could convey the flavor as well as the content. I also spent an intense two weeks in the summer of 1985 doing a thorough chronology and analysis of all key memoranda and information which documented the warning I sought to convey in my letter to President Reagan.

When I am dealing with public officials as part of my official duties I name them. I have kept my observations to the public life of public officials. In some cases I approached members of Congress and private citizens who are friends of the president in an effort to get information to President Reagan. In those cases I have not named the individuals because they were acting on a personal basis rather than as part of their official duties and I want to respect their privacy.

Naturally as each new president assumes office there is a sense of renewal and an understandable feeling that the last administration's problems were due to the top echelon which has ostensibly now been replaced. Every new president and his supporters believe he will avoid those problems. Certainly those of us who supported Ronald Reagan in 1980 and subsequently joined his administration were determined to help him govern effectively in foreign policy and avoid the manipulation and unilateral, unauthorized actions by elements of the foreign policy institutions which had occurred in previous administrations. Although specific individuals are responsible for their specific actions, and some are gone while others are unlikely to serve the president, the problem posed by the subculture of manipulation will remain.

I offer three situations I witnessed from outside that adversely affected three presidents. In 1968 a top-secret cable was leaked and caused a major setback for President Lyndon B. Johnson. I believe that partly as a result of that unauthorized action and its impact, President Johnson announced the next month that he would not run for renomination or reelection. In November 1968 Richard Nixon was elected president.

Reportedly, in 1978 President Jimmy Carter personally telephoned the editor of a major newspaper requesting that it not publish a highly sensitive unauthorized leak about our negotiations with the Soviet Union. The newspaper went ahead and published a story saying that the recent decision of the United States to suspend strategic arms negotiations was only a bargaining ploy and that the Carter Administration would be back at the negotiating table soon.

A February 1988 report said "An American commitment in 1985 to end military aid to the Afghan guerrillas at the beginning of a Soviet troop withdrawal was made without the knowledge or approval of President Reagan, according to White House and State Department officials " (New York Times, February 11, 1988). On February 23, 1988, at a discussion of this issue at the American Enterprise Institute which included Jeane Kirkpatrick and myself, Senator Gordon Humphrey (Republican of New Hampshire) criticized the actions of the State Department saying: ". . . things are not quite as the State Department expresses them in this case and in most cases. It is odd, isn't it, that we agreed to become a guarantor to an agreement before its terms were known? . . . [this] was done behind the President's back . . . without the assent and apparently without the knowledge of President Reagan. . . ." That would mean for twenty-six months one part of the executive branch acted on an issue of major importance to U.S.-Soviet relations, the future stability of friendly Middle East oil states and the millions of long-suffering people of Afghanistan with its own policy rather than one set by the President.

(Partly as a result of these revelations and a bipartisan Senate resolution which called on the president to reject the State Department's formula, one change was made ostensibly affecting the agreement signed April 14, 1988, and guaranteed by the United States and the Soviet Union.)

In all three of these situations strong-minded American presidents of quite varied temperament and management style found themselves being end-run and manipulated by their subordinates. My guess is that the executive branch officials doing the manipulation believed themselves to be acting in the best interests of their country—and perhaps even of the president they were maneuvering against. It seems to me that this improper conduct is the result of a subculture of manipulation that has taken root in elements of the foreign policy bureaucracy—most especially among some, not all, senior career officials of the State Department—the habit and expectation that the decisions and orders of a president are to be observed or ignored or countered depending on their own conception of the national interest.

The dramatic episodes I experienced during the Reagan years would have seemed incredible even to me as a longtime observer of this unfortunate pattern had I not personally lived these events. It is my personal belief that our prospects for defending our freedom while maintaining peace will be much, much smaller unless this form of improper and unethical conduct within the executive is substantially reduced in the future. Contemporary international politics are too dangerous. Presidents already have to share significant authority over aspects of foreign policy with a highly assertive Congress. If our presidents cannot at least count on their own subordinates in the executive branch to behave properly and honorably they will be ever diminished in their capacity to defend and advance our values and interests in the world.

The writing of this book spanned the summer of 1986 to the spring of 1987 with some additional thoughts added after the Iran-contra issue surfaced. I am deeply grateful to my wife Nancy Goldsmith Menges for her loving encouragement and creative ideas and suggestions through succeeding drafts. Nancy's thoughtful insight about people will be evident to the reader, since I often gained important advice from her.

I am also grateful to the many competent and honorable political and career public servants with whom I worked closely at all levels of the federal government. Their hard work and dedication have made an immense difference to our country and were an inspiration to me personally. I had written a "good news" section about a number of these individuals, but limits on length have prevented that from being included. The reader will know who some of these individuals are among the people I discuss in this book. I also want to mention my great respect for White House colleagues who shared my commitment to President Reagan's foreign policy principles and from whom I often recieved important moral support and ideas. They include: White House speech writers Bentley Elliott, Anthony Dolan, Joshua Gilder, Peggy Noonan, Dana Rohrabacher, Peter Robinson; NSC colleagues Kenneth deGraffenreid, Christopher Lehman, Sven Kraemer, Roger Robinson; and others including Morton Blackwell, Patrick Buchanan, Ann Higgins, Mark Klugman, Phillip Nicolaides, Robert Reilly, Faith Whittlesey, Mona Charen—all members of what we came to call the "Reagan underground." My effectiveness and morale were also immeasurably helped by the skills, good cheer and loyalty of my two secretaries in the federal government: Mrs. Judy Huba and Mrs. Laurie Chipperfield. I appreciate the professionalism shown by the federal government organization in their review of my manuscript.

For many months in 1986 and early 1987 I had the good fortune of working with Ms. Mary Wallace, who typed this manuscript. After working forty years for the federal government Mary Wallace opened her own word processing business, and her great competence and goodwill helped me enormously.

I had the good fortune to work with Ms. Jane Dystel of the E. J. Acton Literary Agency and at Simon and Schuster with Mr. Robert Asahina. His suggestions and ideas have always been creative and have contributed to making this a more interesting and readable book.

Since mid-1987 I have been affiliated with the American Enterprise Institute. Its new president, Christopher DeMuth, and Ambassador Jeane Kirkpatrick, as head of the foreign policy program, have provided an exceptionally congenial and stimulating work environment.

INTRODUCTION

In late April of 1987, on the kind of spectacular spring day that occurs in Washington, D.C., the kind of day in which it truly seems as if nothing could possibly go wrong, I walked into the White House for the first time in months. A year ago I had worked there, with the National Security Council.

Today I was to meet a White House attorney, and he would accompany me to Capitol Hill, where I had another, and more ominous, appointment. I was to be interviewed by the chief investigator of the Joint Congressional Committee on the Iran-contra affair.

Once in the Hart Senate Office Building, and past the heavy security, we were taken into a small meeting room where four men and one woman, who turned out to be committee investigators, sat on one side of the table. The White House lawyer and I sat on the other.

There was an exchange of pleasantries and an offer of beverages, and then Mark Belnick, the chief investigator, got down to business.

"When did you join the Reagan administration?"

"In 1981," I answered. "CIA Director William Casey asked me to serve as National Intelligence Officer for Latin America."

"When did you go to work at the National Security Council?"

"In early October 1983, NSC adviser William Clark asked me to serve as special assistant to the president for National Security Affairs with the senior responsibility for Latin America."

I really had no clear idea of what he was after, but his next question served to focus his inquiry and my thoughts.

"Dr. Menges, until when were you responsible for Latin America including Central America?"

I hesitated only briefly, then said, "Until July 1985—when NSC adviser Robert McFarlane told the president and me that I was being 'moved up' to 'broader and expanded responsibilities' for international communications and public diplomacy on all key foreign policy issues."

Suddenly he picked up the pace of his questions, and I followed suit with my answers.

"Did you believe McFarlane?"

"No."

"Why was he removing you from responsibility for Latin America?"

At this point I stopped for a moment. He had brought me, very quickly, to the central reason why I had left the Reagan administration. I simply could not give him an evasive or a noncommittal answer. I took a deep mental breath and plunged in.

"Because," I said slowly and evenly, knowing full well that I might someday have to repeat this testimony before televised hearings and in full glare of national and international publicity, "Mr. McFarlane knew that on a number of occasions I objected to the fact that he and Admiral Poindexter were"—I chose my words with care—"unwilling to provide President Reagan with timely and full information on major events to assure that the president was in charge of U.S. foreign policy. . . ."

Belnick gave no indication as to what he thought of my answer one way or the other. Instead he handed me a copy of a document, which I could see was marked "Exhibit" with a number. He then passed copies to his four associates and still had a considerable pile of them in front of him.

He said to me in a calm voice, as if he were talking about a holiday greeting card, "Did you write this?"

I was momentarily stunned. He had just handed me a copy of the twelve-page letter I had written to President Reagan on August 6, 1985, a letter in which I had tried to warn him that McFarlane and Poindexter were not permitting the NSC to function in the way it was supposed to and were at times actually keeping the president in the dark. Despite my urgent requests to at least three very highly placed people who knew Ronald Reagan personally, I had not been able to get the letter to him.

"Who were these people?" he asked.

"I'm sorry," I said, "but I will not violate their privacy by telling you their names without their permission."

My answer seemed to displease Mr. Belnick. He said, "Most likely the president has not received your letter, since our copy did not come from the White House." And then it was his turn to protect a source.

Of course the president had not received my letter. If he had, there would have been repercussions—either against me or against those I had named as responsible for specific violations of President Reagan's foreign policy orders, and for the absence, after five years, of a counterstrategy against the continuing threat of international terrorism.

I was convinced that if the president had read my letter, he would have acted on it. And if he had acted on it, there would have been a major improvement in the way the NSC worked—and, I believe, the Iran-contra affair, which for a time threatened the Reagan presidency itself, would never have happened.

CONSTANTINE C. MENGES
Washington, D.C.

THE DIFFICULTY WITH MANY CAREER OFFICIALS IN THE GOVERNMENT IS THAT THEY REGARD THEMSELVES AS THE MEN WHO REALLY MAKE POLICY AND RUN THE GOVERNMENT. THEY LOOK UPON THE ELECTED OFFICIALS AS JUST TEMPORARY OCCUPANTS. EVERY PRESIDENT IN OUR HISTORY HAS BEEN FACED WITH THIS PROBLEM: HOW TO PREVENT CAREER MEN FROM CIRCUMVENTING PRESIDENTIAL POLICY. TOO OFTEN CAREER MEN SEEK TO IMPOSE THEIR OWN VIEWS INSTEAD OF CARRYING OUT THE ESTABLISHED POLICY OF THE ADMINISTRATION. . . . IT HAS HAPPENED IN THE DEPARTMENT OF STATE.

BUT I WANTED TO MAKE IT PLAIN THAT THE PRESIDENT OF THE UNITED STATES, AND NOT THE SECOND OR THIRD ECHELON IN THE STATE DEPARTMENT, IS RESPONSIBLE FOR MAKING FOREIGN POLICY, AND, FURTHERMORE, THAT NO ONE IN ANY DEPARTMENT CAN SABOTAGE THE PRESIDENT'S POLICY. THE CIVIL SERVANT, THE GENERAL OR ADMIRAL, THE FOREIGN SERVICE OFFICER HAS NO AUTHORITY TO MAKE POLICY. THEY ACT ONLY AS SERVANTS OF THE GOVERNMENT, AND THEREFORE THEY MUST REMAIN IN LINE WITH THE GOVERNMENT POLICY THAT IS ESTABLISHED BY THOSE WHO HAVE BEEN CHOSEN BY THE PEOPLE TO SET THAT POLICY.

PRESIDENT HARRY S TRUMAN

PART ONE

PRELUDE

1

AN IMMIGRANT'S JOURNEY
TO THE WHITE HOUSE

On a bright spring day in May 1981, I sat on a sofa facing CIA Director William Casey in his spacious office with a vista of the Potomac River and its border of lush green forests. It was my second conversation with Casey; two weeks earlier he had invited me to meet with him for the first time. People he knew had recommended me, and he had read some of my published writings on foreign policy. Now he wanted to talk with me about my accepting a high-level position with the CIA—Casey was suggesting two possibilities—but the conversation took another turn.

Casey's frank manner invited me to be candid, and I was: "I have to tell you I have some serious questions about the competence of the career foreign policy and intelligence agencies, including the CIA. I know there are many dedicated and skilled people, but during the Carter years these organizations just didn't foresee—much less prevent—some real disasters."

To explain my doubts I cited my recent firsthand experiences. I recalled to Casey how, starting in late 1977 and all through 1978, I'd unavailingly warned Carter administration officials that diverse groups seemed to be coalescing to overthrow the then friendly government in Iran. The officials had reacted passively. One cited Carter's 1978 state visit, during which he had turned to the shah of Iran and said, beaming: "I can see how you are loved by your people."

I recalled vainly trying to get their attention again when the communist coup in Afghanistan, in April 1978, increased the dangers of destabilization in next-door Iran. After the fact, a House Intelligence Committee report complained that neither the Carter State Department nor the U.S. intelligence community seemed willing to seriously examine the idea that the friendly government of Iran might be overthrown. By the time the Carter administration saw the threat, in November 1978, even *Time* had been reporting for weeks that a revolution against the shah might well succeed. He left Iran in mid-January 1979, and Khomeini took power in February 1979.

I likewise told Casey of my attempts during late 1978 and 1979 to warn the Carter administration, including the CIA, about the Sandinistas. There had been clear signs that Fidel Castro and the Soviets were sharply stepping up aid to communist guerrilla movements in Central America. I'd predicted the course the Sandinistas subsequently followed: they would probably imitate Castro's example and set up a "united front" with genuinely democratic anti-Somoza forces, promising real democracy in order to fool both their countrymen and the free world media; then they would set up a communist dictatorship, with strong Cuban and Soviet support, providing a haven for guerrillas and terrorists; finally the Nicaragua-based communist insurgencies would target El Salvador and Guatemala, with the ultimate strategic objective of destabilizing Mexico and Panama.

Casey was keenly interested in the Carter people's reactions to my warnings. I recalled that at the National Security Council, the senior Latin America expert (who probably met with me only because I knew his boss, Zbigniew Brzezinski), listened politely, then said simply that Anastasio Somoza, the Nicaraguan dictator, would have to go. Yes, it was important to have "democracy" in Nicaragua, but it would probably be the "Mexican one-party type." I had replied: "No, the Sandinistas are communists."

I'd fared no better at the Defense Department. There the senior Carter official for Latin America, Michael Armacost, seemed a bit concerned but told me that "everyone" expected Somoza to last until the end of his term in 1982. He dismissed my concern about the threat a communist Central America could pose. "Mexico," he said serenely, "can use its surplus oil money to buy its way out of any political problem."*

---

* I have known and liked Armacost since we were graduate students at Columbia University in the early 1960s—but we have had sharply different judgments on key foreign policy issues since 1978. Armacost later served three years as Reagan's ambassador to the Philippines. When he returned to take the top-ranking policy job in the Reagan-Shultz State Department in June 1984, Armacost told me he saw no real challenge to Marcos's rule. Eighteen months later Marcos fell.

I told Casey how I'd called on Frank Carlucci, deputy director of the CIA in early 1979. I'd worked for Carlucci in 1973–1975 and commended him for his foresight and courage in 1975, when, as U.S. ambassador to Portugal, he'd awakened the State Department in time to help stop the cunning communist power grab then under way there. And I'd urged him to rouse the passive Carter administration to thwart an imminent communist takeover in Nicaragua. "You're the only one who seems to be worried about that," he'd said.*

Still, he did set up a meeting for me at CIA in late January 1979. A group of senior officials listened to my analysis but had little reaction. They completely disagreed that Mexico would ever be in any danger, even in the "highly improbable" event that Nicaragua or most of Central America went communist.

I realized, as I spoke, that I was pouring out my frustrations to Casey at greater length than I'd meant to. But he was sympathetic, and he saw my point. I wasn't merely complaining that my own judgments had been rejected. I was calling attention to a problem that disturbed him, too.

The heart of the matter was this: The entire huge network of government foreign policy and intelligence organizations had failed—"refused" might be a better word—even to take these palpable dangers seriously. I wasn't surprised, I told Casey, to find the liberal media adhering to the complacent conventional wisdom. But that hundreds of professional experts, with mountains of current information at their disposal, people whose job it was to anticipate and prevent future crises, should prefer that same conventional wisdom over prudent efforts to assess and if necessary try to reverse highly negative international trends, while even I, as a solitary private citizen, had been able to know better—that was deeply regrettable.

Now the country was paying for their mistakes. And, I told Casey, we could be in for more trouble—in the Persian Gulf and in Central America.

Casey nodded. "I agree with you," he said. "That's exactly why I want to bring in some strong-minded outsiders like yourself, analysts with experience in the real world, to the top levels of the CIA." Casey paused. He seemed to sense my hesitation, so in his direct style he said, "You're so concerned about the threats to our freedom. I'm offering you a chance to help—what are you waiting for?"

---

* Carlucci served as Reagan's deputy secretary of defense 1981–83; NSC adviser 1987; and secretary of defense since December 1987.

Expecting Casey's offer, but reluctant to be affiliated with the CIA, I had prepared for this moment of decision by thinking about my life and my basic political values and commitments.

The family histories of many Americans are tales of human lives shattered by aggressive tyrannies that have driven them or their forefathers thousands of miles across the globe. I know this because it's just what happened to me.

My family's history taught me, early on, the horrible toll that totalitarian dictatorships can take on the lives of individuals and families. Throughout my boyhood and adult life, I have studied and traveled in order to learn more about the world, its people, and their politics. I have learned that many places in the world remain very dangerous for those who want to live in freedom. Therefore, to me the real challenge and responsibility of those who work on foreign policy is to act prudently and wisely so that we maintain peace with freedom and help friendly countries do the same.

These experiences and the facts of history have given me a deep commitment to political democracy, a sense of appreciation for being a citizen of the United States, a firm opposition to dictatorships of the right or left, and an understanding that the Soviet Union and its allies represent the greatest threat to our freedom.

I was born in Turkey, of German parents, on September 1, 1939—the day World War II began. My father, a scholar specializing in the languages and peoples of the Soviet Union, Iran, and Turkey, had been with the Academy of Sciences in Berlin. Since he opposed and publicly spoke out against the Nazis, the dreaded secret police, the Gestapo, arrested and interrogated him in 1936. They released him but ordered him to report back. Instead he fled to Czechoslovakia. In 1937 my father moved to Turkey where my mother joined him. They had foreseen the Munich Agreement of September 1938, in which the European democracies mistakenly sought peace with Hitler by appeasing the Nazi regime.

The anti-Nazi refugees there were afraid that Turkey might take the German side in the war, as it had in World War I. By 1940 the United Kingdom was Europe's last democracy, and it was in mortal danger from Hitler. My parents knew that if Turkey joined the German side, its next move might be to turn the anti-Nazi refugees over to the Hitler government. Their best hope was to reach the United States.

My father had the good fortune to receive an invitation in the summer of 1940 to teach Slavic and Central Asian languages at Columbia

University. He had to travel to New York through the Far East to avoid going through Nazi-occupied countries. Since I was still an infant, my parents felt that such a long trip might be risky to my health, so my father went to New York alone. My mother took me to neutral Portugal, where she hoped to catch a ship to New York soon.

It took her six years. Tens of thousands of other refugees were there with the same idea. Passenger shipping was cut back sharply for years because Nazi submarines made the Atlantic dangerous.

After the successful Allied landings at Normandy in 1944, the seas became safer again, and my mother was able to send me to New York on a special ship designated just for refugee children. I have a vague, pleasant memory of the trip across the Atlantic with a shipful of other children and friendly American volunteers. I arrived speaking German and Portuguese.

When my mother followed in early 1946, her marriage turned out to have been a casualty of the war, and she and my father were divorced. But over the years I have remained close to both my parents, who have always given me love and encouragement.

My father was renting a small room in an apartment near Columbia, so I stayed with his friends, Professor Karl Wittfogel and his wife, Esther, who made me welcome in their spacious apartment and who have been lifelong friends of my family. (In September 1986 we had a festive dinner, celebrating the Wittfogels' ninetieth birthdays.) It was soon apparent that my father could not do his university work and care for me, so he asked the Wittfogels to help him find a foster family. For the next two years I lived with Helga and Jerry Hoffbauer and their daughter, Stephanie, in West Hempstead, Long Island. The Hoffbauers, who were Jewish refugees from Nazi Germany, having arrived in 1937, provided a warm, friendly home which I remember with great pleasure.

I lost track of the Hoffbauers and tried to locate them after graduating from college so I could thank them. But I could not find them. Then, in 1981, their granddaughter saw me on a television program, and we got back in touch. Our families have become friends. The Hoffbauers have visited us in Washington, D.C., and we have stayed with them in Miami. I was happy to see them again and to be able to invite them to visit the White House and join us in the president's box at the Kennedy Center.

In 1950, when I was ten, my father arranged for me to spend a summer with his parents in Frankfurt, Germany. It was a wonderful summer, and it turned out to have an important impact on my life. My paternal grandparents were gentle, devout Christians, still optimistic, though they had lived through two world wars and the Nazi nightmare and though one of their two sons, a doctor, had been killed in his hospital during a bombing raid.

All my German relatives held the Hitler regime responsible for the war and its sufferings. They gave me a sense of the constant fear felt by freedom-loving people trapped in a totalitarian dictatorship.

While my father went on an expedition to Iran for two months, I rode around Frankfurt on a borrowed bicycle. I made friends among German children and spoke the language well enough to pass for a German myself. At the same time, I felt proud to be an American. Now and then, with my premature interest in history and international relations, I got into heated political arguments with my playmates' parents. With the moral self-assurance of my ten years, I would criticize these adults for not having resisted the Hitler regime. Sometimes they responded by politely but firmly showing me the door.

My aunt (Hedwig Menges) later explained to me that many adult Germans who had not resisted the Nazis now felt guilty. They had been paralyzed by fear as they saw Hitler's opposition killed or sent off to the concentration camps. My aunt also told me that no *German* ten-year-old would talk to adults as I did.

Near my grandparents' home was the Gutleut Kaserne—a small military barracks now used by the U.S. Army. I often went down there and chatted with the GIs. They were very friendly toward a ten-year-old American and allowed me to come and go through the sentry posts. Soon they were letting me help clean and reassemble the weapons. Some even let me ride along on their jeep patrols. I was having a great time.

Then, suddenly, everything changed. On June 25, 1950, communist North Korea, with Soviet support, attacked South Korea, and within days President Truman sent U.S. troops to lead the defensive action of the United Nations Forces. The informal style of the Gutleut Kaserne army base changed overnight, and the "American kid" found the base, its weapons, and its jeeps off limits.

Some Germans feared that Stalin might be using the Korean War to distract the West from a direct Soviet military attack on West Germany and the rest of free Europe. The communist takeovers of Eastern Europe and China and the Soviet blockade of West Berlin were recent events. My grandparents prayed that they would be spared a *third* world war. By September the fear had abated, thanks to Truman's firmness and the beginning of American rearmament.

From 1946 to 1950, as my mother struggled to earn a living and cope with the divorce, we lived in about ten places including New York, Miami, and San Francisco. Then, to permit me to see my father more, my mother moved back to New York in 1950. To augment our meager income, I always worked after school and during summers—selling newspapers, working in a shoe repair shop, as a messenger on Wall Street, and then in high-tech jobs or tutoring during college. I was fortunate in attending an excellent high school, All Hallows Institute, from which I graduated in 1956.

In 1957, after my freshman year at Columbia College in New York, my grandparents invited me to visit them again. I crossed the Atlantic on a French coal freighter—a three-week trip that gave me lots of time to work on my French and Russian. After a few weeks with my relatives in Frankfurt, I bought a used motorcycle for a hundred dollars and drove it more than four thousand miles throughout most of Western Europe. I stayed in youth hostels for fifty cents a night and ate in student dining rooms with new acquaintances I met in each country. I returned to Germany for the last weeks of the summer, in time to attend several political events during the 1957 national election campaign. The trip gave me a good feeling for daily life in Europe and helped me decide, after graduation from Columbia in 1960, to study international politics rather than pure science.

My four years at Columbia College had been splendidly stimulating. The faculty and students were challenging and hardworking. I had won a graduate fellowship that permitted me to enroll in Columbia's graduate political science program.

There I was fortunate in the superb quality of the faculty, including Zbigniew Brzezinski, Lawrence Chamberlain, Samuel P. Huntington, William T. R. Fox, Otto Kirchheimer, Juan Linz, Warner Schilling, and Ronald M. Schnider. By the end of the first year of graduate study, in May 1961, I was gaining new insights through systematic learning about international politics, the Soviet Union, NATO, and other foreign policy issues.

I went to Europe again in the summer of 1961. This time I took a Yugoslavian freighter from New York to Tangiers, Morocco. Because I opposed the Franco dictatorship I intended to bypass Spain, but curiosity and the attraction of the culture got the better of me. I spent a month there, exploring the country, frequenting semiclandestine Spanish jazz clubs, where I met some of the cultural and political avant garde, and visiting university campuses, where I'd get into discussions of political and economic trends. My time in Spain sparked a hope that there might be a transition to democracy after Franco. It seemed to me, then as now, that the chance for an evolution to democracy was much greater in an authoritarian system (where politics is controlled) than in a totalitarian one (where the regime seeks control of all institutions).

After a few weeks with my German relatives, I bought a used Volkswagen and, for the first time, visited communist Eastern Europe. There I learned firsthand how much the people of all ages detested the communist regimes. In August, while camping in Hungary with two acquaintances from Budapest, I learned that the communists were building a wall to divide East from West Berlin. I drove straight to West Berlin, which seemed to be surrounded by Soviet and East German troop formations.

This new Berlin crisis provided a focal point for the major international issue of our time: the struggle between democracy and communism. I made daily trips into East Berlin (my passport gave me an access that was denied the West Germans). I met face to face and tried to help the people who were willing to risk prison, and even life itself, in order to get away from communism while they could. I saw the brute military force the Soviet Union and the goose-stepping East German "people's army" used to prevent the United States, Britain, and France from countering this illegal action. And I saw how my West German family and friends again felt the cold chill of fear—just as in 1950.

I returned to my graduate studies in fall 1961 with three ideas crystallized by the summer's experience. First, the democracies had to maintain enough military power to deter the Soviet Union from the direct use of its military forces. Second, the democracies had to find ways to encourage the development of democratic institutions in dictatorships of both right and left. Third, the internal failure of communism, and its rejection by most of the people it ruled, could ultimately lead to the end of communism as an international threat—*provided* the free world prevented the Soviet Union from adding more and more countries to its coalition.

During the spring of 1962 I met Herman Kahn, the brilliant and controversial author of *On Thermonuclear War,* who had come to Columbia to lecture on strategic weapons and arms control. I asked him a number of questions. He answered them generously and afterward invited me to visit the Hudson Institute, the "think tank" he and Max Singer had recently founded.

A few days later I drove out and met Herman's eclectic team of political scientists, physicians, lawyers, scientists, and other specialists who gathered to talk and write on foreign policy and defense issues. Herman asked me to join them for the summer. This was my introduction to analytic work for the government on strategic weapons, arms control, and foreign policy issues, making use of classified information. The institute was a stimulating place, a bridge between the worlds of ideas and action, bringing together the skills of different intellectual disciplines in order to propose practical solutions to major public problems. Later I worked part-time at Hudson while writing my doctoral thesis, and ever since then I have alternated among public service, think tanks, and universities.

In 1963, because I was among the few people then working on both the Soviet Union and strategic weapons, the Columbia University Russian Institute asked me to help prepare a major conference on U.S.-Soviet arms control issues. That same year a faculty member proposed that I write a book-length report entitled "Arms Control in Latin America" for a multiuniversity project that was examining this issue in each region of the world. I accepted. I was fascinated by Latin America and had decided to make it my specialty among the developing regions while continuing my work on the Soviet Union and Western Europe. I decided to begin my research for this project by visiting Latin America.

On the way to Latin America, I spent some time in Mississippi during the "long, hot summer" of 1963 helping volunteers in Martin Luther King's voting rights education project. I admired the citizens of both races who had the courage to press for equal rights by nonviolent means, and I wanted to make at least a small contribution of my own.

We all came to know fear. There was constant harassment not only from the Ku Klux Klan and the White Citizens Council, but also from Black Muslim separatists. I remember vividly how we would meet in the little churches in the evenings and how the songs and prayers really did give everyone courage. I will never forget the black men and women, most of them elderly, who dared to vote that August: they had to pass between opposing rows of cursing, threatening white *and* black extremists in front of the courthouse door. These brave people would have to stay after the volunteers left. Yet I believed even then that Dr. King was right in thinking that most whites as well as blacks wanted the end of legally prescribed segregation and that equal civil rights for all would bring the South harmony and revitalization.

From Mississippi I went through Texas to Mexico, Central America, Panama, South America, and back via Puerto Rico. I spent several months traveling, by bus or hitchhiking, studying a paperback Spanish grammar book along the way. I had plenty of opportunity to apply my new learning. In the two-dollar hotels where I spent each night, no one spoke English.

This low-budget approach was a good way for a twenty-three-year-old graduate student to get acquainted with each country from the bottom up. About half the people lived in poverty far beneath anything in Mississippi. I made it a practice to seek out Peace Corps workers and various religious volunteers who worked with the poor. As they described their experiences, I came to see that practical assistance from abroad very definitely could and did improve the lives of the poor and offer them new opportunities for the future.

It was an eventful summer. In Mexico City I visited with volunteers building housing in the poorest part of the city. At a San Salvador hospital I was visiting with a doctor friend, a woman went into labor at 3:00 A.M.; since nobody else seemed to be around, I had the moving experience of helping to deliver the baby. In Bogota I happened to meet the daughter of a major Colombian figure who had been assassinated some years earlier; her prosperous husband was sympathetic to the communist guerrilla groups receiving aid from Castro.

I sought out students from leftist as well as democratic groups at the major universities. My approach with all of them was to announce at the outset that I believed in democracy and opposed all forms of dictatorship. That usually cleared the air. The young communists, with their ardent secular faith, always seemed surprised, in our impromptu debates, by my knowledge of Marxism-Leninism and Soviet history. On this and many future trips I met many prodemocratic and many communist leaders, including Sandinistas, who would shape events in Latin America over the next quarter century.

As the author of a study on Latin America funded by the Arms Control and Disarmament Agency, I had access to U.S. embassy and Latin American government officials. I learned from them how in several countries—including Guatemala, Nicaragua, Venezuela, and Colombia—the Castro regime was providing arms, money, and training to communist guerrilla and terrorist groups. As long as this was the case, the Latin governments believed they needed larger, more effective military forces, and the prospect for arms reduction was correspondingly reduced.

This 1963 trip gave me new insight into the threat posed by communist insurgency and the means needed to resist it. In Colombia I accompanied the president and the military leadership on a counterinsurgency tour of inspection that included the most dangerous zones. In Venezuela communist students at a university proudly showed me the arsenal of automatic weapons they had hidden in one of the student dorms.

*   *   *

As I was heading home by way of Puerto Rico, my apparent knack for meeting people led to an experience that still amazes me. I was visiting the parents of Joseph Ramos, a good friend from college, when—out of the blue—the governor's office called and asked me to come and meet with him.

Luis Muñoz Marín was already legendary. His leadership had sparked enormous economic development in Puerto Rico. I went to the governor's mansion, with its superb view of the turquoise Caribbean.

After some pleasant opening conversation, Muñoz Marín said he had heard from friends that I was very good at "meeting everyone" in a given country and getting a good feeling for the political situation. Would I undertake a "discreet mission" on his behalf?

A recent military coup in the Dominican Republic had ended what had seemed a promising transition to democracy. Muñoz Marín explained that he was planning to prepare a personal report, with recommendations for action by President Kennedy. He asked me to go to the Dominican Republic and give him a written account of the situation. It might be dangerous, he said, but I had the advantage of being young and unknown in the region.

Of course I agreed to go. I managed to meet most of the civilian and military leaders of the various Dominican factions. But after hectic days and nights in Santo Domingo and the impoverished countryside, I was relieved to fly back to the safety of Puerto Rico, where I gave the governor my report. In the future there would be many occasions when I would say a prayer of thanks as I left a dangerous situation and returned to the security of a democratic order most of us take for granted.

After joining the political science faculty at the University of Wisconsin in Madison, I went to Chile in the summer and autumn of 1964. I had decided to write my doctoral thesis on the Chilean political economy, focusing on the controversial land reform issue. I arrived during the presidential election season, with Eduardo Frei, a Christian Democrat, running against Salvador Allende, leader of a socialist-communist coalition. My own sympathies were with Frei, who won and governed effectively for six years. (Allende was to win in 1970 with a plurality of 36 percent. His coalition wrecked the economy and nearly led to a communist takeover from within the government, until the 1973 coup in which Allende died and democracy was suspended.)

In 1967 I moved to California and joined the staff of the Rand Corporation, then viewed by many as the nation's leading foreign policy think tank. Ronald Reagan was then serving ably, it seemed to me, in his first term as governor. During my four years at Rand I wrote on a range of international issues, including counterinsurgency in Vietnam and democratic development in Latin America and sometimes to Washington to brief government policymakers.

In 1968, while I was still at Rand, I proposed an idea for a government-funded study. I suggested comparative analysis of groups seeking liberalization and democracy in four dictatorships, two of the right-wing (Spain and Portugal) and two communist (Yugoslavia and Czechoslovakia).

For the West it was a moment of both danger and opportunity. In three of these countries the dictators were old, and there would likely be a major period of transition in the early 1970s. In Czechoslovakia the communist regime itself appeared to be trying to liberalize. If the United States could identify the forces that wanted an end to dictatorship, we might adopt a discreet policy to encourage and aid democratic elements within each country. At the same time, I argued, it was probable that the communists in Portugal and Spain were even now preparing to try to gain power when the rule of Salazar and Franco came to an end. (In 1974–75 the Communist party of Portugal nearly succeeded in taking power there.)

Unfortunately my idea was too esoteric for the government policy-makers. I decided to pursue the study on my own. In the summer of 1968 I used my vacation to revisit Spain and then to spend some weeks in Czechoslovakia.

It was the time of the "Prague spring." I believed that the Soviet Union would use any means to crush the Czechoslovakian government's effort to democratize, and I wanted to see the country for myself before the likely crackdown.

I took a bus from Munich and once again felt the chill I always feel when I see the communist border with Western Europe. The evenly spaced guard towers delineate a horizon marked by high barbed-wire fences. Between the towers are cleared areas salted with land mines—all the signs of a huge prison.

On the long bus ride to Prague, I met a university student who later introduced me to many of the younger leaders of the democratic movement. Within days I had met a wide range of prodemocratic government officials, citizens, churchmen, and university leaders. Despite my forebodings about the Soviets, I began to catch the hope these people shared. They believed that by promising to remain in the Warsaw Pact, aligned with Moscow internationally, Czechoslovakia might be permitted to have at least a degree of internal democracy.

In mid-August several of my Czech student friends called and said they had to see me at once. They had heard that thousands of male Soviet "tourists"—of military age—were entering Czechoslovakia at various border crossings. These "tourists" dressed alike and were carrying identical suitcases—just large enough to contain weapons. My sources believed these were Soviet commando units, in disguise, doing advance reconnaissance for a military attack.

I took this information to the U.S. embassy. Jacob Beam, the U.S. ambassador at the time, later wrote in his memoirs that he had received such information and cabled it to Washington, but that it was ignored: it didn't fit the mind-set of the bureaucracy.

Early in the morning of August 20, a Czech friend woke me with the news: thousands of Soviet paratroopers were landing near the Prague airport.

Throughout Czechoslovakia there was a silent, numbed weeping. The people saw that the Soviet Union would not permit even a spark of democracy in one of its colonies. The Soviets declared and enforced their new "Brezhnev doctrine": no communist country allied with the USSR would be allowed to escape. Soviet troops captured the Czech leadership, political and military, and took them to Moscow, chained and sitting on the floor of a military cargo plane.

Within hours, prodemocratic students and workers launched a nation-wide campaign of nonviolent resistance. They hid their key leaders, whom the KBG and Soviet commando squads were hunting. They changed street, road, and railroad signs throughout the country to confuse the four hundred thousand invading troops. They set up secret headquarters to treat their wounded, coordinate sabotage and diversionary actions, and publish free daily newspapers. I stayed and worked with this unarmed resistance for several weeks. I also passed information to Radio Free Europe, which played a vital role by broadcasting accurate news to the Czechs.

I sent a dramatic postcard (published by the resistance) showing Soviet tanks in Prague's main square to my Rand colleague Fritz Ermarth* and to my former Columbia professor Zbigniew Brzezinski.

After some weeks I heard that the KBG was looking for me. Though on vacation, as a Rand employee I had the military rank of major "in case of capture." If the KBG arrested me, there would be diplomatic

---

* Appointed by Carlucci in December 1986 as the senior Soviet specialist on the Reagan NSC staff.

problems as well as the obvious personal ones. It was time for me to leave.

Back in California I tried, by writing and public speaking, to make more Americans aware of the Czechs' courageous efforts for democracy. This searing experience had made me realize anew how passionately people will fight for freedom even against communist dictatorships.

That fall I wrote two related papers at Rand. One told the inspiring story of the Czechs' nonviolent resistance. The second urged free world help for armed resistance movements against *newly* established communist regimes. In 1986 a journalist would discover this eighteen-year-old article and say to me at a White House reception: "You are the originator of the 'Reagan doctrine.' " My reply: "Reagan is the author of the Reagan doctrine." I didn't mention that in late 1968 a top Soviet official, during a visit to Rand, asked for copies of both articles.

In 1969 Robert Drucker, a talented independent film producer who knew me personally, asked me to help prepare a documentary film on economic development projects of the Catholic church in Latin America. I took a few months' leave from Rand to visit Rome, where I met Catholic leaders who were involved in social action and missionary work. Next I traveled through Latin America to select projects for filming. Then I led a film crew to Chile, Peru, and Colombia.

My contact with religious groups opened my eyes to a problem that has grown more serious in the years since: the attraction of some churchmen to communist promises of social justice. Among the dedicated church people who want to improve the lot of the poor, a minority make the mistake of believing that Marxist-Leninist methods, organizations, and even armed guerrillas hold the answer.

They make this mistake for one basic reason: they consider only the rhetorical goals of communism and ignore its actual results. Hardly any of these misguided Christians, in my experience, had any historical knowledge of what communist governments do once they are in power. They made the typical human political mistake: they accepted as a friendly and moral force any group, even armed communists, who shared their opposition to current political and economic institutions they viewed as unjust and irreformable. I saw the tragic results of this gullibility in Nicaragua in 1979, when most religious leaders of that country made what they now realize was a terribly naive move: they supported the communist Sandinistas instead of backing *only* the genuinely democratic groups.

In 1970 my work took a new turn. I accepted an invitation to work in the Department of Health, Education, and Welfare and moved to Washington, D.C. I would serve on Secretary Robert Finch's staff to evaluate the effectiveness of current federal education programs and propose new approaches.

I took this job for two reasons. The activist in me wanted to move from policy analysis at Rand to actual government work. Second, Lewis H. Butler and the late John Veneman, the energetic and talented California Republicans who with Finch were the leadership of HEW, persuaded me that we had to do better at finding ways to help low-income Americans improve their lives. I moved to Washington intending to stay with HEW for two years but wound up staying five—moving from the secretary's staff to assistant director for civil rights and then deputy assistant secretary for education. Late in my stint at HEW, I worked under two men I would later come to know better in the Reagan administration: Secretary Caspar Weinberger and Deputy Secretary Frank Carlucci.

By 1975 I had decided it was time to return to my work on international relations. Just then several White House officials approached me about serving on the President's Domestic Council under Gerald Ford. As I was considering this, the new chairman of the Civil Aeronautics Board, John Robson, contacted me. Knowing I liked action, he argued that instead of sitting in an elegant White House office responsible for issues with which little was likely to happen in the next two years, I should join him in the effort to deregulate a major industry. And, Robson said, my analytic skills and international experience meant that I could help save the economically pressed and important U.S. international airlines and provide the required leadership in tough economic negotiations with, among others, the United Kingdom, Japan, Mexico, Iran, and the Soviet Union.

The two years I spent on this job gave me a new experience in international relations. I also learned a great deal about how the State Department operated, both at home and abroad.

When the Carter administration arrived in 1977, I was naturally out of a job. I felt then and now that a new president must bring his own people into the top policy jobs. I was looking forward to the freedom of private life again. Now I could focus on my long-term interests—how U.S. policy can: encourage peaceful transition to democracy; counter Soviet-supported subversive aggression and terrrorism; and maintain sufficient strategic strength while seeking reciprocal and verified arms reductions. For the next four years I wrote widely and spoke on these isssues.

*   *   *

A new phase of my life began when I left the government—a phase that would culminate in my return as a member of the National Security Council.

I had waited until I was past thirty-five to marry, but it was well worth the wait when I married Nancy Goldsmith, a lovely, perceptive woman. As it happened, Nancy also spoke Spanish and shared my interest in Spain, so when the I left the government in 1977 we used our modest savings to live in sunny Iberia, where I did research for a short book, *Spain: The Struggle for Democracy Today* (1978).

We returned to Washington in December 1977. New international dangers loomed by then, and the Carter administration neither dealt with nor even comprehended them.

Besides my efforts to persuade senior Carter officials to take preventive action—which I described to Director Casey—I began writing short op-ed articles, hoping to alert the government and my fellow citizens through the media.

But I found that no major newspaper would publish my warnings about Iran. Two editors, in fact, said I'd have to be Henry Kissinger to get such an offbeat opinion printed! *The Washington Post* and *New York Times* both rejected more than twenty pieces I wrote on this, the threat of the communist takeover in Nicaragua and other international issues.

The editors of some major papers were harder to reach than the top level of government officials. When I finally managed to meet with a few of them, I found they had the same problem as the government: strong fixed opinions and an ingrained resistance to hearing, let alone publishing, other points of view.

The fact that the shah fell and Khomeini came to power didn't help me sell my warnings about the danger of a communist Nicaragua. One after another, the major papers—except for the *San Diego Union* and the *Chicago Tribune*—rejected my articles predicting that the Sandinistas would make Nicaragua a second Cuba. An exception to what seemed to me to be liberal media self-deception was Martin Peretz, publisher of the *New Republic*, who heard me on television and then decided to publish some of my articles.

This began to change in late 1979, when it was becoming obvious that the Sandinistas were indeed communists in alliance with Cuba and the Soviets. Eventually *The New York Times* published a number of my articles. In 1980 one of these began: "History will mark the events in Iran and Nicaragua in 1979 as a turning point in the invisible war between radical and moderate forces for control of the oil and destiny of the Middle East and for control of Central America and Mexico.'' This remains true.

President Carter was to pay for his foreign policy mistakes (which triggered the oil crisis and economic problems) in the 1980 election—a turning point for me, too.

Early in 1980 Fred Ikle—a distinguished-looking, policy-oriented scholar with a Swiss-German accent—asked me to make a public declaration of support for the candidacy of Ronald Reagan and to volunteer some time to help him get elected. At that point Reagan was by no means the leading contender for the Republican nomination. But Ikle, who had been my boss at the Rand Corporation in the 1960s, knew I was a lifelong Republican who had felt that Reagan did a good job as governor of California and who shared Reagan's apprehensions about communist expansion.

Nancy and I were leaning in Reagan's direction, but we wondered if he knew as much about foreign policy as George Bush. After hearing both candidates speak a few times, we'd concluded that Reagan was better. So when Ikle approached me I had no hesitation. I said I'd be happy to do whatever I could to help Reagan win the nomination and the election.

A few weeks later about forty foreign policy advisers met with Reagan at the International Club in Washington. Each of us participated in several of twelve groups dealing with distinct foreign policy issues, according to our specialities; mine were NATO, the Soviet Union, Latin America, and international economics.

The purpose of the meeting was not only to introduce Reagan to foreign policy specialists who might help him later, but to impress on the media and the voters that if *these* people (many of whom had served at senior levels of other administrations) were endorsing Reagan, he *must* have a serious foreign policy agenda.

But we specialists, at the same time, were putting our reputations on the line by endorsing him. When my name appeared on the published list of Reagan advisers, I got a call from an old friend in the Carter White House. Why, he asked, had I "made the mistake" of lending my name to Reagan? "If you want to help him, fine," he said. "But do it privately. Then if he wins, you're in, and if he loses, which is more likely, it won't hurt you. But by publicly endorsing him now, you've really jeopardized your chances of earning a living in this town."

I told him that I recognized the risk, but that I felt Reagan was the best candidate. "If he loses and it costs me," I said, "so be it." But I thanked my friend for being so candid. "Besides," I added wryly, "everything in Washington depends on bureaucratic networks. My guess is that even if Reagan wins, you'll still be at the White House. And I'll be asking you to help me get a job in his administration." He laughed.

After Reagan's victory all the members of his foreign policy advisory committee expected to be involved in the three-month transition. We naturally thought we'd be called on to map out a foreign policy agenda and recommend staff. It didn't turn out that way: nearly all the Reagan foreign policy experts were sidelined. The newly designated secretary of state, Alexander Haig, was a career military official, and he was more comfortable with the career foreign service officers he had worked with during the Nixon and Ford years. He met once with the Reagan foreign policy team, thanked them for their transition report, and said their services were concluded.

Meanwhile, at the Defense Department, another unfortunate development occurred. The secretary-designate, Caspar Weinberger, wanted to bring in Frank Carlucci as his deputy. But Reagan's defense experts opposed Carlucci because he had served Carter as deputy CIA director, and they felt the Carter CIA had repeatedly failed to foresee trouble in Iran, Nicaragua, Ethiopia, and Afghanistan. They tried to dissuade Weinberger from appointing him.

I thought their opposition to Carlucci was ill-advised. I knew that Weinberger trusted Carlucci like a brother and had great confidence in his administrative skills. Weinberger would insist on the deputy of his choice as he moved for the first time into the complex area of defense.

I tried to warn the Reagan defense team that their attempt to block Carlucci would backfire. But they persisted. So Weinberger met once with the head of the Reagan team, William Van Cleave, took his report, and told him the entire team was no longer needed. It was a pity things worked out that way. Weinberger and Van Cleave, both valuable and talented men who agreed with Reagan's views, might have worked well together.

It dawned on me that neither Reagan nor the key members of his California team knew how the foreign policy agencies in Washington actually worked. That was understandable. But what was worse, they seemed not to grasp that unless a new president, Republican or Democrat, appointed his own competent people to the top policy jobs, the powerful Washington bureaucracies would naturally pursue their own agendas rather than the president's. A president has the authority to appoint about seven hundred top policy officials—a modest number, at that, to work with and lead four million career federal employees, civilian and military. His chance to exert real power would be much greater if he took the time to fill those top spots with able people who shared his goals.

Though Reagan was choosing his cabinet, his interest in appointments seemed not to go much beyond that. Among the original sixty or so Reagan foreign policy advisers, only sixteen joined his administration in any capacity. And very few of those sixteen found themselves in key policy-shaping positions. Reagan's lack of detailed interest in his appointments was an unhappy portent.

Some friends in the Reagan organization sent my resume around, but I had decided I wouldn't "campaign" for a job. The Reagan people had known where to find me during the campaign, I figured, so if they felt I could contribute now, they would find me. Instead of job hunting, I tried to have an impact on how the Reagan transition team would handle two critical issues: defining a counterstrategy against Soviet-supported subversive aggression and terrorism, and formulating a prodemocratic Reagan policy for Central America, with an urgent focus on current developments in El Salvador.

I believed that the communist guerrillas in El Salvador were on the verge of a major offensive to seize power before Reagan's inauguration. But the danger came not only from the violent left. Some right-wing extremists, angry at El Salvador's new land-reform policy, saw Reagan's election as a green light to stage a coup against President Napoleon Duarte's civil-military coalition government.

I wrote a short paper urging the Carter administration to rush military aid to Duarte to help defeat the imminent communist attack. I wrote another paper calling for a clear Reagan endorsement of the Duarte government and unequivocal condemnation of the violent right as well as the violent left. I gave both proposals to Brzezinski, Carter's National Security Council adviser; to Frank Kramer, a realistic senior Carter official in the Defense Department; to Richard Allen, Reagan's designate for NSC adviser; and to Fred Ikle, who had worked closely with Allen throughout the campaign.

Some Reagan supporters felt that my support for the Duarte government was wrong. They had been led by a few Salvadoran rightists into believing that a coup and a rollback of land reform were necessary. Word soon reached me that if I continued my efforts, some powerful conservatives would block me from working for the administration later on. But

I persisted, and the Reagan transition team endorsed Duarte and warned against a right-wing coup.

Some have been slow to appreciate the virtues of democracy abroad—both in improving the well-being of people and friendly relations with us and as a bulwark against communism. Yet virtually all of communism's many postwar conquests have occurred in countries without functioning democratic institutions. The delicate moment when long-established authoritarian regimes are in transition has always been a time of special vulnerability to communist subversion and of opportunity for the building of democratic institutions. During the 1980s I would have the chance to help Reagan make the encouragement of democracy (without the coercion of friendly countries) a major theme and policy priority. During the first six years of his administration ten Latin American countries, with a combined population of 240 million people, returned to democracy.

In late November 1980 Duarte made a private visit to President Carter. He was seeking the resumption of U.S. military aid (cut off since 1977) to repel the communist offensive that he too believed was imminent. The Carter people asked me to set up a private meeting between Duarte and Reagan's top Latin America people. It was a hopeful milestone. Among those attending the meeting was Jeane Kirkpatrick. She understood the importance of Duarte's firm commitment to democracy and was impressed by his realism about the communists. Duarte gave a brilliant analysis of the probable shape of the communist attack. He predicted that it would be massive and would happen before Reagan took office. President Carter, Duarte told us, had personally promised to send El Salvador ten helicopters and to begin rapid military aid. His visit had been an apparent success.

Two weeks after this pledge four American women religious volunteers were murdered and secretly buried. This brutal act seemed to have been committed by a group of Salvadoran soldiers. The already modest U.S. economic aid was suspended, along with any thought of resuming military assistance. Moreover, Carter's ambassador to El Salvador, Robert White, rejected the idea that any major guerrilla offensive was in the offing. When I had warned about this in a public meeting of the Council of the Americas in October, White and the other senior State Department officials assured the audience of hundreds that there would be no such communist guerrilla offensive. These were the same State Department officials who had ignored my warnings about the Sandinistas and now in 1980 realized full well that their policy had unintentionally delivered Nicaragua to communism.

In mid-December I spoke with Brzezinski. I said that even if a faction of the Salvadoran military had been responsible for those murders, it made no sense to make this an occasion for permitting the triumph of a communist insurrection. The killers must be brought to justice, but the people of El Salvador should not be punished. It was essential to blunt the coming communist assault by sending military aid—at once.

On December 27 the Salvadoran communist front trumpeted from its Mexico City progaganda headquarters a boast that it would soon launch a "victorious final offensive to liberate El Salvador." Even then the Carter administration sent no aid.

On January 9, 1981, I attended the funeral of Michael Hammer at Arlington National Cemetery. Hammer, a dedicated and courageous AFL-CIO official, had been gunned down, along with the leader of the Salvadoran peasant union, for helping the union carry out land reform. After the moving ceremony I turned to Robert White.

"Do you still think my concerns about a communist offensive are nonsense?" I asked him.

His eyes narrowed. "Yes," he said, "a guerrilla offensive is coming, and they've been storing lots of weapons. But I still say these are really juvenile delinquents who can't do a lot of damage."

White flew back to El Salvador that evening. At dawn the next day six thousand well-armed and well-coordinated communist guerrillas struck with deadly force throughout the country.

The Carter administration had not delivered the ten helicopters that had been promised in November, and Duarte was unable to move the small and poorly armed Salvadoran forces to any effect. No military aid whatsoever had arrived. Belatedly, on January 16 White urgently requested that Carter send arms.

Within hours U.S. Air Force transports loaded with weapons and ammunition were on their way. The Salvadoran forces reportedly had only enough ammunition for two more days!

This tardy, though sensible, last act of the Carter administration greatly boosted Salvadoran morale and gave Duarte what he needed to defeat the communist "final offensive." And it prevented a third communist takeover in Latin America—after Grenada and Nicaragua—during the Carter years.

El Salvador was a vivid example of a form of Soviet-supported terrorism and armed subversion we would be facing for many years to come. It seemed to me that this was an international threat that very few diplomats or military men understood, and we needed a counterstrategy.

During the transitional months of November and December 1980, I asked eight experienced foreign policy experts from both parties, including Carlucci and Paul Nitze, to meet in a discussion group for the purpose of formulating a long-term plan of action. I prepared two papers; we had several lively discussions; we produced a consensus on strategy and procedures. I summarized the results in a memo that most of the participants signed. Four of them had close personal ties with at least one of Reagan's designated foreign policy cabinet members—Haig, Weinberger, Casey, or Allen—and each promised to hand a copy of the memo to his friend.

Through the early months of 1981 I was busy writing and consulting, and I was often asked to speak at conferences. Usually I was one of the few Republican analysts or Reagan supporters invited. In January 1981, at the Woodrow Wilson International Center for Scholars, I presented a paper entitled "The U.S. and Latin America in the 1980s." There I urged a U.S. policy encouraging democratic institution building in Latin America; providing assistance for economic growth and improved living conditions for the poor; and extending security help to defend against violent extremists of both right and left.

I also proposed that the new administration establish a "National Foundation for Democracy" to help genuinely democratic groups within foreign countries. At the time, this idea was only shared by a very small group of Republicans and Democrats and by leaders of the AFL-CIO and the U.S. Chamber of Commerce. But by the spring of 1982 Reagan had proposed just such a program, and by 1983 the National Endowment for Democracy was a fact.

I was happy enough with what I was doing, but I have to admit I was disappointed that the phone didn't ring with an offer from the Reagan administration. By now my friend from the Carter White House was comfortably ensconced in the Reagan White House—just as I'd predicted. In April 1981 he called to ask if he could help me get a job with Richard Allen, now Reagan's national security adviser, with whom he now worked closely. I reminded him of my sardonic prophecy.

"Yes," he replied, laughing, "you've always been good on the issues, but not so good at promoting your own interests. Send me your resume, and I'll see what I can do."

In May another friend, Dr. Mark Cannon, called. He had just been at a conference with CIA Director William Casey. Casey had told him he was looking for foreign policy experts who could bring a fresh perspective to some top-level positions within the National Intelligence Council. This council, my friend explained, represented the CIA in the policy-making process, coordinated the analytic work of the whole intelligence community (the military and National Security Agency as well as CIA), and reported directly to Casey.

"When I told him about you, he told me he'd read and liked some of your articles, and he'd be getting in touch with you."

"Thanks for thinking of me," I said, "but I doubt I'd consider working at the CIA. I don't know anyone there, and it seems like a huge bureaucracy that wouldn't take kindly to outsiders being brought in at a senior level."

But a few days later I got a call to come out to CIA headquarters and meet with the director. Casey had been Reagan's second campaign manager. I'd never met him. I asked a few knowledgeable people about him, and three adjectives kept cropping up: "brilliant . . . activist . . . mumbling."

The high security and aura of mystery around CIA headquarters make a visit there unforgettable. I drove to the Langley redoubt on a sunny May day and was instructed to park near the main entrance.

A receptionist ushered me into a small private waiting room furnished with Oriental antiques. An elevator door opened silently, and a young man said, "Dr. Menges, please come with me." We took the private elevator up to another elegantly furnished suite of several waiting rooms. A few minutes later Casey's secretary showed me into his large, bright, spacious office.

A floor-to-ceiling window forty feet long framed a spectacular view of dense green foliage beyond which lay the Potomac. Here too the decor was Oriental, with subdued rose and light mauve creating an air of elegant comfort and tranquility.

Casey rose frome his desk and welcomed me with a friendly handshake. He invited me to sit on one of two sofas, while he took the other one. "I've heard a lot of good things about you," he said. "I think the CIA would be strengthened if we brought in a few top-notch outside experts who could mix it up intellectually with the staff we have here."

Casey asked me what I thought were the main foreign policy problems facing the United States. For the next hour I sketched out my views and gave him copies of several of the short op-ed pieces I'd written. I spoke of a counterstrategy against armed subversion and terrorism. I also mentioned that I'd been writing since 1978 that the United States should use its technology to develop a strategic defense system. This was a more sensible and humane way to defend ourselves, we would have a technological advantage over the Soviets, and it was far better than the SALT II approach, which instead of cutting back nuclear weapons permitted each side to deploy up to thirteen thousand nuclear warheads on missiles and bombers. Casey seemed receptive to these ideas.

On Latin America, I told him I thought the United States should pursue a prodemocratic policy that could help the Latin countries defeat both the violent right and the violent left. *If* the communists took over Central America, I said, it was all too likely that Mexico and Panama would fall next. I gave him an article I'd written in 1979 in the hope of alerting the Carter administration that Mexico could be a potential "Iran next door."

I also told Casey about my informal committee to formulate a counterstrategy against what I then called "Soviet-supported political and paramilitary warfare" and handed him a copy of our December 1980 report. Finally I gave him a 1979 *New York Times* article of mine in which I'd pressed the point that the time was ripe for the United States to help the genuine democrats of Latin America move their countries from military dictatorships to democratic civilian governments. I mentioned my behind-the-scenes role in helping the Reagan administration avoid even the perception that it in any way favored a right-wing coup in El Salvador. I noted that on March 5, 1981, the president had given a superb summary of a sensible U.S. policy when he said, "We are opposed to the violent right as well as the violent left in El Salvador. I support the genuinely democratic groups and the land reform."

Casey had probed and asked questions, but now it was his turn to talk. I was struck by his cordiality and his keen, straightforward realism about the Soviets and their partners. Despite his reputation, he didn't mumble.

He told me he had two areas in mind for me. He wanted me to be the CIA's top Latin America person, or he wanted to create a new function at the agency that I might fill.

Casey ended our meeting by saying he hoped I'd seriously think about taking on one of the two assignments he had described. He added that he'd arrange another meeting soon.

I left Casey's office feeling encouraged. I still wasn't sure I'd work for the CIA, but I was glad of the opportunity to present my thoughts to a man in such a key policy-making position. It was gratifying to find that we seemed to see eye to eye and that Casey agreed the United States should pursue a prodemocratic strategy in Latin America. He also understood the importance of keeping the public accurately informed about foreign events in order to maintain political consensus. He knew the dangers posed by systematic communist efforts to misinform and mislead the people, the media, and politicians in the free world countries.

I was at least willing to consider taking a position as national intelligence officer, reporting to Casey personally. When I told my White House friend I was likely to receive an offer during my next talk with Casey, he replied that he thought I could be more effective at the National Security Council.

"Why don't I tell Dick Allen that this is his last chance to make you an offer?" he volunteered. "That would start a competition for you between NSC and CIA."

"Thanks," I said, "but that wouldn't be fair to Casey. He's taken up a good deal of his time to meet with me and read some of my work."

A few days later I saw Casey again. He was very forthcoming. He had read the articles I left with him, he said, and he felt even more strongly that the agency needed a few outsiders like me to serve as intellectual catalysts.

I told him I was interested in the position as national intelligence officer for Latin America because of my concern about the dangerous Central American situation. As to the other option, I doubted that it would be feasible for me, as a new arrival, to establish a new function within a complex and compartmentalized bureaucracy.

Casey understood and sympathized. It was then that I recounted my frustrated attempts to alert the Carter administration leaders and the career agencies to the danger posed in Iran and Nicaragua.

Casey replied that this was exactly why he wanted to bring in some strong-minded and experienced outside analysts at the top levels of CIA. Just before asking me to serve as the new national intelligence officer for Latin America, Casey sketched the duties of the job: initiating, coordinating, gathering, analyzing, and evaluating intelligence on Latin America; calling attention to emerging issues and problems; chairing monthly "warning" meetings among intelligence groups on potential threats to U.S. interests; and representing Casey on behalf of the entire intelligence community in the interagency policy-making process.

Casey's offer posed a tough decision for my future. I was attracted by it, I was impressed with Casey, and I thought we could work well together. But could one man really make a difference at the CIA?

Needing a salary to support my family, I also had to think about the impact of working for the CIA on my future ability to obtain employment in my field. I was one of the comparatively few foreign policy experts who shared the Republican perspective; most research and academic institutions are overwhelmingly liberal.

Before this second meeting with Casey, I had discussed these questions with Nancy. Her answer coincided with my own inner promptings.

"Yes," she said, "there may be unpleasant consequences later. But there is a chance to help our country avoid serious danger. You should take Casey's offer and do your best."

With Nancy and my conscience in agreement, I told Bill Casey I'd accept the job.

Before and during my two years with the CIA, I had some previews of the people I would later work with at the National Security Council.

I first met Robert "Bud" McFarlane in the spring of 1981. At the time he was serving as counselor to Secretary of State Alexander Haig. A retired marine lieutenant colonel, he had worked with Haig in the Kissinger NSC during the Nixon and Ford years.

I was still a private citizen in early 1981—my service with the CIA didn't begin until September—and John Negroponte,* a career foreign service officer, had urged McFarlane to listen to my ideas about Central America.

McFarlane had a spacious office on the prestigious seventh floor of the State Department. He was cordial and invited me to sit on the sofa he reserved for informal conversations.

I spoke about Nicaragua. Though few had noticed, the communist regime there was getting international support not only from the usual suspects—the Soviet bloc, Cuba, Libya, and the PLO—but also from many Social Democratic parties in Western Europe and from Mexico. In a month President Reagan was scheduled to have his first summit meeting with Mexico's president, López Portillo. The United States, I suggested, should inform Mexico about the Sandinistas' internal repression and their aggression against their neighbors through armed subversion. And the president should take the occasion of the summit to urge his Mexican counterpart, politely but firmly, to shift from what amounted to a procommunist foreign policy in Central America and support genuinely democratic forces instead or else become genuinely neutral. I told McFarlane that Mexico was misleading some of our allies in Western

---

* Negroponte subsequently served as U.S. ambassador to Honduras 1982–84; assistant secretary of state for oceans, environment and science; and from December 1987 as deputy NSC adviser to General Colin Powell.

Europe and Latin America—and if not persuaded to stop this would become a serious problem over the next years.

I likewise told McFarlane that Vice President Bush, who was soon to meet France's newly elected Socialist president François Mitterrand, should urge the French government to resist the European Socialist party leaders who supported Central America's violent left. I handed McFarlane a one-page summary of the evidence for my concerns and the draft of a forthcoming *Commentary* article I'd written on this issue.

In his quiet, deliberative way, McFarlane asked a few questions. I could tell from their content and his manner that he didn't really grasp the international implications of having a new communist regime on our doorstep endorsed by Mexico and by many Socialist parties among our NATO allies.

McFarlane, I felt, would do nothing.

The matter was urgent, so I took it up shortly afterward with two other high administration officials. The new assistant secretary of state for Latin America was Thomas Enders, a tall, imperious career foreign service officer, also from the Kissinger-Haig team. Enders asked me to write a paper summarizing Mexico's actions and suggest a strategy to persuade Mexico to stop. I did this. Enders read it but decided to do nothing. (I had lunch with John Gavin, Reagan's ambassador-designate to Mexico. He was surprised by my information: in weeks of State Department briefing, no one had told him about Mexico's two years of procommunist actions.)

I then went to see Richard Darman whom I had worked with at HEW and known since 1970. As deputy to White House Chief of Staff James Baker, Dick was involved in preparing for the U.S.-Mexico summit. Darman listened with interest but felt the matter should be left to the State Department's judgment. This meant that nothing was done to dissuade either Mexico or the new French government from helping the communist side in Central America.

A few weeks after Vice President Bush's visit, the new French president shocked the Reagan administration by publicly endorsing the Sandinistas, selling them arms and giving them economic aid.

Then, in August 1981, France and Mexico jointly proposed that the communist guerrillas in El Salvador be given "international recognition." This would put them on a par with the Duarte government so that a "power-sharing" political settlement could be arranged. Had Duarte and fourteen other Latin American governments not swiftly rejected this misbegotten plan, this Mexican-French mistake would have brought the communists much closer to victory in El Salvador and then all of Central America.

UN Ambassador Jeane Kirkpatrick was like Bill Casey: self-confident, eager for information and ideas, with a grasp of international and domestic politics that was both analytic and intuitive. I had first worked with her during the Reagan campaign, where she showed a team spirit and a commitment to candidate Reagan's foreign policy principles. During my two years at the CIA, she and I met at times to trade information on Latin America and sometimes to share scuttlebutt about the latest State Department plots against Reagan's goals.

In late 1981 Ron Mann, the dedicated Reaganite associate director of White House personnel, first introduced me to Bill Clark, who later would be my boss at the National Security Council. At the time he was Haig's deputy secretary of state. I gave Clark an intelligence briefing on Latin America, showing him photos of the thirty new military bases and the terrorist and guerrilla training camps the Sandinistas had set up in Nicaragua.

A tall, ruggedly handsome man with a Californian style of civility and understatement, Clark asked incisive questions. Then he said in a slightly sad voice: "There are some people at the White House who believe that the only thing that matters to this presidency is the economy. They think that if we close our eyes to what's going on in Central America, it will just go away."

"Who, at the White House?" I asked. He responded only with a smile.

In the summer of 1983, as Clark was considering me for the Latin American portfolio at the NSC, he wanted me to see Admiral John Poindexter, temporarily serving as his de facto deputy while McFarlane was special presidential envoy to the Middle East. Whereas Clark had been interested in substantive issues about the Latin American situation, Poindexter was mainly interested in whether I could and would "get along" with the other foreign policy agencies—especially the State Department.

I told Poindexter that though I strongly believed in teamwork and was reasonably good at consensus building, I would not "get along" by "going along." I told him my view that the job of the NSC staff was to make sure that the president actually made all the key foreign policy decisions. And in order to do this, every president must be able to count on the NSC staff for full information and exposure to a fair debate about alternatives before he makes such decisions. And once a president decides, I said, it was up to the NSC staff to make sure his orders are carried out by the entire government.

Poindexter listened impassively, puffing on his pipe, sitting stiffly behind his desk in a small windowless office in the White House basement. I sensed he found my reply too assertive.

In the late summer of 1983 Clark requested that I move from CIA to the National Security Council. Casey approved.

I was, of course, deeply pleased to have the opportunity to work for President Reagan at the White House. I had spent two tough and interesting years at the CIA, and now I would have the chance to contribute to the making of policy at a crucial moment for Central America and the entire region of thirty-three countries and 440 million people south of our border. Almost as soon as I arrived at NSC in early October 1983, we faced a sudden crisis and opportunity in the Caribbean.

2

GRENADA

The phone rang before 7:00 A.M. on Sunday morning. A voice said, "This is the White House Situation Room. A terrorist bomb exploded at the marine compound in Lebanon during the night, and casualties are estimated at 247 dead. The president is flying back to Washington with McFarlane and Secretary Shultz. There will be an NSC meeting this morning. You are requested to attend and come in to prepare for the meeting."

A wave of sadness swept over me at the thought of the dead and wounded marines and their families, and I said a silent prayer. Though the Situation Room supervisor, prudently, had made no mention of Grenada on the open telephone lines, I immediately wondered whether the tragedy in Beirut would deflect military resources away from the Grenada mission.

It was a somber morning—cold, bleak, and rainy. The weather matched everyone's mood. Ironically, the marine amphibious unit now steaming toward Grenada had been on its way to Lebanon to replace the marine force that had fallen victim to the terrorists. Might the Joint Chiefs of Staff now argue that keeping the U.S. forces for defense or retaliation in Lebanon was more important than the Grenada operation?

I drove to the White House, met Poindexter and North, and commiserated with them about this horrible tragedy that hit their navy colleagues. The Middle Eastern NSC staff had arrived and prepared a factual overview of the latest information from Lebanon. They were also talking with State, Defense, and the CIA to prepare a list of possible retaliatory actions and the U.S. combat forces available to carry them out.

Some of us went out and stood on the south lawn in the rain to watch the president's helicopter, Marine One, land in front of the residence.

President Reagan looked grim as he entered the White House. Soon after, the foreign policy cabinet arrived. This was Sunday, October 23, 1983, just thirteen days after I had arrived at the NSC. What would the decisions be today? I knew they would have major consequences.

MONDAY, OCTOBER 10

Filled with a nervous yet pleasurable excitement, I was attending my first regular senior staff meeting at the National Security Council. Held every morning at seven-thirty in the Situation Room located in the White House basement, these senior NSC staff meetings were regularly attended by William Clark, the National Security adviser; Bud McFarlane, his deputy; Admiral John Poindexter; and the individuals responsible for each of the five regions into which NSC has divided the world, plus the senior people responsible for international economics, political-military affairs, and relations with Congress and the media.

Most of us would arrive about 7:00 A.M. and begin our standard daily reading. Before official Washington began perusing the morning newspapers, we were deep in such fare as the *National Intelligence Daily*, produced by the CIA; overnight diplomatic and intelligence cables, which the Situation Room staff synthesizes for each area; and various items sent to us from State, Defense, and CIA staff. Add a quick look at the daily press and the White House news summary, and it came to a *lot* of information.

At the seven-thirty meeting each of us would give a two- to three-minute summary of key events and issues in our respective areas that might be of interest to the president or might require some action on his part.

Every morning Bill Clark briefed the president on national security issues for at least a half hour. Usually Clark asked the senior staff member responsible for the current "hot" issue to participate, which meant the president would have a direct conversation with that staff member. It also gave the staff member himself a personal sense of the president's perceptions on the issue, which helped when it came time to write the background and decision memoranda for him. President Reagan was pleasant and easy to talk with.

All of us who were experts in foreign policy fields understood the necessity of effective briefing and synthesis of information. We knew that the ability to admit the need for more information and to ask questions was a mark of self-confident leadership, and Bill Clark felt comfortable in bringing the senior NSC staff into frequent and direct comunication with the president.

I would not have my first meeting with the president for another twelve days, but from the beginning I looked forward to it.

TUESDAY, OCTOBER 11

On my second day on the job at the NSC, I went over to the State Department to have lunch with Jim Michael, the principal deputy assistant secretary for Latin America (who in 1987 would be named our ambassador to Guatemala). Whenever I entered the State Department, I felt curious "vibes." I knew that many of the in-group in the Latin American bureau were unhappy that I had moved from the CIA—where I'd worked closely with Bill Casey for two years—to the National Security Council. They knew I was in wholehearted agreement with President Reagan, whereas many of them seemed to believe their calling was to save Ronald Reagan from himself.

The president was far too results-oriented for the careful tastes of some State Department types. Their main approach to foreign affairs was that the United States should make "agreements" with nations that presented problems. That was definitely not Ronald Reagan's style. He believed we should seek sensible agreements, yes, but measure our foreign policy by whether or not in the real world our strategic and democratic interests were advancing or retreating.

At our Tuesday lunch, Jim Michael told me about State's latest compromise proposal, which was intended to help obtain congressional approval for funding the "contras," the armed democratic resistance in Nicaragua. The State Department wanted a Republican congressman to propose that if Mexico (and the three other Latin American mediating countries) concluded that Nicaragua had stopped subversion of its neighbors, then the United States would automatically terminate its aid to the freedom fighters.

That stunned me. It was about as incompetent a proposal as I'd yet heard come out of State.

"Jim," I asked in a calm voice, "what do you think would happen next?"

"I think," he replied, "this would pass the House and the Senate."

I agreed with that reading but said, "If this became U.S. law, what would happen in Central America?"

My question seemed to puzzle him, as if he'd given little thought to the consequences of this action in Central America.

I pointed out that Mexico had been supporting the communist government in Nicaragua since 1979, both politically and with hundreds of millions of dollars in economic help. Indeed, Mexico's 1982 "Peace Plan" for the region totally contradicted President Reagan's policy, because it permitted the Sandinistas to completely ignore the 1979 OAS requirement that Nicaragua become a genuine democracy. Further, the whole process by which Nicaragua provided training, money, weapons, and other support to the communist guerrillas and terrorists was highly secret, disguised, and "officially denied."

Only the United States had the full range of intelligence resources to keep track of these clandestine activities. Mexico and three other Latin American countries had neither the means nor the political will to monitor the Sandinistas' subversive operations—which were done with the full technical aid of Cuba and the Soviet bloc. Furthermore, the United States should not relegate its foreign policy-making to other countries. Any proposed compromise with Congress should specify that only *our* president would make the final judgment about whether or not the Sandinistas were continuing subversive aggression against their neighbors.

Jim Michael looked as if I had just spoiled his lunch. Grimacing, he said, "But I've already discussed this compromise with Ollie North, and he agrees with it."

That surprised me, but I pointed out the possibility that North—as a marine major thinking about the immediate *tactical* objective of winning the next congressional vote—probably had not considered the Central American political dimension, just as State had not done so. I also remarked that Oliver North was in a separate unit of the National Security Council, the political-military unit, which was involved with the specifics of U.S. arms transfers and military aid around the world rather than with overall strategic policy.

WEDNESDAY, OCTOBER 12

Bill Clark and I discussed several Latin American issues. When we'd finished, I told him about my lunch with Michael and the State Department proposal.

"What do you think about it?" asked Clark in his quiet voice.

I answered by telling him what I'd told Jim Michael: "In short, it would be a major mistake."

Bill Clark said, "I agree, it contradicts the president's policy. Let's send State a memo immediately telling them this approach is not acceptable to the president."

And then, because I felt Clark needed to know, I told him that Michael had said Ollie North agreed with State.

"Constantine," said Clark, "*you* are the senior person for Latin America."

At Clark's direction, I wrote a short but pointed memo to State, which stopped—for a time—their misguided effort at a self-destructive compromise with Congress.

This was when I first met Fawn Hall—Ollie North's hardworking, efficient, and always pleasant secretary. My own NSC secretary would be Ms. Judy Huba, with whom I had worked at the CIA, but she was still helping my predecessor "phase out," so I asked Fawn to type my first NSC memo. She cheerfully agreed.

The draft was from me to the assistant secretary for Latin America. Fawn looked up and said—ever so gently—"I have never seen a memo from an NSC staff member addressed directly to someone outside the NSC."

"Oh? What do we do here?" I replied.

Fawn said, "Everything in writing from the NSC is sent either by the NSC adviser or by the president. There is very tight control to make sure the NSC adviser knows what the staff is doing."

"That makes sense, Fawn. Thanks for telling me. Nobody has told me about the procedures here yet. Fine. Let's do this memo, then, from Clark to Shultz." And so Fawn Hall—whose mother, Wilma Hall, worked as McFarlane's secretary—had just helped me avoid a bureaucratic mistake!

On that same day dramatic events were taking place on a little, once idyllic Caribbean island surrounded by warm blue-green waters. The island was Grenada, and there a dissident communist faction had staged a coup against Maurice Bishop, the communist prime minister. The new communist group, which called itself the Revolutionary Military Council, put Bishop and several of his key cabinet allies under house arrest.

The American media paid little attention to the events that led up to the Grenadian coup, but as a specialist in the region I had been watching them closely ever since the earlier coup, in March of 1979, which had brought Maurice Bishop and his New Jewel Movement (NJM) to power.

Following that action, and fulfilling its anti-Western rhetoric, the NJM quickly established diplomatic ties with Havana and, later, with Moscow. Within weeks of taking power it began to receive weapons shipments from Cuba.

In 1979 it had seemed to me as clear as the waters surrounding Grenada that a communist takeover was occurring in the Caribbean—the first since 1959 when Castro took power.

The Carter administration had made some diplomatic efforts to dissuade Maurice Bishop from establishing close links with Cuba and the Soviet bloc, but these suggestions were ignored. The Carter administration then looked the other way. It seemed to hope that if confrontation were avoided, time would mellow what it saw as little more than a *rhetorically* radical movement.

Unfortunately for the people of Grenada, time and events proved less than cooperative. While some in the Carter administration congratulated themselves on not "overreacting," 110,000 Grenadans found themselves virtual prisoners of a small Marxist-Leninist clique that was determined to establish, carefully but inexorably, a totalitarian dictatorship.

By 1981, the year I entered the Reagan administration, we had definitive information that the Bishop regime was acting in classic dictatorial fashion. It had established a secret police; persecuted and imprisoned many of the democratic, civic, and trade union leaders; established "mass organizations" of radicalized teenagers; and built up the previous regime's small police force and army from a total of about three hundred to more than four thousand.

President Reagan had decided to inform the public about the growing Cuban and Soviet-bloc military presence in the region and cited the building of *two* secret military facilities on Grenada, about which the people of that island nation knew virtually nothing. Sometimes, when Soviet or Cuban ships would unload military equipment at night, all of Grenada's lights were turned off! Guards along the route from the port to the secret military camps—which were guarded by Cubans—would keep people from knowing what military supplies the convoy was moving.

Further, the leaders of the nearby, mainly black, English-speaking Caribbean democracies were alarmed that Cuban, Soviet, East German, Bulgarian, and Libyan personnel were on Grenada, indoctrinating and training students and radicals from their countries. By 1981 they saw that Grenada was militarily and politically linked with Cuba and the Soviet bloc and had become a base for subversion directed against their small, vulnerable democratic islands. These leaders also knew that, since their security forces numbered in the tens or low hundreds, a trained and disciplined force of fifty to one hundred people acting with the benefit of surprise might be enough to stage a successful radical coup.

So in 1981 the Caribbean democracies established a regional mutual defense organization within the framework of the OAS called the Organization of Eastern Caribbean States (OECS). In case of problems in one member state, the others agreed that armed force could be used by the OECS to provide immediate help. Grenada was accepted as a member in the OECS in the hope that this might moderate its foreign activities and pull it in a democratic direction. Grenada joined the OECS but became no more moderate.

Now, in October 1983, as I read the reports about the factional battles between the two communist groups, I became concerned about the possible danger to the nearly eight hundred U.S. medical students who were studying on Grenada. Would they be caught in a crossfire as thousands of newly armed, radicalized Grenadians in the revolutionary police, army, and militia forces picked sides? A few years earlier some NJM leaders had publicly threatened to use the American medical students as hostages. Might one faction decide that holding Americans hostage could, as in Iran, give it political leverage?

But in crises there is opportunity, and I believed that this emergency just might present an excellent chance to restore democracy to Grenada while assuring the safety of our citizens. I immediately asked all the foreign policy agencies to provide their latest facts on Grenada. I also sought up-to-date information on any activities by Cuban or Soviet-bloc secret police or military units that might be sent to help one or the other communist faction. Further, I suggested that there be an immediate increase in efforts to detect any movement of Cuban or other hostile military forces toward Grenada.

THURSDAY, OCTOBER 13

At the morning meeting of the senior NSC staff, I provided a short account of the events in Grenada, the actions of hostile governments, and the concerns being raised by the friendly Caribbean democracies. Maurice Bishop had just returned from visiting Castro in Cuba, but the leaders of the coup were known as the hardest-line pro-Soviet group. Was there a tactical quarrel between Havana and Moscow and their respective Grenadian allies?

When I returned to my office, I drafted a one-page plan for the protection of our U.S. citizens and the restoration of democracy on Grenada. It suggested action by an international, legal, collective security force that would include democratic Caribbean countries. I intended to talk to Bill Clark about my Grenada plan at the next NSC staff meeting.

Toward the end of the day, Bill Clark asked us to come for an unusual afternoon NSC staff meeting in the Roosevelt Room. For several hours rumors had been circulating that had nothing to do with foreign policy. Now Bill Clark, in his direct and quiet way, told us he had decided to resign as National Security adviser and would accept the president's nomination to become the next secretary of the interior. We were all surprised and sad. Several people stood and told him publicly how much he would be missed.

I was a great admirer of "Judge" Clark for his calm counsel and his abiding level-headedness. Without him the National Security Council would never be the same. I knew that, but I didn't realize just how different it would be.

In the timeless fashion of Washington, there now began a process of speculation and maneuvering designed to influence President Reagan's decision about a new NSC adviser. Bill Casey and I talked about Clark's replacement, and I told him I thought Jeane Kirkpatrick would bring creative vision and in-depth knowledge of foreign policy issues. My impression was that Kirkpatrick would accept the position, which was probably the reason she discreetly took no part in any of the discussions and maneuverings.

Reportedly, Secretary of State George Shultz wanted to have Chief of Staff James Baker in the sensitive NSC job, and his poweful allies seemed to include Michael Deaver, who had the president's ear. It was rumored that at the last minute Weinberger and Casey talked the president out of naming James Baker, who had no foreign policy experience. The press speculated about possible appointees: Kirkpatrick, Under Secretary of State Lawrence Eagleburger, and Robert McFarlane were mentioned.

Often in Washington, once anyone's name comes up in the press, the next round of stories quotes anonymous sources who either praise or belittle the person in question. The balance between positive and negative anonymous commentary is decided by the personal views of the individual reporters and editors.

The two coalitions maneuvered to make their case to the president both directly and through the media. It seemed to me that Casey and Weinberger favored Kirkpatrick, while Shultz and his allies seemed to be pushing for Eagleburger. But by Sunday, October 16, the rumor mill had anointed McFarlane as the compromise choice. Sure enough, the next day the formal announcement was made; McFarlane moved up from deputy to NSC adviser. He immediately asked the senior staff members for a brief outline of the key issues in our area and informed us that he would continue the daily 7:30 A.M. meetings.

I was not too happy with McFarlane's appointment. I had seen a lot of him while representing CIA on the interagency groups that defined policy alternatives on Cuba and Central America in 1981 and 1982.

During the many weeks of interagency meetings to develop a strategy for Cuba and Central America in the autumn of 1981, McFarlane had always followed the State Department approach.

On several occasions when I felt there had not been adequate discussion, I asked to see McFarlane privately. Invariably his reaction seemed one of annoyance that I was raising uncomfortable issues and taking up his time. He did not find me a "get along by going along" type of person.

However, McFarlane clearly thought of himself as a realist about communism. Still, I thought, he would probably end my brief NSC employment as soon as he felt secure. In fact, that is what I told my wife on Monday evening. But I continued to work on my Grenada plan.

On Friday, October 14, I had given my preliminary Grenada plan to North and to the NSC senior intelligence director Kenneth deGraffenried. I asked both to keep it to themselves, since it was only a personal idea. And absolute secrecy would be needed for success both in getting a decision by the president and in carrying it out. I asked Ollie North to think about the military requirements but not to talk with anyone, and I asked deGraffenried to survey the available intelligence information for clues and to help me get additional information.

Both seemed skeptical that the administration would do anything like this. North in particular viewed it as highly unlikely and seemed to give it no further thought.

*   *   *

MONDAY, OCTOBER 17

I had a private meeting with a senior Defense Department official and talked about the plan with him. He was very blunt: "This plan has no chance whatsoever in this administration. McFarlane doesn't like you. He thinks you're too Reaganite. If you mention this to him, you'll give him the pretext to remove you from the NSC before you even get a chance to do any of the good work I know you can accomplish there. This is a waste of time. Take my advice. Don't do anything about Grenada, and don't mention this plan to McFarlane or Poindexter."

I was surprised by his intensity. But he had confirmed my own hunch that McFarlane viewed me as too "Reaganite." And I too thought the chances of the administration taking military action to restore democracy in Grenada were very slim.

"I know this is risky for me," I replied, "and I know the chances are slim that we will do it, but here's why we should: first, to protect U.S. citizens there; second, to help the Grenadian people and stop the threat the communist regime poses to the neighboring democracies; third, to have a positive political effect in Central America and throughout the Caribbean, encouraging our friends and demoralizing the violent communist groups; fourth—and this is my own personal hunch—I'm concerned that the Soviet Union might send or threaten to send nuclear-armed aircraft or submarines to be stationed in Grenada as a way to prevent us from meeting our commitment to deploy medium-range nuclear missiles in Europe next month."

The Soviets, I went on, had publicly threatened to respond with an "analogous deployment" that would threaten us. They realize that breaking the 1962 Kennedy-Khrushchev agreement by putting nuclear weapons in Cuba would immediately create a major war-threatening crisis. Moscow would not want to risk using Nicaragua because it was too valuable to them as a partner for the destabilization of Central America and Mexico on our mainland. But little Grenada, with a deep-water port that could accommodate Soviet nuclear-missile submarines and the big runway being completed, might be a perfect place for Soviet forces capable of carrying nuclear weapons. Then, if the United States backed down from its decision to put medium-range nuclear missiles in Europe, or removed them, Moscow could offer to remove the nuclear weapons it had "temporarily deployed" on Grenada.

Even if this fourth reason was speculative, the other three seemed to me to warrant action. I also pointed out that our failure to act would be perceived in the region as weakness.

So I was going to take the personal risk and tell McFarlane about the plan the next morning. In the meantime, I asked the senior Defense official to think about the military requirements and perhaps take a look, discreetly, at the 1981 maneuvers that were called "Operation Amber in the Amberdines." (At the time, the press had speculated that this was a rehearsal for action against Grenada, which is located in the Grenadine island chain.) He curtly reiterated his view: There was no chance that the administration would use force, and if I told my plan to McFarlane, I would soon find myself out of the NSC.

The next morning McFarlane presided over his first senior staff meeting. When my turn came I told him I viewed the situation in Grenada as one that required the protection of U.S. citizens and offered the opportunity to restore democracy. I told him I had writtten the outline of a political-military plan to accomplish this, had discussed it informally with a Defense Department colleague, and planned to discuss it today with Bill Middendorf, the U.S. ambassador to the Organization of American States (OAS) and with the State Department.

McFarlane looked at me with a quizzical expression. Had he fully understood what I was suggesting?

"Well," said the new NSC head, "that's okay." He then called on the next staff person. At least he hadn't said that I should stop thinking along those lines, which was a pleasant surprise, nor had he told me not to discuss the idea further.

Later that day I met with William J. Middendorf, Jr. A good-natured, hardworking, and enthusiastic conservative, by profession a banker, Bill Middendorf had served previous Republican administrations as secretary of the navy and as ambassador to the Netherlands. I had met him during the 1980 Reagan campaign when I'd served on an advisory group he chaired with his customary energy and style. He was one of the select few Reagan supporters who had received a policy-level presidential appointment in the Department of State, and he totally supported Ronald Reagan's foreign policies in Latin America.

Middendorf came over to my office in the Old Executive Office Building next to the White House for our meeting. We discussed the overall situation in Latin America for a while, and then I outlined my plan. I asked, "How many OAS members would oppose, and how many would support, a military action in Grenada—done with or without other Caribbean countries?"

Unlike my Defense Department colleague, Middendorf reacted positively and without hesitation. His eyes lit up, and he said, "If it could be done, this would be a great step for freedom." He promised to give the plan serious thought and to come up with his best judgment on how the OAS members might react and how they might get involved.

As he was leaving my office Middendorf said, "It's a great idea. But if I were you, I wouldn't get my hopes up."

I called one of the many competent foreign service officers at the State Department with whom I had worked very productively during the last couple of years, and asked about the thinking over at the Latin American bureau. He told me that not much had been done, even though Ambassador Milan Bish, a Reagan political appointee in Barbados, had sent urgent cables describing the deep concern of all the Caribbean democratic leaders. At the same time, another skilled Reagan political appointee, Ambassador William Hewitt in Jamaica, had informed Washington that Prime Minister Seaga, who was also quite worried, was planning to meet with six eastern Caribbean prime ministers.

Clearly, I was not alone in my concern about the situation in Grenada.

Right after the NSC staff meeting, I had a breakfast meeting with Bill Doherty of the AFL-CIO. For many years Bill had been head of the American Institute for Free Labor Development, which had trained more than 350,000 democratic union leaders from all the Latin American countries.

At breakfast Bill introduced me to several Grenadan labor leaders who had been persecuted by the communist government. I was pleased to meet them and asked questions about which Grenadan prodemocratic, political, labor, and civic leaders were in prison, which were still in Grenada, and which were in exile.

Doherty also told me that all the democratic union leaders throughout the Caribbean feared that the coup could lead to serious bloodshed since *both* communist factions were ruthless. And he expected the free trade unions of all the Caribbean countries to issue a resolution the next day or two denouncing both communist groups on Grenada. Doherty reminded me that a year before we had both been concerned about the movement of the military dictatorship in Suriname toward Cuba. Our concern was based on the fact that the same Cuban secret agent—Oswaldo Cardenas—who had helped Bishop take power in Grenada had also turned up in June 1982 as the new Cuban ambassador in Suriname. Doherty recalled that Castro, Bishop, and Bouterse—the dictator of Suriname—became allies in October 1982 after Bishop's visit to

Suriname. At the time, Bishop had told Bouterse the way to treat the democratic political and labor leaders who were protesting against the growing communist ties: "Either you eliminate them, or they will eliminate you." (The State Department ignored my written warnings about the grave danger to the democratic leaders in Suriname.) In December 1982 Bouterse, with Cuban secret police present, had rounded up, tortured, and murdered about fifteen of Suriname's key democratic leaders.

Now, the Grenadian labor leaders told us that there could be many executions in Grenada.

WEDNESDAY, OCTOBER 19

Today, the State Department held a meeting to explore one contingency in case it should become necessary: alternate ways of conducting a "quick in and out" military rescue of U.S. citizens on Grenada, with or without the consent of the revolutionary Military Council (RMC). State included representatives from the Joint Chiefs of Staff (JCS) and from CIA.

I learned of this meeting from friends at State, despite the fact that the Latin American bureau had "forgotten" to tell me or anyone from the NSC.

Why that happened involves a little known fact about the Reagan administration. From the administration's first days to the present, the State Department convened, and chaired, all the regular interagency meetings on foreign policy issues below the presidential level. The intention was to avoid the pulling and tugging between the NSC staff and the State Department by giving State the lead.

Theoretically, in exchange for this clout the State Department would provide a regular forum for participation by Defense, CIA, and NSC. If issues could not be agreed upon or required a major decision, the Restricted Interagency Group (R/IG) would move the question to the Senior Interagency group (S/IG) chaired by State or to the National Security Council, where the president would make the final decision. For this arrangement to serve the president, State had to be fair in the exercise of its authority.

The only problem was that things did not work out that way. In the highly charged and controversial process of making decisions on Central

America and Cuba during 1981–82, in my observation, State was definitely not fair.

During months of intense meetings and memoranda writing during the fall and winter of 1981, Assistant Secretary of State Thomas Enders had totally excluded Roger Fontaine and General Robert Schweitzer of the NSC staff from these meetings. And this was obviously done with McFarlane's full consent, as he chaired these meetings for Secretary of State Haig.

As a result, I would visit Fontaine and Schweitzer, and I would brief them about the debates at these meetings, show them the written memoranda, and ask their views on the issues. I did this out of respect for my colleagues and also because I knew they had to write the background memoranda for the president when it came time for final decisions to be made. It seemed essential that they be informed. I had also protested unsuccessfully to both Enders and McFarlane against their excluding the NSC staff.

In 1983 Enders had pulled the same trick by excluding me, then a CIA representative, from some interagency meetings. His method was to have the formal interagency meetings cover only routine issues and leave policy questions for "informal discussions" by his personal invitation only. Enders had been removed in May 1983, and the new assistant secretary for Latin America was Tony Motley, who kept all of Enders's top people. I had seen signs that their response to my move to the NSC might well be to play, or to replay, the same bureaucratic game: only those people who hewed the State Department line would get invited to interagency meetings.

Later on Wednesday, October 19, I learned that the drama in Grenada had intensified. A large pro-Bishop crowd had surged along the winding streets, freed Bishop and the four cabinet ministers who had been arrested along with him, and then gone up to Fort Rupert, which overlooked the picturesque harbor.

But then the jubilant Maurice Bishop and his followers were surprised at the fort by troops under the command of the Revolutionary Military Council. They put Bishop and his cabinet ministers against the wall and killed them. Then the troops turned their weapons on the crowd. In all, about fifty people died.

The Revolutionary Military Council then imposed a twenty-four-hour shoot-on-sight curfew. A short time later its troops reportedly surrounded the living quarters of the American medical students.

We received this news in the afternoon, and I worked through the evening to gather all available information and prepare three one-page overviews. First was a short, factual summary of what had happened. Second, I put together, from information I'd gathered over the previous few days, a summary of the reactions from the Caribbean governments, trade unions, democratic political parties, and religious groups—all of which denounced the bloodshed and urged action to prevent more deaths. Third, I described on one page the prodemocratic leadership and institutions that could provide the basis for the restoration of democracy.

I then urged McFarlane and Poindexter to convene the Crisis Pre-Planning Group (CPPG). Ordinarily only the State Department could convene subcabinet foreign policy meetings* but there was one exception: if the National Security Adviser decided there was a situation that might require presidential action involving the use of force, or the threat of force, he could take the inititative and convene the CPPG at the subcabinet level. And this, obviously, was such a case.

McFarlane and Poindexter agreed to convene the CPPG the following day. Next, I called Bill Middendorf and Under Secretary of Defense Fred Ikle on a secure phone and told them that they were invited to the CPPG, which would be about Grenada. I also talked on the secure phone to Bill Casey about other issues—he was about to leave on a trip—and I almost mentioned the Grenada plan but didn't want to get his hopes up.

By now my wife, Nancy, was wondering why, ever since the coup in Grenada, I left at six-thirty in the morning and did not return until midnight. I couldn't tell her, except to say that we were all very concerned about the safety of our citizens there. As a precaution, I asked her not to mention my long hours to anyone.

THURSDAY, OCTOBER 20

At 9:00 A.M., the National Security Council convened the Crisis Pre-Planning Group meeting on Grenada in room 208 of the Old Executive Office Building. At one end of the long wooden table sat John Poindexter, puffing on his pipe.

Room 208—"admission was by invitation only"—was the new crisis

---

* Defense chaired the subcabinet interagency meetings on defense policy and CIA could chair those on intelligence—but virtually all major issues were defined as foreign policy and therefore in State's domain.

dictate the first drafts of the various memos, Ollie would add his ideas, and Fawn Hall would type them into final shape for McFarlane and the president.

We were a good team, and I enjoyed working with Ollie and Fawn— we all wanted to see the United States act with strength.

At one point Ollie said to me, "When you showed me the plan last week, I never thought it would get this far. Maybe we'll really do something for a change."

Still, North remained basically dubious. He said he'd seen other occasions when nothing was done: after the terrorist bombing of the U.S. embassy in Lebanon in April of 1983, and in September 1983 after the Soviets shot down a civilian Korean Airlines flight. He predicted that the State Department would oppose action and argue for negotiations and that the Joint Chiefs of Staff would also oppose any military action.

North's prediction notwithstanding, the issue was now a serious item on the foreign policy agenda. I figured the opponents of action would most likely include White House Chief of Staff James Baker, Vice President Bush, and Secretary of State Shultz, all of whom tended to see things the same way. Unknown to most at the White House was the fact that I knew Baker's deputy, Richard Darman. Despite our different views on some issues, we had a cordial relationship that we had maintained over many years. Still, I was surprised when I started to work at the White House, and one of Darman's aides told me, "Dick thinks you are one of the most intelligent and creative people in government."

After trying unsuccessfully to see Richard Darman, I went to Philip Hughes, Vice President Bush's deputy adviser on foreign policy. Hughes had told me that when he worked with Admiral Murphy, Bush's chief of staff in the Carter Defense Department, he'd been appalled by the lack of effective action in the growing danger spots of Grenada and Nicaragua. I thought it likely Hughes would be preparing the background material for the vice president's participation in the NSC meeting, so I gave him copies of the same material I'd wanted to show Darman.

Shortly before 6:00 P.M., the participants began to arrive: Vice President Bush, Weinberger, Meese, JCS Chairman General Vessey, Acting CIA Director McMahon, Eagleburger, Motley, Ikle, Middendorf, North, and myself. We all went into the Situation Room in the White House.

President Reagan was traveling, as were Bill Casey and Jeane Kirkpatrick. I was pleased that McFarlane had agreed to my request that

Middendorf attend in order to provide information on the OAS aspect because I felt it could be a decisive factor.

The Situation Room is in the basement of the west wing of the White House. It is small, with comfortable chairs around a conference table and walls paneled in dark wood. The table seats twelve and is small enough so that all can speak to and hear one another. Around the wall are another fourteen chairs so each NSC participant can bring one of his staff.

Vice President Bush sat in the president's chair. McFarlane was at the opposite end. The cabinet members sat around the table. I thought about the significance of the issue, the short time they had to become briefed and the possibility that I might have to explain the situation. I could feel my mouth begin to go dry. But I knew from experience that if I felt the need to speak up, I wouldn't have a problem.

A factual update was the first order of business. Then the discussion moved to the availability of military forces and how long it would take to ready them. The objective, right from the beginning, was to plan a rescue that would guarantee quick success, but with a minimum of casualties on either side.

Secretary Shultz arrived late—he had been briefing Senator Helms and others on the secret contents of the 1962 Kennedy-Khrushchev accords on Cuba. The State Department representatives had made clear that the Caribbean democratic leaders wanted action and were deeply frightened by the bloodshed on Grenada. These Caribbean leaders would hold a summit meeting the next day to decide whether or not to make a formal request, under the terms of the OECS treaty, for collective military action.

I knew from our information that these leaders had a practical problem: what if they asked formally for military help from the United States and then were refused? Would the RMC take retaliatory actions? Might Castro? Their problem was very real.

It seemed to me as I listened intently that a gradual shift within the NSC group was taking place in favor of action.

As the entire discussion had already been framed in terms of the action being a combined rescue and restoration of democracy, the next issue had to do with who, or what, would replace the RMC.

As soon as I heard the question "Are there any democratic leaders and groups?" I was ready with the one-page overview I'd prepared. I gave copies to McFarlane, who passed them around the table while I briefly told the group that there were genuine democrats who could establish an interim government leading to fair and free elections.

There were a few more minutes of discussion, and then the one-hour meeting drew to a close. I felt a clear majority was tilting toward action. The first suggested presidential decision was to prepare for possible military action by shifting navy ships, which were taking a marine unit to rotate forces in Lebanon, plus other naval units, toward Grenada.

Secrecy was imperative. All government leaders would continue with their announced schedules, except for the cancellation of a trip the secretary of state was to have made to Central America the next day, Friday (a trip on which I was to accompany him). We hoped the atmosphere of normalcy would mislead the Soviets and Cubans into concluding that no military action was imminent.

As part of this plan, there would also be no change in the schedule of the top man. President Reagan and his new National Security adviser would travel to Augusta, Georgia, for a golf weekend. Secretary of State Shultz would go, too, further proof of the relaxed situation in Washington. In fact, however, the final decisions on the military operation would be made at an NSC meeting* on Saturday morning, October 22.

Plans for this NSC meeting began to take on a decidedly clandestine air. According to the plan, cabinet members would arrive at the White House complex using different entrances. And none would use the entrance most visible to the White Houses press corps—and watched by who knew who else in this day of bugged embassies—for that Saturday NSC meeting, which was to be held in room 208 of the Old Executive Office Building, a site chosen over the customary but more visible Situation Room.

Any leak, or even active speculation, could have jeopardized the mission and the lives of the American students.

Right after the Thursday evening meeting in the Situation Room, McFarlane, Poindexter, North, and I conferred briefly. We outlined the National Security Decision Directive (NSDD) that would serve as the president's written prepare-for-action order to all parts of the government. I went back to the office, wrote the directive, and showed it to Ollie North for his comments.

Then I wrote a memorandum from McFarlane to the president that summarized the facts, the discussion, and the consensus of opinion at the Thursday evening meeting and added the recommendation that the

---

* I shall use the term "NSC meeting" to include both the full NSC and the more restricted National Security Planning Group (NSPG) meetings of the president and his cabinet-level foreign policy advisers.

president sign the attached NSDD to indicate his approval of the preliminary actions.

Other work kept me in my office for hours. I didn't get home until almost three in the morning. I was dead tired, but I was becoming ever more hopeful that the United States would help restore democracy to Grenada.

FRIDAY, OCTOBER 21

I arrived early—having had three hours' sleep—and checked all the latest information so that I could give McFarlane a full report at the 7:30 A.M. meeting. I told him that State was preparing the detailed political plan that would be reviewed at a noon Restricted Interagency Group meeting.

"Fine," said McFarlane, "but we also need to have a CPPG meeting in room 208 late this afternoon to prepare for tomorrow morning's NSC meeting."

The noon meeting at the State Department, which was led by Assistant Secretary Motley, continued for two hours of increasing intensity. Motley and his staff, with career foreign service officer Richard Brown as chairman of the Grenada Task Force, had done a very good job in preparing a political plan for the rescue and the establishment of an interim government. Each of us—from Defense, CIA, NSC, and State—had a few ideas and suggestions.

I was pleased to see the State Department taking the lead, for once using the skills of its professional officers to plan for a successful move against a communist government. Why this positive leadership? Because Secretary Shultz, to my welcome surprise, had taken a firm position in favor of the Grenada rescue operation.

While we were meeting in Washington, the Caribbean democratic leaders from Jamaica, Barbados, Dominica, St. Lucia, St. Vincent, Montserrat, and St. Christopher-Nevis were meeting on Barbados. All believed a collective military intervention was necessary—and legal under customary international law and the terms of the 1981 OECS treaty.

Not only were hundreds of our medical students terrorized and surrounded by hostile forces, but many citizens from these Caribbean countries were also trapped by the twenty-four-hour shoot-to-kill curfew. Jamaica and Barbados, as the largest countries, were willing to provide substantial military forces, while the smaller island countries could offer only token contributions, some of which numbered in the tens or hundreds.

As these leaders decided what to do, they thought about the balance of regional military forces. Not only was there a 4,000-strong Grenadan "people's revolutionary army," but, more important, the leaders feared the 230,000-strong Cuban military, which included about two hundred jet fighter aircraft, fast torpedo boats, and even two submarines.

To them, the Cuban threat loomed large, particularly when they recalled the experience of recent years. These Caribbean leaders had witnessed, with astonishment and disbelief, the Ford and Carter administrations stand by passively while Fidel Castro sent 20,000 Cuban troops to help the communist faction take power in Angola and Mozambique in 1975; an additional fifteen thousand Cuban troops to help a pro-Soviet military group consolidate power in Ethiopia two years later; and, since 1979, more thousands of troops, secret police, and other operatives sent to prop up dictatorships in nearby Grenada and Nicaragua.

The Caribbean leaders also felt vulnerable. They knew that Cuba, the Soviets, and Libya were training some of their own citizens to disrupt life on their islands. For example, in 1980 the Cuban ambassador to Jamaica had been caught supplying gangs of radical terrorists with weapons and ammunition during the national election campaign. They also knew that Cuba could fly troops into Grenada quickly, and that most of their territories could be attacked by Cuban jet aircraft. Most important, these leaders knew that each year the Soviet Union provided $4 billion to Cuba (one-third of its gross national product), a sum that included tens of thousands of tons of weapons. That Moscow backed, paid for, and encouraged Castro's aggression in Africa and Latin America was a simple fact of life to them.

The Caribbean leaders hesitated to suggest military action in Grenada—an ally of Cuba—unless they were certain that the United States would participate. If the United States were unwilling to join them, the best they could do would be to deplore the violence on Grenada and avoid arousing additional hostility from Cuba or the new communist faction that conrolled Grenada.

At the same time, some in our government were hesitant to act unilaterally. It was my view that a collective security action was by far the most desirable for political and strategic reasons, but that if the Caribbean countries were too afraid to ask for help, the United States had the right to act alone to protect American citizens.

This was a time that called for courage by these leaders. Since no final decision had yet been made by President Reagan, it was not possible to give them a guarantee that if they asked for military help, the United

States would say yes. The answer could well be no, and then where would they be?

However, the skilled and energetic Reagan political appointee in Barbados, Ambassador Milan Bish, could tell the Caribbean leaders that the probability of U.S. military action would be much higher if they requested military action collectively. Still, for them such a step would be risky. I really did not know what they would do. Two thousand miles away, in Washington, we wondered, "Will they or won't they?"

Late Friday afternoon Poindexter chaired the CPPG meeting in room 208. The State Department had revised its preliminary action plan, and copies had been distributed. Now the tone of our discussions had shifted from whether we would act to how this could be accomplished with minimum casualties while insuring speed to avoid the likelihood of Cuban or Soviet counteraction.

I felt we also had to prepare, as a matter of prudence, against the possibility of harassment—or even more serious actions—Soviet accomplices, say, East Germany against exposed West Berlin, North Korea against South Korea, Libya or Syria targeting terrorists against U.S. airplanes, embassies, or other facilities.

Just the day before, Poindexter had said that the most secure means would be used to order U.S. ships to change course from Lebanon toward Grenada. Nevertheless, ABC news had learned about this and was broadcasting it.

It pleased me to see that now our government was working as a team, with all the subcabinet officials from State, Defense, CIA, and NSC carrying out their respective tasks with seriousness and collegiality. That evening Ollie North and I worked together for four and a half hours, writing the background and decision memoranda for the next morning's secret NSC meeting. Early in the evening Poindexter reviewed our first draft and made a few minor revisions. Then the Grenada memoranda were sent to the president, Shultz, and McFarlane at the golf course in Georgia.

SATURDAY, OCTOBER 22

I was in early to prepare for the 9:00 A.M. NSC meeting. Once again I pulled together all the new information on the situation on Grenada, the Caribbean, and the worldwide activities of Cuba and the Soviets that had arrived during the night.

The good news was the unanimous vote of the Caribbean democratic leaders to make a formal request for U.S. military participation with them to restore order in Grenada under the 1981 OECS treaty. Further good news was that the Cubans did not seem to be sending or preparing to send military reinforcements to Grenada. Castro undoubtedly felt that his political overtures and propaganda would deflect the United States from any military action—after all, for many years no one had taken any serious action to halt Cuban intervention in Africa, Grenada, or Nicaragua, nor impeded the training of thousands of terrorists in Cuba. Thus Castro's confidence and his contempt for American political leaders reduced the need to prepare for action against Cuban forces—or military targets—in Cuba.

Using the secure phone, I called Motley and briefed him on the agenda for the meeting. I told him President Reagan, Shultz, and McFarlane would participate from Georgia using two-way (secure) speaker phones. I also called and briefed Fred Ikle at Defense, who by now was beginning to believe that something might actually happen. Ollie North and I were working together closely, having essentially divided the coordination. I handled the political and strategic issues, while he dealt with the Joint Chiefs of Staff on the military operations. General Vessey, chairman of the JCS, had flown back to Washington on a special aircraft at 1:30 A.M. and assembled a secret group to begin serious planning for the combined military operation.

Shortly before 9:00 A.M., members of the foreign policy cabinet began arriving at the White House—all out of sight of reporters. The participants included Weinberger, Vessey, and Ikle from Defense; Eagleburger and Motley from State; McMahon and an operations officer from CIA; and Poindexter, North, and myself from NSC. Vice President Bush chaired the Washington group.

All participants were escorted to room 208, which many had never seen before. The vice president sat at one end of the long table and Poindexter at the other, with speaker phones positioned so that everyone could hear President Reagan, Shultz, and McFarlane.

The meeting began with an overview and an update. The State Department then told about the unanimous request for military assistance from the OECS Caribbean democracies and State's consultations with other interested governments. Furthermore, the larger Caribbean democracies, Jamaica and Barbados, were also willing to provide military forces for a joint operation with the United States.

We then took up, in broad terms, the military aspects of the operation. There were animated discussions about just how many Soviet-bloc,

Cuban, and Libyan hostile personnel were on Grenada. Views differed as to the combat capabilities of the Grenadan and Cuban forces. The conclusion was that by early Tuesday, October 25, the United States and allied forces would be in position to initiate military action that could assure rapid success with few casualties. As the first troops landed, U.S. ambassadors would inform Moscow, Havana, and other governments with hostile personnel on the island that captured noncombat personnel would be treated correctly and repatriated as quickly as possible.

The only legal authority on Grenada was the governor general, Sir Paul Scoon. He was a Grenadan citizen appointed by the British crown—the same procedure as in other independent commonwealth countries—who served as head of state (the late Prime Minister Bishop had been head of the government).

Sir Paul Scoon had gone into hiding right after the violence, and he was still there, on the island. Ingeniously, he had smuggled out a request for external help in restoring law and order. U.S. commandos would make the rescue of the medical students and Sir Paul Scoon their first priority.

The detailed hour-by-hour plan was circulated to everyone at the meeting. There was also a short discussion of the War Powers Resolution, which requires the president to get approval of Congress if he intends to deploy U.S. troops in combat for more than sixty days. There was little question that U.S. combat forces would be out before that time, and the Caribbean troops could provide internal security for the interim government.

The president had participated and asked questions over the speaker phone; he made his decision. The United States would answer the call for help from our Caribbean neighbors. We would assure the safety of our citizens. U.S. forces, along with those from several other Caribbean countries, would land in Grenada early Tuesday morning, October 25,1983.

The NSC meeting ended at about 11:30 A.M. The president clearly had the unanimous agreement of his foreign policy cabinet and other key advisers. I went back to the office to draft McFarlane's memorandum to the president, along with the National Security Decision Directive, which the president would use to order actions by State, Defense, and CIA.

Ollie North took a look at the NSDD before I gave it to Poindexter for his review. Poindexter made a few changes. I then got on the secure telephone to read the draft NSDD to several senior officials while Poindexter called others—he wanted to be sure they agreed that the draft presidential order accurately reflected the president's decisions and that its meaning was clear.

By 2:10 P.M. I had finished writing the decision memorandum and final NSDD for signature by the president. Poindexter, as acting NSC adviser, obtained authorization from the president and then sent signed copies to State, Defense, and CIA. The American government now moved into full gear to carry out the decision.

I felt an enormous sense of satisfaction about this important decision. Now it was vital that everyone keep the secret and carefully monitor Cuban and Soviet actions to prevent their interference. I told Poindexter that we had just received information that the Revolutionary Military Council was going to reopen the airport and permit flights to enter, and that General Austin wanted to talk with us. Poindexter's reply was one of the few times I heard him joke.

In a mock-serious voice he said, "Constantine, tell the State Department to inform Grenada that we will send some people to talk, and that they will arrive early next week."

While Ollie North continued work on the military issues, I spent the rest of the afternoon preparing the political aspects, such as a draft of the president's public announcement, a fact sheet to be used by the White House press office in briefing the news media on Tuesday, and talking points for the president, McFarlane, and Poindexter to use as they briefed congressional leaders the night before the operation and as they met with congressmen and the media on October 25.

I had never before realized that the first draft of nearly everything a president says or writes about foreign policy is written by the NSC staff and then often given to the White House speech writers, who have the talent to turn analysts' facts into memorable presidential prose. Over the next years I would work often and closely with the creative men and women of the White House speech writing staff, ably led by Bentley Elliott and, later, by Anthony Dolan.

After touching base with North and Poindexter in the early evening, I returned home at about 8:00 P.M.

SUNDAY, OCTOBER 23

After receiving the seven A.M. telephone call with the sad news about the Beirut terrorist attack on our marines, I went to the White House and watched Reagan's helicopter arrive. Shortly after, the president began leading a series of NSC meetings, first on Lebanon and then about Grenada, which lasted until about seven that evening. Participants in these NSC meeetings included Bush, Shultz, Weinberger, Vessey, McMahon, Poindexter, and McFarlane. Along with Tony Motley, Fred Ikle, and Under Secretary of State Lawrence Eagleburger, Ollie North and I took part in the Grenada discussions.

During the first round on Grenada, the president was given an update on the political and military situation, which included a status report on the military planning and combat deployment. Reagan questioned us, probing, in his very genial and quite effective way, to make sure that he had everybody's honest viewpoint about the coming Grenada operation. This was certainly not the detached Reagan about whom I had read so much. He was somber, sensible, and energetic as he carefully weighed whether the tragedy in Lebanon should affect the decision on Grenada that he had made the day before.

During the time Lebanon was being discussed in the Situation Room, we in the "Grenada group" waited next door in McFarlane's office. I had never met Under Secretary Eagleburger before, although I knew about him. He was a career foreign service officer who had been Henry Kissinger's right-hand man for nearly eight years (1969–76). I had worked closely with one of Eagleburger's staff in 1982, helping to persuade members of the foreign policy cabinet to support the excellent proposal for the National Endowment for Democracy. So I opened a conversation by complimenting Eagleburger for his leadership in that project. I then suggested that once Reagan reaffirmed his Grenada decision, we should prepare for three additional tasks.

First, we should plan to persuade friendly countries in Latin America and Europe that this was a correct and necessary action. I suggested that Mexico and some European Social Democrats would most likely condemn the Grenada rescue, and I proposed that Eagleburger send Michael Ledeen, who had worked in his office as a special assistant to Secretary Haig, to Europe. Ledeen could help explain the facts about internal communist repression and external subversion from Grenada. I also urged that Eagleburger or Ikle assure that government film crews would go in with the troops. They could film the opening of the political prisons and do interviews with democratic leaders who had been held there. Also, the film crews should show the world what the secret military facilities on Grenada looked like and what was found there.

"Past experience," I said, "tells us to expect that the worldwide communist apparatus will tell lies about our actions and motives. We have to counter this by showing the truth in a highly visual and vivid way."

Second, I felt we had to assure the humane deinstitutionalization of the communist dictatorship. This meant that all combat forces should be instructed to assure proper treatment for all prisoners and especially to protect former Grenadian officials, including those of the secret police and military, from any torture or physical abuse by other Grenadians who might, after four years of dictatorship, want revenge.

We also needed to establish a system of photographing, fingerprinting, and questioning all prisoners from the communist regime, which would permit us to identify the key leaders and distinguish them from the majority rank and file, who could then be released soon.

Only the top communist leaders need be held in prison, and they should be given a fair trial using the English legal procedures that were customary in the former British colonies of the eastern Caribbean. I said these concerns for due process and humane treatment were important because of our political values, but also because it was essential to show the people working in and fighting for communist regimes in Nicaragua, Angola, Afghanistan, and elsewhere that their defeat would not mean abuse, torture, death, or prolonged imprisonment. Grenada could be a positive example of reconciliation after liberation from communist dictatorship.

Third, I suggested we assure that an interim government would be composed of respected individuals who were genuinely committed to political democracy. Standing by while a communist dictatorship was replaced by an anticommunist dictatorship would be a major mistake. We should be prepared to help the genuinely democratic groups organize themselves right from the start. Perhaps the new National Endowment for Democracy could play a positive role in this regard, as could Bill Doherty's AFL-CIO free labor group.

Since we had to wait for an hour or two while the NSC discussed Lebanon, I thought this would be a good time to discuss the actions we would need to take after the military operations began on Tuesday morning. Fred Ikle supported these ideas and made some suggestions about how the military might be prepared for its postcombat role in temporary civil governance.

To my surprise, Eagleburger said practically nothing in response, and Motley seemed not to grasp what I meant by "humane deinstitutionalization of the dictatorship."

We had our last discussion with President Reagan and the NSC from about 5:00 to 6:00 P.M. Then Ollie North, a few of the others, and I waited ouside the Situation Room for another hour while Reagan and the foreign policy cabinet had a final discussion about both Lebanon and Grenada.

North was very pessimistic. He thought the Grenada operation would be canceled in the name of retaliation in Lebanon—which would then also not happen. He said the Joint Chiefs of Staff simply did not want to use U.S. military forces in limited combat operations. My guess was different. I felt that Reagan would stick with his decision on Grenada, but I had no sense as to what, if anything, would be done in Lebanon. At 7:00 P.M. we learned the answer: the Grenada operation would take place as scheduled, early Tuesday, October 25.

That night Nancy and I were meeting Judith Hernstadt, Max Singer, and his wife, Suzanne, for dinner. I apologized for arriving an hour late. Assuming I'd been held up by the crises in Lebanon, everyone asked what would be done about the killing of our marines. All I said was that there was a great deal of thinking going on. Then I changed the subject.

MONDAY, OCTOBER 24

The NSC convened another CPPG meeting to review the situation and plans. Fortunately, though the students remained surrounded, they were not under any tighter control. The rescue operations still seemed feasible.

I had another assignment that afternoon: I was to brief Attorney General William French Smith on the forthcoming operation. McFarlane wanted to be sure that the attorney general knew what was about to happen and that he concurred in the NSC interpretation of the War Powers Act and other relevant laws. I had never been to the Justice Department before and was struck by the majestic decor and size of the attorney general's suite and formal office.

Attorney General Smith had an elegant small private office behind a nearly hidden wooden door, and this is where we had our discussion. Robert Kimmitt, the NSC legal counsel and executive secretary, was with me.

Back at the NSC, I saw Ollie North briefly and asked him how the military preparations were going. "Fine," he said. I didn't ask for any further information.

Weinberger and Vessey had decided that only the president and a few others—probably including McFarlane and Shultz—should know the details of the military plans in advance. My two years at CIA had conditioned me not to probe where I did not have a "need to know."

Besides, the problem of unauthorized leaking of information to the news media was so pervasive that many of us preferred not to know sensitive detailed information outside our scope of direct responsibility so that we could not even be *suspected* of having leaked such information. My work concentrated on the international political strategy of this operation. Since I had no expertise to contribute to the military planning, I made no effort to find out any specifics.

Later that afternoon McFarlane asked me to update the public briefing materials I had prepared on Saturday and to assure that he and the president had all the information needed to field questions from congressional leaders that night and from the media the next morning. Personally, I was apprehensive about the reaction of some in the congressional leadership to the Grenada operation once they were briefed in advance later in the evening. Would they all keep the secret? I had been surprised by the unwillingness of many Democrats in Congress to face up to the reality of dramatically increased Cuban and Soviet subversive aggression through support for communist guerrillas in Central America—even after the Reagan administration had declassified definitive evidence in 1981, 1982, and 1983. Clearly, the post–World War II bipartisan agreement about foreign policy facts, methods, and objectives was gone, and I hoped that none of the congressional leaders would try to derail the Grenada operation by telling the media.

At about eleven-thirty that night, McFarlane, Poindexter, North, Bob Sims (the NSC media liaison), and I sat around the Situation Room table for a final review. McFarlane told us how the congressional leaders had reacted: House Speaker O'Neill "understood the reason for the action"; House Majority whip James Wright "supported the need to take a stand against communist subversion"; Senate Democratic Majority Leader Byrd opposed the action and would say so publicly after it was announced tomorrow; Senate Republican Leader Howard Baker thought it was "bad politics," an enormous burden for him to carry; and House Republican Leader Robert Michel was "strongly supportive."

McFarlane was, I thought, genuinely surprised by Howard Baker's lack of support and by Tip O'Neill's willingness to give his assent to the action.

McFarlane then asked, "How are we going to sell this to the public?"

I answered, "By telling the truth about the need to rescue our students and by stressing the positive results that will come from the restoration of democracy and the ending of a communist dictatorship."

McFarlane then assigned several among us to brief a few members of the House and Senate Foreign Relations committees that night. He said that the CIA would brief the intelligence committees early the next day.

Poindexter, in one of the few personal comments he made to me in three years, said, "Well, Constantine, your initiative worked. Tomorrow we'll see the results." Then he added in a quieter voice, "I heard a rumor that you were involved in the fall of Allende in Chile."

That surprised me. I said, "No, John, I have been interested in Chile since living there in 1964, but in 1973 I was at HEW trying to help poor children get a better education."

That apparently surprised *him*, because all he said was, "Oh."

I went back to the crisis management center in room 208 and checked on the latest information. Later I went to Ollie North's office and found him asleep on his sofa. Obviously he was going to be spending the night in the Old Executive Office Building. I covered Ollie with his overcoat, then called the Situation Room to let them know where he was, since he would probably not hear the telephone or his beeper.

I arrived home at about midnight.

TUESDAY, OCTOBER 25

The first units of the combined Caribbean and U.S. forces landed before dawn. Fighting was heavy, especially at the main airfield where U.S. Rangers were parachuting into positions defended by the military-trained Cuban construction battalions. I pulled the information together into a one-page situation report on the battle, including political reactions by hostile governments such as Cuba, Nicaragua, and the Soviet Union, plus the initial reaction of friendly governments. Then I walked over to the White House for what turned out to be one of the most interesting experiences of my life.

The State Department had had the excellent idea of inviting Mrs. Eugenia Charles, the prime minister of Dominica, to appear with President Reagan when he made the public announcement at 9:00 A.M. Prime Minister Charles was the chairperson of the Organization of Eastern Caribbean States, and it was she who had signed and transmitted the formal request for United States assistance.

An air force plane had flown Mrs. Charles from the Caribbean early in the morning, and I met her as she arrived at the White House just before 7:30 A.M. We chatted for a few minutes, and I told her that we would be joining President Reagan, Secretary Shultz, and Robert McFarlane in the Oval Office for coffee and juice. I mentioned that if she agreed, she and President Reagan would appear together to make the public announcement at nine, and that the U.S. government would welcome her speaking with members of Congress and the media about the reasons for the Grenada operation as perceived by her fellow democratic Caribbean leaders.

Mrs. Charles, an intelligent and dignified black woman in her fifties, was exceptionally articulate and charming. Some described her as "a Caribbean Jeane Kirkpatrick." She was obviously a bit tired from her predawn airplane trip but was clearly optimistic. She said the Grenada operation would save many, many lives and would restore peace in her region.

We walked from the White House basement to the Oval Office. I had never been there before and as a new arrival still had my temporary White House identification.

"Excuse me, sir?" said the oh-so-polite but nonetheless surprised Secret Service guard when I asked him how to find the Oval Office. Senior staff members who have first-thing-in-the-morning access to the president, and who are escorting an obviously important visitor, usually know how to find that office themselves.

"Prime Minister Charles," I said quickly, "has a meeting scheduled with the president." He nodded and gave me directions.

Moments later we entered the Oval Office. The president warmly welcomed the prime minister. After wishing me good morning, he escorted her to one of the two facing armchairs, waited for her to sit down, then took the other chair.

A fire was crackling in the fireplace, and the early-morning light was already filtering through the large windows of the Oval Office. The ambience was one of serenity.

Secretary Shultz and Bud McFarlane, who were already there, stood to greet Mrs. Charles. A steward brought in coffee and orange juice. We sat, and I experienced a distinct sense of appreciation at being part of this historic moment.

Prime Minister Charles opened the conversation by thanking the president for having decided to help. She said that year after year the Grenadian dictatorship had gotten worse. And, she added, the faction that had overthrown and murdered Maurice Bishop were the most hard-line, dangerous, and pro-Moscow communists.

The president, in turn, said that we and the eastern Caribbean states shared a common democratic heritage and a desire for peace. He described the contents of his public announcement and asked the prime minister if she would be willing to accompany him to the White House press room later that morning and answer questions from the media.

"I would be pleased to appear with you, Mr. President," said Mrs. Charles, and added that she would be most willing to speak out during her visit so that the American people could learn the truth about the situation in Grenada.

I remember being struck by the realization, as we sat in the Oval Office, of the absolute *rightness* of the decision the president had made.

Thirty minutes later I escorted Prime Minister Charles to the White House dining room, where we were to have breakfast with Deputy Secretary of State Kenneth Dam. I had known Ken Dam slightly when he served on the domestic policy staff of the Nixon White House and I worked for HEW Secretary Elliot Richardson. Dam was an old friend of Secretary of State Shultz's from the time they both were on the faculty of the University of Chicago. When Shultz succeeded Haig at State in July of 1982, he brought Ken Dam in as his deputy, and I had occasionally briefed him.

I introduced the prime minister to Ken Dam, and the three of us talked for a while about the Grenada operation. Then I steered the conversation toward the kinds of questions—hostile and difficult—I guessed the media and our opponents in Congress would be asking.

Prime Minister Charles said, "I have heard that the White House press corps is very assertive. Is that true?"

Both Dam and I said something, but I'm sure we ducked the question. I had yet to see a presidential press or news conference in person. I was sure that the reaction of the U.S. media would be essentially negative. For the next ten minutes I played the role of devil's advocate, posing—as diplomatically as I could—as an interrogator and asking the hardest and most hostile questions I could think of. Then we worked on the phrasing of brief yet substantive answers. (In the future at the White House I would do this quite often, helping visiting heads of state prepare for the skeptical, occasionally hostile questions of the media.)

At a moment when Mrs. Charles was out of the room temporarily, I was handed the latest draft of the president's imminent announcement about the action in Grenada. I was surprised to see that the State Department had deleted, as one of our stated purposes, "to restore democracy." I quickly suggested to Ken Dam that it was important for the president to say this because we wanted people to know that our purpose was also to see a real democracy—not any type of new dictatorship—in place in Grenada. I was pleased that he agreed and we could make the change.

Just moments before 9:00 A.M., I followed President Reagan, Prime Minister Charles, McFarlane, and Motley into the White House press room.

The media, who knew by now that the military action had already begun, were very angry. Part of that anger stemmed from the fact that only yesterday, in answer to a direct question about the possibility of such action, Admiral Poindexter had told the press that it was "preposterous." Further, the administration had decided that until the fighting ended, there would be no media presence with the forces in Grenada, and, obviously, no members of the media had been asked to make the trip.

Suddenly the television lights were on, and the room quieted down. Momentarily.

President Reagan gave his brief statement. When he'd finished he introduced Prime Minister Charles, who made some brief, extemporaneous statements that emphasized the legal nature of the action and the OECS request for assistance from the United States, Jamaica, and Barbados. Mr. Reagan and Mrs. Charles stayed for a few more minutes of questions. Then Assistant Secretary Motley took the podium and, along with Larry Speakes, handled mostly hostile questions for the next half hour.

At 10:00 A.M. McFarlane and Poindexter, who had been giving background briefings to the media, called me to the Situation Room and told me that the president would be giving a national television speech on Lebanon and Grenada. We discussed themes for that speech for about half an hour. I was instructed to write the Grenada portion. In one hour I came up with a ten-page draft, which I gave to Poindexter.

I then made a special visit to see Dick Darman. I wanted to explain exactly why, in my opinion, the Grenada rescue was a positive step from the standpoint of national security.

Next I kept a previously arranged lunch with Bill Doherty. He was overjoyed at the news reports. Doherty told me he would get down to Grenada as soon as the fighting ended to help the democratic labor unions start up again. I asked him to talk to Lane Kirkland, president of the AFL-CIO, and suggest some labor movement support for President Reagan's courageous action.

After lunch I met with Bentley Elliott, who in just a few hours transformed my rough draft and my fact sheets into a polished first draft of the president's speech.

At five o'clock I was asked to brief a group of embassy officials from the United Kingdom and some British Commonwealth countries. For the next few days I did quite a bit of that, providing the administration's point of view, through a series of radio interviews (done by telephone) set up by the White House media office.

Just as I'd suspected, the initial reaction from the major media was negative. And those Democrats in Congress who regularly opposed the president used such words as "totally opposed," "outraged," and "ashamed." Tip O'Neill, who had been described as supporting the action, changed his mind and was sharply critical.

Meanwhile, on Grenada the fighting continued all day long. Many of the medical students and Sir Paul Scoon had been rescued quickly, but armed resistance flared up throughout the day. At the NSC we received frequent reports and the news grew increasingly encouraging.

In the first twenty-four hours we took about 560 Cuban prisoners, plus several thousand Grenadian troops. It was evident that the people of Grenada *welcomed* the combined U.S. and Caribbean forces, recognizing them as liberators from a frightening, oppressive regime. Our forces learned that one out of every one hundred Grenadians had been held as political prisoners (the equivalent number in the United States, given our relative population, would be 2.4 million people). And they were telling tales of suffering and torture.

Combat ended on Thursday, October 27, but there was still the need to be watchful lest Castro or the Soviets decide to retaliate.

The U.S. interagency group that had put together the rescue faced several immediate tasks: helping the OECS and the Grenadians organize an interim government and a temporary security force; identifying and questioning Grenadian prisoners; identifying and repatriating the Cuban, Soviet-bloc, Libyan, and North Korean operatives who'd been taken prisoner; and assisting in the restoration of normal utilities, communications, and public services.

Even though the number was relatively small, there *were* casualties: 18 from the U.S. forces were killed and 116 wounded; Grenadian casualties included 45 killed and 337 wounded; and of the almost 800 Cubans, 29 were killed and 59 wounded.

By November 9, 49 Soviets, 10 East Germans, 3 Bulgarians, 15 North Koreans, 17 Libyans, and all but 2 of the Cubans had been returned to their countries. By December 15, all the U.S. combat forces had been withdrawn, which left only training, medical, police, and logistical support elements to help the Caribbean forces.

A November 1983 CBS poll taken in Grenada found that 92 percent of the people there welcomed the rescue forces. Within days of the event

U.S. public opinion polls showed that the overwhelming majority of the American people agreed that President Reagan had done the right thing. A bipartisan congressional delegation visited Grenada shortly after the rescue, and virtually all of the congressmen—including some of the Democrats who had been most critical—returned to say that they had talked to the Grenadian people and seen the warehouses filled with Cuban weapons, and they now agreed with the president.

After ten days had passed I urged that the captured files be carefully and systematically reviewed, along with the weapons and facilities used for the subversive training. We had a unique opportunity: Grenada was the first country where a communist regime had been toppled. That meant there had to be a rich vein of knowledge and insight to be mined by carefully analyzing the methods that had been used to consolidate power internally and the techniques of subversive cooperation with Cuba and the Soviet bloc.

The president ordered this systematic analysis be done, and the result is a unique archive, available to the public, that has already provided much valuable information, both through U.S. government publications and the work of scholars (such as Professor Jiri Valenta).

Among the findings that have been documented are these:

- By 1983 the New Jewel Movement had fully revealed itself as a Marxist-Leninist totalitarian party, complete with Central Committee and Politburo.
- The New Jewel Movement had a secret police and many political prisoners.
- The army and revolutionary militia totaled four thousand—stronger than the combined forces of all its OECS neighbors.
- There were almost nine hundred military advisers and other personnel on Grenada from Cuba, the Soviet Union, East Germany, Bulgaria, North Korea, and Libya.
- Grenada had concluded five secret military agreements—three with the Soviet Union, one each with Cuba and North Korea.
- Soviet-bloc weapons (starting with Cuba's first shipment in April of 1979)—far more powerful than those possessed by any neighbors—included artillery, armored personnel carriers, rocket launchers, and antiaircraft weapons; there were enough infantry weapons and uniforms for a force of twenty thousand.
- Documents and other evidence proved that Grenada was working with Cuba and the Soviet bloc to support subversion in the English-speaking Caribbean.

*   *   *

From the beginning we had said that the first and most important reason we went into Grenada with force was that the lives of American citizens were in danger. Initially skeptics claimed we exaggerated the danger to have an excuse to take on the communists. Which side was right? The answer to that question was provided by the returning students themselves.

After the rescue I was in the White House watching the live television coverage of the students' return. Some of us were apprehensive, knowing that some of these students would be political liberals who, because of their general opposition to Ronald Reagan, might minimize the danger they'd been in (now that they were safe) and denounce the whole operation. Stranger things had certainly happened.

So, as we in the White House watched the first few students come down the ramp from the plane, we knew the media would search for critics. We knew that if the media found even one, two, or three among the eight hundred students, these would be featured on every network news program, and they'd have their minutes of celebrity.

As the first students reached the ground, instead of walking over to the bank of microphones and press people, they stopped. I watched with amazement—and happiness—as one knelt and *kissed the ground*. Obviously it was a moment of great feeling for them—and also for us at the White House.

One student said simply, "I support President Reagan's move. . . . He really did save our lives."

A few weeks later the president invited some of the brave American soldiers who had fought in Grenada, and the medical students they had rescued, to the White House, where some of the soldiers were given medals. Then the two groups of young Americans had a chance to meet each other, as well as President Reagan, Secretary of State Shultz, National Security adviser McFarlane, and the rest of us who had worked behind the scenes in anticipation of this happy moment.

I looked out the White House window and across the green lawn to the Washington and Jefferson memorials. I felt pride in the fact that President Reagan had acted with courage, that his entire administration had performed correctly, competently, and with real teamwork. It was a grand feeling, but it was one of the few times I would feel that way for the next three years.

PART TWO

CENTRAL AMERICA

3

CENTRAL AMERICA: MISSERVING THE PRESIDENT

A communist Central America poses the grave risk that one hundred million people from Panama to our open southern border will come under the control of pro-Soviet dictatorships. Violence and a human tidal wave of refugees will then cross into the United States.

PRESIDENT RONALD REAGAN
TELEVISION SPEECH,
MAY 9, 1984

It was a sunny summer day, and through the large windows of the Cabinet Room I could see the colorful flowers in the Rose Garden. An intense NSC meeting had just ended with President Reagan making an important decision—one that had sharply displeased Secretary of State Shultz.

Reagan got up from the table and began to walk toward the Oval Office when Secretary of State Schultz also got up, continuing to pursue his point. Shultz's large frame blocked the narrow space between the table and the windows, bringing the president to a halt.

Reagan's face took on a quizzical look at this sign of Shultz's intensity. He paused, listened for a few moments, and said genially: Very interesting, George, but I have to go to my next appointment. Shultz moved aside, and Reagan went out.

Moments later, as I was gathering up the written agenda pages from the meeting, I saw Secretary of Defense Weinberger finish a short chat and move toward the door. Shultz now moved into the doorway, blocking his path. Pointing his forefinger at Weinberger's chest, Shultz rumbled angrily: "If you can't support negotiations in Central America as the president ordered, you should leave the administration!"

I tried not to listen, but Shultz's tone and anger made such discretion impossible.

Weinberger looked his former colleague and boss right in the eye and replied in a voice that was quiet with suppressed indignation: "All of us—Casey, Kirkpatrick, the president, and I—favor negotiations. If you can't obey the president's clear orders on the *objectives* of those negotiations, *you're* the one who should go."

This encounter reflected the intensity of the inside struggle over U.S. policy in Central America.

Throughout his administration, Ronald Reagan has been fighting a policy battle over Central America. The public knows his usual opponents: those Democrats in the Congress who year after year have disagreed with him about the seriousness of the communist takeover threat in Central America and—if that occurred—potentially in Mexico as well.

What the public does not realize, however, is that some members of the president's own foreign policy cabinet have also acted against his policy decisions on Central America. Believing in their own good intentions, they have conducted an invisible campaign to pursue their own foreign policy agenda, in Central America and elsewhere.

Of course differences of opinion exist within any administration, and infighting can be fierce. Honest differences are part of the process of forming policy, and the president is best served by having two or more clear choices about which he has been fully informed. But once he decides, his appointees should regard his decision as final.

During my five years "inside," I witnessed seven major episodes where some of President Reagan's closest advisers tried to short-circuit the process. Even after the president had clearly stated his policy—both in public speeches and in formal, written National Security Directives—one cabinet member would follow a critically different course of action. And that cabinet member would make every effort to keep his initiatives secret, not just from his colleagues, but—it seemed—even from the president himself. In several cases only a last-minute intervention saved the president's policy—and thereby averted the slide toward a major setback.

Starting in early 1984 Michael Deaver and White House Chief of Staff James Baker arranged for Shultz to have at least one and sometimes two completely private meetings each week with President Reagan. (This continued, and in 1987 former White House Chief of Staff Donald Regan told the Iran-contra congressional investigators that during 1985 and 1986 Shultz had met ninety-nine times alone with Reagan.) These meetings gave Shultz the means to keep the president informed about foreign events. But they also offered a setting where Shultz could try to maneuver the president toward the policies preferred by the State Department—without having to contend with the often differing views of the rest of the foreign policy cabinet as occurred during meetings of the National Security Council. Shultz couldn't have pulled this off without the acquiescence of the NSC adviser, Robert McFarlane, whose *job* it was to make sure that President Reagan was fully informed and not preempted by any part of the government.

A few of us within the NSC, upon learning of surreptitious efforts to counter the president's stated policy on Central America, tried to persuade McFarlane and Poindexter to give the president all the facts and call an NSC meeting so that there could be a full and fair debate. But time and time again this counsel was simply ignored until I took vigorous action to assure that the issue reached the president.

In my opinion the stakes for our country were extremely high. I was convinced then, and remain firmly convinced now, that the unintended result of the secret plotting would have been just what the president predicted: a communist Central America and, in turn, the very real possibility of a communist Mexico and Panama.

Those of us in the administration who supported the president's policy agreed with him that only by helping the Nicaraguan people establish genuine democracy in their country would both dangers be avoided.

The State Department side, however, felt that the way to avert this possibility was to strike a political bargain with the Sandinistas: if they promised to stop helping the communists take power in the rest of Central America, we would not object to a communist Nicaragua. In other words, you can *be* communists, just don't *spread* communism. The State Department also dismissed the idea that communist victories in Central America would likely lead to an alliance among those new regimes and the communist movement within Mexico.

The president's supporters could have blocked the approaches that went against his policy had they been openly and fairly proposed through officially prescribed procedures. But both before and after George Shultz became secretary of state in mid-1982, some people at the State Department were conducting their own Central American policy through a variety of time-tested bureaucratic tactics: bypassing normal channels, making secret diplomatic contacts, suppressing and withholding information, delaying the release of key documents, holding private parallel meetings instead of doing business at regular ones, furtive networking, leaking to the press, dealing opponents within the administration out of the action, undercutting responsible officials, and, of course, simple backbiting.

I was to see all these techniques in action. I would even be the target of a few of them myself.

The key to President Reagan's Central America policy has been a realistic commitment to democracy. It sounds so obvious: who can be against "democracy"? And this policy is based as much on geopolitical realism as on American political ideals. Unfortunately, as we shall see, not everyone had grasped this—even within the Reagan administration.

For some years now three competing groups have been waging a dramatic struggle in Central America: first, those committed to political democracy, whose views cover the spectrum from the democratic left to the center and democratic right; second, communist guerrillas, terrorists, and political organizations: and third, a small violent right.

Since taking office in January 1981, President Reagan had ordered a prudent and balanced policy of helping the people of Central America expand and strengthen democratic institutions, defend themselves against both violent extremes, and improve their living conditions.

As of early 1988 the good news from the Reagan years is that the number of democracies among the five Central American countries has increased from one in 1980 to four by 1985; the number of communist guerrillas and terrorists has declined from a peak of about thirteen thousand to about four thousand; and the violent right in El Salvador and Guatemala had virtually ceased to function. However, this progress is fragile and remains reversible as long as the people of Nicaragua are kept in the grip of the communist Sandinista regime. This is true because the Soviet bloc and Cuba provide thousands of military and secret police operatives, hundreds of millions of dollars in weapons, and full support in the aggression by armed subversion against its neighbors, which the Sandinistas initiated in 1979 and have continued ever since.

There would be major historical consequences from either a fully democratic Central America, including Nicaragua—which is of course

Ronald Reagan's objective—or a communist Central America. The success of the genuinely democratic groups would mean real peace and improved living conditions for the one hundred million people in a geographical area that stretches from Panama to our two thousand-mile open southern border.

A democratic future for the people of Nicaragua is attainable for three reasons: the courage of the unarmed and armed resistance combined with the revulsion of most Nicaraguans at the reality of life under communism; geography and the power of the United States, which—under Reagan—will prevent communist or other Sandinista allies from sending troops to crush the armed resistance; and third, the approximate ten-to-one ratio of guerrilla to conventional forces that could continue to prevent victory by the Sandinista military over the estimated 20,000 freedom fighters. And, provided external support continued, they could expand to 30,000 or 35,000, leading to the crumbling of the Sandinista dictatorship as it was unable to add the 100,000–150,000 additional soldiers.

The people of Central America have not asked the United States to send troops; they have proven ready and able to fight for their own freedom. But they do need the assistance requested by President Reagan from Congress for all aspects of his balanced and prudent policy—including for the Nicaraguan freedom fighters.

The defeat of communism in Central America could also provide an example every bit as dramatic and constructive in its historical impact as that which occurred in 1947, when President Truman decided the United States should help the people of Greece and Turkey defend themselves against Soviet-backed guerrillas and subversion.

Then, the defeat of those communist attempts to take power through force played a major role in assuring the freedom and prosperity of Western Europe. The stability of our alliance with free Europe has, in turn, helped maintain world peace. All those positive results derived from the bipartisan consensus of 1947 that the communist takeover of Eastern Europe, North Korea, and Soviet military aid to communists seeking control of China and Vietnam—all violations of the UN charter and the summit agreements that ended World War II—would not also be allowed to succeed in Western Europe.

So, too, American-aided success for the brave democratic leaders and people of Central America could have a very positive impact. It would slow the process of communist efforts to take power in other parts of Latin America, and it would provide a positive example for all developing regions. Already we see that the restoration of democracy in Grenada sharply reduced the subversion aimed at the nine Caribbean island democracies. During the Reagan years the failure of the communist power grab in the rest of Central America has contributed to the successful transition to democracy of ten Latin American countries.

On the other hand, there is a potentially very dark future. The communist regime in Nicaragua seeks to defeat and isolate the internal democratic resistance groups, both armed and unarmed, by means of a defective political treaty that results in the dismantling of all foreign support or through the misguided action of the U.S. Congress in cutting off military aid to the armed resistance. If that defeat were to happen—according to President Reagan, former Secretary of Defense Weinberger, the late CIA Director Casey, and former UN Ambassador Kirkpatrick—there is a high probability that communist guerrilla groups would ultimately take power throughout Central America.

This might happen through both a paramilitary and a political process. Ending U.S. and other free world help for the armed resistance inside Nicaragua could demoralize and frighten all the democratic leaders in Central America and would reenergize all the communist elements and perhaps the violent right as well.

Should the armed democratic resistance inside Nicaragua be neutralized, the Sandinistas could then sharply increase their military support to communist guerrillas and terrorists in Central America. They could also infiltrate thousands of their own 140,000-strong trained military forces into El Salvador and Guatemala disguised as communists from those countries. For example, Nicaragua could infiltrate 100 ''guerrillas'' a day, or 3,000 per month, which means 24,000 could be inside El Salvador within eight months. Since governments usually need about ten soldiers to contain one guerrilla, President Duarte of El Salvador would have to expand his military forces quickly from about 50,000 to almost 300,000 an almost impossible task in a short time, even in the unlikely event the United States would provide the required massive ($2 billion per year) increase in military aid.

Some Americans might feel that while a permanently communist Nicaragua or Central America would be unfortunate, we could live with it as we've learned to coexist with Cuba.

That viewpoint misses two fundamental realities. One is the tens of thousands of deaths already caused by Cuban and Nicaraguan actions (aggression that increases with each success); and the second reality is that the Mexico of the late 1980s is a very fragile land.

Since 1982 this sun-drenched but poverty-racked nation has been in the throes of a visible economic and hidden political crisis that threatens its political system. If Central America went communist, Mexico would be like a proud but wounded animal in plain view of a dangerous, powerful predator.

For years I had warned about the potential fragility of Mexico while also concluding that *if* the communists are stopped in Central America, it is likely that Mexico will not become communist. But I believe President Reagan's judgment is correct: if communist groups succeed in taking over most of Central America, this will likely produce a major communist effort to take power in Mexico—which could well succeed so rapidly that we would have very little chance to help the Mexicans head it off in time. Mexico is vulnerable because of the continuing extreme poverty compounded by its years-long economic crisis, the growing disaffection from the governing party, and the small but well-organized communist movement that includes political parties, labor unions, peasant organizations, and a network of front groups. With help from the Soviet bloc Cuba, *and a communist Central America,* the Mexican far left could well bring down the current system.

This would mean that after two centuries of secure borders, for the first time the people of the United States would be face to face on land with one hundred million people under communist control and allied with Cuba and the Soviet bloc.

This somber prediction is not just mine or President Reagan's: the late Democratic senator Henry Jackson warned about this in 1982, and in January 1984 the bipartisan commission appointed by President Reagan and led by Henry Kissinger, which also included AFL-CIO president Lane Kirkland and former Democratic party Chairman Robert Strauss, agreed with this somber forecast. It said that the result of a communist Central America would be millions of refugees fleeing communism into the United States. In addition, the bipartisan commission said new communist regimes in Central America would become Soviet-Cuban allies and initiate armed subversion against their neighbors—just as the Sandinistas have done. It concluded there would have to be a major increase in the U.S. defense budget to hold off this new threat on our southern border. And there would also be a sharp reduction in our ability to meet commitments to friendly countries in the Middle East, Asia, and even Western Europe.

Think for just a moment of a long red "Cuba," an aggressive, militarized communist Central America and Mexico stretching from Panama to the open, two-thousand-mile-long U.S. border. That would truly change world history and sharply increase the danger to our freedom.

And I have no doubt that if that came about, we would view today's lost opportunity to stop it—*without* the use of our forces—with the same deep sense of regret the European democracies of the 1930s felt looking back at their failure to stop Hitler before he had fully built his military machine and started World War II, which took 60 million lives.

Opponents of the Reagan policy within the administration, of course, did not want such a disastrous outcome. The problem was that they failed to imagine it seriously and therefore failed to understand how crucial it is that the Sandinista regime be held to its 1979 pledges to the OAS—the commitment to institute genuine democracy in Nicaragua and remain nonaligned that was the basis of its diplomatic recognition. A brief glance back at recent history may help to explain why there has been so much disagreement about U.S. policy toward Central America.

Like most former Spanish colonies in the New World, the countries of Central America became independent in the 1820s. Various attempts at Central American unity failed in the nineteenth century; the five countries all shared the Spanish heritage and language but developed separately. In the early part of the twentieth century, the United States sought to prevent European powers from using internal turmoil or the recurrent financial problems of the Latin American countries as a cause or pretext for sending their armed forces into this hemisphere. As a result, on several occasions during the early part of this century, the United States sent small numbers of troops to help various Nicaraguan governments maintain order and conduct elections.

This policy changed, however, after Franklin Roosevelt became president in 1933. A major element of his "good neighbor" policy toward our southern neighbors was that the United States would deal with whatever government was in place; we would no longer use economic, political, or military means to influence the internal politics of friendly countries. So, when the Nicaraguan National Guard under General Somoza staged a coup in 1934, and the U.S. representative urgently requested that Roosevelt intervene to reverse it, FDR decided to take no action. The Somoza dictatorship held power until its removal in 1979.

In the late 1950s Fidel Castro pledged to restore democracy to Cuba and persuaded most democratic Cuban leaders, the U.S. State Department, and most of the U.S. media. But within weeks of taking power in

January 1959, Castro began building his dictatorship and providing weapons, training, and money to communist guerrillas who were launched from Cuba to attack Panama, Nicaragua, the Dominican Republic, democratic Venezuela, and Colombia. In 1961 Castro helped a small Marxist-Leninist group from Nicaragua establish the "Sandinista Front for National Liberation" (FSLN).

During seventeen years of political and terrorist operations, the Sandinistas had little success; in 1978, however, the murder, by persons still unknown, of a popular anti-Somoza newspaper editor shocked the country into activism aimed at bringing about real democracy. In March 1979 Castro decided Nicaragua was ripe for communist revolution. He had shrewdly sized up the internal political opposition to Somoza and the Carter administration's passivity toward three recent communist takeovers (in Ethiopia, Afghanistan, and Grenada).

Castro brought twenty-seven of the top Sandinista guerrilla leaders to Cuba for a pep talk. He urged them to follow his own example: promise democracy and thereby gain leadership of the entire anti-Somoza coalition, including the unarmed, genuinely democratic groups. Most likely, Castro told the Sandinistas they could replace Somoza if they could deceive the Nicaraguans, the U.S. State Department, and the Western media—just as he had done. Finally, Castro helped unify the three Sandinista factions by having them pick three from each to form the nine-person Sandinista directorate that still rules Nicaragua.

The Sandinistas accepted his tactical advice. Castro then sharply increased the number of Cuban covert agents helping them and shipped hundreds of tons of weapons to the expanding guerrilla forces. In April 1979 the Sandinistas, following the script, promised democracy and joined in a coalition with the genuinely democratic anti-Somoza groups.

Next Castro took a farsighted and fateful move: in May he visited the president of Mexico. A few days later the Mexican president appointed a new foreign minister and initiated what has become a continuing two-track Mexican policy in Central America: maintaining relations with existing governments, while providing active support to the Sandinistas and permitting communist guerrilla movements to have propaganda and political headquarters inside Mexico.

Over the next years Mexico provided $600 million and its full, active political support to the Sandinista regime. Following Castro's visit, the Mexican president publicly called for the overthrow of Somoza. Then he worked with Costa Rica, Venezuela, Panama, Colombia, and Cuba to provide aid for the Sandinista guerrilla forces. As a result the Sandinista guerrillas expanded from about five hundred in early 1979, to about six thousand six months later.

Mexico also took an unprecedented diplomatic step. It worked with the Carter administration, Costa Rica, Panama, Colombia, and Venezuela in the OAS in June 1979 to bring about the first withdrawal ever of diplomatic recognition from an existing government. On June 23, 1979, the OAS voted to terminate diplomatic recognition of the Somoza government and transfer diplomatic recognition to the exile coalition of communist Sandinistas and genuine democrats then based in Costa Rica. The OAS made diplomatic recognition of the exiles contingent on three actions by the new government: (1) holding genuinely democratic elections; (2) remaining nonaligned in foreign policy; and (3) maintaining a mixed economy. The Carter administration supported this and then made a belated effort to have the OAS provide a multinational military peace force that would assure these three conditions would in fact be carried out by the new Nicaraguan government. But Mexico took the lead to block and defeat this proposal.

For anyone who wanted to know, there was no mystery about what the Sandinistas were. In 1977 the State Department's official, unclassified country paper on Nicaragua had accurately described the Sandinistas as "a small, Marxist-Leninist, pro-Castro terrorist group."

On July 12, 1979, following intensive negotiations in which the Carter State Department had a leading role, the Sandinistas sent the OAS a written assurance that they would establish real democracy in Nicaragua "within months." A week-long diplomatic process had produced a "negotiated political solution" in which the OAS removed Somoza and recognized the exile coalition government. In return the Sandinistas pledged genuine democracy, nonalignment, and a "minimal military corps."

Many of the Western media were deceived by the Sandinistas. *The New York Times* reported in June 1979, "A doctor . . . praised the young rebels. 'They're not communists,' he said. 'That's a fairy tale that Somoza invented and only the National Guard believes.' " Days after the Sandinista-led government took power on July 19, 1979, *The Washington Post* wrote: "The new [Sandinista laws] project the new government as highly moralistic, concerned about state security, politically liberal in a social democratic mold."

The Carter administration hoped to make the democratic promises come true by receiving Daniel Ortega in the White House in September 1979, being friendly, and immediately providing full diplomatic and economic support. The Carter administration provided $118 million in direct bilateral aid, supported $262 million in aid from U.S.-funded international development banks, and encouraged the generous refinancing of $500 million in private bank loans. In addition, other democratic countries provided additional millions of dollars in aid to Nicaragua during the Sandinistas' first two years.

Nevertheless, *within weeks,* and very clearly by September 1979, the Sandinistas were acting anything but democratic. They were establishing a communist dictatorship internally; forging military and political links with the Soviet bloc and Cuba; and providing weapons, training, and full support for communist guerrillas from all over Central America, who were then being infiltrated back to attack their neighboring home countries. From 1981 on the Reagan administration would declassify extensive amounts of information and photographs to document these aggressive actions initiated by the Sandinista government despite the friendly U.S. actions toward the Sandinistas during 1979–81. By 1983 even the Democratic-controlled House Intelligence Committee agreed with the facts and said so in an unclassified report.

Which brings us back to a major point of contention of my time at the NSC: the objectives and nature of an acceptable political settlement for Central America.

The president himself was clear: he instructed the government to seek the political settlement he would describe in his public speech of April 4, 1985. A genuine peace treaty would require the Sandinistas to establish democracy as promised the OAS in 1979; terminate its subversive aggression against their neighbors; remove the military, secret police, and other personnel from the Soviet bloc, Cuba, Libya, the PLO, and other anti-Western terrorist organizations; and reduce its military forces to parity with those of neighboring countries. And of course all of this had to be done with effective verification.

The the State Department's Latin America bureau had other ideas. While it did sometimes produce speeches of strong support for the president's objectives, it had already decided that all four were unattainable. And under George Shultz's direction from mid-1982 on, the State Department would repeatedly act to encourage and facilitate a "political solution" that *would not assure implementation of genuine democracy in Nicaragua but instead would recognize the communist regime as permanent.*

State's approach was based on the hope of a trade-off: the United States would end support to the armed resistance fighters inside Nicaragua, and in return the Sandinistas would *promise* to cease armed subversion (which they officially denied engaging in anyway), reduce the Soviet-Cuban presence, and cut the size of their armed forces.

Real democracy? The Sandinistas declared they already had it. Besides, this was strictly an "internal matter."

Of course State said that any Central American peace treaty must contain language binding Nicaragua to "make progress toward pluralism" and "observe human rights." But, curiously, the same State Department that had taken the lead in producing the "negotiated settlement" with the OAS in 1979 was now willing to accept even more vague Sandinista promises, though the specific democratic promises made in 1979 had been flagrantly violated for years.

It seemed to me that in State's view Reagan's firmness and realism were merely intransigence and naiveté, and his policy was therefore not to be implemented but circumvented. Realism, State Department style, would mean acknowledging that the Sandinistas are here to stay, and dealing with them would mean making concessions in exchange for new promises to keep their old promises. In practice, State's "realism" would mean getting nothing for something and implied that the president himself was an obstacle to a "peaceful settlement" in Central America. These views coincided with and were reinforced by the activist Democrats in the Congress who have energetically opposed President Reagan's policy since he took office.

Naturally, anyone who takes this view of Ronald Reagan is unlikely to make keeping the president fully informed a high priority. I myself saw the State Department run seven major attempts to conduct its own Central America policy rather then the president's. In my view, nobody did this more aggressively than Thomas Enders, the foreign service officer whom Haig appointed in 1981 as the assistant secretary responsible for Latin America.

The first attempted end run occurred in August 1981. Without interagency agreement, Enders went to Nicaragua and told the Sandinistas normal relations depended only on their ending subversion of their neighbors—not also implementing the democratic commitments to the OAS. A few days after I entered the Reagan administration in September 1981, I had a private meeting with Enders. I gave him a copy of a one-page plan I had written as a private citizen for U.S. actions to help the people of Nicaragua attain real democracy and remove the communist dictatorship before 1983. Enders read my plan, looked angrily at me, crumpled the page in his fist, and smashed it down on his table saying: "Constantine, this is the real world. Get serious. There is no chance for democracy in Nicaragua."

The second attempted State Department end run on Central America occurred in March 1982, when Enders brought on a diplomatic crisis. Despite all that he knew about Mexico's procommunist activities in Central America, he advised Secretary of State Alexander Haig to have two lengthy private meetings with the pro-Sandinista Mexican foreign minister. At the same time, Enders sent Special Ambassador Vernon Walters to meet secretly with Castro in Havana. This, just days before El Salvador was to hold its first democratic elections in many years. Communist guerrillas there had refused to participate and had been backed by the Mexican president's call for "power sharing" between Duarte and the communists instead of democratic elections.

Within two days all the friendly leaders in Central America knew about both visits, and strong rumors were circulated that the United States was negotiating a "sellout" of its friends. Remembering Vietnam in 1973, the shah of Iran and Somoza in 1979, these friendly regional leaders were struck with fear. They knew Mexico was helping the communists. Therefore, they viewed any U.S. tilt toward Mexico as an indication that Washington had decided against helping them defeat the communist threat. And of course these fears of a U.S. sellout were fanned by a certain element: the chorus of far-left agents of influence in each Central American country who would whisper into the ear of each beleaguered president, "You can't trust the United States: look at Vietnam, Somoza, Iran!" There was talk of some key leaders seeking deals with Cuba and Nicaragua.

This panic had been halted only when Bill Casey told NSC Adviser Bill Clark, who in turn told Haig about the impact of his meetings with the Mexican minister. Haig had apparently not intended this, and, now understanding the situation, he publicly rejected the Mexican approach to Central America. He also affirmed his support for Ronald Reagan's policy endorsing the imminent elections in El Salvador and calling for real democracy in Nicaragua.

As mentioned earlier, in the first days of the Reagan administration State was made "chairman" of all subcabinet meetings on foreign policy. This meant that the State Department assistant secretaries for the five global regions became dominant: they could decide when and whether to convene an interagency meeting that would normally include Defense, CIA, and NSC along with State. Such meetings were to be held each week to permit a systematic sharing of information about current trends and actions, to look ahead to possible dangers or opportunities, and to make sure that the president's foreign policy decisions were being carried out.

But leaving the initiative to State permitted abuse. I felt that Enders manipulated the subcabinet meetings as illustrated by the third attempted end run. I believe this was Enders's most ambitious attempt to make his own foreign policy. It turned out to be his undoing. This was the "two-track initiative" he had launched in January 1983 (while I was still at CIA).

Shultz had replaced Haig in the summer of 1982, and by late 1982 Enders had become his sole policy adviser on Latin American issues. Enders had used his foreign service friends such as Lawrence Eagleburger (then Shultz's top aide on policy) to outmaneuver such State Department peers as Bill Middendorf and the noncareer directors of political-military affairs and of the policy planning staff. After Bill Clark appointed McFarlane deputy NSC adviser in early 1982, Enders had an ally at the National Security Council. Enders then placed in the Latin American section of NSC one of his favorite career officials, who, on Central America, gradually edged out the Reagan appointee on the NSC staff. Next, Enders would exclude some senior Defense officials and me from what were ostensibly interagency policy meetings. As I saw it, Enders then worked with McFarlane and his other NSC ally, to avoid having the NSC staff alert Clark or the president to the full implications of new State Department initiatives.

In January 1983 I learned from sources within the State Department that Enders was formulating a new Central American strategy. A friend told me Enders was going to use our consensus about the need for increased military aid to El Salvador to help Shultz sell this new approach to the president.

Concerned, I went to Bill Casey and gave him what information I had. I told him that State was up to something, but I didn't know what it was because the few remaining Reagan subcabinet officials were now being excluded by Enders.

Within hours, Casey gave me a sixteen-page "two-track" strategy proposal that Enders had written for Shultz to send to the president. Casey asked for my evaluation.

I read it carefully and was dismayed. In essence Enders wanted to work jointly with Mexico to "Latinize" the conflict.

His proposed strategy completely ignored what we all knew: since

Castro's May 1979 visit, Mexico's policy in Central America had been deeply at odds with that of the United States. In February 1982 the Mexican president had gone to Nicaragua and announced a regional "peace plan" that (1) abandoned the OAS requirement that Nicaragua adopt a genuine democracy, (2) opposed the coming March 1982 elections in El Salvador, urging instead "power sharing" between the Duarte government and the communist guerrillas, and (3) opposed any aid to the Contras.

Virtually all the democratic leaders in Central America perceived Mexico correctly as a political ally of communist Nicaragua and Cuba. Even Haig, Enders's friend and former boss, had publicly accused Mexico of permitting communist guerrillas to train and conduct other operations from its territory. Our friends in the region referred to the Mexican ambassador in Managua as the "tenth commandante."

The deep anxiety Enders had helped cause in March 1982 was still a fresh memory to Casey and me, but Shultz would not know about this because he had still been in private business. Besides asking me to evaluate the draft Enders/Shultz proposal, Casey asked me to write a brief memorandum from him to Shultz summarizing these and other facts about Mexican policy and actions in Central America.

On January 28, 1983, I went with Casey to the State Department, where he met with Shultz, Under Secretary Eagleburger, Enders, and Steven Bosworth, Enders's deputy.

After this meeting Casey told me he had asked Shultz to read and consider the facts presented in the analysis that criticized the State proposal. He had asked Shultz not to send the proposal to the president until after his, Shultz's, forthcoming China trip. When Shultz returned from China, Casey argued, there could be a full NSC discussion of the State proposal. Casey held that rather than joining with Mexico, the State Department should be trying to persuade Mexico that it would be in its own interests to stop appeasing Nicaragua and either become genuinely neutral or help the real democrats in the region.

Casey felt optimistic after the meeting. He told me he thought Shultz would wait and give further thought before sending Enders's proposal to the White House.

The next day Bill Clark told Casey that Shultz had endorsed and sent President Reagan the Enders proposal then left for China. We were both surprised by Shultz's action.

Clark and Casey both judged that the State Department proposal was self-defeating. Clearly the president agreed. After studying it, Reagan decided instead to write an encouraging letter to each of the friendly heads of state in Central America and the presidents of several other Latin American countries such as Venezuela, who were concerned about trends in Central America. And for special emphasis, he sent Ambassador Kirkpatrick to deliver it personally, with assurances of continued U.S. support.

Kirkpatrick's trip was a big success. All the Latin American leaders she visited received her warmly. They also welcomed Reagan's letter of support.

When she returned I went to her State Department office to get her personal impressions. I could see immediately that she was in fine form, well pleased with the results of her journey.

"Every president I talked to was very happy to get the letter from Reagan," she said buoyantly. "They respect him, and they count on our strength."

I said that was good news.

"I want to tell you more and find out what's been happening back here," she said, "but I've just talked to Bill Clark on the phone and he wants to see me right away. Why don't you ride over with me? I want to show you something."

"Fine."

Trailed by her security guards, we went down into the basement garage. As we settled back in Kirkpatrick's limousine for the short drive to the White House, she lowered her voice confidentially: "I want to show you the item I'm going to give to Bill Clark. You won't believe it!"

I knew this would be something she'd obtained on the trip. A hot report on planned Sandinista actions, perhaps? Whatever it was, it didn't sound like good news.

She reached into her leather briefcase and pulled out a State Department cable stamped "Eyes only for the U.S. Ambassador."

"Tom Enders sent this to every U.S. embassy I visited with the president's letter," she said, handing it to me. "Of all the ambassadors I saw, only one dared to tell me about it; he gave me a copy."

I read the cable carefully. In effect, Enders told each ambassador: There is a new Central American strategy coming; it hasn't been formally approved yet, but as soon as Shultz returns from China, it will be; so meanwhile, just ignore Kirkpatrick and the letter she is carrying from Reagan.

I could hardly believe my eyes. Here was Enders, a professional foreign service officer with more than twenty years in government and now occupying a presidentially appointed position, telling United States ambassadors to disregard their president's letter and his emissary.

It was a shock. Naturally, this was perceived as incriminating evidence of insubordination and brought demands from the White House for Enders's dismissal. This disloyalty (to his president) was beyond the pale.

But there was worse: Shultz *endorsed* this behavior by fighting tenaciously to keep Enders on!

A few months later, however, Clark and Casey had the final ammunition. They showed that Enders had held up for months the publication of an unclassified information report on Central America we had prepared in January for the predictable stormy congressional debates of February through May 1983. At that point Shultz was given no choice but to remove Enders—though rumor had it that Shultz at first resisted by threatening to resign. Enders left on May 23 and the declassified Central American paper was published by State and Defense on May 27, 1983.

By the time I arrived at NSC in October 1983, Enders's replacement, Langhorne Anthony "Tony" Motley, had settled into the job. The good teamwork among all concerned during the Grenada operation led me to hope that the State Department would now finally give full support to Reagan's policy. Motley was a vigorous Republican businessman from Alaska who had grown up in Brazil, spoke fluent Portuguese, and had made a positive impression as Ambassador to Brazil from 1981 to 1983. And I had been encouraged by an early meeting Motley had had with a few of us "Reagan people" who worked on Latin America: we had given him information on policy issues, had told him about some of Enders's attempted end runs and Reagan's rejection of the two-track strategy, and had suggested competent foreign service officers and outside experts as candidates for the top five jobs in his bureau.

But Motley decided to keep all of Enders's foreign service officers in those top jobs. Since, as they say, "people are policy," this was the first sign of the troubles to come.

In mid-November 1983 I suggested to Motley that there should be an overall review of Central American policy and that it be done via an NSC meeting. This would allow the president to set the course for 1984 by giving him the latest information and a clear debate on policy alternatives.

There was, however, one big problem with this idea: Motley's actions showed the State Department still did not like NSC meetings. They provided an opportunity for the president to compare the views of Casey, Kirkpatrick, and Weinberger with those of George Shultz.

Motley told me there was no need for such a review. Or for an NSC meeting. But McFarlane did the correct thing and, writing "for the president," ordered the strategy review with the NSC meeting as the final step.

When Motley kept all of Enders's top staff, a number of us worried that the same unfair, devious, interagency process would return—and in time it did. As events unfolded we concluded that Shultz had probably ordered Motley to keep Enders's staff and continue the same State approach in Central America. (This is supported by a May 1983 memo from Shultz to the president which was declassified in 1987.)

One of the first to discover what this meant was former Florida Senator Richard Stone.

As a Democratic senator during the Carter administration, Stone had distinguished himself repeatedly by calling attention to Soviet-bloc, Cuban, and Sandinista activities in support of terrorists who were attacking our friends in both Central America and the Middle East. In 1980, though he was and remains a member of the Democratic party, Stone publicly endorsed Reagan for president.

As an experienced legislator and a prominent Jewish leader, Senator Stone brought great talent to the post when President Reagan appointed him, in 1983, as special ambassador for public diplomacy on Central America. Stone was responsible for providing accurate information on events in Central America to leaders and citizens in the United States as well as in friendly countries, especially in Latin America and Europe. A few months later, as part of the effort to encourage a genuine negotiated political settlement of the conflicts in Central America, Ronald Reagan named Stone as presidential envoy.

Stone had the old-fashioned idea that the president's policy should be followed. As a result, he and the Latin American bureau of the State Department usually had a dispute about the content of his negotiating instructions.

Secretary of State Shultz would back the Latin American bureau, but the draft instructions had to be sent to the White House for final approval since Stone was a presidential envoy. Naturally, once the draft instructions came to my desk at NSC, they would be changed as needed to assure they reflected the president's policy. And then these new White House instructions would be sent back to the State Department.

In December 1983 Vice President Bush was chosen to lead the U.S. delegation to attend the inauguration of the first democratically elected president of Argentina in many years. This was a grand moment, because President Reagan had consistently encouraged the region's peaceful transition from dictatorship back to democracy. Nearly all heads of state from Latin America would be attending the festive inauguration in Buenos Aires, which provided a good opportunity for useful meetings. Presidential Envoy Stone was being sent to meet with many of the assembled leaders, including Daniel Ortega, the Sandinista strong man.

Now, in the wake of the Grenada rescue, we noticed a heightened interest on the part of the Sandinistas in knowing precisely what the Reagan administration saw as the basis for a political settlement. Stone's written instructions from the White House clearly reflected the president's policy that there must be genuine democracy in Nicaragua, an end to its armed subversion, and the verified removal of the Soviet-bloc-Cuban-PLO operatives. Special Envoy Stone would also be telling the presidents from Central America, Venezuela, Colombia, and other key countries the same thing he would be telling Ortega, so they too would know Reagan's position.

The first sign that Motley might repeat Enders's sly maneuvers had come in late November. The State Department refused, as part of the Central America strategy review, to produce papers on three topics that had been included in the NSC directive defining the tasks to be done in the strategy review. Motley and his staff did not want to write papers about proposed diplomatic strategy and tactics to attain the president's objectives in 1984; how to persuade Congress to provide funds for the armed resistance; and how to more effectively inform U.S. and foreign leaders and citizens about the facts in Central America.

I had told McFarlane that several weeks of effort to persuade State to produce these papers had failed, and he should take this up with Shultz in their weekly meeting. In early December I told McFarlane that we could not hold the NSC meeting then scheduled for just before Christmas unless the interagency group had been able to review State's proposals on these three major aspects of our strategy.

We—Stone, Middendorf, Ikle, and myself—wondered why State seemed unwilling to put its proposals on paper. Was it just a bureaucratic turf battle in which the Latin American bureau felt this did not concern the president or the rest of the foreign policy group? Or did Motley and his top staff have something planned but wanted to avoid revealing it or lying about it on paper?

In early December Motley and Stone flew to Argentina with the vice president, sitting together for ten hours on Air Force Two.

Shortly after each began his rounds of meetings in Argentina, Stone called me with startling news. The president of a major Latin American country had just told him that Nicaragua's Ortega was chortling up and down the hotel hallway, telling each Latin American president that he and Motley would be having "secret negotiations"—just as Kissinger used to do with the Vietnamese communists.

Ortega was telling the Latin American presidents to ignore whatever Stone said about Reagan's policy because the "real negotiations" would be with Motley on a "second track."

Yet Motley had not said a word about this to Stone. When confronted by Stone, Motley had admitted that, yes, he and Ortega were going to meet, but this was to have been "totally secret." He said he was surprised Ortega was boasting about this. When I heard this, I mused that this was State's fourth attempted end run—secret talks with no presidential approval or direction.

Stone told me that this apparent duplicity undermined his and President Reagan's policy, adding, "There is no point in my continuing with any further discussions. The administration has no credibility right now."

I suggested that Stone continue with his meetings and told him I would ask McFarlane to take corrective action immediately, as the NSC had no knowledge of Motley's plan.

As it turned out, it was fortunate that I was in Washington rather than along on the trip to Argentina as had originally been planned. A few days before the vice president's delegation left, Ollie North stopped me in the hallway and said that Admiral Poindexter, the deputy NSC adviser, had just informed him that he, Ollie, was to take my place on the trip to Argentina and Central America.

"I told him you should go and not me," Ollie said, "but Poindexter insisted on it, said that military matters will be discussed down there and I should be the one to go."

"Fine," I said, "have a great trip."

It struck me as an odd decision, though, since the fundamental purpose of sending a high-level delegation headed by Vice President Bush was to express support for transitions to democracy. This was a political issue. And the discussions in Central America would focus on the president's letter to the leadership in El Salvador saying they must oppose the violent right as well as the communists. I had been writing and saying this for five years and had a major role in persuading the administration to take this action. But since Ollie clearly wanted to go, and I thought cooperation among the NSC staff was more important, I decided not to ask Poindexter to keep me on the trip.

Since I was still in Washington, I could quickly explain to McFarlane and Poindexter the negative political effects in Latin America of Motley's "secret," and unauthorized, initiative. On hearing the news, they immediately checked with State and were told by Under Secretary Eagleburger that he and the State Department had not known of this Motley-Ortega meeting. (Could this be true? I wondered.)

In this case, McFarlane acted precisely as the president's NSC adviser should. I was told to draft a cable of instructions to Motley that would repeat President Reagan's negotiating objectives precisely as they were stated to Presidential Envoy Stone. Further, Motley was instructed not to deviate from this at all and to make a full report of his meeting with Ortega in writing. Eagleburger said that State would transmit these instructions to Motley at once. I so informed Stone and urged him to continue his planned meetings, which he did.

Days after this episode, unnamed "senior State Department officials" were quoted in the U.S. press as saying that "democracy in Nicaragua cannot be obtained," and that negotiations meant the United States would have to "give up some of its objectives, like democracy" in Nicaragua.

By mid-December everyone was back from the trip, but the State Department still had failed to provide drafts of its proposals on the three important topics. I recommended to McFarlane that he write Shultz and request these three papers within a week and also inform Shultz that the scheduled NSC meeting was being postponed until early January because of State's failure to complete its work. I also told McFarlane that Motley's meeting with Ortega showed that the State Department continued to pursue its own policies and was most likely refusing to write these three papers in order to avoid having the president reaffirm or once more make decisions on these topics. Again McFarlane showed leadership. He sent the memo to Shultz and postponed the NSC meeting until early January.

I telephoned Motley and suggested that in the less busy days between Christmas and the New Year he and I might have lunch and discuss the recent episode. I told him that I was concerned he might be being misled by the Enders crew. I wanted to tell him the inside story of how the president had previously rejected State Department unilateral initiatives and how what I preceived as insubordination to the president had cost Enders his position as assistant secretary (though Shultz gave Enders a plum job as U.S. ambassador to Spain). Motley said he did not "have time" to meet with me for a private discussion.

In early January 1984 the NSC meeting on Central America took place in the White House Situation Room. With President Reagan presiding, the entire foreign policy cabinet was present—Casey, Kirkpatrick, McFarlane, Shultz, and Weinberger. A red folder with the agenda and copies of the strategy paper were at each place around the table. Despite McFarlane's memo to Shultz, the State Latin American bureau had not provided the three requested papers until 9:00 P.M. the night before. This tactic, the "last-minute memo," was a classic device to avoid real debate about policy proposals. By delaying so long, State technically "complied" with the order to produce the papers but knew they could not be read before the NSC meeting by members of the subcabinet, the cabinet, or President Reagan himself.

In this case the tactic didn't work. Each member of the foreign policy cabinet had clear ideas about the need for far more effective State Department action in the three areas. Casey, Kirkpatrick, and Weinberger candidly expressed their views to the president, who felt the same way. Naturally, before this NSC meeting, I had the opportunity to discuss the agenda and the strategy paper with most of the key participants, except Shultz. The result of the NSC meeting was a very clear and comprehensive written NSDD from the president to members of his foreign policy cabinet. President Reagan reaffirmed his balanced policy and made it clear that the U.S. goal was a democratic Central America including Nicaragua and the defeat of communist subversion. He also ordered a full-scale and vigorous effort to persuade Congress to fund the contras and tell the truth about Central America to citizens and leaders in the United States and friendly countries. This presidential decision directive, which reaffirmed a number of previous decisions, was the basis for many presidential speeches and became the strategic guideline for U.S. policy over the next years. But if certain of "the president's men" had had their way, it would never have happened.

If a picture of unremitting struggle between the State Department on the one hand and a diminishing band of Reagan loyalists on the other seems to be emerging from this narrative, well, that's the way it was. What is impossible to know, however, is how often Secretary of State George Shultz was acting with full knowledge and how often his staff was misleading him.

That question was on my mind on the first and last journey I took with

Shultz. It was a February 1984 trip to Central and South America. We were together for ten days, along with Presidential Envoy Stone, the Defense Department's Nestor Sanchez, and Motley.

Stone and Motley were managing an uneasy truce after their December showdown. In fact, the five of us were civil at all times. Shultz would occasionally convene our group for an informal discussion of the issues—either in our hotels or on the plane flights from Central America to Venezuela, Brazil, Barbados, and Grenada. On economic matters Shultz was always insightful; this was his field. But when he moved on to international politics, he seemed totally dependent on his staff. I told him facts that surprised him (which at first surprised me), and he seemed to incorporate them into his views. But the strong impression I had was that as soon as he got back to Washington the State Department bureaucracy would inundate him with its own views and bring him back into line. Nonetheless, I hoped the shared experience of the trip would lead to better relations back in Washington.

Unfortunately, within days of our return Senator Stone fell victim to the "resignation ruse." Stone got word of another Motley maneuver. The president of a major Latin American country was being misled about U.S. policy in Central America, and Stone was the obvious choice to fly down and meet with him. A highly placed official at State telephoned the U.S. ambassador in that country and asked him to send a cable requesting a visit from an American spokesman—but not Senator Stone. That cable was sent and then used against Stone in the State Department rumor mill . . . "too controversial" . . . "not effective."

When Stone found out about this little trick he was livid. He phoned to tell me he had written a letter of resignation. "I'm sick and tired of this sophomoric double-dealing by people who are supposed to be my colleagues!" he told me.

I told Senator Stone not to submit the letter. I suggested that, instead, he write a different kind of letter, this one documenting that this had been done to him by a State Department official. Then, I said, he should inform Secretary Shultz, while I would do the same with Bud McFarlane.

But Stone had already written his resignation letter and taken it to Shultz, telling the secretary of state that if Motley and the Latin American bureau did not work in a fair way, his resignation would be in effect. Reportedly Shultz said he would "look into it"—but the letter stayed on his desk.

The next day I got a call asking if I wanted to review the press announcement of Senator Stone's resignation.

"That can't be," I said. "He is a presidential appointee, and his resignation has to go through NSC, which means I would have seen it and McFarlane would have urged the president not to accept it."

No, I was told, Shultz took it to either Jim Baker or Michael Deaver, and the two of them went right in to the president and advised him it was routine and he should accept it.

The Shultz–White House axis had triumphed again. Where was Bud McFarlane on this one? In my view: in his office with the door closed, playing it safe despite his assurances to Stone of help.

I had clearly explained to both McFarlane and Poindexter that State wanted to remove Senator Stone not because of any "clash of personalities," as State had professed, but because Stone was refusing to knuckle under to the Latin American bureau's policy preferences and was standing up for President Reagan's negotiating objectives. That is why he was removed and replaced by a career foreign service officer who would "go along" with the State Department.

Should anyone think I might be exaggerating this account of what happened to former Senator Stone, let me pass on an anecdote that did not come to my attention until the summer of 1987. I was talking about l'affaire Stone with an American ambassador (who requested that he remain anonymous), and he said that some months after it had happened, he was talking about it with Tony Motley. According to the ambassador, "Motley's comment made such a strong impression on me that I jotted it down in my journal. He said, 'I got Dick Stone. I cut his head off, and he didn't even know what hit him.' "

Following Stone's departure in late February 1984, McFarlane seemed increasingly afraid to take on Shultz. He turned a deaf ear to my repeated requests that he ask Shultz to order Motley to hold regular subcabinet interagency meetings. Motley began violating his earlier promise that he would not repeat Enders's pattern of holding few, or simply pro forma, meetings with the real discussions taking place in his private office.

By his passivity toward Shultz in the removal of Senator Stone and on the matter of regular interagency meetings, McFarlane was effectively tilting control of Latin America policy to the State Department. The plain fact was that on many issues the CIA, Defense, and NSC were at odds with State. That was why Motley wanted to avoid meetings. At these subcabinet Restricted Interagency Group meetings chaired by State there were many (not all) issues where it was Defense, CIA, NSC staff versus State—just like at the NSC meeting chaired by the president. The solution for State was obvious—avoid, delay, or end-run such meetings.

There was another angle. The fewer interagency meetings there were, the more operational control State enjoyed. On a day-to-day basis, the State Department directs all U.S. embassies and ambassadors. It can make things happen by sending instruction cables or making phone calls. It can order our ambassadors to provide or withhold information to or from foreign governments and can then use real or prompted reactions from those governments to tilt Washington's policy its own way. Simply put, without the NSC meetings—or some equivalent process—the State Department bureaucracy will control virtually all U.S. foreign policy actions virtually by itself.

I now experienced a series of State Department maneuvers against Reagan's policy: the Mexican persuasion campaign that did *not* occur; the "Mexican letter" not sent; a surprise Shultz visit abroad; and the secret four-step plan for Nicaragua.

These reflected State's preference to act—without "interference" from others, up to and including the president. For example, in the episode of what I called the "Mexican persuasion campaign," it showed that it was willing to disregard even an important, direct presidential order.

In November 1981 President Reagan had given written orders that his administration should step up its efforts to tell the truth about Central America to friendly countries. This included Mexico. Reagan had tried to improve our traditionally cordial relations with Mexico by holding an annual summit with the Mexican president and, when Mexico plunged into economic crisis in 1982, helping to obtain billions of dollars in emergency financing.

In late 1983 the leaders of a key friendly Central American country visited with Vice President Bush in Washington. They were seeking more economic aid, but they told us they were deeply troubled by the recent visit of a high-level Mexican delegation to their country. Like all our friends in Central America, these leaders knew and said that Mexico was acting in full partnership with Cuba and Nicaragua. They knew that one Mexican foreign minister always consulted with top Cuban and Nicaraguan officials—often in Havana and Managua—before coming out with the latest Mexican proposal on Central America.

They said that the Mexicans had told them that for years Mexico had been "kicking the U.S. in the teeth on Central America," yet had still been receiving enormous amounts of economic help from the United

States. "But," they told the Central Americans, "you are getting much too little economic help even though you are taking big risks by being an ally of the U.S. You should do what we are doing. You too should kick the U.S. in the teeth, stop working with them against the Nicaraguans, and instead be friendly to Cuba and the Sandinistas. That way you will be safe from the power of Castro and his friends the way Mexico is safe, and you will get more economic help from the U.S."

This was disturbing information. To me it meant Mexico was contemptuous of the United States and was going beyond support for the Sandinistas and appeasement of Cuba to the undermining of U.S. relationships in the region.

Shortly after the January 1984 NSC meeting, Reagan had ordered the Department of State to design and carry out a Mexican persuasion campaign that in a systematic way would tell the truth about Central America to all the key leaders and to the general public in Mexico. The president further ordered that this be done in time to have an impact before the coming May 1984 visit of Mexico's President de la Madrid to the White House.

Three weeks later State had still done nothing. During the trip with Shultz, I had told him all about Mexico's destructive actions in Central America since 1979. "I didn't realize that," he said. Right after the trip Motley asked me to write a plan for the Mexican persuasion campaign. Within two days I had given State my proposed plan; it was now mid-February, and only twelve weeks remained before the Mexican state visit.

A few more weeks went by. State took no action except to produce a paper opposing economic pressure to stop Mexico's hostile activities in Central America.

I countered that all agreed economic pressure should not be used or even considered. But, I added, the United States had every right to present factual information about Central America to the people and leaders of Mexico.

More time passed. Soon there were only seven weeks until the Mexican president would visit Washington, D.C. In response to my next inquiry, the State Department people said that John Gavin, our ambassador to Mexico, "doesn't like the idea." I had a cordial relationship with Ambassador Gavin, who is fluent in Spanish and also has a master's degree in Latin American Studies from Stanford. A former film actor, he was a longtime friend of Ronald Reagan and Bill Clark. So I called Gavin on the secure telephone and asked him his opinion of the Mexican persuasion campaign.

"Is it feasible?" I asked. "Does it make sense?"

"Yes," he replied. "Let's go ahead with it and do our best." I told him the State Department people said he objected to the plan. "They must have misunderstood me," he said, surprised.

So I went over to State for the third time and met with the two top people in the Motley-Enders group—Craig Johnston (later appointed U.S. ambassador to Algeria) and James Michael. Three of us had a friendly meeting. Fine, they said: if Gavin agrees, then we'll go ahead with the Mexican persuasion campaign.

The next week I was in Hawaii on vacation with my family when I got an excited call from my office. I was told *Newsweek* had just run an item describing the "Constantine Menges plan" to put economic pressure on Mexico to force a change in its Central American policy. In turn, this had produced angry outbursts of protest in some of the Mexican press.

According to the caller, *Newsweek* said the State Department did not want to do this, but it will have to "follow White House orders," even though it's a bad idea.

I said, "Let's have the White House and State make clear that no economic pressure of any type has been ordered. Further, State should finally actually carry out the Mexican persuasion campaign."

But in fact I knew that "someone" had used the classic insider's weapon—the leak of distorted information in order to kill an idea.

When I returned to Washington, McFarlane refused to put any pressure on State, and there was no Mexican persuasion campaign. The State Department had found a way to ignore the president's orders.

Unfortunately, I was now hearing stories from other NSC colleagues about McFarlane's passivity on other serious issues. My colleague Roger Robinson, a Reagan supporter and also a Bill Clark recruit, was responsible for international economic issues. He noted the same pattern in his area, where Shultz and the secretary of commerce were always pushing for additional economic relations with the Soviet Union.

Robinson knew Reagan's position: any economic benefits for Moscow would come after, not before, progress on political and arms control issues. But when Robinson brought evidence that this policy wasn't being honored, McFarlane proved reluctant to schedule timely NSC meetings so the two sides could square off before the president.

Now and then Robinson would have to alert Weinberger and Casey on some hot issue, and they in turn would push for an NSC meeting with the president. When given the choice between Shultz-Baldrige's "Let's open trade and credits'' and Weinberger-Casey-Kirkpatrick's "Only after there is real progress,'' Reagan invariably decided to continue with the latter which was his stated policy.

Ironically, it was precisely because Reagan was so consistent, when faced with clear and fully argued alternatives, that one faction within his administration wanted to keep presidential involvement to a minimum. And this faction, unfortunately, increasingly gained control of access to the president—with plenty of help from Robert C. McFarlane.

By May 1984, I could clearly see McFarlane's ever-growing reluctance to bring important issues and facts to Reagan whenever doing so might mean crossing Shultz.

While the president was in China in early May, I prepared a plan to help persuade the House of Representatives, on his return, to vote for increased economic and military aid to the fragile Central American democracies. McFarlane approved the plan, which included a national television speech by Reagan. He told me to write a first draft, to be turned into presidential prose by Ben Elliott.

When Reagan returned on a Friday afternoon, after a twenty-hour flight from China, he was given Ben's draft at Camp David. At ten the next morning we were given more than six pages of handwritten changes by Reagan.

On May 9 Reagan gave his televised speech to the nation. On May 10 he won the crucial House vote for more aid to El Salvador (212–208).

Now we had momentum in Congress we could use. Chris Lehman (the senior NSC staffer responsible for liaison with Congress) and I urged McFarlane to take advantage of it. The Senate had voted 72–22 for military aid to the Nicaraguan armed resistance, and we should push the House to vote for it, too—before the Fourth of July recess. Casey, Weinberger, and Kirkpatrick said the same to McFarlane and Shultz. Lehman, Ollie North, and I were optimistic that the president could win this vote, too.

Then, suddenly, McFarlane seemed to pull back. At the morning staff meeting Lehman and I pressed him to carry through with the campaign to win the contra-aid vote in the House. McFarlane shook his head.

"I've discussed this with Baker and Shultz,'' he said, "and they think it's better to put off the vote until the end of September.''

"Why, Bud?'' I said. "By then the presidential campaign will be in full swing, and we won't be able to get bipartisan support. It doesn't make sense, politically. Besides,'' I added, "this is a major decision the president ought to make for himself.''

McFarlane looked at me, then looked away. His silence told me he would not dare go to the president and disagree with Jim Baker and Shultz—he would do nothing.

It wasn't until late June that Reagan finally had a chance to hear Casey, Weinberger, and Kirkpatrick urge an all-out effort to win the contra vote. I heard Reagan reply, with obvious emotion, that he would do whatever they thought was needed—lobby members of Congress, make more speeches,—to win the vote *now,* before the Fourth of July recess. He expressed surprise that such an effort wasn't already under way.

But by then it was already too late. Only days remained before the recess and the onset of the election season. At the end of September the Democrats refused to support the president. When the new fiscal year began in October, contra aid had been cut off.

Thus was planted one seed of the scandal that would later weaken the Reagan administration: for the Democrats' mistake in ending congressional funding for the contras ultimately led to the scheme to provide aid by unauthorized means.

But another seed of the Iran-contra scandal was sown, indirectly, by the actions of George Shultz. Aided by Michael Deaver, it seemed to me that Shultz began trying to circumvent the NSC decision-making process by using his private, informal Oval Office meetings with the president to launch major policy changes over the heads—and behind the backs—of the rest of the foreign policy cabinet.

One top Reagan appointee later observed, when Iran-contra made the disastrous results of circumventing the NSC process clear to the whole world, that "Deaver's arranging these private meetings between the president and Shultz turned out to be one of the most destructive developments of the entire Reagan presidency."

Shultz's attempt to dominate foreign policy-making became dramatically clear in two episodes: his surprise visit to Nicaragua and his pursuit of a secret four-step plan for Central America. Both seriously threatened the sound but delicate course Reagan had always followed, a policy that depended above all on the extent to which the friendly but frightened Central American governments felt they could depend on Reagan's word—as every one but the State Department seemed to understand.

In May 1984 the president of Mexico arrived in Washington for a state visit. I enjoyed the colorful welcoming ceremony on the south lawn of the White House. And part of the reason I enjoyed it was that Reagan's welcoming speech pointedly criticized the Mexican president's pro-Sandinista policies.

At the first working meeting the two presidents met privately for an hour, with each trying to persuade the other of his views on Central America. During this time, the Mexican foreign minister and Secretary Shultz led their respective delegations in a discussion held in the Cabinet Room, right next to the Oval Office. Then Secretary Shultz hosted the president of Mexico and his foreign minister at an elegant lunch. This was followed by discussions that excluded all non–State Department staff.

Within hours I had a copy of the interpreter's transcript of the two presidents' one-on-one conversation. Reagan had been superb in presenting the case for his policy, and both presidents were very candid. But I was concerned that the policies President Reagan had conveyed in the private meeting might somehow be misconstrued by the Mexican foreign ministry. So I suggested to McFarlane that we should give the president talking points, so he could repeat his private statement of U.S. policy for the Mexican president at the next morning's larger breakfast meeting, which would officially close the state visit. McFarlane agreed, and I immediately got this to his office.

The next day this draft came back with Ronald Reagan's handwritten comment: Bud, these are good, they arrived too late for the breakfast meeting, but let's send this out as a letter right away. We immediately put the talking points in the form of a letter from Reagan to the president of Mexico, and my colleague Jacqueline Tillman took it right over to Motley and told him that President Reagan had approved the substance and wanted the letter sent.

The reply was, "Shultz is going to have problems with this." Days passed; we called State and were told the letter was "on the way back with a few small changes," but still nothing came back.

I was scheduled to travel with Shultz to Central America on June 1. On the day before the trip, McFarlane told me that Raymond Burghardt, a career foreign service officer he had recently assigned to me, would be going along, too.

I hadn't asked for a second deputy, but in light of the killing work weeks Jackie Tillman and I were putting in, giving me Burghardt might have seemed a considerate gesture on McFarlane's part. Still, I wondered. Ray Burghardt had just spent two years in Honduras—he was an honest man, and I liked him personally. But he frankly agreed with the State Department rather than with the president's policy on the terms of a settlement with Nicaragua. I had tried in vain to persuade him that State's approach would reverse all the gains democracy had made in Central America since 1981.

Even so, I didn't suspect what was coming.

"Okay," I told Bud. "There's no reason for two of us to go, not with all the work we have here. I'll stay."

The next day, June 1, John Poindexter called me over to his office. He handed me a press announcement. "This is being issued now," he said.

I read it. What it said floored me.

Shultz was now in Nicaragua to meet with the Sandinista leaders.

This was a complete surprise. I reread the press release to make sure it said what I thought it said. Unfortunately, it did. This visit initiated direct U.S. bilateral negotiations with Nicaragua.

Now I understood why the State Department had stalled and resisted sending Reagan's letter to the Mexican president: the letter had reaffirmed Reagan's opposition to U.S.-Nicaragua bilateral talks and repeated his insistence that the Sandinistas should negotiate with their own domestic opponents, civic and military. The Sandinistas, for their part, had maintained that their opponents at home were mere "puppets" and demanded direct talks with the United States, the "puppet master." They would use Shultz's visit, and the direct bilateral talks to validate their position and frighten our allies.

I left Poindexter's office and called Casey on the secure line. "State sent people to see Cap, Jeane, and me simultaneously," he growled. "We were all surprised, and we agree this is a hell of a bad development. It looks like Shultz doesn't feel he has to talk with any of us now that he has his private get-togethers with the boss."

Later I was told that Motley had boasted to the press aboard the airplane carrying Shultz to Managua: "Menges knew nothing about this. He and the NSC are finished interfering." I noted the implication that the NSC's normal participation was "interference."

This major change in policy had occurred without an NSC meeting where the president would most likely have heard Casey, Kirkpatrick, and Weinberger state the case against this unilateral initiative. None of them had known in advance. In fact, the State Department had written an orderly plan to have Casey, Kirkpatrick, and Weinberger informed just before the public announcement—just as Poindexter had done with me!

Apparently Shultz and, perhaps, McFarlane had simply had a general conversation about this with the president. And, of course, on January 17, 1986, Reagan made the fateful decision to sell weapons directly to Iran after exactly this same type of Oval Office conversation with a group, selected to exclude those who were opposed (Weinberger and Shultz, with whom I would have agreed on this issue).

So as I now look back, it seems to me that in May of 1984, McFarlane and Shultz planted a seed of the future Iran scandal, by their willingness to ignore the NSC process, keep their cabinet colleagues uninformed, and, in effect, manipulate a trusting president.

A few days after Shultz's visit to Nicaragua, Ortega, the Sandinista strong man, showed his interest in "peace" by taking another of his trips to Moscow, where he said Nicaragua had a right to obtain jet fighter aircraft.

I knew that State was preparing negotiating instructions for the new presidential envoy, Harry Shlaudeman, who was scheduled to leave for Central America on June 19, and meet with the Nicaraguans on June 25. I had heard from my sources at State that a whole new approach was being prepared. But since the State Department refused to tell anyone at NSC, Defense, or CIA what they were planning, the only way to find out would be an NSC meeting with the president.

At the morning meetings of the senior NSC staff I repeatedly asked McFarlane to convene an NSC meeting so the president could review the secret new State Department approach with the benefit of advice from his entire foreign policy cabinet. "Bud," I wanted to shout, "this is our *job*! It would be for the president's *good*!"

Day after day McFarlane said nothing and did nothing. His only response to my urgings was the slight clenching of his jaw which I learned to recognize as the normal signal of his irritation. I knew I was putting my job on the line.

When I got nowhere with verbal requests, I started writing memoranda to McFarlane urging an NSC meeting. No reply. The days kept ticking by.

Finally I told McFarlane: "I will have to inform Casey, Kirkpatrick, and Weinberger about the rumors. They might then be talking to you— or the president—about the need for an NSC meeting."

At last, and with obvious reluctance, McFarlane asked for a briefing by Assistant Secretary Motley and Presidential Envoy Shlaudeman. We met with Poindexter, North, and Burghardt in the Situation Room the day before Shlaudeman was scheduled to leave for Central America.

At this last-minute meeting, those of us who were from the NSC were told *for the first time* that, yes, State was formulating a new four-step approach.

"Could we see a copy of it?" I asked.

A photocopy of "step one" was passed to us across the table. I scanned it and groaned inwardly.

Under its provisions the Sandinistas were required to send only a small fraction of the Cuban military, secret police, and other personnel back to Cuba (no effective means of verification were specified) and to close the radio command and control facilities for the communist guerrillas in El Salvador. In return, the United States would among other concessions offer access to tens of millions of dollars in international aid and sharply limit the present and future U.S. military presence in the region.

Poindexter immediately noted that one U.S. aircraft carrier held more personnel than the State plan's proposal would allow. "Does that mean," he asked, "that the navy can't sail aircraft carriers in the waters near Central America?"

I objected that the proposal conceded too much and lacked provisions for verifying that the Sandinistas would keep their new promises. North agreed with me.

Could we see the entire four-step plan? "No," Motley said. "It is not finished yet."

Shortly after the meeting I had a copy of the complete four-step plan. It had been signed by Shultz days before.

I immediately provided copies for McFarlane and Poindexter and told them they had apparently been lied to directly by two presidential appointees, and that this plan totally contradicted the president's written policy directives. Further, if given to Nicaragua on June 25, as was now State's intention, I believed the Sandinistas would pass it along to the other Central American countries to prove to them that the United States was going to sell them out.

This was the fifth attempted end run of the president and had to be stopped. I immediately told Casey, Kirkpatrick, and Ikle, plus Curtin Winsor, the U.S. ambassador in Costa Rica, who was visiting. Winsor's years of work on Latin America and longtime activism in the Republican party made him a strong supporter of the president's Central American policy. He was appalled by State's proposed plan and felt it would create fear among friendly leaders, which could cause the situation in the region to unravel.

Winsor had an idea he hoped might save the day. He had known Vice President Bush for some years, and he just happened to have an appointment to see him about another matter.

"Why don't you come along," he suggested, "and tell him what State is up to? He might agree to alert Reagan that we need an NSC meeting before the thing gets launched."

Vice President Bush greeted us cordially. Winsor opened the conversation.

"I appreciate your taking the time to see me," he said. "I was going to give you an update on the situation in Costa Rica and Central America. But I believe Constantine here has some information that should take precedence. It could be of great importance to you and the president. I'll just let him give you the facts."

I'd been in many meetings with Bush, but this was the first time I'd ever had occasion to ask him on an urgent basis to help the president. I wondered if I'd be able to help him understand just how serious this matter was.

"Mr. Vice President," I began, "I have a copy of a new four-step proposal for Central America, signed by George Shultz, that State intends to give to the Sandinista government in a matter of days. As far as I know, President Reagan has never seen it. Neither have Casey, Kirkpatrick, and Weinberger. In my judgment, this proposal countermands the written policy directives of the president."

I handed him two documents: a copy of the State proposal and a copy of the NSC directive that spelled out the president's policy. Bush had been listening closely, his eyes sharply focused. Now he studied each document briefly and then looked up.

I continued: "Before such a major change in policy is undertaken by one cabinet officer, it seems to me that there has to be a chance for the president to review this proposal in the context of a National Security Council meeting. That way, he can make a decision based on hearing Shultz's views and, most likely, the strong objections of Casey, Kirkpatrick, and Weinberger."

"Besides, if this document is given to the Sandinistas at the meeting scheduled for the end of this month, I believe they'll immediately give it to our Central American allies and say, 'This shows you that the United States is ready to make a deal with us and won't stand by the contras, or by you. You'd better accept our offer: if you go neutral right now, we'll leave you alone later.' "

Winsor spoke up: "I agree completely. The Costa Ricans and our other friends are continually being told that the State Department will make a deal with the Sandinistas. They were *shocked* when Shultz told them— just hours before he flew to Nicaragua—that he was going to start bilateral negotiations. They have all sorts of fears about what will happen in those talks, and this proposal would confirm their nightmares.''

We expected some questions and perhaps some discussion of what might be done to get an NSC meeting. Instead, the vice president said the information was "interesting," but he made no comment about taking any type of action. We both left convinced that Mr. Bush would do nothing.

By now, however, McFarlane realized State had gone too far, and he scheduled an NSC meeting. Shultz then had Motley lobby Casey, Kirkpatrick, and Weinberger and for the first time gave them copies of the four-step plan. As I heard it, all three were appalled by the incompetence and bad judgment reflected in the State proposal, and they were determined to tell the president why he should reject the Shultz proposal and continue with his current policy.

When the NSC meeting convened in late June, Shlaudeman was already meeting with the Sandinistas in Mexico. We had arranged a telephone code that would tell Shlaudeman whether or not to present the new State proposal to Nicaragua.

I believed that the stakes were none other than whether the president's sensible policy would continue or would be unraveled by State's misguided proposal. Would the president be taken in by Shultz's siren song that this was only a negotiating proposal that was fully compatible with Reagan's policy? Or would he agree with the counterarguments of Casey, Kirkpatrick, and Weinberger?

The NSC meeting, the stormiest I ever attended, ran a full hour longer than scheduled—an extremely rare occurrence, given the tight schedule every president lives on. When it ended, Shultz had lost again. The president had held to his policy and rejected the State proposal. And the National Security Council had served its intended purpose: to give the president all sides of a major policy issue and assure that he was in charge.

Right after the meeting McFarlane, the president, and I met briefly to outline the presidential decision directive. I immediately wrote a draft and got it to McFarlane. The president signed it, and within two hours of the meeting couriers delivered it to Shultz, Casey, Kirkpatrick, and Weinberger. Shlaudeman was ordered not to give the Sandinistas the new State plan. The president had rescued his policy just in the nick of time.

Soon thereafter I went to the White House entrance to escort a visiting Latin American president-elect and Secretary of State Shultz to the Oval

Office. The long black limousine drew up, and the president-elect, whom I knew, got out and greeted me warmly.

Then Secretary Shultz got out. I said, "Good morning, Mr. Secretary," and extended my hand. Shultz looked down at it, then he looked me in the eye, with a long cold stare, and walked right past me. We filed into the Roosevelt Room, just across from the Oval Office, and I tried to involve Shultz in the conversation with the visiting president-elect while stewards served us coffee. Shultz refused to talk to me. We then went into the Oval Office, where President Reagan was his usual charming self with his visitor and with us.

That night I told my wife, "Nancy, today I was snubbed by the secretary of state. Shultz is angry because I believe the president should control foreign policy. We'd better save our pennies, because Shultz will pressure McFarlane to remove me, and I can't look for a new job while I'm still at the White House."

I made several requests for a private meeting with Secretary Shultz so that we could briefly discuss the issues. In early July 1984 a State Department employee told me that he had heard Motley in his staff meeting allege that I had described Shultz as "a potential Soviet agent of influence." My State Department friend saw this as part of an ongoing defamation campaign against me and said, "You have to counter it."

I replied, "I have never said or even *thought* anything so silly. I believe Shultz is a loyal American who thinks he is doing what is best for our country. But if he won't see me even for five minutes, I can't set the record straight. And I don't know how I can counter a lie like the one you tell me Motley is spreading."

In mid-July, while flying back with the president on Air Force One from a meeting with the Caribbean heads of state, I was seated with Shultz's friend and deputy secetary of state, Ken Dam. I explained why I believed Shultz was being misled on the substance of policy and that the president had to be in charge of foreign policy and asked him to urge Shultz to spend fifteen or twenty minutes with me. When Judy Huba called for an appointment, she was told Shultz had no time available.

I had told McFarlane and now told Ken Dam that, despite the president's decisions at the June NSC meeting, State was *still* pushing its four-point proposal. McFarlane wasn't making it any easier for me to cope with State's machinations: with each passing month he had been giving Poindexter more and more authority over the issues I had been dealing with. I recalled that when I first came to the NSC, Poindexter had made it clear to me that he and McFarlane wanted the NSC staff to "get along" with the foreign policy bureaucracy, especially State.

By late July I realized that I had to press for another NSC meeting. The last one, amazingly, hadn't "taken" at State. Shultz's latest stratagem was both cunning and completely in character.

After receiving the written orders from the president in late June, Shultz had replied with a memo that seemed to accept the decision. But in an appendix Shultz added subtly that the four-step plan would be one of the means State would continue to use to carry out "the President's objectives."

Normally all memos to the president about Latin America would come to me first, and I would write a draft reply. In this case McFarlane handled the memo himself without telling me: sent it to Reagan with a short note saying, "This looks OK to me," and the president suspected nothing irregular. But I got a copy from my own sources anyway. It was definitely not "OK."

Since State continued to push the four-step plan, the rest of the foreign policy cabinet was also asking McFarlane to schedule another NSC meeting. McFarlane and Poindexter had no choice. The meeting was held at the end of July in the Cabinet Room.

I sat behind the vice president, facing the president, who was flanked by Weinberger and Shultz. Weinberger read aloud some of the concessions State had put in "step one" of its pet proposal.

Hearing these, Reagan actually flushed with anger. I had rarely seen him so emphatic. He shook his head: "No!"

The debate was tense and heated, and once again Reagan stuck to his guns. When the meeting ended, there was no doubt that he wanted to continue with his policy.

It was after this NSC meeting that Shultz, still refusing to accept defeat, stood and blocked Reagan from leaving the room. It was an unbelievable performance. My guess was that Shultz believed he had gotten Reagan's approval for the four-step plan and that Reagan was now going back on their "understanding." I felt it was as if Shultz felt the president were being insubordinate.

This was also when Shultz blustered at Weinberger, who stood his ground. Again, State's four-step plan seemed dead. It just wasn't George Shultz's day.

Right after this, Shultz had lunch with Casey and vehemently blamed Under Secretary of Defense Ikle and me for Weinberger's "hard line."

A few minutes after the NSC meeting, I walked into Poindexter's office to review with him the outline of the presidential decision directive I would be writing. Poindexter had attended the NSC meeting and had witnessed the dramatic Shultz-Weinberger confrontation. Now he looked up from his luncheon tray and shouted at me, "You are causing all this trouble. It's your job to see that these problems don't come to the president. You're not doing your job." I was surprised by this outburst from a person who had always appeared so devoid of emotion.

I replied quietly, "The State Department chairs the interagency policy groups, and, as I have told you, most of the time State refuses to hold the meetings, and then simply ignores the fact that on many issues its position is opposed by Defense, CIA, and NSC staff. Therefore, as long as State tries to disobey the president's foreign policy decision, the NSC meeting is the only way to assure presidential authority."

Again Poindexter shouted, "You are making too much trouble for us. Don't write the presidential directive. I'll have Ollie do it. Get out of my office!" Since Ollie had not been at the NSC meeting, I of course helped him write the decision directive, and he gave it to Poindexter.

Later I was told that Secretary Shultz had continued to lobby the president about the text of this new NSDD during a five-hour flight to Los Angeles where President Reagan would open the 1984 summer Olympic games.

Obviously Shultz had complained vigorously about me to McFarlane and Poindexter, and I fully expected to be fired any day. Some weeks later, my able and well-informed secretary, Mrs. Judy Huba, told me that her sources said the plan was to fire me right after President Reagan's reelection. Why this did not happen I really can't say. In the meantime, I did the only thing I could do, and that was to work just as I'd always worked.

4

A SOUTH AMERICAN JOURNEY WITH VICE PRESIDENT BUSH—RONALD REAGAN TO THE RESCUE

Vice President George Bush is always a gracious host, and his West Wing office has a cozy elegance. But I felt a little tense as I met with him one August morning in 1984. I was there with several others, including Tony Motley, to brief Bush on key issues for his August 10 trip to the inauguration of León Febres Cordero, the newly elected president of Ecuador.

A lot was riding on this trip and on how Bush used it. Its formal purpose was to celebrate another positive step in the return of democracy to Latin America. All the elected leaders of Latin American countries would attend to mark the occasion of Ecuador's second consecutive democratic presidential election. But it was also an important opportunity for the vice president, on behalf of Ronald Reagan, to meet privately with the presidents of Ecuador, Venezuela, Colombia, and Bolivia and to counter the active pro-Sandinista diplomacy of the Mexican government.

At the two recent, dramatic NSC meetings, both of which Bush attended, the president had firmly restated his position: he sought a genuine political settlement in Central America. And this meant the explicit stipulation that Nicaragua would carry out its 1979 pledge to the OAS to establish genuine democracy, along with an effective system to guarantee compliance. Only when that had occurred would aid to the Nicaraguan armed democratic resistance—the contras—be ended.

But in June 1984 the Mexicans had drafted a treaty that met neither of these conditions. Reagan opposed this defective draft treaty—the Contadora Treaty, as it was called—all four of the other Central American countries had also rejected it. But unfortunately the Mexican foreign minister had persuaded his counterparts in Colombia, Venezuela, and Panama to endorse it.

If this Mexican-drafted treaty were to be signed, the results would likely be tragic. The Nicaraguan freedom fighters would be dismantled, and military aid to El Salvador would be cut off. In return, there would be only vague promises that the Sandinistas would "make progress toward pluralism." The treaty was toothless: it had no effective provision for verifying that the Sandinistas were cutting off their own aid to communist guerrillas in neighboring countries (aid the Sandinistas denied they were giving), or that they were reducing their military forces, or that they were moving out the vast Cuban-Soviet-bloc contingent of military and intelligence personnel (we put the number at several thousand, but the Sandinistas said two hundred, averring that the rest were "teachers and medical personnel").

I had foreseen the Mexican role earlier that year. In February I'd presented my analysis at a meeting in El Salvador chaired by Shultz and attended by the U.S. ambassadors to the five Central American and four Contadora countries.

Mexico, I had told the group, would probably take the lead to draft a false treaty in favor of the Sandinistas, in keeping with all of Mexico's previous public and private "peace proposals." Then Mexico would work hard to persuade the other three mediating or "Contadora group" countries—Venezuela, Colombia, and Panama—to go along with its draft, unless the State Department could persuade their presidents and foreign ministers to write a sound peace treaty of their own. Failing this, Nicaragua would probably endorse the defective treaty. Then the four mediating countries would put intense political pressure on the four friendly Central American countries to sign it.

This, I said, would shift the political equation among the nine countries. Instead of the present seven to two alignment for a genuine treaty, with Mexico and Nicaragua isolated, this political–diplomatic campaign could in time produce a seven to two alignment for the false treaty, with El Salvador and Honduras isolated.

During that February meeting in San Salvador, as I looked around at the group of senior U.S. officials, I sensed that several of them agreed with me. But Shultz's expression told me that he dismissed or failed to understand my analysis.

Time and events proved my impression to be dead right. From February to August the State Department did almost nothing to counter what I called the cunning Mexican-Cuban-Nicaraguan "false treaty trap."

Now, in August, the trap was set to close on our friends in Central America. By speaking, Bush could head this off in Ecuador. If properly briefed, he might just do so.

I felt I had to walk a careful line with the vice president. I wanted to be sure he understood exactly why I called the Contadora draft treaty "false" and "defective," but I didn't want to insult his intelligence by acting as if I had to oversimplify things for him.

I was tempted to draw him a chart, with the "friendlies"—Guatemala, El Salvador, Honduras, and Costa Rica—on one side and, on the other, Nicaragua and the four Contadora countries—Venezuela, Colombia, Panama, and the self-appointed leader of the group, Mexico.

But getting the players straight was only half the task. The other half was to appreciate the lines of force, the dynamics of the interaction among all these different countries and their leaders. For example, it was essential to know that for years diplomats from Cuba and the Soviet bloc had been working in parallel with Mexico as the point man in an intensive propaganda campaign. The aim was for Mexico to mislead its fellow Contadora countries, who were the external mediators in the area. Then those countries, led by Mexico, would work on one after another of the "friendlies," trying to induce each of them to sign the false treaty the next time it came up for action.

This was in fact and in effect the political front of the communist war for control of Central America. In order to counter it, the United States had to take the lead and rally Venezuela, Colombia, and Panama to get behind the four friendly Central American countries—or they might ultimately be swayed by Mexico and Cuba into going along with a treaty that, in effect, guaranteed the power of the communists in Nicaragua.

It was into this invisible but churning vortex of political-diplomatic conflict that Vice President Bush was about to step. As the number-two man to a president who trusted him, he had great potential influence. If he understood the stakes and was playing his cards right, he could be the catalyst that would keep Colombia, Venezuela, and Panama out of the Sandinista diplomatic net and persuade them to support the four friendly Central American countries. Given the timing, Bush had a golden opportunity to bolster the president's policy.

Tony Motley briefed Bush first, summarizing the issues State recommended for discussion at his official meetings in Ecuador. These had to do almost entirely with routine bilateral economic and technical issues such as the reasons for our delay in providing spare helicopter parts for Colombia. To my surprise, Motley said next to nothing about the most urgent subject of all: the need to reaffirm, emphatically, the president's position on the terms of a genuine peace settlement for Central America.

When Motley had finished I spoke up: "Mr. Vice President, I strongly urge—in fact, I think it's crucial—that you spend a few minutes with each Latin American president on the issue of Central America. They want to know our views, and unless we ask them to support the democratic forces and firmly oppose the procommunist forces in Central America, their tendency is to be ambiguous and simply go along with the Mexican treaty formulations which *sound* harmless. This also allows them to avoid the risk of any demonstrations or violence from their own domestic far left. For example, in the case of Colombia, President Betancur Cuartas, I believe, has gone along with Mexico partly to appease Castro, in the hope that this could lead to a truce with the ten thousand or more communist guerrillas in Colombia who receive support from Cuba."

To my great relief Vice President Bush listened intently, with evident interest in what I was saying.

I then urged Mr. Bush to emphasize three main points about Central America with each of the South American presidents he would be meeting. The first was that Nicaragua had been committing aggression against its neighbors through armed subversion since August 1979, and we had the evidence (photos and declassified intelligence already released); second, Nicaragua had not complied with its 1979 OAS requirement to implement genuine democracy, and evidence showed that the forthcoming November 1984 elections there were virtually certain to be a Soviet-style fraud.

The final point was that the June Contadora treaty was fatally flawed because though it in no way guaranteed the implementaion of democracy in Nicaragua, it did require an end to all U.S. military aid to Central America and the immediate cut off of aid to the contras. And it failed to provide for an effective verification system.

"We certainly ought to try to get this message across," Bush said.

Gratified by his reaction, I told him: "We'll write up one page of talking points to summarize this, and I'll bring it to the airplane tonight."

At about 1:00 A.M. that night much the same group, plus the vice president's personal and security staff along with the accompanying press, assembled at the VIP lounge of Andrews Air Force Base for the six-thousand-mile nonstop trip to the heart of South America.

We slept for a few hours on the flight and the next morning changed into our business clothes for the formal receptions that would begin at planeside. When we were all ready we went forward for a meeting that included the vice president, Admiral Murphy, Tony Motley, Philip Hughes, and myself. I handed the vice president and my colleagues copies of the page of talking points I'd promised on Central America and the Contadora peace treaty negotiations.

I told him that there was a Mexican-Cuban-Nicaraguan ploy of trying to use the annual September/October meetings of the United Nations General Assembly to obtain votes against us on the Central America issue. These three countries had been lobbying together against our policy in Central America for years, with a certain degree of success. And for the first time, the ten foreign ministers of the European Economic Community were to meet with the nine "Contadora" foreign ministers in Central America at the end of September. Thus, I believed that Mexico, Cuba, and Nicaragua would most likely produce some kind of false second Contadora draft, hoping to have it endorsed by the UN General Assembly and our European allies.

"Mr. Vice President," I said, "your discussions with the two Contadora-member presidents from Venezuela and Colombia really offer us a major opportunity. You can ask them to take the lead away from Mexico and its 'false treaty' approach, and get the Contadora peace process on the road to a genuine peace treaty. Also, a defective September treaty would definitely be used by some Democrats in Congress as a reason for not supporting the president's request for aid to the Nicaraguan armed resistance. That vote comes up before the end of the fiscal year on September 30."

Phil Hughes agreed, but Tony Motley shot me a look that could kill. Motley then took up, briefly, some of the economic and technical issues. Although George Bush asked very few questions, he again seemed to agree with the suggestions, and he seemed to understand the coming international and domestic political events that made it urgent that he persuade the presidents of Venezuela and Colombia to take the lead away from Mexico in the Contadora process. That's where the meeting ended.

We returned to our seats, and soon we could see, through the clouds, the majestic snow-capped Andes. Moments later we landed at the beautiful Spanish-colonial city of Quito, nestled in a mountain valley almost ten thousand feet above sea level.

After a gracious ceremonial welcome at the airport, the vice president and his group got in assigned cars, and the heavily guarded convoy raced through blocked-off streets to our hotel headquarters. The tight security was highly visible: armed soldiers rimmed the arrival area at the airport, and military snipers were poised on rooftops at the airport and on buildings along the route. All the streets leading to the large, modern hotel were cordoned off by the Ecuadoran military police. Inside, uniformed and plainclothes police were everywhere.

As in the February 1984 trip with Secretary of State Shultz, I was amazed at how quickly and efficiently all elements of our government are able to set up a miniheadquarters abroad, complete with White House security and communications; the secretariat to receive and distribute the stream of incoming classified and unclassified cables and news from Washington, D.C. and around the world; the "mail room" where each of us had a file with our name for copies of incoming information; and the scheduling office from which we received detailed, minute-by-minute timetables listing the vice president's activities and our own participation.

Mr. Bush had a full and demanding day ahead of him. We arrived at the hotel at about 9:30 A.M. That morning Bush attended a special mass at Quito's magnificent cathedral, and then he met with the outgoing president who had taken over when his democratically elected predecessor, Roldos, was killed. (Roldos died in an airplane crash that many observers believe was caused by communist guerrillas from Colombia. They had threatened Roldos because he had cooperated in the extradition of their comrades, who were using Ecuador as a base area.)

The next stop for George Bush was a large formal inauguration lunch with the incoming and outgoing Ecuadoran presidents and many of the attending heads of state or delegation from Europe and Latin America.

Back at the hotel, there was only time for a quick change before our auto caravan, with its heavy security, drove to a nearby hotel where Mr. Bush would meet the five Latin American presidents.

This was it. This was the first of the vitally important meetings with leaders of countries whose actions could stave off the false treaty forces. George Bush had the kind of opportunity to do good for America that seldom comes to a vice president. I prayed he would make the most of it.

Since the vice president went to visit each of the five presidents who outranked him, in protocol, we went to the hotel conference room that would serve as our temporary staging area. For a man who had just gone through several hours of ceremonies and diplomatic small talk, George

Bush looked vigorous. He greeted us as we arrived to join him, and I quickly pulled out one of my copies of the talking points on Central America. I asked if he had any questions I could answer and whether he wanted to have an "extra," which was a tactful way of offering him another copy in case he had misplaced his. But no, he pulled out his copy, glanced at it, and in a few minutes we all were walking briskly down the hotel corridors to meet with President Lusinchi of Venezuela.

In our morning discussion on the airplane, I had briefly reminded the vice president of the fact that in 1958 the fragile new Social Democratic government of Venezuela had just replaced a right-wing military dictatorship. This group of Venezuelan social democrats had believed Castro's line that he wanted to bring democracy to Cuba, and they had given him political and economic support during the last year of his fight against the Batista dictatorship. But Castro repaid their help by providing training, money, and weapons to communist guerrillas and terrorists who, in the summer of 1959, began a bloody ten-year-long war against Venezuela's new democratic government, which was then headed by President Jaime Lusinchi's party.

Because of this bitter history, the faction of the Venezuelan Social Democratic party headed by Lusinchi had, along with the Christian Democratic opposition party in Venezuela, always been realistic about communist subversion and terrorism. Unfortunately, however, the Venezuelan foreign ministry was going along with the Mexicans on Central America because it had been left on its own in the Contadora diplomatic process: the State Department had not yet tried hard enough to persuade Venezuela that it was making a serious mistake.

With that in mind, I said to the vice president, "Your meeting represents a perfect opportunity to ask President Lusinchi to put the political and economic weight of Venezuela on the side of President Reagan's search for a genuine peace settlement. You could be the one to persuade Lusinchi to reject the Mexican proposals for a false Contadora treaty."

And if this change also moved Panama and Colombia away from the Mexican approach, it would boost the morale of all the friendly, democratic leaders in Central America who were disturbed by Mexico's ability to mislead and dominate the other three mediating "Contadora" countries.

We arrived at the meeting room. Bush and Lusinchi were then seated with an interpreter between. The bright lights for the TV and still cameras focused on them for the "photo opportunity." Suddenly the lights were doused, the press left, and (with Motley and me present) the substantive conversation began.

President Lusinchi, a warm, outgoing physician-turned-politician, had a number of urgent matters on his mind. He began by talking of the scourge of narcotics, noting that the vice president was head of the task force charged with reducing the imports of illegal drugs into the United States, and said that he and four other democratic Latin American presidents were going to issue a joint communiqué calling for member nations of the Organization of American States to contribute to a joint antinarcotics fund that would be administered by the OAS.

Vice President Bush agreed that the problem was serious and said the United States would study this proposal with genuine interest. Lusinchi went on to express his concerns about the danger that President Siles of Bolivia might be destabilized, adding that the Latin democracies were thinking of ways to head off any such problem. Still leading the conversation, Lusinchi discussed his country's progress on its economic debt problem and asked for U.S. help. After twenty-five minutes the time for the meeting had expired. There were warm handshakes and farewells; it was all over. And not a word had been said about the Contadora treaty.

As we walked back down the hotel hallway to wait for the next meeting, Bush turned to me. "Well, Constantine," he asked, "how do you think that went?"

Inwardly, I was deeply disappointed. Mr. Bush had responded to each of Lusinchi's points pleasantly, sensibly avoiding any commitments for new U.S. funding, but he had failed to initiate discussion on *any* topic. He had said *nothing* about Central America or the Contadora negotiations. That, I felt, would be taken as a sign that Washington was in agreement with Venezuela's having followed Mexico's lead. (This was a continuing and very serious problem: our failure to denounce the false treaty would make it look like tacit approval, and then Cuba, Nicaragua, and Mexico would crank up the pressure on our friends in Central America.)

My answer to the vice president was straightforward. "I think it's unfortunate that you said nothing about Central America or Contadora to one of the most important Latin American presidents, and the one most likely to be on our side. That means it's all the more urgent that you be very explicit about President Reagan's viewpoint when you meet with President Betancur of Colombia."

The Vice President said nothing.

After a meeting with President Siles of Bolivia, and a brief wait in our headquarters at the hotel, where there was just enough time for a sip of coffee or fresh fruit juice, the vice president's entourage was again on the move. This time it was his meeting with the president of Colombia, Belisario Betancur, who was clearly looking forward to this encounter. He opened the discussion with a recitation of all the risks he was taking in order to fight the narcotics smugglers. In a passionate voice he spoke of the recent assassination of his attorney general and of the frequent death threats against himself and his family, threats that would certainly increase if he were to go through with the planned extradition of Colombian drug lords to the United States for trial.

Betancur continued by describing the need for more U.S. cooperation, including a greater U.S. contribution to the OAS antinarcotics effort. He gave an animated description of how Colombia had mobilized its military for antidrug operations. But these could be far more effective, he said, if the United States would finally deliver the spare parts for about twenty helicopters that "the State Department" had promised months and months ago.

This implied complaint about State Department inefficiency raised Tony Motley's hackles. Almost interrupting, he immediately jumped in to explain, heatedly, that the delay was due to the Colombian government's failure to provide some needed information.

To my astonishment, Betancur and Motley then proceeded to have an *argument*. Motley raised his voice and pointed his finger at the Colombian president, seemingly livid at Betancur for having embarrassed him in front of the vice president. After some minutes of this, Bush interjected that both governments would work this out quickly.

Unfortunately, the time was now up. Again Bush had not conveyed any firm, clear message about Central America or the Contadora treaty. My concern deepened: both Venezuela and Colombia would interpret his silence as U.S. agreement with their having gone along with Mexico.

There were other substantive meetings that day and festive dinners and concerts that evening, and the next morning the vice president had a very warm and upbeat meeting with León Febres Cordero, the new president of Ecuador. By the early afternoon we were speeding along toward Air Force Two. Suddenly the convoy screeched to a halt, and my car and several others in our motorcade actually crashed into one another. Fortunately it was an accident, not an attack, and the vice president's car had not been involved. I was slightly shaken up but happy that the light machine guns carried by the security personnel in our car did not go off. We continued on to the airport. We had a spectacular view of the Andes as we took off toward the west. A short time later we landed at the Pacific port of Guayaquil for refueling and refreshments at the Ecuadoran military air base there.

After our return to Washington on August 11, I got caught up on my work, which included writing an overview for Bud McFarlane of what the Latin American group had accomplished during my first ten months and requesting a meeting to discuss how our work might improve. There was no reply.

After a welcome family vacation I flew to Europe on September 5 to brief European government, party, and media leaders on Central America.

Once I arrived in Paris, I learned that in the three weeks since Motley had heard (and ignored) my concerns about the Europeans, a preliminary meeting of the European foreign ministries had prepared a draft declaration on Central America for their September 28 meeting there. This first draft by our democratic European allies was very adverse; it failed to give clear support to the region's genuine democrats, and it failed to condemn the aggression of communist Nicaragua.

But while I was still in Europe, things began to go wrong in the Americas.

On September 7 the Mexicans did what I had warned about. They produced a second-draft Contadora treaty with a smattering of cosmetic adjustments that again fell far short of a sound peace agreement. The delighted Nicaraguan junta announced it would sign this treaty provided there were no changes and challenged the four Central American countries to do the same.

Now, in the United States, in Latin America, and in Western Europe, the entire Sandinista Soviet bloc and Cuban propaganda apparatus went into high gear to obtain a bandwagon of endorsements for this new "peace treaty" from Western governments, political parties, religious and civic groups, and, especially, the media. The propaganda line was that the Central American four should sign immediately—to show that they were really committed to peace and to prove that they were not being "pushed around" by the Reagan administration.

In the United States this seriously defective Contadora treaty was proposed as the "peaceful alternative" to any more congressional funding for the Nicaraguan freedom fighters. The argument: Congress should deny funds for the contras so the Reagan administration would have to endorse a "negotiated solution." This last view was shared by the leadership of the State Department's Latin American bureau.

As those drums began to beat, I heard a simultaneous and equally disturbing sound. A fifth round of secret bilateral talks between the United States and Nicaragua was held in Mexico, with Ambassador Shlaudeman and Raymond Burghardt representing the U.S. Contrary to President Reagan's written instructions of June 1984, the State Department gave the Nicaraguans a copy of its "calendar of reciprocal steps." *This was the same four-step proposal that Ronald Reagan had rejected at the late June NSC meeting.*

One change had been made: the words "the U.S. will take into account" replaced the earlier State Department description of specific U.S. reciprocal actions (such as helping Nicaragua obtain additional tens of millions in international economic aid or specific limits on the U.S. military presence in the region).

Within days Fidel Castro had a copy. And as he met with journalists from Latin America and Europe, Castro showed them the document and said that the constant repetition of the phrase "the U.S. will take into account" proved that Washington was deceptive and totally unserious in its bilateral negotiations. Therefore, Castro declared triumphantly, the only real "peaceful solution" was the September 7, 1984, Contadora treaty draft.

My conversations with our European allies focused on the same points I had hoped the vice president would raise in Ecuador. In addition, I gave each European leader a White House folder containing several one-page summaries of our position on issues, President Reagan's May 1984 national television speech on Central America, and our latest photo-illustrated unclassified "white paper" on Central America. I also provided them with a translation into French, or German, or Spanish of my one-page summary of our policy and trends in Central America. I'd been meeting with many of the same leaders almost every year since 1981, and we always had a frank and friendly exchange of views. It helped that I could give the briefings in French, German, and Spanish.

I urged the Europeans not to endorse the September 7, 1984, Contadora treaty draft. I pointed out that since the Sandinistas had stubbornly refused for five years to implement real democracy, the EEC should become a force for genuine democratic elections in Nicaragua in November 1984 by warning that all West European economic aid would be cut off if the election turned out to be a typical communist-style fraud.

As my return flight neared home, I had a growing sense of unease. I felt trouble right at hand.

*   *   *

On my return, I learned that Curtin Winsor, the U.S. ambassador in Costa Rica, was deeply concerned over Costa Rica's seeming readiness to sign the September 7 treaty. Winsor told me on the secure telephone that according to his information, Mexico had been putting heavy pressure on Guatemala to sign, and that its foreign minister was inclined to do so. This was very bad news, as it suggested the very thing I had feared in February: a possible seven to two lineup in favor of the false treaty.

Winsor told me the Costa Ricans believed that communist governments never sign treaties with any type of multinational verification system. Therefore, the Costa Ricans believed they could sign the Mexican treaty without any qualms, because Nicaragua would then back off and be revealed as the real obstacle to peace.

Speaking on the secure telephone, I asked Winsor whether he had ever received the excellent unclassified summary of communist violations of four war termination treaties since 1953 that had been prepared for Dr. Fred Ikle at the Defense Department. In July I had prepared a memo asking McFarlane to send a copy of that document to each of our ambassadors to the Central American and Contadora countries, as well as to President Reagan and the members of the foreign policy cabinet. The reason I wanted it sent was to head off exactly the kind of wishful thinking that Winsor was running up against in Costa Rica. But McFarlane had never answered, and now it dawned on me that this analysis had never been sent to anyone. What was going on? I grew even more uneasy.

I quickly arranged for the analysis to be sent to Ambassador Winsor and the other U.S. ambassadors in Central America. Next, I wrote McFarlane a memo summarizing the information from Winsor and other sources, which showed that two and perhaps three of our four Central American allies were seriously considering signing the defective draft treaty. Only President Duarte of El Salvador, I told him, remained completely firm in recognizing the immense danger this posed.

I recommended to McFarlane he propose to President Reagan that he send a personal letter—which had been drafted by NSC and then reviewed by State, Defense, and CIA with no objections—to each of the four Central American presidents *at once*. Reagan's letter defined a genuine political settlement, stated clearly that because the Mexican September 7 treaty did not meet those criteria, it would be very harmful, and pointed out that if the Central Americans signed the document, they would have to live with the consequences.

The president's letter was implicitly warning the Central American presidents not to believe they could sign defective treaties and assume that American soldiers would rescue them from the consequences of such irresponsibility.

President Reagan's letter went on to say that open and democratic governments respect a peace treaty when it is signed. He strongly urged them to inform the Contadora group that additional negotiations were still required since the draft treaty had not reached agreement on arms reductions, the actual implementation of internal democracy in Nicaragua, verification, and other major issues. President Reagan also reminded the four Central American presidents that decades of experience with four negotiated agreements with communist governments (Korea, 1953; Vietnam, 1954; Laos, 1962; Vietnam, 1973) showed there are likely to be continuous communist violations, along with efforts to prevent any multinational verification group from functioning in an objective way.

I told McFarlane in my September 24, 1984, memo that it was urgent this letter be sent promptly. If Costa Rica or even one other country announced its intention to sign, this could leave El Salvador isolated. That would practically guarantee that the European community foreign ministers would also endorse the draft treaty on September 28.

McFarlane approved the letter, the president agreed and signed, and it was immediately sent to the State Department for telegraphic transmission to each of our four ambassadors.

Meanwhile, the plot *still* thickened. Motley had been away from Washington for several days, and when he returned to find this approved presidential letter, *he delayed sending it.*

I learned of this delay because I had told our ambassadors on the secure telephone that the president's letter was coming, and they called me back, puzzled, to say it hadn't arrived. I inquired at State but got no reply from Motley's office.

An amusing rumor that I can't confirm came from a State Department source: Motley allegedly called Shultz several times to complain that the "Menges letter" had not been cleared with State. This rumor suggested that Motley was using President Reagan's letter with Shultz as yet another reason to have Shultz push for my firing. But, the rumor continued, Shultz told Motley to leave him alone about Menges so he could concentrate on his meetings with Soviet Foreign Minister Gromyko at the United Nations.

By the second day after the president had signed his letter, it had still not been sent out by State. Could it be that State didn't understand either the seriousness or the timing—or both—of what was going on?

All during the two and a half weeks since the September 7 announcement of the second treaty draft, Mexico, Cuba, Nicaragua *and* the foreign ministries of the three Contadora countries were putting steady pressure on the four Central American presidents. They urged them to announce their support for the treaty.

While Mexico, Cuba and Nicaragua probably couched their public pressure in the words of "peace," I am sure it is fair to surmise that various communist agents of influence had more threatening messages to pass on. It would have been perfectly in character for them to whisper to the Central American presidents that unless they saw things the communists' way, Castro and the Soviets would step up their aid to terrorists and guerrillas in their countries. And who knew what might happen to them and their families?

No one had trouble recalling that communist guerrillas had kidnapped the daughter of one Central American president in 1983, and in 1985, during a similar round of pressure, communist guerrillas kidnapped the adult daughter of El Salvador's President Duarte. The potential results of these communist pressures were dead serious.

Bud McFarlane called me at home very early in the morning and asked if the letter had gone. I replied that as far as I knew, not yet. McFarlane seemed very angry and, for a change, at State, not me. He said he'd make sure it was sent at once, and within a few hours the U.S. ambassadors had the cable text of President Reagan's letter.

They delivered it to the four Central American presidents, and shortly thereafter all four issued statements *rejecting* the September 7, 1984, draft treaty.

Once again Ronald Reagan had come through in the nick of time with a strong, positive action. And so had Bud McFarlane.

A day or two later the European community foreign ministers concluded their meeting in Central America with a general call for peace, but they did not avoid endorsing the draft treaty. In New York the Mexican UN delegation, after frantically trying to obtain the votes for a UN General Assembly endorsement of the September 7 treaty, told a number of UN delegations, falsely, that all the Central Americans except El Salvador had signed the draft treaty.

But the Mexican ploy failed. Ambassador Jeane Kirkpatrick and her U.S. delegation worked hard to get the facts out, and that stopped any UN endorsement of the draft treaty.

I thought of how close we had come to losing a major political battle and how much easier it might have been if the vice president had raised these questions in his meetings in Ecuador. Again I wondered why Motley had delayed sending out the president's letter.

But these thoughts were pushed aside by my overwhelming sense of relief. President Reagan had again rescued his Central America policy. His letter gave the four Central American presidents the courage to face the facts, reject the false draft treaty, and continue working for a genuine peace settlement.

Little did I know that a far worse political threat was in store. It was a plot directly related to Congress' refusal to approve new military aid for the contras in the next budget year beginning October 1984.

5

ELECTION EVE SURPRISE

The usually bustling halls of the State Department were empty and silent as I walked to Jeane Kirkpatrick's office. It was a Saturday morning—October 13, 1984. In my briefcase I was carrying evidence of what I considered a plot against the president's policy in Central America.

For the past week, at the regular morning staff meetings and in memoranda, I had once again been asking McFarlane to inform the president and to convene an NSC meeting where the president could hear George Shultz make his case while Casey, Kirkpatrick, and Weinberger made theirs. But it seemed to me that Shultz, after his setbacks at the June and July NSC meetings, had come up with a new and more direct approach to get his way on Nicaragua. Further, McFarlane would not tell the president or convene an NSC meeting.

Therefore, my only recourse was to inform the three other members of the foreign policy cabinet about the information I had. They might decide to reach the president. The day before I had given Ikle the facts so he could inform Weinberger, who was in the Middle East. This morning Casey and Kirkpatrick had asked me to meet them in Kirkpatrick's office and to bring all the relevant documents.

Kirkpatrick greeted me warmly; her former executive assistant, and now my associate, Jacqueline Tillman, joined us, too. Bill Casey arrived a few minutes later. Coffee was brewing in the small room next to Kirkpatrick's large office, and each of us poured a cup and sat down on the sofa and armchairs around her table.

Casey opened: "Okay, Constantine, let's see what you've got. It sounds bad, but I've got to see for myself."

146

I pulled out two copies of a more than sixty-page "peace treaty" for Central America written by the State Department and handed one to him and one to Kirkpatrick. Next, I handed them a brief memo to McFarlane (and Motley) that summarized the agreed views of the CIA, Defense, and NSC subcabinet members of the interagency group that this draft treaty was contrary to the president's policy and would have negative effects in Central America. Last, I gave them copies of eyes-only cables between Shultz, then on a trip to Central America and Mexico, and McFarlane.

I quickly reviewed the series of surprising events and clues since early October that had gradually led me to understand what was happening. I concluded, "These cables were the final proof to me: Shultz and McFarlane want to go ahead and have the Central Americans take the lead. And if that happens, I don't have to tell you, this treaty will essentially unravel the president's policy. Unless he's informed and does something about it, the State Department plan is to have this defective treaty signed by the end of this month—just before the presidential elections."

"If it happens, I'll resign immediately. If this is done without the president's authority, we clearly don't have a properly functioning government, and if he approves, I couldn't support such a decision."

Casey and Kirkpatrick studied the documents intently. When they looked up Casey said: "The president has to know. We have to tell him about this. My guess is that Shultz and McFarlane think they're doing him a favor—producing an election-eve 'peace treaty' they think is in our national interest and will also help him win the election. They're wrong on both counts. This treaty will be a disaster for our friends in Central America, and it will set the president back politically. Liberals will call it a politically motivated sham, and conservatives will say, rightly, that it's a sellout."

The four of us compared information from all our sources and talked for about half an hour more. Casey wound up the discussion by promising, "I'll get the facts to the boss this weekend."

I walked back to the White House wondering, Would Casey get through? Would the president understand? Would he take action?

October 1984 had begun with clear blue skies, invigorating coolness, the hint of fall colors in the magnificent parklands surrounding the Lincoln and Jefferson memorials. The presidential election season was moving into its final days: the president would frequently be away on the campaign trail. Some of us wondered if Michael Deaver's 1984 campaign to portray the president as "a man of peace" might result in an "October surprise"—a presidential election-eve announcement of a peace agreement in Central America.

Looking ahead to the next six weeks from October to mid-November, I wrote McFarlane about the two major Central American issues and what we should do about them: the Nicaraguan presidential election of November 6 and the continuing series of international meetings—including the secret U.S./Nicaragua bilateral negotiations—about a peace settlement for Central America.

Possibly the Sandinistas had scheduled their presidential elections two days after the U.S. presidential election in the hope of expanding their international support among U.S. democratic allies by deceiving them into believing their election was genuine. The Sandinistas considered every democratic country or group they fooled a means of self-protection in case Reagan were reelected.

During the spring and summer of 1984, members of the unarmed Nicaraguan democratic opposition had come to Washington to discuss the election with me. They were in a quandary. They knew that a fair election was unlikely, given the internal political control, secret police surveillance, telephone tapping, government "neighborhood committees" spying on everyone, controlling the vital ration cards, pervasive fear, and thousands of secretly held political prisoners in nineteen new, clandestine prisons. Yet to refuse to participate until all the Sandinistas' well-disguised internal controls were dismantled could be perceived as a confession of weakness. The Sandinista propaganda machine would tell the outside world the democratic parties were afraid that participating in the election would prove "the people" overwhelmingly supported the government. Their question to me was simply: What should we do?

I told them that they had done an excellent job in unifying nearly all the democratic political parties, democratic trade unions, cooperative, business, and civic federations into one "democratic coordinating group." Now they would have to decide for themselves whether to compete or not—the United States government could not take a position on that issue.

They came up with an ingenious decision. Arturo Cruz, the presidential candidate of the genuine democrats and, until his defection, the former Sandinista ambassador to the United States, told me: "I and most of us democrats refused to participate in the phony, controlled elections of the Somoza dictatorship, and we're not going to participate in communist-type controlled elections, either." But Arturo Cruz and the democratic coordinating group decided they would make a genuine effort to campaign for the presidency of Nicaragua and let the results illustrate whether or not it was possible.

At great personal risk, Cruz returned to Nicaragua. During the "campaign," secret-police-controlled mobs attacked him and frequently disrupted his attempts to speak publicly. The Sandinista regime made certain there was virtually no access to radio or television for the democratic coordination group. Constant secret police harassment and threats made it impossible to build a larger nationwide campaign organization.

Robert Leiken, an American academic, witnessed all of this. He published a highly influential article in the liberal *New Republic,* which described the communist Sandinistas' use of violence, their methods of intimidation, and their denial of freedom of speech, assembly, and organization to the democratic political coalition.

In September of 1984, after three months of trying to withstand this constant bullying, Arturo Cruz and his group decided to withdraw from the Nicaraguan election. They stated that since both the electoral campaign and the counting of the votes were under Sandinista control, the outcome would be a fraud.

The Sandinistas were prepared for this contingency. Several other small Marxist-Leninist parties were competing, and two of them were ostensibly farther to the left than the Sandinistas. They pointed to these as evidence to Western visitors of their own comparative "moderation." Two small, genuinely democratic political parties had also decided not to join in the boycott. Later in October, when one of these small parties convened in order to vote on whether it too should withdraw from the election, the Sandinistas sent one of their secret police mobs to attack the party members. This broke up the meeting, thus preventing a vote for abstention. So even though the democratic coordinating group had withdrawn from the elections, the Sandinista propagandists could point to an election with five other parties on the ballot. Nicaragua invited delegations of sympathizers and government observers from Latin America and Western Europe for the purpose of observing the election, which on the surface was made to appear orderly, normal, and competitive.

For months our NSC staff had been urging Tony Motley as chairman of the Restricted Interagency Group to prepare a systematic U.S. effort to inform our friends in Latin America and Western Europe about what was really going on behind the deceptive Nicaraguan propaganda. In the spring of 1984 Jacqueline Tillman had written a brief, sensible plan to explain Sandinista manipulation of the political campaigns *as these events were occurring.* This was one of several urgent proposals that we had privately given Motley, hoping he would move it forward as his own concept. That didn't work, either. So, on October 3, 1984, we again proposed to McFarlane that he take up this issue with Shultz, in order to energize fully the information and diplomatic resources of the U.S. government to tell the truth about the coming Nicaraguan "election."

That same day Tony Motley and Presidential Envoy for Central America Harry Shlaudeman, a foreign service officer, met with Daniel Ortega in New York City. This was another secret U.S./Nicaragua bilateral meeting of the sort that made our Central American allies so nervous. Although the terms of reference for such U.S./Nicaragua bilateral meetings should have been reviewed by the president and National Security Council, State had provided no information, and I had not known about this meeting in advance.

Remembering the dramatic events of June and July, I immediately became suspicious. And concerned. So I included in my October 3 memo several actions that McFarlane could suggest to Shultz in order to increase the chance for a genuine rather than false political settlement for Central America.

Was State hatching a new scheme? For eight weeks Motley hadn't convened a single meeting of the Restricted Interagency Group (State, Defense, CIA, NSC). My memo to McFarlane urging these actions on Shultz seemed to be the only way to counteract whatever State was doing. All NSC staff members concerned with Latin America signed the memo. But McFarlane made no reply.

On Friday, October 5, I flew to New York to attend a formal luncheon given by Secretary Shultz in honor of all the Latin American foreign ministers and ambassadors attending the UN meetings. Earlier that morning Shultz, Motley, and Shlaudeman had met with the foreign ministers of the four Central American countries. For the first time in more than two years, Shultz had invited Ambassador Jeane Kirkpatrick to participate in the formal meeting that had followed the "informal discussions."

Not long after that I met with Ambassador Kirkpatrick in her office at the U.S. mission to the UN. "It was unusual for Shultz to invite me," she said, "and at the end of the meeting he suggested we have a group photo with the four Central American foreign ministers.

"But," she continued, "I felt uneasy about this sudden interest in me and in a photo, so I said I was sorry, but I had to leave for an appointment.

"Then at the doorway, a Shultz assistant asked me *again* if I could stay for the photo, and again I said I had to go. Finally, while I was waiting for the elevator, another Shultz assistant came out and said it was very important to Secretary Shultz that I be part of the group photo. But I said, 'Sorry, I'm already late,' and I left. What are we to suppose that was all about?"

"I doubt it was just the social graces," I said.

"That's what I was thinking," Kirkpatrick said with a wry smile, "but I was afraid I was being cynical. What does State have up its sleeve this time?"

"Maybe," I suggested, "they want some sort of implied endorsement from you. They must be up to something new in Central America."

"What?"

She had me there. But both of us were seen by the Latin Americans as "Reaganites"—strong supporters of the president's policies. As a result, many Latin American leaders tried to convey messages to the U.S. government through us, especially via Ambassador Kirkpatrick, rather than through the State Department. Time and again they would complain that State "cannot be trusted."

So we began to compare notes from our various Latin American contacts' conversations, after which we compared perceptions from recent intelligence and diplomatic reporting, all of this in an effort to guess what the State Department was up to. Earlier that week, Ambassador Kirkpatrick told me, another member of the foreign policy cabinet also had the uneasy feeling that some plot was being hatched by State.

She then used the secure phone to call Secretary of Defense Weinberger, to tell him about the "group photo" and ask what he had heard.

They chatted for a minute and then Kirkpatrick's deputy, Ambassador José Sorzano (who would be appointed by Frank Carlucci in January of 1987 to be responsible for Latin America at NSC) came in. We asked him if he had heard anything. No, he replied, but he told us a story.

A few days earlier, Sorzano said, some State Department officials from Washington had asked to use his office for a few hours for meetings with some of the Soviet delegation accompanying Gromyko for his meetings with Shultz. "When I returned to my office the next day I noticed that something was missing—my Norman Rockwell prints, patriotic scenes of American life. I called up the State Department officials to find out what happened. They told me they'd removed the paintings. They were afraid such patriotic themes might offend their Soviet visitors! They'd forgotten to put the prints back up afterward—that's the only reason I found out." He shook his head in dismay.

None of us would have believed such a pathetic display of self-initiated appeasement had it not happened right in the next office. Sorzano left, and Kirkpatrick and I joked about how hard it was to know what the State Department was plotting for Central America.

"Perhaps," I said, "someday we should write a satirical TV series called *State Department Plots*." I left for the Shultz luncheon promising to keep Kirkpatrick informed if I came across any clues.

Daniel Ortega, Nicaragua's strongman and "candidate for president," made a big mistake during his speech to the UN: he said the United States was going to invade Nicaragua on October 15, 1984.

Since a number of Democratic congressmen had been saying much the same thing for the last four years, and since the Sandinistas believed they could more easily deceive a Mondale administration, Ortega should have "predicted" that *if reelected*, President Reagan would invade Nicaragua by *November* 15!

In reply, some of us in the administration pointed out that this was the tenth time the Sandinista government had forecast a U.S. invasion. We "predicted" that on October 15 Ortega would once again be proven wrong. We also tried to remind the media and the public that in his 1981 speech at the UN, Ortega had proudly introduced the communist guerrilla leaders from El Salvador as the rightful government and proclaimed Nicaragua's full support for them. Ortega's actions were tactical mistakes, and mistakes from the communist side were always welcome.

It was then that I got wind of another blunder—on *our* side. Over the weekend of October 6 and 7, I learned from my sources at State, the Latin American bureau was working around the clock in a frantic effort to write its own version, in English and Spanish, of a Central American treaty.

On Wednesday, October 10, Shultz would be leading the U.S. delegation to attend the inauguration of Nicholas Ardito Barletta, the newly elected president of Panama. All the Central American and Contadora leaders would be at the inaugural festivities. It seemed to me that State planned to use the opportunity to persuade the four friendly Central American countries and Nicaragua to *sign its new draft treaty*!

Now I began to understand the secret meeting with Ortega, followed by the efforts to have Kirkpatrick "in the picture."

On Monday, October 8, I went over to State hoping to be able to pick up an advance copy of the treaty draft. But I was told it was on "close hold." The draft would be "reviewed" at a Restricted Interagency Group meeting the next day, I was told. The "last minute memo" tactic again!

At the Tuesday, October 9, 7:30 A.M. senior staff meeting in the White House Situation Room, I had told McFarlane about the State Department's draft treaty. "No one at NSC, Defense, or CIA has seen the draft yet," I said, "but State will give us a peek later in the morning at a Restricted Interagency meeting. All this secrecy by State makes me worry that this is a formula for a false political settlement, contrary to the president's policy, as we saw in the June and July four-step plan."

I added my fear that State would try to push this draft on the four Central America allies during and after Shultz's October 10–12 trip to the presidential inauguration in Panama and during his stop in Mexico. By this point I no longer had *any* doubt: State was trying to bring about a false peace agreement just before the U.S. presidential election!

McFarlane was characteristically noncommittal, but this information portended an urgent matter. I expected him at least to ask me some questions or to suggest that I let him know later whether or not Motley and State were willing to modify the draft treaty. But McFarlane said nothing.

Now my concerns mounted. Had I failed to communicate the importance of what State might be planning? Or worse, did McFarlane already know? And was he just going along with Shultz?

A few minutes after that senior staff meeting, Bob Kimmitt, McFarlane's top administrative person, a veteran of eight consecutive years on the NSC staff and the reputed "Deaver ally" inside NSC, came over to me and said, "Constantine, Bud has decided that you will not be going with Shultz on the trip to Panama tomorrow."

"Why not?" I asked, a little jolted.

"Motley called and said Shultz doesn't want you to represent NSC."

"I think it's a little odd," I said, "for the State Department to decide whom McFarlane sends to represent him and the president on foreign trips."

Kimmitt shrugged. "That's Bud's decision, Constantine." Indeed, Bud's decision seemed to give me my answer: McFarlane *was* cooperating with Shultz. He seemed determined not to let President Reagan hear any debate about this draft treaty at an NSC meeting.

The 10:00 A.M. Restricted Interagency Group meeting in Motley's office was unusual in two ways. First, it was occurring. Second, Motley was exceptionally calm and confident.

These interagency meetings often made Motley irritable and defensive: often there seemed to be broad agreement among Defense, CIA, and NSC against the State Department's position. And Motley, like Enders before him, disliked being confronted by me or by *anyone* else who had a different view and the facts and arguments to back it up. Motley felt defensive about getting into a debate with me because I had the annoying habit of bringing along copies of the president's National Security Decision Directives or excerpts from his major public statements. I'd show them to Motley and the other subcabinet members in order to document and clarify the president's foreign policy, which we were *all* supposed to be implementing.

This morning each person had copies of the NSC memorandum objecting to the State Department treaty draft, and the Defense and CIA participants spoke up to verify that they had the same problems. Motley said the draft treaty had been quickly written, and that State "would try to take the suggested changes into account." Of course Motley and his staff had less than twenty-four hours to make any changes: Shultz had to have the final version for his trip to Panama the next morning.

We quickly turned to the key implementing sections on democracy and verification. Beneath all the grand-sounding words about democracy, pluralism, and verification, the State Department draft was only slightly better in content than the Mexican September 7 Contadora treaty draft! It failed completely to provide any means of assuring Sandinista compliance on the issues that President Reagan had always included in his written decision directives—simultaneous implementation of genuine democracy in Nicaragua and the military provisions, plus a verification system that would work.

"Tony," I said, pressing for a commitment, "will you accept the key proposed changes on democracy and verification?"

Motley was evasive. "We'll look at these suggestions and do our best to include some of them."

Motley adjourned the meeting, and we all realized we had just been through a charade: the formal interagency "consultation" had been arranged all right, but again, the "last-minute memo" tactic meant there would be no way for anyone outside State to see the final draft Shultz would have on the airplane the next morning. What was more, with the president on the campaign trail, and with McFarlane apparently unwilling to stand up for the president's position against Shultz (and with Menges removed from the Shultz trip), this time there could be no last-minute actions by the president to undo the State Department's plan.

Motley seemed supremely confident, and even civil, as we conversed privately in his office after the meeting. Trying to appeal to his sense of our national interest, I quietly made the same case to Motley that I would make to McFarlane in another memo later that day.

"Tony, the State Department draft treaty is contrary to the president's policy. We'll be in a much better bargaining position with Nicaragua *after* the president is reelected because the Sandinistas will then be more worried about their future. Now, on the eve of our election, is not the right time to push for a final treaty. After all, it's a standard communist tactic in negotiations to use the natural political desire of either Democratic or Republican administrations for some type of preelection 'peace breakthrough' to achieve more favorable terms for their side."

Now, on October 9, there simply wasn't enough time for the Nicaraguan democratic opposition to mount a nationwide campaign, even if the Sandinistas would actually permit real freedom of speech, assembly, and organization for the remaining days of their "campaign." Therefore, I said, "The Sandinistas will profess their willingness to abide by the democratization provisions of the treaty in the *next elections*, maybe in 1990, but they'll argue that their November 1984 election is already set and will be held before this treaty can take effect."

During our discussion, one of Motley's secretaries came in, apologized for interrupting, and said, "Michael Deaver is on the line." I offered to leave so Motley could have privacy, but he told the secretary he would call Deaver back in a few minutes. Was this a clue to Motley's new demeanor toward me? He was calm and clearly sure of his control over the coming events. Was this because Shultz, McFarlane, and Deaver had all agreed on an election-eve Central America peace treaty? It certainly looked that way to me.

Months before the dramatic confrontation in June 1984, I had asked for a fifteen- or twenty-minute private chat about Central America with both Deaver and the president's chief of staff, Jim Baker. I wanted to help them understand the vulnerability and fragility of our four Central American allies and their fears of a U.S. sellout. I hoped to explain why a false political treaty would likely unravel all the democratic progress to date. I also hoped to enlighten them on the cunning diplomatic maneuvers of the Mexican-Nicaraguan-Cuban coalition.

I understood that neither Deaver nor Jim Baker had the time to follow the details of the situation in Central America. Most likely they were going along with what they assumed was good advice from Shultz. And if McFarlane seemed to be going along, too, there was every reason for Deaver and Jim Baker to think this State treaty draft was fine.

I knew Tom Enders still visited Jim Baker for a friendly chat from time to time. White House friends told me that Deaver had little international knowledge, but that he wanted the president to "look good" and was therefore susceptible to the State Department's desire for some diplomatic "successes." I'd also heard rumors that Casey, Weinberger, Kirkpatrick, Ikle, and myself were always described to Baker and Deaver as "militarists" who itched for a U.S. invasion of Nicaragua.

My belief in the good intentions of Deaver and Baker—and in the power of facts—led me to hope that a one-on-one conversation, where they could pose all their questions and I could reply, would persuade them that all of the "Reagan realists" sought real peace, that none of us wanted a U.S. invasion of Nicaragua, and that we all supported a key element of the president's strategy: to help the people of Central America defend and liberate themselves, with their own citizens carrying the direct responsibilities. But I had been unable to obtain an appointment for an informal conversation about Central America with either Deaver or Jim Baker (who did meet with me after these events in January 1985).

After fifteen minutes of discussion, I could see that Motley remained totally unmoved by my comments. When he courteously walked me to his office door, I asked, "Tony, why did State request that the NSC not send me along on the trip tomorrow?"

"Because," he said, "Shultz doesn't want you on his airplane."

Naturally I asked, "Why not?"

Motley said, "Because Shultz has been informed that you have described him as a potential Soviet agent of influence."

There it was again! The exact phrase I had first heard in early July 1984 from a colleague at the State Department. He had called and said he had to see me urgently and then told me he had heard Motley say, in a meeting of some of his senior staff, that "Menges considers George Shultz a potential Soviet agent of influence."

Now, standing in his doorway, I asked calmly, "Tony, are you the one who's been saying that? I want to make it absolutely clear that my strong disagreement with him, and *you*, on policy doesn't imply any questions about his or your loyalty."

Motley said loftily, "I'm not going to violate the secretary's confidence by telling you the source of his information. But I *can* tell you he heard it from someone he trusts."

Well, I thought, that's a clever way to avoid either telling me the truth or lying directly.

After the meeting we had all analyzed the bulky draft in detail. Then my colleagues and I at NSC immediately consulted with our counterparts at Defense and CIA. They had all reached the same conclusion we did: the State Department draft treaty could never produce a genuine political settlement. By midafternoon I had sent Motley a memorandum summarizing the comments of the subcabinet-level members of the Restricted Interagency Group from Defense, CIA, and NSC.

This memorandum stressed that we *all* believed the State treaty draft was contrary to the president's decisions. The memo highlighted the two major criticisms, along with some relatively minor ones. For each deficiency we suggested new treaty language to bring the draft into conformity with Reagan's policy decisions.

I had already told Ikle that this latest draft treaty signaled a vigorous State Department push for some type of Central America "peace settlement" to be negotiated before the U.S. election. Now I reminded him that in October 1968, and October 1972, there had been hints from the incumbent Johnson and Nixon administrations of an "October surprise," a peace settlement that would end the Vietnam War. In October 1980, too, there had been hints that the Carter administration might bend very far toward Khomeini to reach agreement and free the U.S. hostages in Iran.

I told Ikle my suspicion that the State Department had made the argument to the political advisers of the president, especially Deaver, that a Central American "peace treaty" on the eve of the presidential election would appear to be a positive achievement. Also it would answer the accusations made by some Democrats that a reelected Reagan administration was likely to invade Nicaragua. Deaver might think, What better way to guarantee the reelection of the president!

I pointed out to Ikle that in light of the media consensus that President Reagan had done "less well than expected" in his first national debate with Walter Mondale, some Reagan political advisers might feel the need for such a "breakthrough." It seemed, in early October, that Mondale's support was growing, and I speculated that the State Department would use this anxiety among the political advisers to make its case for the diplomatic approach, which it had been pushing so diligently all year.

"But all this is just speculation," Ikle replied. "I agree with your criticisms of the State draft treaty, but I don't think they'd push for a peace settlement before the election.''

"Constantine," he said, "you're just too suspicious of the State Department."

After my meeting with Motley, I felt deeply worried that this time State would succeed in its sixth attempted end run around the president's policy. There *had* to be something more I could do. But what?

At five-thirty in the afternoon I learned State would make none of the key changes proposed by Defense, CIA, and NSC. I then wrote McFarlane another memo urging him to call an NSC meeting and intervene with Shultz against the State Department's draft treaty.

In this one I proposed two simple, practical changes in the State text: first, that *all* aspects of the treaty would enter into force only when the Organization of American States had certified that Nicaragua had implemented genuinely democratic elections and thereby met the 1979 OAS requirement; second, that the verification system be organized and managed by majority vote of the five Central American countries, and that the OAS constitute its ultimate point of authority in the event of disputes.

I reminded McFarlane that President Reagan had told the four Central American presidents in his September 24, 1984, letter the communist record in four post–World War II treaties had been one of evasion and manipulation. Therefore, I wrote McFarlane, giving Nicaragua a veto over the membership and procedures of the verification system, as proposed by the State Department's draft treaty, removed any chance for effective verification.

Once again, it was "us" versus "them," and "them" was our own State Department. Jacqueline Tillman and Oliver North also signed this memo to McFarlane. But Raymond Burghardt wouldn't sign. His heart seemed to be with State.

The next morning, Wednesday, October 10, I informed McFarlane at the senior staff meeting that I and two other NSC staff members had sent him this memo objecting to the State Department draft treaty. Further, I said, "The State Department draft treaty is contrary to the president's policy directives, and, therefore, a meeting of the National Security Council with President Reagan is urgently needed before Secretary Shultz tells our allies it represents the new position of the United States."

McFarlane said and did nothing. I was disappointed but no longer surprised.

The pieces of the puzzle were falling into place. I had heard that recently the Shultzes had invited McFarlane and his wife to spend a quiet weekend at their country home. Was that when Shultz and McFarlane had settled on a plan for an election-eve Central American "peace breakthrough"?

Now I could see that the real purpose behind the early October State Department discussions with the four friendly Central American ministers and of the secret Motley-Shlaudeman meeting with Ortega in New York the week before had been to initiate the process of agreement on this new treaty draft.

Most likely, Ortega and the Sandinistas had remained adamant in their key positions on avoiding any enforceable requirement for democracy and having a veto over the verification system.

Later I saw Motley's report to Shultz on his meeting with Ortega. I had guessed right.

So, as often before in its history, the State Department and its leadership simply gave in to the opposition. That is why State wrote the draft, hastily, over the October 7–8 weekend following those consultations in New York.

Kirkpatrick's instinct was correct when she avoided the "group photo" with Shultz, Motley, and the four Central American foreign ministers. Such a photo could have been used as evidence that she had joined and supported the discussions that shaped the "peace arrangement."

Later that same morning I received word of the events taking shape.

During the four-hour flight from Andrews Air Force Base to Panama, Shultz had convened his own Restricted Interagency Group meeting on the airplane. It included some of the same State, CIA, and Defense participants as the previous day's meeting in Motley's office—except that I was back in Washington.

From the airplane, Shultz sent McFarlane an eyes-only cable: We have to move quickly in order to have a signed Central America peace treaty by October 31, 1984. Therefore, the differences within the U.S. government on the draft treaty have to be resolved. That has now been done at the interagency meeting held aboard the airplane. "Only Menges," Shultz wrote, "stands in the way of complete agreement."

Then Shultz summarized for McFarlane the "compromise language" that had been "agreed to by all" on his airplane.

My copy of this Shultz-to-McFarlane cable had McFarlane's answers written on it in his distinctive, very neat writing: "Okay" to each Shultz proposal. In the best bureaucratic tradition of covering himself by having a staffer back him up, McFarlane then routed the Shultz memo *around me* by marking it "eyes only" directly to Raymond Burghardt for "an opinion from the staff." Burghardt agreed with McFarlane that all the Shultz compromises were fine. McFarlane then sent a message to Shultz, in flight, approving all the State Department proposals. Again, one of "us" had gone over to "them."

When the McFarlane message to Shultz came into my hands on Wednesday, I realized that this was his answer to the concerns I had expressed. He would permit no NSC meeting with the president that might allow Ronald Reagan to decide whether he wanted to make this change in his policy. McFarlane had decided not just to go along: he was actively joining Shultz to push for this self-defeating treaty.

It was time to marshal support for the president's policy.

I told Oliver North and Christopher Lehman about the latest events and about the messages between McFarlane and Shultz. They agreed that this was counter to Reagan's written directives and would likely lead to the unraveling of all the progress that had been made in Central America. We all tried to think what step to take next.

The situation was grim. The combination of pressure from Cuba, Nicaragua, Mexico, *and* the United States State Department could well lead our Central American allies to sign this badly flawed treaty. This would likely be followed by the de facto neutralization of Honduras and Costa Rica. It definitely would undercut any chance for future funding of the Nicaraguan armed resistance. These events would permit the Sandinistas to isolate and defeat the anti-Sandinista forces.

Next, Nicaragua and all the communist countries would step up their military support to the communist guerrillas in a now isolated and frightened El Salvador. Nicaragua might even infiltrate thousands of its own troops disguised as Salvadoran communist guerrillas. This would threaten the hard-won democracy in El Salvador and could lead to a communist Central America.

We had thought McFarlane agreed with this analysis, so we were disheartened that he would go along with Shultz and the State Department. There was speculation that McFarlane wanted to assure his reappointment as NSC adviser in the second Reagan term by joining with the Shultz-Deaver "election-eve peace treaty" team.

I had told McFarlane that I believed it my duty to inform Weinberger, Casey, and Kirkpatrick—all members of the National Security Council along with McFarlane, the vice president, and the president—they had to be brought up-to-date, fast. I called Casey and Kirkpatrick and gave them a quick summary on the secure telephone. Weinberger was out of town, but I spoke with Ikle, and he promised to tell Weinberger everything.

All three asked to see copies of the State draft treaty and the October 9 memorandum summarizing the agreed-upon objections of their representatives. I sent those items immediately. But I still worried they might reach the president too late: thanks to McFarlane, State now had an official "clearance" to push for its treaty while in Panama.

That Wednesday, as it happened, I'd invited John Negroponte,* a foreign service officer then serving as U.S. ambassador to Honduras, for lunch at the White House. It was always a pleasure to see John and get the latest news from him, but now I wanted to ask him about a certain episode in recent history.

In October 1968 the Johnson administration had participated in stepped-up negotiations on Vietnam, and in October 1972 the Nixon administration had done the same. Both times John had been directly involved. I asked him to tell me about how these two earlier attempted "October surprises" had been initiated. Had it been the political wings of the two administrations that had pushed for a quick—even if rickety—preelection deal?

"No," he replied. "In both cases the pressure for using the opportunity of an election-eve peace agreement came from State."

"How did it happen?" I asked.

"Well, the State Department negotiators knew they could find allies on the White House staffs—people who just wanted to win the election and didn't care much about the fine print in any peace treaty. And they made their White House coalition in 1968, and they did it again in 1972.

"I don't have to tell you what a blunder it was, both times. The communists understood our political timetable, and they tried to exploit it to get the agreement they wanted. In Paris in October 1972, the chief North Vietnamese negotiator brought their *completed draft* of a treaty to the *first* meeting with Kissinger. He said to Henry, 'You are in a hurry, aren't you?' Very considerate!"

I was beginning to understand that feeling of being "hurried" toward an event I strongly opposed.

Negroponte went on to say that at Kissinger's insistence he and several others stayed up all night, in spite of jet lag, trying to rework

* Appointed deputy NSC adviser by General Colin Powell in November 1987.

that very one-sided communist draft treaty instead of starting the negotiations on a more even basis. Ultimately Negroponte had refused to go along with what he viewed—correctly, as history grimly proved—as a very bad Vietnam peace treaty (for which the Nobel Peace Prize was awarded). He was punished by being "exiled" to Ecuador and commercial issues, until he returned to a key position in the Reagan administration.

I asked John what he knew about Shultz's imminent meeting in Panama.

"*Something's* up," he said, "but I really don't know what. I'm not part of Motley's in-group, and they don't tell me these things."

The next day, Thursday, October 11, at the morning staff meeting, I again urged McFarlane to convene an NSC meeting so the president could review the draft treaty. He made no reply. Later that morning, though I had not spoken with any members of Congress, a few supporters of the president in the House and Senate had learned about the impending treaty and began calling McFarlane to ask about it. Later I was told he assured them there was no reason for concern about a "phony treaty." (A conveniently ambiguous reply!)

Some of these same Congressmen called Edward Meese, the affable and articulate Californian who since 1981 had served as counselor to the president. Meese was perceived as someone to whom Reagan supporters could appeal. Before noon I got a call to come over to Meese's large corner office to talk to Ken Cribb, his able and judicious assistant. With Ken was Robert Reilly, a creative and effective member of the White House public liaison office who strongly supported the president on Central America. Both Ken and Bob had heard rumors from congressional sources, and Ken asked me, on Meese's behalf, "Is it true that State is planning a late October peace treaty?" I confirmed the facts without going into all the details. Cribb told me that McFarlane had already told Meese there was "nothing to worry about." (Again, the convenient ambiguity.)

Fred Ikle and I met later that day to review his "eyes-only" message to Weinberger, who was out of the country. "And I had thought you were too suspicious of State!" Ikle laughed ruefully. It was a welcome relief that he now understood how serious this was. Ikle had prepared an excellent summary of recent events for Weinberger and a suggested draft message from Weinberger to the president summing up the Defense Department's objections to the State Department treaty. After we talked, Ikle sent his cable to Weinberger.

* * *

On Friday, October 12, the *Washington Times* carried a short but explosive story contending Shultz was pushing for a defective Central America treaty, and that it would be "finalized" when he visited Mexico on his way back from Panama.

I later learned, from a person who was traveling with Shultz, that this report immediately alarmed the State Department group. They told Shultz there were rumors that congressional sources had given this story to the *Washington Times*, but the congressmen had learned about this "from the NSC."

According to my source, Tony Motley told Shultz emphatically that I was the source of this story. As a matter of fact, I had spoken with no one in Congress and no one in the media. Be that as it may, the *Washington Times* story brought a new barrage of questions for McFarlane from Republicans in Congress. I was told this made him furious. Later I would have direct proof of his anger.

It was at this point on Saturday morning, October 13, that Jeane Kirkpatrick, Bill Casey, Jacqueline Tillman, and I had met in Kirkpatrick's office to review the situation. Casey and Kirkpatrick agreed that the president had to be informed immediately, and that Casey would talk with Reagan at Camp David during the weekend.

But would Casey be able to get to the president? Again and again I was seeing the truth of the political saying, "He who controls the access controls the man."

The Saturday-morning streets were nearly empty as I walked the short distance from State to the White House complex. I carefully read through the incoming cable traffic to keep up with the latest on the negotiations and other events in Latin America. In midafternoon I went to the White House Situation Room. There I was told that McFarlane had just received an "eyes-only" message from Weinberger to the president, and it involved Central America.

I called Ikle, who told me: "Weinberger was deeply upset to learn about the State Department's maneuver, and he sent the president a message, as I suggested."

Another message. But would *it* get through? That depended on McFarlane.

White House sources told me McFarlane was enraged when he read the Weinberger message to the president. Several hours after the message had arrived, I was told McFarlane had *not* yet sent it to the president at Camp David!

I called Casey and told him that the Weinberger protest had arrived, but McFarlane was holding it.

Only hours later on that same crisp Saturday afternoon, I was crossing from the White House to the Executive Office Building when I saw McFarlane coming the other way. I said hello, and he gave me a look that I read to mean: Why is Menges here now? I thought how sadly ironic it was that the man who just one year ago had had the courage to bring the Grenada rescue plan to Reagan for action now seemed in effect, to be hiding a major event from his president.

After a welcome Sunday at home, I got up at about six on Monday, October 15, in order to arrive even earlier than usual for the morning meeting with McFarlane and the senior staff. I needed the extra time to review all the incoming cable traffic and reports to get a sense of the status of the Shultz negotiations. Besides, President Duarte of El Salvador was meeting that day for the first time with the communist guerrilla leaders at the town of La Palma.

Since Duarte would be traveling to a known place at a specific time along a limited number of routes, he would be in danger. Several times in the past Fidel Castro had sent assassination teams to kill him: Castro recognized that a democratic reformist leader like Duarte was the most effective opponent of communist conquest. The violent right in El Salvador also hated Duarte (because of the 1980 land reform), and I was concerned that either violent extreme might use the truce talks to kill Duarte, perhaps by staging an attack that would make the other extreme appear to have done it. For example, the violent right might contrive through a third party to hire former or current communist guerrillas, or Castro might arrange to pay criminals or ex-military personnel to commit such a murder.

Fortunately, nothing in the incoming cable traffic suggested an assassination plot. There was no need for me to bring up any special preventive actions at the morning meeting. That left only one topic: the State draft treaty.

As I was leaving my house that morning, I had said to Nancy: "I really should try one more time to tell McFarlane that this draft treaty is a terrible mistake. It's just *totally* contrary to Reagan's policy."

My ever-perceptive wife shook her head. "Constantine, you've already said this. You have done all you can. If you want my advice, for the moment say nothing."

The White House Situation Room is small and it's perfect for quiet conversation. This particular morning I sat along the wall rather than at the table, and when my turn came I said quietly, "Bud, I want to stress again that I, Ollie North, and Jackie Tillman all agree that State's draft treaty will fail to produce peace, will cause the unraveling of the democratic progress we've made, and will likely lead to a communist Central America. I believe we urgently need an NSC meeting with the president on this issue."

The soft-spoken, unemotional Bud McFarlane glared at me. And then, in a voice I had never heard from him before, he shouted, "Constantine, your actions in this matter have been *subversive*! You talked to the press, and you've talked to Congress! Your actions are totally out of line!"

The entire room froze. Few of us had ever seen or heard McFarlane angry—certainly nothing like this. I realized that my wife had been right.

Quietly and firmly I replied, "Bud, I have acted correctly and properly to keep the members of the foreign policy cabinet informed about this major development in my area. I have spoken to *no* one in the media or the Congress about this, and I am willing to take a polygraph test on it. I have always been honest with you; I told you last week I would brief the NSC cabinet members about this. I am willing to be held accountable for my actions, but not for inaccurate rumors about my actions."

After I finished, McFarlane, who was still smoldering, said, "That is contrary to information that has been given to me."

After the meeting, I followed McFarlane into his office hoping for at least a minute to set the record straight. He was at his desk as I came in and said, "Bud, may I speak to you?"

He scowled at me, picked up his telephone, and said, "As you see, I'm busy now." With that, he turned his back on me.

I left McFarlane's office and went to the White House dining room for breakfast. Two of my colleagues joined me. Both agreed that McFarlane's explosion would be that day's hot news on the gossip circuit. "We'll try to organize some defensive support for you," one of them said, "because it looks like your days are numbered."

After breakfast, I wrote a short letter to McFarlane repeating that I had not spoken to the media or Congress and requesting the chance to talk for a few minutes. I got no answer from him.

That night at home I recounted the scene for my wife and told her she had been right. What I didn't tell her was that I was now certain I would be fired right after the election.

The next day, when I reached Bill Casey on the phone, he told me he had good news. I held my breath and listened.

"I spoke with the president on Sunday," he said, "and raised the objections Kirkpatrick, Weinberger, and I all had to the State treaty. Reagan agreed right away: the chances for negotiating a decent settlement would be much better *after* the election than now." So the president decided there would be no rush toward an artificial and partisan preelection deadline. We had won!

Finally I understood the real reason McFarlane had shouted at me on Monday morning. He blamed *me* because Weinberger and Casey had told the president what was happening and persuaded him to uphold his policy and kill the Shultz election-eve "peace in our time" treaty.

National Security Council
senior staff for most of the period, October 1983-June 1985

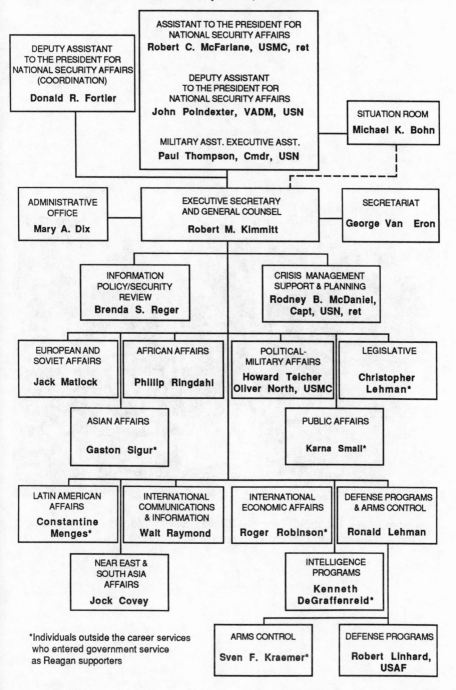

Constantine Menges, George Shultz, Edwin Meese, John Gavin, James Baker, and Ronald Reagan (May 15, 1984)

WHILE THE PRESIDENT'S AWAY...
THE WHITE HOUSE AND STATE
DEPT. "ACCOMMODATIONISTS" WILL
PLAY.

MENGES

The Washington Times, May 5, 1986

6

THE BATTLE OF THE AMBASSADORS

It was a sunny Wednesday morning, December 19, 1984, when Edwin Meese hurried into the Oval Office. As counselor to the president, and one of Reagan's oldest friends and advisers, Meese had access to Reagan whenever he needed it.

This morning he brought in a piece of paper with a disquieting message. After the reelection and his reappointment as secretary of state, Shultz was intending to remove nearly all the U.S. ambassadors to Latin America who were Republican political supporters of the president. Reaganite senior officials at the State Department were targeted, too. Shultz would replace his intended victims with career foreign service officers.

Reportedly, Shultz had told Reagan that most of these Reagan supporters were ready, even anxious, to return to private life. Besides, such changes at the end of a four-year term were routine.

Meese had very different information, and handed Reagan a one-page memorandum signed by one of the ambassadors appointed by Reagan to Central America. This note named Reagan-appointed ambassadors and said that, far from wishing to return to private life, they were willing and eager to continue serving President Reagan as ambassadors for another four years.

The memo also summarized the extensive experience and training of these ambassadors: three had Ph.D.'s in Latin American subjects and decades of experience in the region. All this contradicted the misinformation State had spread in the press that these men were all political

170

hacks, "amateurs." I believe Meese took the explosive memo directly to
Reagan because he had learned that McFarlane, who should have been
giving Reagan the facts, was simply going along with Shultz and Deaver,
the engineers of this ambassadorial purge. And Meese didn't want to see
the president manipulated, misled, or misinformed.

Probably, he also realized that if Shultz succeeded in staffing our
Central American embassies entirely with career foreign service officers,
the State Department could more easily pressure these new appointees
toward its policy rather than the president's policy in this crucial region.
Meese knew about the election-eve "peace treaty" and about some of the
previous State Department end-run attempts. He understood the maxim
that "people are policy," and he wanted to be sure that Reagan had all
the facts before he acted on the Shultz proposals at the Thursday
personnel meeting. Three people made the recommendations on the
appointment of ambassadors: McFarlane, Deaver, and Ken Dam, Shultz's
deputy. All would agree with the State Department plan.

When Reagan read the memo and heard what Meese had to say, I am
told his face flushed with anger.

Only minutes after Meese had finished his conversation with Reagan in
the Oval Office, I learned the president's reaction. But it still wasn't clear
what would happen on Thursday; Reagan hadn't actually committed
himself. Would he still be angry, and would he nix the State Department
plan? Or would he be persuaded that the diplomatic turnover was a good
idea after all?

As I left Ed Meese's sunny corner office in the West Wing and walked
down the corridor, I saw a short trim man coming toward me. Michael
Deaver looked at me as if wondering why I had just come from Meese's
office.

On October 30 President Reagan presided over a full NSC meeting that
had been called at the urging of Casey, Kirkpatrick, and Weinberger to
review the situation in Central America. The president reaffirmed his
four-part policy, including his negotiating objectives with Nicaragua.

After McFarlane had shouted at me in the senior NSC staff meeting and
subsequently refused to talk privately with me, I figured I would be
removed from the NSC right after the presidential election. So in the last
days of October and early November, thinking I wouldn't have the
opportunity much longer, I invited a number of friends to join me for
lunch at the White House mess (dining room) so we could enjoy the
special ambience and spirit of this historic home of our presidents.

Often it was Ron Jackson, the manager of the White House mess, and his competent staff who provided most of us on the senior White House staff with the only moments of calm and serenity during our always hectic work days. We appreciated that very much and usually invited colleagues in government who were pleased to "lunch at the White House." The White House mess also was very important in building positive relationships with such White House colleagues as the speech writers, the people responsible for liaison with the Congress, and the very effective public outreach staff headed by Ambassador Faith Whittlesey. Unfortunately, the frequency of these "business lunches" meant there was little time for inviting personal friends to lunch at the White House, so I was trying to make up for that just in case these were my "last days"!

After lunch, if time permitted and the president was elsewhere, I would take my personal visitors on a short stroll past the Oval Office and the Cabinet Room, then out under the colonnade to the main residence, alongside the beautiful Rose Garden. If we were lucky, we could also walk through the elegant hallways and rooms on the first floor that presidents used for official entertainment: the East Room; the Red, Blue, and Green rooms; and the State Dining Room. Ironically, these short interludes with visitors were virtually the only moments when I could pause long enough to appreciate the beauty of the American heritage so visible in the art and furnishings.

As a subcabinet official, I could not participate in any campaign activities, but obviously I hoped the American people would reelect Ronald Reagan. On election night I shared the good news of his forty-nine-state landslide with my family and friends at one of the many gala parties in Washington. The splendor of competitive politics in a genuine democracy is that despite what the opinion polls may suggest, we are never certain of the election result until all the votes are counted. This uncertainty helps to keep all elected officeholders more humble and attuned to their fellow citizens.

Contrary to the self-induced fears of some, *none* of the "Reaganites" working on Latin America issues viewed the reelection as a mandate for a military invasion of Nicaragua. But on the eve of our presidential election, the news media had begun a flurry of speculation about U.S. military action against Nicaragua. It reported that not one but several Soviet-bloc ships were arriving in Nicaragua carrying large crates on their decks that "could be" Soviet-made jet fighter aircraft.

The Soviet bloc had been shipping ever-increasing amounts of weapons to Nicaragua since 1979 (two billion dollars' worth by 1987). As it normally took five to seven weeks to ship such large weapons, it was quite obvious that the Soviet Union intended them to arrive right after the U.S. presidential election on November 4 and about the same time as the pseudoelection to be held in Nicaragua on November 6. Perhaps the Soviets wanted to wait until after the U.S. election to avoid alarming the American public, or giving President Reagan new evidence, of the communist threat on the North American mainland. And Moscow most likely wanted its Sandinista allies to have the new weapons immediately after the U.S. election, since they may have believed a reelected Ronald Reagan would be far more assertive.

Whatever their reasoning, its effect on the American media was electric. Alarm bells went off, and they were heard by Congress and the administration. After the initial stories, some in the media speculated that the administration had purposely leaked the fact of these Soviet ships' delivering weapons in order to have a pretext for military action against Nicaragua. This was not true.

After a flurry of activity triggered by the Soviet deliveries of heavy weapons to Nicaragua (helicopter gunships, not jet fighters) there was a postelection lull. President and Mrs. Reagan flew to their California ranch for a Thanksgiving vacation after weeks of active political campaigning. I wrote three brief strategy papers on foreign policy opportunities for the second Reagan administration.

The first described the "significant, but fragile and reversible progress" in four of the five Central America countries since 1981. It summarized the resources and likely tactics of the genuinely democratic groups and of the communist left and its international allies. I assessed three U.S. strategies: (1) the State Department's "containment" approach; (2) U.S. military invasion; and (3) continuation of the president's policy with resources adequate to ensure continued progress in the four Central America countries and assure that the Nicaraguan people achieved real democracy within the next several years.

My judgment was that "containment" would fail, that it would lead to a communist Central America, which would then be used to help the internal far left take power in Mexico, Panama, and probably other Latin American countries. I also opposed a U.S. military invasion as not being necessary or in our best interests and as likely to result in too many killed and wounded on all sides. I recommended the third strategy, which I felt could succeed if the U.S. government became more unified and competent in persuading Congress and friendly Latin American countries to provide political, economic, and other support while isolating the aggressor Sandinista regime.

The second paper proposed a counterstrategy against Soviet-sponsored subversive aggression and terrorism that had several obvious benefits: it was legal, prudent, and sustainable.

My third post-reelection proposal was that the Reagan administration lead a renewed and greatly expanded effort on the part of the world's industrial democracies to encourage peaceful transitions to *genuine* democracy in countries that truly wanted this form of government. If the people and genuinely democratic groups sought democracy, then those of us who already enjoyed it should give them encouragement and practical help without, however, coercing friendly regimes.

In the next several weeks President Reagan was scheduled to receive Prime Minister Thatcher of the United Kingdom and then Prime Minister Nakasone of Japan. I suggested to McFarlane that this expanded democracy initiative might appeal to both of these leaders, and that the three countries could jointly establish a "coalition for genuine democracy" that would receive public funds but be independent of day by day government control as were the West German political action foundations.

This coalition could invite other genuine democracies to join with all new members requiring at least a two-thirds favorable vote for admission. The coalition would be nonpartisan—it would help all genuinely democratic groups, from left to right. It could link individuals in one country who had recently participated in a successful transition to democracy with those of another who were then in the middle of this difficult process. Equally important, the coalition could try to create a prodemocracy and free market presence within many of the international organizations that had been under unremitting pressure from the antidemocratic combination of the Soviet bloc and many dictatorships in the developing world.

I pointed out to McFarlane that this idea would likely have bipartisan support, because it coincided substantially with proposals suggested by Max Kampleman, Penn Kemble, and Ben Wattenberg as leaders of a sensible group within the Democratic party, the Coalition for a Democratic Majority. Their proposal had also included the clear need to "encourage humanization and democratization within the communist world," as well as in other types of dictatorships.

This international prodemocracy coalition would only be permitted to support genuinely democratic groups that refrained from any form of violence. And there would have to be an annual professional audit to ensure reasonable oversight and the correct expenditure of the funds. In describing my written proposal to McFarlane at the morning senior NSC staff meeting, I suggested that he meet with his five senior staff members for the world's geographic regions, so that we could explore reactions and comments together.

To my surprise, McFarlane responded positively. "Constantine, this is an interesting idea. I'll try to arrange for follow-up. Do you have a copy of that memo with you?" I did and gave it to him across the table, pleased that for once there might be a chance for a few of us to discuss a strategic issue with McFarlane.

So what happened? Nothing, as far as I could tell!

I waited for a number of days. Several senior NSC staff members told me they were interested in the democracy idea and would look forward to a discussion with McFarlane. But the time for the Thatcher and Nakasone visit was approaching, and neither McFarlane nor Poindexter seemed to be doing anything to include this subject in President Reagan's conversations with them.

I asked for a private meeting with McFarlane to discuss my suggestions. One was scheduled for Saturday morning, December 8, 1984; McFarlane and Poindexter were both there.

McFarlane's reappointment as National Security Adviser had been announced in late November, and shortly after that my secretary told me she'd heard through her personal grapevine that McFarlane had decided not to fire me—"at least not for a while." But, the rumor went, McFarlane and Poindexter were going to work with Ollie North and Raymond Burghardt on the "sensitive" Central America issues, exclude me, and hope I would be sufficiently demoralized to leave voluntarily. This was a classic bureaucratic way to remove people without taking the risks of actually firing them.

Shortly before that meeting with McFarlane, I had discovered that he had asked his then deputy Donald Fortier, Ollie North, and Raymond Burghardt to produce a strategy paper on Central America. By coincidence my strategy paper and theirs had been sent to him on the same date.

On a bright December Saturday morning, I entered the White House and walked into McFarlane's basement office next to the Situation Room. He and Poindexter were civil, but distant as always. I got right to it. First, I briefly summarized my Central America paper and suggested that there should be an early NSC meeting to assure that the president would set the strategy for 1985, just as had been done for 1984. I gave them both copies of the Central America strategy paper and asked if I could answer any questions. "No. Anything else?"

I said we still had no counterstrategy against terrorism and could expect further attacks and setbacks. Then I gave them my one-page synthesis of my proposal. McFarlane looked at the document, clenched his jaws a few times, and said once again, "Anything else?"

"Yes," I said, "the coalition for democracy idea should be discussed by the interagency groups so that the president can make a final decision at an NSC meeting before Thatcher and Nakasone arrive. The president could announce this new initiative in his 1985 State of the Union speech."

There was no discernible reply, and then Poindexter got up, his subtle way of indicating our "discussion" was over.

As far as I could tell, my three proposals were simply languishing at the NSC, despite the fact that these weeks right after the election were supposed to be the time in which everyone in the government reflected on the first Reagan term and came up with initiatives for the second. But as several of my NSC colleagues observed, with a feeling of surprise that matched mine, Bud McFarlane didn't seem to be interested in *any* of our suggestions for the second term.

Not everyone in the Reagan cabinet was as "laid back" as the National Security adviser. I was told that George Shultz planned to put a little something in the Christmas stockings of Ronald Reagan's politically appointed ambassadors to Latin America. And that little something made a lump of coal look good!

In early December a State Department official I knew well called and asked me to meet with him privately, but not at my office. I got the feeling that he didn't want the White House computerized record of appointments to show that he had met with me. I suggested we meet at my home.

Once we were seated in the living room, he told his story. "The State Department's Latin American bureau has made a list of virtually all the American ambassadors appointed by President Reagan, and they've talked George Shultz into firing them all! It's going to be 'Merry Christmas, and by the way, you're out of a job.' "

State's plan was to replace each and every one of them with a career foreign service officer who supported the State Department's position on Central America. This would avoid the "embarrassment" caused the State Department when ambassadors sent honest cables reporting the fear and panic among friendly Central American leaders that had been triggered by the repeated schemes for defective political treaties.

"What's more," my source continued, "Shultz is also going to get rid of the few Reagan appointees in policy jobs at State." He mentioned hardworking loyalists such as Bill Middendorf at OAS, Richard McCormack, the assistant secretary for economic and business affairs, and William Schneider, under secretary for security assistance.

This news was the first salvo in what I came to call "the Battle of the Ambassadors."

I mentioned this information to McFarlane at the next senior NSC staff meeting. "Our friends in Latin America, especially Central America," I said, "would see any wholesale change of ambassadors, especially the removal of known Reagan supporters, as a political event. It would signal a policy change, and they'll fear the worst."

I hoped McFarlane might share my concern. He could be sure the president understood all the facts and implications of State's intentions. If so, Reagan might well decide to block any such plan. McFarlane said nothing and looked annoyed.

Later, one of his favorite staffers approached me at breakfast in the White House mess.

"Maybe you don't realize it," she told me, "but you're getting on Bud's nerves. You keep bringing up touchy subjects at the morning meetings."

"I was getting that impression," I said, understating the matter.

I visited a member of the foreign policy cabinet at his home and told him the rumor.

"You might want to call around and find out if Shultz really means to do this," I suggested.

"I will. This could really wreak havoc with our policy down there, if it's true."

Two weeks before Christmas Joseph Kraft, the widely read *Washington Post* columnist, published the rumor. He approved of Shultz's plan, so it had presumably been leaked to him. As he put it, State was going to replace "amateur" ambassadors with foreign service "professionals" and remove "ideologues" from senior positions.

The wire services picked up the story, and soon the word had spread throughout the United States and Latin America.

This leak seemed to come from State and suggested to me that State was now confident that Shultz couldn't be stopped. It was also an advance hint to the Reagan ambassadors: start packing.

As soon as this news broke, a number of the targeted ambassadors called me on their secure telephones. They told me that as startling as this published rumor was that no one had spoken to *them* about their removal. Was it true? they asked.

My careful answer was that the rumor probably was an accurate reflection of George Shultz's intentions, *but* I had no evidence that State had taken any of the procedural steps needed to bring about such a major decision by the president—and only Ronald Reagan could remove them. This paperwork from State would normally come through my office, and I had seen nothing yet.

All the ambassadors with whom I spoke told me they were surprised at the story that they wanted to leave. They would be pleased to continue serving President Reagan, and they'd had no indication that he wasn't just as pleased with them.

I did my best to calm their fears, but I had a sinking feeling that we were in the first act of this drama.

One of the "marked men," Ambassador Curtin Winsor in Costa Rica, asked me for specific advice: "Should I fly to Washington and take this issue up personally with George Shultz and the White House?"

I said, "If I were in your position, that's exactly what I would do. Reagan's whole Central America policy is at stake."

Bad as the first part of the rumor was, Winsor said, the second part was almost its equal: the new ambassador-designate to Honduras was to be a foreign service officer who, while working for both Enders and Motley, had been a leading opponent of the president's Central American policy.

Only weeks before, this "ambassador-intended-for-Honduras" had said to Shultz, in the presence of one of my NSC colleagues, that "it was time to think about a Central America policy without the contras." Winsor said if that person became ambassador to Honduras, he could manipulate events there to undermine the cause of the Nicaraguan freedom fighters. I agreed.

So, for both policy and personal reasons, Winsor decided to fight the State Department. He arrived in Washington on Sunday, December 16, 1984.

Several days earlier the U.S. ambassador to Colombia, Dr. Lewis Tambs, had been told that Motley wanted him to resign immediately, and that he should write a letter of resignation to the president. The person who told him this was a third-level foreign service officer.

Dr. Tambs, who was serving as ambassador while on leave from

Arizona State University as a professor of Latin American history, had lived, worked, and traveled in Latin America for more than twenty-five years. He spoke fluent Spanish and was thoroughly familiar with the region. This was another of the so-called amateurs President Reagan had appointed.

As the president's representative in Colombia, Ambassador Tambs had performed all his duties extremely well and had helped the Colombian government shut down a huge narcotics factory that had been protected by communist guerrillas. Tambs had also encouraged the Colombian government to battle the powerful, and deadly, illegal narcotics smuggling gangs. For Tambs's excellent service, President Reagan had written him a letter of commendation. The Colombian narco-terrorists, however, announced that they had placed a $400,000 (later increased to a round million) murder "contract" on him. Tambs, along with his wife and newborn child, had survived several assassination plots by the drug smugglers *and* the Colombian communist guerrillas.

Understandably, Tambs had been deeply distressed by the sudden, undignified notice of his ostensible dismissal. Unfortunately, Tambs did not call me to check the facts. He had assumed that the foreign service officer would not have told him to resign unless President Reagan had already approved. With deep sadness at this surprising request, Tambs wrote and signed his letter of resignation. He then returned to Colombia to tell his wife and begin the move home.

Meanwhile, Ambassador Curtin Winsor, who *had* called me before deciding what course to take, checked in with me as soon as he arrived in Washington, D.C. Winsor had done a superb job in Costa Rica. He and his wife, Anne, both spoke Spanish very well and, along with their five children, had made an effective team. After college Curtin had served as a foreign service officer for five years, but then left and obtained a Ph.D. degree in Latin America studies. He had worked in banking, managed two businesses, and also had worked for Senator Dole. He was an active Republican, a financial contributor to his party, and had known Vice President Bush for many years. In fact, Winsor had actively supported Bush for president early in the 1980 campaign then strongly supported Reagan in the general election and had served on the Reagan transition team for the State Department after the 1980 election. Winsor also had about twenty years of direct experience with Latin America. This was another of the "amateurs" Shultz was going to remove from public service.

Curtin Winsor had also known McFarlane for some years and had hoped to speak with him about this unexpected development. I had brought up his request for a five-minute meeting on three occasions at the senior NSC staff meeting, but McFarlane decided not to take the time to see Winsor. Apparently McFarlane was going to stand aside from "the Battle of the Ambassadors," just as he had in the case of Senator Stone's removal.

On Monday, December 17, I invited Ambassador Winsor to an early breakfast at the White House. We compared notes, and I gave him the news that McFarlane was unwilling to see him. Later Winsor, former Senator Richard Stone, and I met at the Metropolitan Club to discuss the situation over lunch. Winsor wanted to get Stone's advice about a political strategy to get this issue to the president, so that Reagan could make an informed decision. Stone told us a few more details about how the State Department had stabbed him in the back and how McFarlane promised to help but in fact had done nothing. And they both agreed that given the three-member ambassadorial committee—State-Deaver-McFarlane—unless the NSC adviser gave the president the facts, Reagan would naturally go along with a unanimous recommendation to replace all these ambassadors and other Reaganites.

Stone told us a joke that had become popular with the ever-dwindling number of Reagan people working on foreign policy: "A liberal Democrat tells his friend that presidential candidate Mondale said, 'If you vote for me, we'll get rid of all the Reagan people in foreign policy.' Well, I voted for Mondale, and now they're getting rid of them!"

Winsor described his strategy. "I'll try to let the president know that I've spoken with five of the ambassadors scheduled for removal, and that all of us want to stay on. But how can I reach the president?"

Winsor pursued several approaches simultaneously. Within the White House, he tried to get the facts to Ed Meese, who was perceived as a person who wanted to make sure the president was not manipulated. Ambassador Faith Whittlesey, then in charge of public liaison, backed him up. So did Ken Cribb, Meese's right-hand man. Winsor found Senator Lugar, the Republican chairman of the Foreign Relations Committee, unwilling to get involved, but Senator Dole and Senator Helms both promised their support. Winsor wrote in his diary, "I spoke for twenty minutes with Senator Helms, who spoke to President Reagan at length. He told me, and I believe it, that Shultz is lying to Ronald Reagan."

Winsor also spoke with Congressman Jack Kemp, who, as chairman of the House Republican Conference, was a key leader. Kemp was very helpful. He tried to reach Ed Meese and later announced that he would delay support for the State Department budget if this purge of Reagan people were carried out. Within the Reagan cabinet, Winsor spoke with Bill Casey, who said he would do what he could, and with Ambassador Kirkpatrick. About their discussion, Winsor wrote in his journal, "She compared my situation with her own when Haig was out to get her. Jeane did a great job of cheering me up. She was emphatic that I must not resign under any circumstances except at Ronald Reagan's request."

Winsor had one friend, Richard Whalen, who had known the president for some years and understood the harm the State plan would do to U.S. policy. Whalen told Winsor that he had met with the president and given him some information about what was going on.

Winsor also tried to see Vice President George Bush. Although Philip Hughes of Bush's foreign policy staff tried to arrange an appointment, the vice president remained "unavailable." This disappointed Winsor, because he felt it was part of Bush's duty to alert the president when important facts weren't being given to him.

My sources had told me that the president would be given Shultz's list of new foreign service ambassadors on December 20 and told that the current ambassadors who would be replaced "were ready to move on." These sources said Shultz was presenting this to the president as an entirely routine shift at the end of the first administration. Was Shultz deliberately misleading the president, or was he too being misinformed by his Latin American bureau? We had no way of knowing. The pressure remained on all the Reagan ambassadors.

On Tuesday, December 17, a small group of us met to discuss the situation over breakfast at the Metropolitan Club. We all agreed that the president was being deceived, and that it was McFarlane's job to assure that the president knew the facts so he could decide whether or not to go along with Shultz on this. But McFarlane seemed determined to do nothing, except sign off on the Shultz-Deaver list.

On Wednesday, December 19—the day before the final decisions were to be made—Winsor then took a courageous step. He wrote a one-page memorandum for the president, briefly describing the extensive Latin American expertise of several Reagan political ambassadors. Winsor added that he had spoken with these ambassadors whom State intended to remove and had received their authorization to tell the president that all of them wished to continue in their posts. Any information the president was being given to the contrary by the State Department was incorrect. But how to get this signed statement to President Reagan?

There *was* one White House adviser who would understand the full significance of the State Department's misleading the president about so many of his appointees—Ed Meese. I took Ambassador Winsor's statement to Ed Meese's office in the West Wing. Ken Cribb, his assistant, read the statement and understood immediately. Obviously he was able to transmit that understanding to Meese, for within hours Meese had given the Winsor statement to President Reagan in the Oval Office. Meese's fast delivery proved one axiom about presidential power: access is no problem when you have it.

I also learned that Shultz's plan had upset the director of White House personnel, John Herrington (who later became secretary of energy in the second term), and his boss, Jim Baker. My sources said Herrington and Baker were surprised and angered that Shultz seemed to be acting as though they didn't exist.

Ambassadorships and the top positions at the State Department are very important presidential appointments. And for all presidential appointments, it was customary for the cabinet officer to propose his candidate to the White House personnel office, which might or might not decide to propose its own competing candidate for the president's final decision. Also, White House personnel expected to be involved and to present the decision to the president before any senior presidential appointee was removed against his or her wishes. I was told that Baker and Herrington thought Shultz now felt so powerful—as a result of his alliance with *both* Deaver and McFarlane—that he could unilaterally remove Reagan appointees and place career foreign service officers in their jobs without really consulting Baker *or* Herrington.

Baker, I was told, felt Shultz was now treating him like a rubber-stamping clerk. The news that a junior State Department official had demanded and received a letter of resignation from Ambassador Tambs would offend both Baker and Herrington. The president had *made no such decision,* and reportedly, State had not even submitted such a recommendation to White House personnel—not even for a pro forma concurrence.

Winsor decided to telephone Tambs, who had returned to Colombia. Winsor wanted to tell Ambassador Tambs that since no personnel decisions had yet been made by the president, the State Department request for Tambs's resignation was *unauthorized.*

Winsor telephoned Tambs through the White House switchboard and urged Tambs to communicate directly with the head of White House personnel and inform him of the State Department's request for his resignation. Further, Winsor proposed, Tambs should formally withdraw his letter of resignation and express his wish to continue serving President Reagan.

Then Winsor made an unusual suggestion: he urged Tambs to avoid the normal government channels and send this word directly to John Herrington at White House personnel using a commercial telegram.

Tambs was happy to hear that the president had not approved the removal of all the Reagan ambassadors. Yes, he said, he would be sure to send a commercial telegram to the director of White House personnel as soon as the telegram offices opened at nine the following morning.

Why did these two men agree on the use of a private, commercial telegram service? The answer is sad. They did so because they knew they couldn't trust the State Department to pass Tambs's telegram to the White House.

At seven-thirty the next morning Ambassador Tambs received a surprise. George Shultz himself telephoned him, commended him for his exceptional work, and told him the request for his resignation had been a "misunderstanding." Shultz told Tambs that both he and the president wanted Tambs to continue serving as an ambassador in Latin America.

After recovering from his surprise at this call from Secretary Shultz, Tambs said he would be pleased to continue serving. Shultz replied that the department would be in touch later about the specific new assignment—which turned out to be Costa Rica, where Curtin Winsor had been serving.

On that same day I waited for news that Tambs had sent his telegram to the White House. Several of us felt that this documentary evidence of the State Department's preemption of the president, combined with the Winsor memorandum, would raise serious questions in the president's mind about State's actions—and perhaps about its veracity.

But the news we awaited didn't come. After receiving Shultz's phone call, Tambs decided not to send his telegram to the White House. The central question now became why. Why would Shultz telephone Tambs the morning after Winsor had called him? Had calling through the White House switchboard compromised the privacy of the Winsor-Tambs telephone conversation? Or was it simply a coincidence?

There was another curious incident in the diversion of a letter from the president of Costa Rica to President Reagan in support of Ambassador Winsor. This letter had been carried to Washington by the Costa Rican foreign minister, who presented it to the State Department for transmittal to President Reagan. This letter warmly praised Ambassador Winsor's contributions to cooperation and cordial relations between the United States and Costa Rica.

But a State Department representative told the foreign minister—before President Reagan had made any final decision—that "Winsor was already out," so State refused to forward the letter to the White House.

Winsor learned of this and asked the Costa Rican foreign minister to submit the letter to the NSC. This was done on December 18. *But I could find no trace of it.* Chris Lehman and I both wanted to be sure it reached President Reagan before he made decisions on December 20. No luck!

Later, Lehman told Winsor that the then deputy executive secretary of the NSC, a foreign service officer, had "misplaced" this letter, a letter from one president to another, until January 5, when it arrived "too late."

At the Wednesday-morning NSC senior staff meeting on December 19, I again told McFarlane of the damage threatened by the wholesale removal of the Reaganite ambassadors and appointees.

McFarlane's reaction was to clench his jaws and give me a look that was even *colder* than usual.

Later that same day, after Ed Meese had given Winsor's memo to Reagan, Shultz was apparently alerted that the president had learned that, contrary to what State had told him, not all these Reagan appointees were in a hurry to "move on."

The next day President Reagan decided against removing his ambassadors. He put a "hold" on most of these personnel decisions until after the Christmas holidays. Now *that* was a Yuletide present.

That night my wife and I went to the gala Christmas dinner dance given by President and Mrs. Reagan for the cabinet and senior White House staff. The Christmas decorations were magnificent and created an elegant, cheerful scene. There was delicious eggnog, excellent food served in the State Dining Room, and an atmosphere of conviviality. Each couple was given the opportunity to greet President and Mrs. Reagan and to have a picture taken with them in front of the opulent White House Christmas tree. President Reagan and the First Lady were warm, thoughtful, and relaxed with all their guests. I introduced Nancy—my Nancy—to members of the cabinet and my colleagues.

Months later I would be told by a usually well-informed official that "the Battle of the Ambassadors" had made President Reagan so angry that he was very close to removing Shultz during the Christmas-New Year holidays. I do not know if this is true.

As 1985 began, Shultz remained in his job but did step back—somewhat—from his plans to remove most of the Reagan people at the State Department. Ambassador to the OAS Middendorf was offered and accepted a new job as ambassador to the European Economic Community. Dr. Richard McCormack, instead of being removed, was shifted from assistant secretary for economic affairs to become the new ambassador to the OAS. Under Secretary William Schneider remained until late 1986.

Unfortunately, Ambassador Winsor, the authentic hero of "the Battle of Ambassadors," a man who tried valiantly to defend the president's authority and policy, was targeted for removal by a determined State Department. He left in early 1985.

The other Reagan ambassadors were forced to accept a new and apparently neutral method for removal devised by the State Department in April 1985. By then Jim Baker and John Herrington had left to become members of the cabinet. With Michael Deaver backing the State Department approach, and McFarlane seeming to acquiesce, as usual, the State Department succeeded in promulgating a new and completely arbitrary "time limit" for ambassadors serving abroad. Foreign service ambassadors would have to be shifted after three years, and political ambassadors could serve no longer than two and a half years. Exceptions were made for some political ambassadors, including the ambassadors to the United Kingdom, Japan, and Italy.

The effect, of course, was to remove or transfer virtually all the Reagan ambassadors in Latin America.

One revelation for me was that Michael Deaver played such a major role in these events. He had announced in January that he was leaving the White House in May 1985 to set up a public affairs business, so I hadn't expected to see him in the thick of things.

I learned about Deaver's role in the replacement of ambassadors when current political ambassadors came to see me—in great distress. In virtually every case, the first word of their impending removal had come from Deaver, who simply used his regular telephone to call and tell them that their time was up and they would soon be getting a formal notice from the State Department.

One ambassador told me that *weeks* passed after Deaver's phone call with no formal notification to him. Since the international telephone call was probably tapped, he assumed his host country leader probably knew about it. He asked me, "Is this a real decision of the president? Should I, to maintain my reputation for candor, tell the head of government? Should my wife and I make plans to move? Or should I fight this decision, especially if it only represents the views of Deaver and Motley, and not Shultz and the president?"

I told this ambassador what had happened in December, pointing out I did not know if President Reagan had actually agreed to these actions; and the reason I didn't know was that McFarlane and Poindexter refused to tell me anything about the latest State Department gambit. This ambassador— a lifelong Republican, a multimillionaire, a major Republican contributor who had known George Bush for many years, and a man who had performed with great skill and distinction—said to me, "I'm ready to leave if I know this is a decision taken by the president. I can't get any straight answers at the State Department. If I'm to depart, the least I think any of us has the right to expect—whether we are career or political ambassadors—is two or three months official notice, so we can leave in a dignified way that maintains respect for our country and its ambassadors."

"You're absolutely right," I said. "The president wouldn't like it if he knew about this disorganized and uncivilized way of changing ambassadors. Unfortunately, I can't persuade McFarlane to let you meet with the president and tell him yourself. But since you know Bush so well, I'm sure you can see him. Just tell Bush the facts. He has a private lunch with the president every week, and he can *easily* alert Reagan to this problem."

My visitor went on: "After many years in business and as an active Republican, I took this job to serve our country and this president. For more than thirty years, I've been a contributor to the Republican party. Now I accepted the physical risks that go along with being an ambassador today. If the administration can't treat people with some modicum of dignity, we're not going to be there in 1986 and 1988 and beyond when the Republican party wants our help again."

He was visibly upset, and I sympathized with his feeling of abandonment. I told him that Ambassador Winsor had fought in December and as a result delayed this process by many months. Then I said, "I hope you use all your contacts and try to see Secretary Shultz and Vice President Bush, and tell them exactly what you told me."

He did see Vice President Bush and received a noncommittal response. Not long afterward he returned to private life.

*   *   *

In early May another skilled and effective Reagan ambassador—who spoke better Spanish and had a greater knowledge of his host country than virtually anyone at the State Department—told me about a Deaver aide's telephone notice to him.

"I told him," he said, " 'You're violating security regulations by making this kind of call on an open line. Don't you understand the delicacy of our relationship with this country? The president appointed me and when he wants me to leave he can tell me. Until then you can shove this telephone up your ass!' "

This person was almost the ideal ambassador. He was deeply knowledgeable about his host country, one he had lived in and visited frequently since his youth; and he was totally fluent in its language and conversant with its culture. He had known Ronald Reagan and many of his top political supporters for more than twenty years. His university work included Latin American studies. He had wide professional experience, a vivacious wife, and, incidentally, he was so handsome that the secretaries at the NSC always eagerly anticipated his visits to my office. Unfortunately, a person with this combination of attributes had been seen as a potential rival by both Enders and Motley—so they had treated him badly.

He had come back for one of his regular visits when I chatted with him. Usually so upbeat and vigorous, he now seemed frustrated if not dejected. I told him I knew there was an effort to remove him. Several mutual friends of his and the president's had advised him not to fight.

"What do you think I should do, Constantine?"

"Fight!" I answered. "Use all your connections to get a meeting with President Reagan or the First Lady. Talk to congressional leaders you know are close to the president and get through to him on the telephone. He thinks very highly of you, and knows you have done an excellent job. The president is probably being told that *you* have taken the initiative to resign and that *you* want to return to private life. You shouldn't write a letter of resignation unless you're certain that the president *knows* you want to serve at least another year, and knowing that, still requests your resignation now."

Fortunately, he took my advice. A few days later he left word for me to call him at about 7:00 P.M. I was playing soccer in the park with my son and walked with him to the nearest pay phone. Then I dialed the White House switchboard requesting the other number and was delighted to hear the ambassador say, using a prearranged code, that he would be staying.

Later, the State Department's under secretary for management, foreign service officer Ronald Spiers, called this ambassador in and explained that it had "never been the State Department's intention to remove him." The Deaver-instigated phone call had been a mistake, a "misunderstanding."

The ambassador looked at Spiers and said coldly, "You're lying."

To prove it, he gave him a copy of a formal letter Spiers's own office had sent weeks earlier to more than thirty corporate presidents. This official State Department letter said there was an "opening" for a new ambassador to the country in question and asked the recipients to submit their nominations for this "open" ambassadorship. Under Secretary Spiers was aghast at being confronted with this evidence. But if he apologized, the ambassador didn't mention it to me.*

Like many of the conflicts about foreign policy within the Reagan administration, the Battle of the Ambassadors had pitted Shultz (representing the dominant faction in the foreign service bureaucracy), his White House ally, Deaver, and McFarlane against a few Reagan supporters who wanted to be sure that the president had all the facts when he made his final decisions.

In this case, thanks to Ambassador Winsor, President Reagan had at first prevented Shultz's complete success. But the State bureaucracy kept on plotting. And, months later, it finally succeeded: many competent Reagan appointees were removed or sidelined. Only months later when I read about Deaver's hundreds of thousands of dollars in public affairs contracts from a number of foreign governments did it occur to me why Deaver might have been so interested in ambassadorial appointments—he may have wanted access while State wanted control.

Shortly after President Reagan's second inauguration, a story in *The Washington Post* caught my eye. Written by Don Oberdorfer, it was headlined SHULTZ FIRMLY IN COMMAND.

Obviously written from the State Department's angle—it seemed State usually provided the *Post*'s inside dope on foreign policy—the story was

---

* In the spring of 1987 the press reported that this same under secretary for management shared the principal responsibility for ensuring proper security at the U.S. embassy in Moscow. The public had just been told by the press that the State Department had resisted implementing counterintelligence measures that had been recommended repeatedly since 1982.

In May of 1987 the *Washington Times* reported that Mr. Spiers would be the recipient of a ten- to twenty-thousand-dollar "performance bonus."

perceptive. Oberdorfer noted that "Secretary of State George P. Shultz has become the central figure in U.S. foreign policy." Only too true.

I read on: "In undramatic fashion, through gradual accretion of authority and steady elimination of rivals"—exactly!—"Shultz has become the senior executor and shaper of President Reagan's global policies."

An unnamed State observer was quoted: "He is the tortoise who moves ever so slowly, but he just keeps coming and finally wins the race against the hares." A nice image, though he might have mentioned that this tortoise also tried shortcuts.

The story continued: "Through personal attention, Shultz has made an ally of the presidential national security adviser, Robert C. McFarlane." It named Caspar Weinberger as Shultz's chief remaining rival but said that "those who have seen them in their weekly breakfast meetings and on social occasions said they have never observed any personal enmity." I smiled at this. "To the dismay of some conservative political figures, those who have lost Shultz's confidence have been removed, whether by design or accident, from the foreign policy process." Less accident than design. I had come close to the brink myself in the last few months; so had others. Plenty of us had "lost Shultz's confidence."

But one section of Oberdorfer's story gave me a jolt:

> Shultz's penchant for negotiations and affinity for the professional Foreign Service have aroused some distrust, despite his generally conservative views.
>
> Last October, for example, national news organizations were informed by telephone calls from Capitol Hill that Shultz, then on a visit to Panama and Mexico, was on the eve of signing a secret four-part deal with Nicaragua.
>
> It was denied by senior officials and didn't happen. State Department officials said they traced the reports to the office of Senator Jesse Helms (R.-N.C.) and Constantine Menges of the National Security Council staff.

Here I was, being publicly, and falsely, accused of leaking—and by an anonymous leaker! The leaker was lying on a second count: the attempted deal was a fact. I had seen the Shultz-McFarlane messages and still had copies of the unclassified State treaty draft. So did Casey, and probably Ikle and Kirkpatrick. The messages and the treaty draft both called explicitly for the treaty to be signed "on or before October 30, 1984."

By rewriting history State's way, the *Post* story wasn't merely reporting on Shultz's increased power: it was serving to increase it further. I was angry at its leaker's brazen charge that I was the one circulating false stories. I always worked within the government when I was in public service, I didn't leak. Now, ironically, I was reading a false rumor that I spread a false rumor. And now, even after initially losing the Battle of the Ambassadors, George Shultz was still "firmly in command."

7

EASTER EGG

When McFarlane confounded the secretarial grapevine by not firing me right after the 1984 election, the whisper was that he had been concerned about the implications for his own career if he got rid of me. I was one of the few remaining "Reaganites" on the NSC staff. He was already in bad odor among congressional Republicans, who knew he'd conspired with Shultz on the preelection "peace treaty."

McFarlane was angry at me because he knew I had made sure the president found out in time to stop Shultz. He also thought I was the one who had told some members of Congress. I wasn't. They'd heard about it through someone else on the NSC staff.

This man knew I hadn't told the congressman. He also knew I had not and would not tell McFarlane and Poindexter that *he* had told them, not even to clear my own name. In December 1984, weeks after McFarlane's outburst, this colleague told me that he'd confessed his role in it to McFarlane and Poindexter to put me "back in their good graces." I wish I could have believed him. But by then I knew Ollie North well enough to guess that though he would claim to have told McFarlane and Poindexter the truth, he'd probably done nothing of the kind.

Working with and getting to know Ollie North well proved to be one of the most interesting experiences of my government service. It was always easy to like him, as the American people saw during his televised testimony in July 1987. Oliver North is highly intelligent, articulate, persuasive, and patriotic—all with a down-to-earth personableness that makes him credible to a broad cross section of our society. North has the natural talents of a skilled politician in dealing with people and putting them at ease. He always conveyed the firm sense that he really believed whatever he was telling a listener.

I first met U.S. Marine Major Oliver North in the spring of 1983; he was then thirty-nine years old (I was forty-four, and McFarlane was forty-six). Since 1981 he had been a member of the political/military group within the NSC. This consisted mainly of military officers who handled arms sales to foreign countries. In 1983 North was assigned responsibility for the Nicaraguan armed resistance. Since the CIA operations directorate (the "spy" side of the agency) had the management responsibility for the then legal U.S. efforts to support the armed resistance in Nicaragua, North developed close relationships with that group. Since I was the senior person for Latin America on the analytical side of CIA, on good terms with Casey, and a firm adherent of the president's policies, North was always friendly toward me.

When Bill Clark asked me to take over responsibility for Latin America at the NSC, Oliver North was extremely cordial in welcoming me when I began my work there in October 1983. For the next four months he and I worked together on Grenada and the major review of Central America strategy. The two individuals who had been working on Latin America left the NSC as I came on board, which meant I was the only staffer for Latin America. Ollie's energetic help on some issues made a major contribution to keeping the work going until Jacqueline Tillman joined the Latin America group in mid-February 1984 with Raymond Burghardt coming over from State a month later.

From my point of view, Ollie North was an important ally on behalf of the president's policy. In late 1983 and 1984 I found Ollie's energy and skills important and valuable in the effort to promote the success of democracy and the defeat of communism in Central America.

In the fall of 1983, during my first months at the NSC, Ollie, Chris Lehman, and I would often go for breakfast in the White House mess after the seven-thirty senior staff meeting. Slowly but surely I came to know the personable and persuasive young major.

To anyone who didn't work directly with him, Lieutenant Colonel Oliver North appeared a model marine—disciplined, dedicated, thorough. Certainly he was patriotic. He had his military hardware and tactics down cold. But the few of us who worked closely with Ollie North on the inside came to see there was another side to the man.

One thing I started to notice was that when the conversation turned to colleagues whom he saw as rivals or obstacles, Ollie found some slightly insidious way to discredit them.

About one he said, "Well, he was an academic. He didn't know how to 'make the bureaucracy work.' " About a senior Defense official he said, on several occasions, "He has no influence because Cap Weinberger doesn't listen to him." More than three years later, when the Tower Commission Report published notes from Ollie to McFarlane and Poindexter in which Ollie reported allegations that one of his colleagues, a potential competitor on the project, might be earning money from the sale of weapons to Iran, passing the unflattering rumor along seemed in character for Ollie North. (That person was subsequently "cut out" of the Iran military sales when he questioned its continuing value.)

In 1984 with the passing months I reluctantly concluded that North regularly exaggerated and reshaped events. He was more and more likely to seek to impress people through "personal hype." For example, North once told me, complete with highlights of the conversation, about a dinner he'd had the previous weekend with then Ambassador Jeane Kirkpatrick. Not long after, in a meeting with Ambassador Kirkpatrick, I asked if a certain subject had come up during that dinner. The ambassador looked blank. "I've never had dinner with Oliver North," she said.

One of my earliest recollections involves my sitting in Ollie's office and listening to him tell a caller, "Henry Kissinger is here visiting me," and "I have to get back to him." Thinking Ollie was joking with his caller, I did a quick (and rather poor) Kissinger imitation, saying loudly, "Ya, Ollie, we haf got to finish dis discussion."

Several months later I and other colleagues would decide that when Ollie told us about his "dinner with Jeane Kirkpatrick," his "weekend spent writing the Kissinger commission report" with one of its celebrity members, and later his alleged "conversation with Nancy Reagan," these were simply rather childish examples of an overactive ego. Sometimes we tried to tease Ollie into admitting these were "tall tales," but mostly we just shook our heads and concluded everybody had his weak points.

Another early-warning sign I ignored was one I came to call Ollie's "memo maneuver." The NSC executive secretariat would distribute incoming actions on Central America to me, and if the issue involved the contras or military matters, a copy would go to North. Initially the usual procedure would be for the Latin American group to prepare the action memo and then show it to Ollie (or to Roger Robinson if it involved economic issues) for comments or concurrence. One morning in late 1983 I came in to see that a memo had gone out to Bud McFarlane with my name on it, mine and Ollie's. "Oh," North said when I asked, "I called you at ten-thirty last night, but you weren't in your office, and this had to get done." Very clever. I told him, in no uncertain terms, that if an urgent matter could not have waited until the next morning at seven for my review, he should simply have had the White House operator call me at home or via my beeper and I would come back to the office. He agreed. But then it happened again and again.

After Jacqueline Tillman had observed this for a couple of weeks, she advised me that I had to protest vigorously to both North and McFarlane because a bad precedent was being set.

"Ollie doesn't have the knowledge of the politics of Central America to make good judgments on broader issues," she said. "If you let him get away with this, soon he'll take over Central America policy."

I replied, "I've asked Ollie not to do this. As it turns out, so far I have no major disagreements with the memos *I've seen* where he's put my name alongside his. If I had a strong disagreement, I can assure you I'd immediately write a countermemo to McFarlane and bring it up at the morning senior NSC staff meeting." But I said I didn't want to raise what would look like a "bureaucratic turf" issue. We had to work with Ollie to help keep State in line, and State would have liked nothing better than a feud within the NSC. Besides, I added, McFarlane was too busy to have to worry about bureaucratic details like this.

"I understand," Tillman replied, "but I think you're making a mistake."

Some days later, after a few more run-ins with North, she came to me and said, her voice thick with emotion, "I've worked here at the NSC for some weeks now with Ollie North, and I've concluded that not only is he a liar, but he's delusional, power hungry, and a danger to the president and the country. He should not be working on the NSC staff."

I was surprised by these harsh opinions. I said, "Ollie is dedicated, energetic, and on the president's side. Yes, he is always name dropping and boasting about his exploits. And yes, he does seem to try to put himself in the limelight and take credit for everything; yes, he does try to take over actions that might involve contact with the president. But to me this seems like just more than the usual amount of self-promoting behavior you see anywhere. It doesn't strike me as a danger the way you put it."

In the summer of 1984 Tillman told me a disturbing story. A journalist friend of hers had described, in colorful detail, certain events that occurred in flight on the June 1984 Shultz trip to Nicaragua. In a casual office chat, she had related the events to Ollie. About two weeks later Ollie told her the same stories and said that a journalist who had been on Shultz's plane had related this to *him*.

Startled, Tillman reminded Ollie that *she* had originally told *him* this story. Yet Ollie insisted, for about twenty minutes, that this had been *his* rather than *her* experience. When she told me about this, she was worried for him: Ollie seemed to be having trouble distinguishing between his fantasies and objective reality. (In November 1986, when the Iran-contra crisis first broke, I was told that Ollie's credibility with some who worked closely with him had fallen to such depths that one of those NSC colleagues joked that the reported unauthorized funds for the contras "were probably another of Ollie's fantasies.")

In late 1985, according to Robert Reilly, a skilled White House colleague, Ollie claimed to have received a congratulatory phone call from Max Rabb, the U.S. ambassador to Italy, on the capture of the Achille Lauro terrorists. A few days later Reilly met with Ambassador Rabb in Europe and mentioned that he knew Oliver North at the NSC. The ambassador looked blank and said, "Who is Oliver North?"

In late 1986 the television news carried recordings of Oliver North claiming, in some of his briefings to citizen groups, that he frequently met alone with President Reagan, including a few times at Camp David. The White House promptly issued a statement that from January 1985 to November 1986 North had been in nineteen meetings with the president but never alone. Testimony in the Iran-contra hearings and reports said that Ollie frequently told pro-Reagan activists about ostensible one-on-one conversations with Reagan. I am told Ollie had a very moving fictional story about how he bent over a map of Grenada with the "old man" in the Oval Office to persuade Reagan to make the rescue decision! Fawn Hall, his secretary, later told the Iran-contra investigating committee that Ollie had *never* met alone with the president.

As McFarlane and Poindexter gave North a freer and freer rein, exercising less and less supervision, Ollie began to feel that he could do everything better than his colleagues. One of our common tasks, under Chris Lehman's leadership, was to brief individual members of Congress hoping they would vote for contra aid. Lehman worked Capitol Hill full-time and knew how to build a coalition to help the president win. But in early 1984 Ollie decided to run his own operation. Not long thereafter Lehman got a call from a leading Republican congressman who barked,

"Keep North off Capitol Hill. He's doing the cause more harm than good." Then the congressman called McFarlane and gave him the same blunt message.

McFarlane said he would call Ollie in and set him straight, but within a few days we got reports that the irrepressible North was back on Capitol Hill. When Lehman confronted him North denied that he was still meeting with congressmen on his own. But Lehman told Ollie exactly where and with whom he had been meeting.

Like the rest of us, Chris Lehman found it hard, despite all the evidence, to change his positive impressions of Ollie North. Lehman told me that as late as 1986 he had dinner with Ollie and sat, a rapt believer, as North recounted a tale of his "personal conversation with the president about the hostages in Lebanon."

In April of 1987, Lehman said, hindsight or no hindsight, he initially believed North about the conversation—"because he was *so* sincere." Lehman made an apt analogy: "Ollie's like a chain saw. He can do constructive work if supervised, but let loose he can cut a tragic swath."

If this kind of exaggeration had remained on the level of office politics, it might not have mattered. But it soon began to go beyond the walls of the NSC.

What particularly worried me was Ollie's use of the phrase "We must cause this to happen."

"No," I'd say, "we don't *cause* things to happen. The president is the one who decides what the government will do, and our job as his staff is to give him the facts and point out the alternatives so he can make an informed decision."

"No," Ollie would say to me, "you're *wrong*. We have to box him in so there's only one way he can go—the right way."

For all the certitude with which Ollie North pursued "the right way," there were any number of times in which he was misled, especially on political issues, into endorsing the way of State Department instead of the president. And, as we have seen, the two were indeed different.

With each passing year in the Reagan administration, I found myself using the phrases "It's an imperfect world" or "We human beings are very imperfect" more and more often. Or so my wife pointed out. And it was true, for I found myself increasingly dismayed by the deception, the manipulation, and the trickery that I saw in the foreign policy decision-making process.

In Central America alone, the situation was very dangerous. A brutal, ruthless communist movement threatened the whole area, and in two key countries there was a small but violent *right*. At the same time, those of us who backed the president's policies were opposed by a large group of misguided congressional Democrats, media that were often misinformed, and many left-wing activists. Worse, we had a State Department pursuing its own foreign policy rather than that of the president.

Because North and I shared so many values, it took me some time to reach the reluctant conclusion that his good qualities and good intentions were marred by serious flaws of judgment and character. My method had always been to work in as civil and cordial a way as possible with everyone in the U.S. government, whatever our differences. But in December of 1984 an unexpected event brought the question of Ollie North's maturity and sense of public responsibility into sharp focus for me.

A private citizen in Los Angeles approached me with an idea for an operation (neither in Latin America nor the Middle East) that he believed could benefit the West and make millions of dollars from foreign sources directly available, legally, to the armed resistance in Nicaragua. I told this man that my listening to his idea did not in any way constitute an *endorsement*, either by the NSC staff or the U.S. government. But I told him I would do some preliminary analysis to check some of his factual information, and then I *might* pass the idea to the appropriate authorities to begin a formal process of decision by the president. I stressed that the law specified a strict process for *all* types of U.S. action abroad, and that the Reagan administration was determined to obey the letter of the law.

I later mentioned the idea to one other NSC person but cautioned that Ollie North should know nothing about it unless the president decided to go ahead. Why? Because I was afraid that Ollie might make the mistake of trying to encourage someone abroad to carry it out, even *without* a presidential decision.

It surprised me that I had come to feel this way. Ollie and I shared the president's conviction that the Democratic majority in Congress had made a major historical mistake in cutting off aid to the Nicaraguan armed resistance. But I felt that the surest way to prevent the president from winning future congressional support was to act outside the law or contrary to proper procedures within the Executive.

Ollie knew I felt deeply on these points. That knowledge, and his desire for total control, probably explains why he never told me anything about his "private activities."

*   *   *

The first days of 1985 brought changes in the top ranks of the administration.

Michael Deaver, Shultz's closest ally, had announced that he would be resigning in a few months. I heard a rumor from a reliable source that the president himself had demanded Deaver's resignation during the New Year's holiday in Palm Springs. The reason? A cabinet member had told Reagan something important in strict confidence. Only hours later a White House press person had phoned the cabinet member to ask about that same private matter. Shocked and angry, the cabinet official went immediately to see the president, who assured him he had told no one— except Michael Deaver.

At about the same time it was announced that Jim Baker and Dick Darman were going to lead the Treasury Department, while Don Regan would leave Treasury to become the new chief of staff. Looking back, I now understand what Deaver's and Baker's departures and Don Regan's arrival meant to McFarlane and Poindexter: more than ever, they needed to maintain good relations with Shultz.

I had witnessed a vivid scene between Regan and McFarlane after one NSC meeting. They were standing by the French doors of the Cabinet Room facing the south lawn. I was waiting for McFarlane, and only the three of us remained.

To my amazement, Regan jabbed his finger several times into McFarlane's chest and said assertively, "You just stay out of that! You stay out of it!"

I was standing a discreet distance away, but I could see the muscles in McFarlane's jaw clench. For a moment I wondered if he might want to take a swing at Regan, but he said nothing.

As he and I walked back to his West Wing office, McFarlane seemed subdued. I reflected that he had a lonely job. The more an NSC adviser works in the president's interest, the more inevitably he'll come into conflict with one, two, or more strong-minded cabinet members. When Bud did his job right, he was likely to have cabinet members complain about him. That explained a lot, even if it didn't ultimately excuse him.

Within weeks of Don Regan's arrival we heard rumors that the chief of staff was cutting back on the NSC adviser's special access to the president. In fact, North told me that McFarlane no longer had his own direct phone line to President Reagan at Camp David. The Don Regan era had begun. Things didn't bode well for relations between Regan and McFarlane, which only increased the already obvious McFarlane tilt toward the State Department.

*   *   *

My work on Latin America continued. We were never short of things to do. Politically delicate transitions to democracy were under way in a number of countries, and U.S. action could be helpful. The $400 billion Latin American debt crisis continued; it required a mixture of sensible financial and political steps to avoid even deeper economic setbacks in the region.

At the NSC, Roger Robinson had the lead responsibility on this. Robinson was an energetic Reagan supporter who had many creative and sensible financial ideas; I helped with political insight and suggestions. In our work together we tried to persuade the State Department to drop its opposition to U.S. economic sanctions against Nicaragua as a counter to its subversive aggression.

There were also opportunities to help settle a number of simmering international disputes. I kept pressing a reluctant State Department to give some time and energy to encouraging peaceful settlements to the United Kingdom-Argentine conflict over the Falkland-Malvinas islands; the Guatemala-Belize territorial dispute; and the Honduras-El Salvador territorial dispute, which in 1969 had led to a brief war. Further, there were a number of countries where most of us in the subcabinet working on Latin America believed prudent action *now* could avoid serious problems later.

The State Department continued to convene the Restricted Interagency Group only intermittently. What's more, the State Latin American bureau's leadership saved most of its real interest and energy for pushing its version of a Central American treaty: I came across State Department memos written for Shultz in early 1985 that in essence suggested ways to *pretend* a Central America treaty would include democracy in Nicaragua.

One of these memos was written by a former Kissinger staffer who had seen President Ford sign the 1975 Helsinki agreements. A decade of history had shown that by 1985 the Helsinki agreements had meant the United States had, in effect, ratified communist control of Eastern Europe in return for Soviet-bloc promises of human rights and political liberalization—*which were never carried out.*

Now, despite the ten years that proved the incompetence of this diplomacy, this same person suggested that State "play up" the treaty language on democratization and "trumpet it like the human rights language of Helsinki." And a senior foreign service official wrote Shultz encouragingly about the prospects for movement toward a treaty, telling Shultz it was in the Sandinistas' interest to accept the State Department proposal since *in fact* it "would require them to do nothing on democratization."

Bill Casey told me that George Shultz had promised him that during the second term he would stop the unilateral initiatives and work in a more collegial way with his foreign policy cabinet colleagues. Perhaps, he suggested, Shultz had been sobered by his lack of success in end-running the president and wanted to start the second term on a better footing. "I hope so," I replied, "but actions speak louder than New Year's promises."

At the NSC in early 1985, McFarlane and Poindexter had decided that Donald Fortier, Oliver North, and my deputy Raymond Burghardt should have the key responsibility for Central America and for winning the congressional vote on aid to the contras. Fortier, who'd worked as a staff member in the House of Representatives, had met McFarlane when they both joined the Haig State Department in 1981–82. In 1982 he had come with McFarlane to the NSC, where McFarlane put him in charge of the NSC political-military directorate. Recently, since McFarlane and Poindexter liked his low-key style, Fortier had been promoted. He was now the second deputy NSC adviser.

Fortier, North, and Burghardt produced proposals on Central America that I was not supposed to see. Chris Lehman and I were both being excluded, but we understood why. Our judgment about congressional strategy differed from that of McFarlane and Poindexter, and (just as they would later do on the Iran scandal) their reaction was to shut out staff members who spoke up with uncongenial views.

Nevertheless, in early January 1985 I wrote up, on one legal-sized page, a strategy to win the contra vote and sent it to McFarlane and Poindexter with copies to Fortier, North, Burghardt, Lehman, and Tillman. The final House vote was expected in mid to late April. I suggested week-by-week activities to inform members of Congress, the public, and friendly countries.

In drawing up this suggested plan, I consulted closely with Chris Lehman, who really understood the Congress, and with Ambassador Otto Reich, a Reagan appointee, who did a first-rate job under difficult circumstances as the State Department point man for public diplomacy. In fact, I worked with informed officials in all the departments. And my proposed actions were keyed to relevant forthcoming international or domestic political events and historic anniversaries.

Although I wasn't supposed to see copies of the Fortier-North-Burghardt documents sent to McFarlane, I did. My purpose in writing up my own suggestions was not to upstage them, but rather to help: I felt that their suggestions lacked a sense of strategy. I also went to see Dick Darman and asked him to make his successful experience on legislative strategy available to McFarlane and Poindexter before he and Jim Baker left for the Treasury Department.

Darman's reply was prophetic: "*Colonel* McFarlane and *Admiral* Poindexter are military officers. They have no sense of political strategy. They're bureaucrats who deal with everything one day at a time. They think they can drift along, let the months go by, and then use a flurry of last-minute activity by the president to win this vote. They're wrong, of course. Every difficult vote we've won needed a consistent strategy over many weeks and months. Usually there has to be wheeling and dealing to win over some of the needed votes—this requires political decisions. But the colonel and the admiral won't take advice from me or Jim [Baker], and they'd consider any suggestions I might make interference with their turf. Sorry, Constantine. You'll have to do the best you can from inside the NSC, and by working with your friends in the cabinet."

That was a sobering conversation. It made me realize I needed all the allies I could get. I decided to have a private talk with Oliver North, whom I now rarely saw, since McFarlane and Poindexter were trying to exclude me on Central America.

Snowflakes were falling as North and I spoke briefly on the street between the White House and the Old Executive Office Building.

"Ollie," I said, "we both know McFarlane and Poindexter are trying to cut me out of Central America. There's nothing I can do about that right now. But you and I have often worked together—we make a balanced team. You're the military man, you've got experience there, but lots of this is political, and new to you, while I have twenty years of international political experience. So what I'm saying is, just come and talk to me about ideas before they become action. I don't want any credit. But I can help."

"You're absolutely right," Ollie replied. "What they're doing to you is reprehensible, and those wimps McFarlane and Poindexter are just going along with Shultz. He wants to sell out. But we won't let him."

That *sounded* great. But from early 1985 on, Ollie never really talked with me about Central America issues, major, minor, or otherwise.

In early 1985, as we in the NSC "strategized" about how to persuade the Democrats in the House to support the president on aid to the Nicaraguan freedom fighters, we agreed on one thing: past experience in

1982, 1983, and 1984 showed that the State Department couldn't be relied on to pursue this administration's objectives effectively.

Yes, Secretary Shultz and Assistant Secretary Motley could give tough-sounding speeches, and sometimes their personal testimony in Congress was first-rate. Occasionally, at White House meetings with the president, Shultz could outdo even Bill Casey in stating the national interest in supporting the Nicaraguan freedom fighters. But for the previous three years we had seen that in the battles with the isolationist congressional Democrats, time and time again, the State Department's leadership and tactics had simply failed.

For example, back in 1982 Enders had recommended that the administration endorse the first Boland restriction on aid to the Nicaraguan armed resistance. The isolationist Democrats obtained this Reagan administration endorsement by using the standard, and clever, bargaining tactic of threatening to pass the Harkin amendment, which would have cut off aid to the contras.

The State Department had the choice of either agreeing to the Boland "compromise" or energetically building a congressional coalition to defeat it. Alone in the subcabinet, I argued that the administration could and should prevent such congressional foreign policy interference with the president's constitutional authority.

Bill Casey called me at home one evening in early December 1982. What was my opinion of the State Department's recommendation that the administration endorse the Boland restriction? I advised him to oppose it on constitutional and policy grounds. Later he told me ruefully, "You were right—we should have fought the first Boland amendment. The defeat of the Harkin amendment by 408 (among 435) votes proved the Democrats had fooled the administration with an empty threat."

In 1983 there had been much too little systematic State Department briefing of the Congress before the crucial House vote in July. Enders had deliberately held back the government white paper on Central America from February until it was publicly released on the same date he was removed, May 27, 1983. While Motley was in the process of being confirmed, the Enders appointees controlled the Latin American bureau and failed to brief Congress effectively.

In July 1983, two days before the dramatic closed-door secret debate of the entire House, Bill Casey phoned me while I was having a luncheon meeting at the Cosmos Club. And he was angry.

Members of Congress were telephoning him and asking him for

information about Central America and the freedom fighters, so they could help President Reagan.

Casey said, "I was told that State was taking care of this, but they seem to have done very little. Constantine, put together the relevant set of your short, unclassified briefing materials, get up to Capitol Hill immediately, and brief the House Republicans."

And in 1984, as already related, Shultz and McFarlane made the mistake of delaying the contra vote until autumn, when the presidential election campaign was in full swing.

Now, in early 1985, all of us at the NSC knew that winning the vote would depend on White House leadership and good judgment—since we could not count on the State Department. But even within the NSC staff there were differing views about how to win.

McFarlane, Poindexter, Fortier, Burghardt, and usually North felt that the only way to win was to offer the Democrats a "compromise." I felt that Poindexter and North were always being led into endorsing this "compromise" approach because they lacked the political understanding to see how it would backfire. The State Department Latin American bureau agreed with and reinforced this approach: it hoped for a compromise that would provide the administration with what some termed a "face-saving way of phasing out the contras in the context of a peace agreement."

The other view was held by Republican congressional leaders like representatives Jack Kemp, Henry Hyde, and Trent Lott, along with Chris Lehman and myself. This view was that the president should wage a vigorous campaign for a yes-or-no vote on aid to the Nicaraguan freedom fighters. Whatever the outcome, we deeply believed the administration should, of course, obey the decision of Congress and let the American people and history judge whether the Democratic majority in the House had acted wisely. We thought that since the president had a solid 170 Republican House votes, and needed only 48 of the 253 Democrats to agree with him, this approach could and would succeed.

Why were we so confident? Because among the more than one hundred Democratic congressmen from the South and Southwest, there was a great potential sense of realism. We believed many could understand the fragility of Mexico and the tragic consequences that would follow if history proved that terminating U.S. support to the contras led to a communist Mexico.

The customary way of politics is compromise. And as the son of a former congressman, McFarlane understandably tended toward this method of resolving disputes. Nonetheless, Chris Lehman and I contended at the morning staff meetings that on *this* issue, the isolationist Democrats had become so effective—after three years of outmaneuvering the administration—that success would most likely be achieved only by sticking with a yes-or-no vote and mounting a vigorous, systematic persuasion campaign. We pointed to the precedent of President Carter's massive and successful information campaign to obtain Senate ratification of the Panama Canal Treaty.

McFarlane said nothing.

Easter and spring came early in 1985, and still the issue of aid to the contras had not been resolved. On April 4 the president of Colombia, Belisario Betancur, came to Washington for a state visit. Jacqueline Tillman had done an excellent job for the NSC in preparing President Reagan. She provided him with firm and clear talking points about Central America to use with President Betancur. These highlighted the crucial difference between a genuine and a destructive peace treaty for that region.

At the senior NSC staff meeting that morning, McFarlane had turned, beaming like a proud father, to Ollie North and announced that today the president would be revealing Ollie's "Easter peace initiative." According to that initiative, the United States would hold up on military aid to the armed resistance for sixty days *after it was passed by Congress*—if the Sandinistas entered into a dialogue with their internal democratic opposition. And if *both sides* requested the U.S. aid be held up further, the president would abide by that.

Chris Lehman and I were both stunned by this. We hadn't heard a word about it.

In fact, it was a useful idea except for one problem: it was proposed at the wrong time. Our count showed that the Republican Senate would definitely vote for aid to the contras. So Lehman had recommended that the Republican Senate leadership be encouraged to call a vote on contra aid a few days *before* Speaker O'Neill scheduled the House vote. That way, the positive vote in the Senate would create a sense of momentum that would help the president in the House.

Unfortunately, McFarlane, Poindexter, and North—not having discussed this idea with their legislative expert, Chris Lehman—made a major mistake in timing. The president's initiative should have been held up until after the Republican Senate voted "yes," then used as the *final offer* in the last hours before the House voted.

As soon as I'd learned this surprising news I did several things. First, I worked with Ben Elliott so that the president's speech announcing the initiative would state his policy clearly.

After I talked with Lehman I wrote McFarlane a memo headed "Today's Nicaraguan peace plan—first thoughts about steps to prevent negative consequences." I warned that three independent coalitions might try to turn the peace plan against the administration: communist Nicaragua and its partners; neutralist political groups within the four friendly Central American countries; and misguided domestic opponents of our policy, including the isolationist Democrats in Congress. For each set of possible negative events, I suggested preventive actions to be taken immediately.

I argued that the congressional Democrats opposing the administration would "pocket the peace initiative and demand much more. They would continue to oppose any military aid, they would seek to have nonmilitary aid channeled via the UN or other international organizations but not through CIA, and they would seek to postpone any final vote until the sixty days had been used for "genuine negotiations." What's more, they would probably demand that a congressional group monitor or certify the "validity" or "good faith" of U.S. negotiating efforts. To cope with these potential demands, my April 4 memo urged that the administration should make clear "that there will be absolutely no change in this proposal." That was the bottom line: vote "yes" or "no." I gave copies of this memo to Fortier, North, Burghardt, Lehman, Tillman, and State.

Unfortunately, the congressional Democrats performed as I predicted: they pushed McFarlane for more concessions. On April 18 McFarlane and Poindexter caved in to the Democratic senators who opposed contra aid. They agreed to a "compromise" in which the president *dropped* his request for military aid but retained the request for nonmilitary aid and the lifting of the second Boland restriction (section 8066). Bill Casey correctly called this "the retreat from the retreat."

Again, neither Lehman nor I was consulted or knew in advance. So, on April 19, hoping to help McFarlane salvage at least this much in the House, I wrote him another memo: "Nicaraguan democratic resistance— avoiding possible defeat of your April 18 compromise."

I told McFarlane about two possible ways the isolationist Democrats in the House could try to defeat even this retreat and turn the administration compromise into a fund for phasing out and resettling the armed resistance. Then I suggested five actions McFarlane could take to avoid total defeat. As before, McFarlane made no reply one way or the other.

Later that day democratic Congressman Michael Barnes proposed a joint resolution for the House and Senate that would have done exactly what I had warned McFarlane about. This Barnes proposal, representing the isolationist view, would have prohibited all funding for military or paramilitary operations inside Nicaragua (meaning no nonmilitary aid to the contras). Instead, Congressman Barnes and his allies would provide $10 million through the UN or the international Red Cross for "humanitarian assistance for Nicaraguan refugees who are outside Nicaragua, regardless of whether they have been associated with the groups opposing the governments of Nicaragua by armed force."

The vote in both the Senate and House was now scheduled for Tuesday, April 23. At 5:00 P.M. on Sunday, April 21, the president, Vice President Bush, George Shultz, Caspar Weinberger, William Casey, Don Regan, and Bud McFarlane met with a bipartisan group of eight senators. The meeting memo written by the White House legislative liaison staff succinctly laid out the purpose for President Reagan: "To negotiate a resolution on funding for Nicaragua [the contras.]" This meeting, which took place at the initiative of Senate Democratic leader Robert Byrd, illustrated the shambles that had been produced by McFarlane's mistake in having President Reagan tell the country his bottom line (the "Easter peace initiative" on April 4) instead of winning in the Senate first.

Bill Casey called me at home a few hours before that Sunday meeting to ask me if I could meet him in his White House office to exchange ideas about next steps. On the phone, Casey asked whether he should also invite North. "Yes," I said, "since he seems to have been one of McFarlane's key advisers on the tactics that produced the current situation."

So there were four of us with Bill Casey that Sunday afternoon. I mentioned that I had suggested to McFarlane that the president meet privately with Tip O'Neill for a one-on-one talk about Mexico and the dangers that a communist Central America would bring to our neighbor. But McFarlane had scrawled one word across that idea—"hopeless."

Casey was sitting behind his desk, and North was sitting to his left, both facing the rest of the group.

"That fat old Irish fart," Ollie said without warning.

Casey did a double take. Apparently he thought Ollie was talking about *him*. "That fat old Irish fart *O'Neill*," Ollie amended. "What does he know about Central America?"

Casey wanted to hear what North and I considered a sensible political strategy to get the most aid possible from Congress. I repeated the Jack

Kemp-Chris Lehman judgment: the president should request a "yes" or "no" vote.

For the last six weeks, I went on, both Chris Lehman and I had been urging McFarlane and Poindexter to propose to Don Regan that the president give a national television speech a few days before the House voted on contra military aid. We believed that the president could *guarantee success* by speaking on national television.

"Unfortunately," I said, "Regan's decided that the president should give a national speech on the budget on April 23 [the day the contra vote was expected]. But Ben Elliott and Tony Dolan have each written an excellent Central America speech. It's all ready for the president. Bill, can you possibly persuade Regan or the president to shift the speech to Monday, April 22, and make it about Central America instead of the budget?"

During the weeks of February, March, and April, Chris Lehman and I did our best to persuade McFarlane and Poindexter that they should personally urge the president to give a Central America TV speech before the contra-aid vote. We understood that as in 1984 they faced a tough decision. Would they take an issue that we believed was of major national security importance directly to the president, even though a strong-minded chief of staff disagreed?

Senior White House sources told me that at the White House meetings chaired by Don Regan, only Pat Buchanan was arguing the case for scheduling this speech on Central America before the April 23 vote. McFarlane was either silent or agreed with Don Regan that the speech should be on the budget. At least that's what I was told.

Gently, I had reminded McFarlane and Poindexter that, last year, if they had challenged Shultz and Jim Baker, President Reagan would have agreed with the NSC, and the vote would likely have been won in May or June rather than lost in the massive $500 billion budget resolution in September. But as far as I could learn, McFarlane again took no action.

I had arranged for well-known former foreign policy officials (from both parties) who supported aid to the contras to meet with the president on April 15. Attending the Oval Office meeting were former Carter NSC adviser Brzezinski, former Secretary of Defense and Energy James Schlesinger, former UN Ambassador Jeane Kirkpatrick, and Vice President Bush. I admired the willingness of these prominent leaders in national security from both political parties to come forward and declare their agreement with President Reagan on this issue. They stood behind the seated president while he made a short pro-freedom fighter statement to the assembled media and television cameras.

Then the reporters let loose a barrage of questions for all the participants, who were bathed in the glare of television lights.

I happened to be standing near Don Regan, so I turned and said, "Mr. Regan, I believe the president can win the contra aid vote if he gives a national television speech on *that* subject, rather than on the budget."

Regan, perhaps surprised that a staff member one level down had spoken to him, replied: "We need to make progress in fixing this budget problem, too."

"The budget," I said, "is a perennial issue, and final congressional action never occurs until the end of the fiscal year in September. The administration has positive momentum *now*, because the MX vote was won in March. If the president gives a procontra TV speech, he'll win this vote, and this will add to the political momentum needed to win those budget votes later. But if the president loses this vote, he'll be weaker on the budget, and the communists could make future gains, which would ultimately cost many billions in new security and refugee settlement expenditures."

Across the Oval Office I caught sight of McFarlane watching me chat with Don Regan. I'll bet he doesn't like my talking with Don Regan, I thought.

Regan was civil. He said, "The plans are set for the budget speech."

I persisted: "The speech writers have two excellent Central America speeches ready to go if you give the word. Could you give me about five minutes in the next day or two to spell out the dangers I see if we lose this vote?"

By now, however, the impromptu press conference had ended, and the TV lights were being doused. I had to escort our visitors out of the Oval Office.

The chief of staff answered, "I am very busy."

I never did get those five minutes.

Leaving the Oval Office, I told McFarlane that I had just been trying to convince Don Regan of the need for a procontra national TV speech.

I remember April 23, 1985, vividly. The Oval Office was brightly lit for the president's 8:00 P.M. TV speech on the budget, and Chris Lehman and I were right across the hall in the Roosevelt Room watching the final count of the House vote on contra aid on a TV monitor. We had said, repeatedly, that forty-eight Democratic votes were needed—and were virtually certain *if* the president gave a national TV speech *before* the vote.

That evening, without the national TV speech, the president got forty-six Democratic votes; and he lost contra aid by two votes (213–215).

A few minutes later President Reagan began his TV speech on the budget, a speech that quickly vanished into the extended political debate on this important subject.

At the end of September 1985 the administration was able to obtain $27 million in *nonmilitary aid* for the armed resistance from the Congress. But neither Defense nor CIA was allowed to administer this, so the State Department had to establish the "Nicaraguan Humanitarian Assistance Office." In addition, the Congress placed the second "Boland Amendment" restriction on the fiscal year 1986 Defense Appropriation Act. The restriction stated, "During Fiscal Year 1986, no funds available to the CIA, Department of Defense, or any other agency or entity of the U.S. involved in intelligence activities may be obligated or expended for the purpose or which would have the effect of supporting, directly or indirectly, military or paramilitary operations in Nicaragua by any nation, group, organization, movement, or individual."

Only after the revelations of the Tower Commission and the joint Senate-House investigation has it finally become clear that this second annual failure to persuade Congress to provide military aid to the Nicaraguan armed resistance is what started McFarlane, Poindexter, and North down their road paved with good intentions.

8

"MOVED UP"

In July 1985 Bud McFarlane was riding high. He'd just reaped media glory for his role in securing the release of forty American hostages held by the terrorists who hijacked a TWA airliner—the most sensational news event of the summer.

His secretary, Wilma Hall, had summoned me to meet with him in his office. It would be our first real conversation in more than a month, but this time I wasn't pleased to be seeing him. This meeting was his idea. He was dealing from strength, and I guessed he was now ready to fire me.

What I didn't know as I was walking to McFarlane's office was that there was another factor at work here: an exchange of letters about me between Ronald Reagan and one of his personal friends who had a secret code that got his letters through without being opened by anyone but the president.

One late April afternoon in 1985, as I was speeding into the West Wing of the White House, I saw Tony Motley waiting outside Poindexter's office. He looked depressed, reminding me of how he had looked the morning after President Reagan had rejected Shultz's four-step Central American plan at the late June 1984 NSC meeting. When Motley saw me, he gave me a look that seemed inquisitive and accusatory. I simply said, "Hello, Tony," and continued on my way.

The next day I attended a luncheon meeting to review the status of the Caribbean basin initiative, President Reagan's three-year-old plan to increase economic growth and jobs. Among those present were Prime

Minister Eugenia Charles, whom I had last seen at a meeting with Shultz and all the Caribbean leaders on Barbados in early 1984. Also present was Governor Hernandez Colon of Puerto Rico (I had represented President Reagan at Governor Colon's inauguration in January 1985) and David Rockefeller in his role as chairman of the Council of the Americas.

After the luncheon meeting I had about thirty minutes until my next appointment. I decided to enjoy the beautiful spring day and walk the dozen or so blocks down Pennsylvania Avenue to my office. When I got there Judy Huba handed me a press release, saying, "I think this will interest you."

It was a brief White House announcement: the president had accepted the resignation of Assistant Secretary Motley and had nominated Elliott Abrams to succeed him.

Now I knew why Motley looked so crestfallen.

Following the time-honored Washington custom, Motley and his supporters told the media that he had been planning to leave for some months to become a lobbyist. Some of us wondered whether Deaver, who would leave the White House to open his new lobbying firm the second week of May, would continue in the private sector the close operation he and Motley had established inside the government.

What had happened to Tony Motley? The Enders team in the Latin American bureau seemed to believe (incorrectly) that I had sparked the removal of Enders in 1983 and now, phantomlike, had struck again, zapping Motley. Perhaps that explained the look I had seen on Motley's face.

What really happened? One story that made the rounds was that Motley had resigned in anger because McFarlane, Poindexter, and North had done to him what State so often did to the rest of the government. Reportedly, Motley had known nothing about the April 4 "Easter peace initiative" and had been caught as totally by surprise as I was. If true, this might well have been the first time that the NSC preempted a regional assistant secretary of state, though my guess is that McFarlane would have told Shultz.

Right after that April 1985 initiative, the State Department had been instructed to seek endorsements from the presidents of Central America and other Latin American countries. These came in, and State was able to assemble the quotations of endorsement on a briefing paper, which was then sent to Congress and the media. At an important congressional hearing a few days before the vital April 23 contra-aid vote, a Democratic opponent of the president's policy asked Motley if any Latin American leaders supported this initiative publicly. Apparently Motley said something like "None that I know about."

By chance, Nancy heard this exchange on the car radio as she was driving home from work and mentioned it to me at dinner. "Somebody should give Reagan a recording of Motley's testimony," she said. "He certainly didn't make a very good case for aid to the contras. *I* was upset by what *I* heard, and I think Reagan would be, too."

I told her it was astonishing that Motley would be so obvious in an open hearing, especially since the State Department had published a compendium of endorsements by many Latin American presidents.

A few days after Motley's resignation, a senior official told me that somebody had indeed gotten a transcript of this testimony to President Reagan. And the president had decided it was time for Motley to leave. According to this rumor, Shultz did not try to fight the decision.

For my part, I thought the nomination of Elliott Abrams was a good idea. One of the "neoconservative" Democrats who had been in the Reagan administration since 1981, Abrams had served as assistant secretary of state first for international organizations and then for human rights. Although not well versed in the political history of Latin America (this had also been true of Enders and Motley), Abrams had written several perceptive op-ed articles about Central America. He seemed to have a real understanding of the importance of the struggle there for our national interests. He was also the highly intelligent son-in-law of Norman Podhoretz and Midge Decter, two of America's most lucid and thoughtful writers on public affairs. Even so, after four years of Enders and Motley, a number of conservatives were upset that neither the president nor the secretary of state had chosen a competent Reagan supporter with Latin American experience. My answer was that Shultz and Reagan had made their decision. I thought Abrams would be a big improvement; we all should try to help him. And we should suggest competent candidates for the four or five deputy assistant secretary positions from inside the foreign service and experts from the outside.

For my part, I congratulated Abrams and offered to meet with him and share whatever information would be helpful—both about Latin America and about the political battles for the president's policy. Abrams took me up on this, and we had several in-depth discussions during May as he prepared for his confirmation hearings in June. I emphasized the need for a regular, fair interagency policy process at the subcabinet level. He expressed full agreement.

That night I told my wife that perhaps after four years of deception and trickery I might finally have the pleasant experience of working in a normal, collegial environment.

Later, I heard another rumor about Motley's departure, and it involved me as well. Jacqueline Tillman told me she'd heard that Shultz and McFarlane had made a deal: the price for Motley's removal was my removal as well. Tillman said the grapevine had it the plan was for McFarlane to move Ray Burghardt into the senior Latin American NSC job.

"That's no surprise," I said, "since McFarlane and Poindexter have been trying to use Burghardt to end-run me since last October. I'm getting uneasy about having the nominal authority for Latin America while McFarlane and Poindexter manipulate their own staff to exclude those of us who have independent experience or judgments on some issues that differ from theirs."

At first I thought only one or two of us were having problems with McFarlane and Poindexter. But at a May 1985 breakfast meeting in the White House mess, a group of senior NSC staffers got together to discuss what had evidently become a common problem. Ever since the beginning of the second term, it was harder and harder to get a meeting with either McFarlane or, more recently, Poindexter. Until we got together to compare notes, however, each of us thought his own lack of access was a purely individual problem. Now we could see that, indeed, both men had become more and more remote from all of us.

No matter how urgent the matter, we couldn't get even five or ten minutes of Bud's time. Only Karna Small, his media liaison person, Oliver North, and possibly one or two others had McFarlane's ear.

Chris Lehman had many urgent legislative strategy issues that he could not discuss; Roger Robinson found that often he could get no hearing on some time-sensitive international economic finance, trade, and debt questions; and Gaston Sigur, although he was responsible for all of Asia, confided he had not been able to get a serious private discussion with McFarlane for months.

I went to see Robert Kimmitt, who served as both the legal officer and the executive secretary of the NSC, having worked at NSC since the Ford administration. He was in the powerful position of controlling the flow of all action assignments and documents. Kimmitt's office was a few feet away from those of McFarlane and Poindexter, and he had worked closely with them for four years. Surely he would have some advice.

"Bob," I asked, "what can I do to improve my working relationship with Bud? I need about five to ten minutes, at least, once every few weeks with him on major issues.''

He startled me by saying something like: ''Constantine, don't think it's just you McFarlane doesn't have time for. The situation is the same with ninety percent of the senior staff. He has to spend a lot of time traveling with the president, and he's decided to spend a lot of time with the media. One of the reasons Bud doesn't talk with you all is that he honestly believes he doesn't need you. Sure, he needs you to write all the memos to the president, but he feels he knows as much as anyone on his staff about any issue. I really think Bud would be happiest if he and Wilma could simply work alone. Sorry to be so bleak, but I don't see any way to change his work pattern right now.''

Several of us on the senior staff decided on a different tack. We would get together and trade ideas on how we could help Bud understand that we wanted to work more closely with him and our ideas could offer useful foreign policy opportunities for the president. Because each of us on the senior staff was also working at such a fast pace, it took about a week to find a half hour when we could all meet together.

Our group discussion didn't include the senior director for Europe (including the Soviet Union), or the senior directors for Africa and the Middle East. We felt that if it came to a hard choice, as foreign service officers they would tilt toward the position of the State Department.

Those of us who belonged to the ''Reagan appointee group'' obviously shared the career officials' concern for our national interests, but with a difference: we were also deeply concerned with the successful foreign policy of *this* president and *this* administration.

We all met in my office in mid-May. The group consisted of Chris Lehman, Roger Robinson, Gaston Sigur, Kenneth deGraffenried, and myself.

Each person took a few minutes to summarize his experience. Each described McFarlane's months-long virtual refusal to grant his request for a brief meeting and mentioned one or two urgent issues in his area that weren't being properly dealt with as a result of Bud's inaccessibility. Next, we discussed submitting a letter to McFarlane that would contain a few practical ideas for improving our ability to help him and would urge him to meet with us at least briefly. Chris Lehman closed the discussion: ''This letter has to make clear that we're trying to help Bud by making our expertise available to him before he makes decisions and before the president is preempted by the bureaucracy or by events. We're not trying to put pressure on Bud in any way.''

Before we could make our suggestion, however, the rumor reached us that McFarlane was considering a "reorganization" of the NSC staff. Some recalled that it was McFarlane who—in the name of "reorganization"—when he arrived with Judge Clark in January 1982 had removed about eight Reagan foreign policy experts who were in second-tier NSC jobs. Further, we all knew that McFarlane was most comfortable working with career foreign service or military staff. As he himself had said on a national television program, "I have been a career bureaucrat for twenty-five years." So we immediately guessed that "reorganization" meant the removal of the few remaining Reaganite senior NSC staffers.

On May 20 I was summoned to see McFarlane. Neither I nor my secretary thought his request for a meeting was to discuss any of my three strategy papers. But just in case, I took copies to leave with him, intending to urge Bud to give those issues (and the senior staff) some of his time. Naturally, as I walked across to the West Wing, I assumed this was the day of dismissal.

McFarlane had moved up from the basement office to the bright, cheerful northwest corner office that Ed Meese had until his confirmation as attorney general. The sun streamed in from the long windows, and there was a large globe of the world on a stand next to an imposing desk. McFarlane invited me to sit on a blue armchair, while he sat on the matching blue sofa.

In his deliberate, somewhat singsong, formal style—it would become familiar to TV viewers during the Iran-contra hearings in 1987— McFarlane told me, "You are a person with a lot of very good ideas about what the administration should be doing in foreign policy. You have sent me some interesting papers. But President Reagan has decided on a cabinet form of government. That means the initiative in foreign policy, as in domestic policy, rests with the cabinet leaders of the individual agencies. Our job here at the NSC is mainly clerical. We simply process the incoming suggestions from the various departments and make sure that these get to the president, or are otherwise acted on as appropriate."

I had heard McFarlane talk about "cabinet government" at various public briefings, though never in such a self-deprecating way as to suggest that he and the NSC staff were hardly more than paper shufflers. As McFarlane talked, I could scarcely believe he was giving me this line. He knew that I knew about the daily work of the NSC. Did *he* believe it at all? Later, I heard him repeat a bit of his "cabinet government" spiel during his opening statement to the Iran investigating committee (May

11, 1987). But as I listened to him in May of 1985, I mentally reviewed a few of the things I had done in the last few days. I had written a first draft of three presidential speeches; I had flown to New York on a presidential jet to meet President Duarte of El Salvador and have a long private chat on the flight back to Washington and then escorted him to a meeting with President Reagan in the Oval Office; I had met with another visiting Latin American president; I had been asked to brief a number of congressmen from both parties on the president's Central American policy; and I had written the talking points for the president's meetings with several leaders on Latin American issues. We NSC "clerks" certainly do keep busy, I thought to myself.

McFarlane continued to his second point. "Constantine, you are a first-rate conceptualizer, analyst, writer, and communicator. But the work of the NSC staff requires mainly bureaucratic skills which are best learned through long service in one of the foreign policy agencies. You don't like bureaucratic work, and this is understandable. Academics always consider it limiting and tedious. Therefore, I suggest that this is a good time for you to make a move to a policy position at an appropriate level in the Department of State or at Defense. I would like the NSC to be more involved with policy, but that is not the president's wish, and I think you would be more effective in one of the cabinet agencies."

I didn't say anything, but I thought to myself that this was certainly a careful, and clever, approach. Obviously McFarlane wanted to give me a clear message—since I had ignored the months of explicit bureaucratic exclusion and other carefully calculated insults. Therefore, I needed to be "invited" to leave the NSC. But, apparently, he still didn't want to take the political risk of simply firing me. In a courteous and even tone, I asked, "Bud, have you talked with Shultz or Weinberger about specific opportunities for me to contribute to their work?"

"No," he said, "but you are welcome to explore that, Constantine."

"Bud," I said, "your description of the NSC staff work as 'clerical' overlooks the most important part of our work: all the tasks we do to make sure the president is really in charge of foreign policy. And they have to be done, whether or not you want to describe them as 'cabinet government.' The NSC staff has to keep him supplied with full information, monitor the agencies so they carry out his decisions, call attention to new opportunities and threats . . ."

Even though I could see Bud's eyes narrowing and his jaw setting, I plunged on. "That's why I wrote the three strategy papers and gave them to you last December. There's one really urgent issue where five years of Reagan administration history has proven the cabinet agencies incapable of moving beyond rhetoric to effective action, and that's terrorism. They haven't provided a real counterstrategy.''

It was McFarlane's turn to interrupt. "There is a lot of bureaucratic work here, and people tell me you are not a good bureaucrat.''

In reply, I handed him a memo and said, "Last August I sent you this memo. It summarizes my first ten months' work here. During four of those months I worked virtually alone. Then Jackie Tillman joined in mid-February, and Ray Burghardt in late March. During my time alone, I produced about 290 memos. Our group has sent you more than eight hundred memos in these ten months. And, as you know, I have never missed a single deadline on policy-related issues. This memo also summarizes the Latin American directorate's contributions—the issues where we sought timely preventive action—and the indifference we usually met at the State.

"In this same memo, Bud, you'll note that I asked you to meet with me so that you could tell me how our work might improve. Your handwritten answer was, 'See me after the election.' I've tried.''

As he read through my short memo, McFarlane began to look perturbed. Being a career bureaucrat, he understood that my memo made it harder to use the pretext of bureaucratic inefficiency against me. My memo documented both our work and my good-faith effort to obtain specific management guidance, which he had consistently failed to provide.

Finally McFarlane looked up from my memo and said, "Let me study this, and then let's have another discussion.''

But before I left I wanted McFarlane to know exactly how I felt about his suggestions.

"Bud, I think the work of the NSC is important and interesting, and that my experience on Latin American issues can be helpful to you and the president. If I were to leave the NSC, given what I have seen of the policy-making process in this administration, rather than continuing in the government, I would return to private life and my work as a foreign policy expert and scholar.''

However, I knew the die was now cast. McFarlane and Poindexter would be huddling to decide on just the right approach to use in removing me.

In late May we began another round of maneuvering to bring before President Reagan in an NSC meeting an issue Shultz and McFarlane had managed to delay action on for months: launching Radio Martí broadcasts to Cuba.

I'd first heard about the Radio Martí idea in 1980 when I was speaking in Miami where Judith Hernstadt, a vivacious and politically involved radio station owner, introduced me to Jorge Mas. As a young man Jorge Mas had, with so many others seeking democracy, joined Castro's revolution against the rightist dictator of Cuba. When Castro began establishing a communist regime, Mas again tried to fight for real democracy. In 1960 he fled, arriving nearly penniless in the United States. Along with many of his generation, he eagerly joined the liberation force so ignominiously abandoned at the Bay of Pigs in 1961.

A good-looking, energetic, deeply patriotic man, Jorge Mas and his wife, Irma, worked hard, raised a family of three successful "new Americans," and became one of the many prosperous Cuban American families living in Miami. Now he had written a concept paper for Radio Martí—a program of daily, objective broadcasts about Cuba into Castro's Cuba. This could serve as the "free press" for the information-starved Cuban people. Having experienced firsthand the good work of Radio Free Europe, I immediately supported his plan.

Jorge Mas also had another important idea. He and a group of successful Cuban American businessmen decided to establish the Cuban American National Foundation, a nonprofit educational organization.

They wanted to help opinion leaders and citizens in both the United States and Latin America get up-to-date, objective information in concise and readable form about the realities of life in Cuba—and also about the hostile international activities of Castro. Using their own funds, they established offices in Miami, Florida, and Washington, D.C., and hired the creative and hardworking Frank Calzon as executive director.

Judith Hernstadt had told Jorge Mas that I was an adviser to Ronald Reagan's 1980 campaign. Naturally he asked me whether I could urge the candidate to endorse this idea. I promised to try and I did. Jorge Mas had many high-level Republican friends and eventually saw there were results. The Reagan administration proposed legislation supporting Radio Martí in 1981, and two years later it passed Congress.

Like all dictators, Fidel Castro feared the truth. He did not want Cubans to hear independent corroboration of the corruption, elite privilege, repression, and international violence perpetrated by his regime. Thus, Castro threatened that if the United States began Radio Martí broadcasts—using legal frequencies—he would turn Cuban transmitters on full power (even though such an act would violate international law) and block out radio broadcasting in the southern part of the United States.

In fact, Soviet-bloc technicians began to arrive in Cuba and immediately started to build new and bigger antennas to carry out this threat. There were occasions when Cuban radios did jam a good part of the nighttime radio in the southern United States, all the way to WHO in Iowa—Ronald Reagan's first employer.

One significant faction of our government—led by the State Department—seemed intimidated by the Cuban threats. At the NSC McFarlane chose to define Radio Martí as a "communication" rather than a Latin American issue, thereby removing it from my area of responsibility.

The months dragged on and on, yet still no Radio Martí broadcasts— even though the staff had been ready since late 1984. By mid-May of 1985, Jorge Mas had spoken with Vice President Bush. But nothing happened. I brought it up at the senior NSC staff meetings, where Poindexter reacted negatively and nervously.

Finally Jorge Mas found the ally he needed: Charles Wick, who had a natural interest in this topic because he was director of the U.S. Information Agency that managed Radio Martí. Besides, the Wicks and Reagans were friends. Jorge Mas prevailed upon Wick to break the log jam.

Wick agreed, and the NSC meeting was held in late May of 1985 in the Situation Room. Since it wasn't my issue, I was not present, but I learned that Secretary of State Shultz opened the meeting by giving reasons why this was *not* the right time to launch Radio Martí. As I heard it, the president interrupted Shultz to ask if we were set to go. Wick replied, "Everything is ready for Radio Martí to go on the air within two days." The president then gave the order to begin broadcasting by Monday of the next week.

When I heard the news I was elated. Once again President Reagan had shown his good judgment and decisiveness—when he finally got the chance!

Castro didn't carry out his threats and Radio Martí has been a great success with the people of Cuba.

Shortly after this happy event, which for some reason seemed to annoy McFarlane, Dana Rohrabacher, a talented presidential speech writer and friend, alerted me to a *Newsweek* item in early June of 1985: REAGAN HARD-LINER ON LATIN AMERICA—Constantine Menges is to be shunted aside and replaced by veteran foreign service officer Raymond Burghardt.

I told Dana that McFarlane did seem to be moving in that direction, and that the story, which had obviously been planted, could have come from the NSC or could have been wishful thinking by someone at the State Department.

A few days later some of my White House colleagues arranged for me to have a private conversation with a senator who was especially close to Reagan. After a cordial greeting I told him that the president had an effective Central America strategy, but that the State Department had repeatedly gone off on its own, directly counter to Reagan administration policy. And I said, "The foreign policy decision-making process isn't working properly because McFarlane has often been unwilling to see that the president had timely and full information, plus the chance to hear a fair debate at an NSC meeting." I pointed out that it took repeated pressure from Casey and other cabinet members to prevent McFarlane from keeping important information from the president.

In a voice filled with concern, the senator asked, "Why doesn't the president understand what the State Department keeps doing?"

"This president," I replied, "like any president, has too many domestic, international, political, and ceremonial responsibilities to keep track of all the maneuverings by the State Department on Central America, unless his NSC adviser gives him a concise outline of the facts. Besides, the State Department can always point to—or prompt—an initiative from some foreign government that can be used as the pretext for reopening a decision the president has already made. As you know, the president tends to trust people. He assumes that McFarlane would tell him about deviousness in any part of his administration. But every time I'd write a summary of previous presidential decisions at the start of a memo for a new NSC meeting, McFarlane or Poindexter would delete the chronology. It seemed to me that they didn't want Mr. Reagan to ask why, since he had already made a decision, the same issue was coming up again."

The president's friend shook his head. I knew this was hard for him to believe or understand. I had given him a one-page overview of several such previous episodes entitled "The Department of State vs. the President." And though he knew me by reputation, he frequently spoke with McFarlane, whom he probably considered to be a hardworking and sensible person.

Then I turned to a second topic I felt the president needed to know about. I predicted that partly because we still had no counterterrorism strategy, we could expect additional tragic attacks, and I gave him a few examples of terrorist threats we'd received. This calm, courtly man became agitated: "Why doesn't McFarlane take the lead and develop a counterterrorist strategy?"

"Because," I replied, "he is busy with each day's tasks. He and Poindexter think in terms of day-by-day actions, not strategic approaches that may take months or years to achieve visible results."

This was the first time I had discussed these problems with anyone outside the executive branch. The president's friend seemed alarmed. Nevertheless, I sensed he would probably take no action. I began to think I should write Reagan a letter and find a friend of his who would get it into his hands.

A few days later America and the world reacted with shock and horror when terrorists hijacked a TWA jetliner and held more than forty American citizens and the crew hostage. Television teams raced to the scene and shot dramatic and poignant coverage of this latest terrorist attack. Daily TV reports featured the desperate plight of the victims, the fierce anti-Americanism of the hijackers, and the prayerful vigil of the victims' families.

McFarlane and a small group within the NSC took the lead in U.S. efforts to save the victims. Poindexter handled the morning staff meeting and virtually all Bud's other responsibilities, while McFarlane became the "crisis manager."

In late June McFarlane reappeared at the morning staff meeting and spoke about his satisfaction with the result. He said, "The president was very pleased with the favorable outcome, and he was very pleased with the NSC's contribution. This should strengthen the role of our staff in the future."

Clearly McFarlane felt he had done a great job in obtaining the release of the TWA passengers and crew. The administration had declared publicly over and over that it "would not negotiate with terrorists" and had said it would not ask Israel to meet the hijackers' demand and release hundreds of Lebanese prisoners being held as convicted or suspected members of terrorist organizations. Israel said publicly it would consider releasing some of these prisoners to help the United States if our administration asked it to. Repeatedly the McFarlane-led "crisis management team" answered that there would be "no negotiations" with terrorists. As it turned out, shortly after the TWA passengers and crew were released—the event having been used for propaganda by the terrorists—Israel *did* release hundreds of Lebanese prisoners.

To many of us on the NSC staff, though we had no knowledge of what actually had happened, it *seemed* to have been an exchange of the U.S. hostages on the airliner for Israeli-held prisoners. And our suspicion grew when the administration issued a statement thanking Syria for its assistance—despite Syria's known cooperation with the Soviet bloc in supporting anti-Western Palestinian terrorist groups.

Then McFarlane made a decision that all but confirmed our suspicions.

On July 8, 1985, President Reagan gave a major national speech on terrorism to the American Bar Association. The first draft of the speech mentioned that certain countries were known to cooperate actively with the Soviet bloc by supporting anti-Western terrorists: Cuba, Nicaragua, Vietnam, North Korea, Libya, and Syria.

On McFarlane's orders, the mention of Syria was deleted. This strongly suggested that there had been a negotiated exchange brokered by Syria. That would fit with a standard PLO tactic: one terrorist faction takes hostages, and another "assists" the target government "to resolve the crisis" by meeting some of the terrorists' demands. Did this experience persuade McFarlane that negotiations with terrorists could be denied publicly but pursued privately?

In early July McFarlane's secretary called and asked me to meet with him on July 8. I told Nancy that my dismissal time had arrived.

I felt that the "good press" about the resolution of the TWA hijacking would make McFarlane and Poindexter feel confident enough to remove Chris Lehman, Roger Robinson, and me, the three noncareer government employees and Reagan supporters willing to raise difficult issues in the senior staff meetings.

Chris Lehman had already told me that he had decided to leave the NSC; he was fed up with the McFarlane-Poindexter antics and felt it was time to live a more normal, less hectic life and to see more of his wife and two young children. By summer's end Lehman and Robinson had both resigned from the NSC staff.

I hadn't been in McFarlane's office since our May conversation. This time I sat on the blue sofa and he sat on one of the antique chairs. To my surprise, his voice didn't have the somber tone one associates with a dismissal. In fact, Bud sounded quite civil.

He began by telling me I was being promoted.

"You've done a superb job," he said blandly, "and the good news is that things in Latin America are going very well. The president's policy is working. So now the NSC is really only dealing with routine issues on

Latin America, and these routine bureaucratic issues aren't worth your time and attention."

"Well," I said cheerily, in the spirit of the moment, "I'm delighted things are going so well. But until Nicaragua has a genuinely democratic government I wouldn't say things are routine. . . ."

"Therefore," McFarlane went on as if I'd not spoken a word, "the president and I have talked about your work, and he and I have decided that you should move up to broader and expanded responsibilities where your abilities will better serve the country.

"You have often said the administration needs to do more to inform foreign and domestic leaders and citizens about Central America and other major issues so that there will be support for President Reagan's policies. You have said that such support is essential in a democracy in order to permit these sound policies to continue. I agree, and the president also believes that we need to do more. Therefore, the president and I want you to assume major responsibilities for communicating the facts about our foreign policy and the international situation, not only on Central America but on all major issues."

I was caught totally by surprise. McFarlane was using the classic bureaucratic technique of the "move up" as a means of separating me from Latin American policy issues. But why?

I knew that after *Newsweek* had published the rumor that I would be replaced by a career foreign service officer on Latin America, four separate group letters of protest had been sent to President Reagan by a total of about fifty senators and congressmen. These letters praised my work, cited the *Newsweek* rumor, and said they hoped it wasn't true, since I was one of the few remaining Reagan foreign policy experts on the senior NSC staff. But I guessed that, as mostly seemed to happen with letters from members of Congress, none of the four letters had reached President Reagan. Replying, I said, "Bud, you're correct! It is an important task. But I've had many years of experience on Latin American issues, including four with this administration. Given the continuing need to help the democratic groups in the whole region, I think I can do the most good by staying on as senior director for Latin America. Perhaps with your approval I should allocate thirty percent of my time to getting across the facts about our policies."

There was an oh-so-cordial tone to McFarlane's immediate reply. "Constantine, that would not be fair to you. That would mean asking you to do two full-time jobs. No, the president and I have discussed this, and the decision has been made. You need to tell me 'yes' or 'no.' " Then he looked at his watch and said, "I have another meeting. Get back to me with your answer in the next couple of days."

I left, realizing that this move up had been carefully cooked up by McFarlane and Poindexter. I was inclined to resign—I knew this was a phony proposal, and that if McFarlane had in fact discussed it with President Reagan, he had to have misled the president about his real intentions. Naturally I discussed the idea of resigning with several senior foreign policy officials and White House colleagues.

But all advised me to spell out in writing the broad range of responsibilities McFarlane had mentioned (appearing on media talk shows, writing op-ed and other articles in the major media, briefing foreign and U.S. leaders, and so on) and then to accept.

My colleagues all argued that I could "do more good inside the administration than outside." They also said that McFarlane's exposition of my "broader and expanded" responsibilities offered many opportunities—especially because I was to work on all major foreign policy issues. Nonetheless, I still had not made up my mind when Poindexter telephoned a day later and asked abruptly, "What's your answer to Bud's offer?"

"I need a few more days to think about it," I said.

With that, Poindexter snapped, "We need to move on this right away. I need your answer now."

I accepted.

A few days later I found out why I was moved up instead of out. A close friend of President Reagan's had been given one of the four congressional letters sent to the president about me; the letter had been signed by about twenty members of Congress, all staunch supporters of the president. With a handwritten note, this friend had sent President Reagan a copy of this congressional letter in late June and urged him to look into the *Newsweek* rumor. My letter got through only because a very few of the president's personal friends have been given a special code to put on the envelopes so their letters will be opened and read *only* by President Reagan himself.

That is why, on July 2, 1985, President Reagan replied to his friend, also by a personal note, that "Constantine Menges is a good man. . . . He's not being ousted . . . he's being moved up. . . ." In mid-July the president's friend met with me. He showed me copies of both letters and asked, "What really happened here?"

"Unfortunately," I said, "the president has been deceived. This isn't a real move up. One obvious sign is that I'm no longer invited to the senior NSC staff meetings. Maybe I've 'moved up' so far that I am above the mundane issues discussed there—like policy! Frankly, my guess is that it was only your letter that caused McFarlane and Poindexter to concoct this deception instead of just removing me from the NSC. When you got through the 'iron wall' around the president, they must have decided to use this method to get me out of their way on Latin American isssues.''

A few days later I was invited to a lunch with a group of senators who were all strong Reagan supporters. The president's friend had given one of the senators a copy of Reagan's letter about me, with permission to show it to his colleagues. The letter was passed from senator to senator. Then they turned to me and asked what was really going on.

I explained it as part of the removal of Reaganites from semi-policy jobs in the NSC and continued, ''This is just one example of a serious problem. The NSC process that's supposed to give the president a fair and full debate on the major policy issues isn't working properly. The State Department keeps trying to carry out its own policy on Central America. And, with one terrorist episode after another, the administration *still* lacks a counterstrategy.''

I suggested that it was essential to warn the president on both issues: the need to restore a fair NSC decision-making process to assure that the president really governs in foreign policy; and the need to formulate a counterstrategy against terrorism. These senators were interested and concerned, but I sensed they didn't feel able to do anything either. Later I learned that McFarlane had told a skeptical Senator Paul Laxalt that this was indeed a genuine move up!

I was learning that the president's supporters in the House and Senate meant well, but they too were unable to get a message through to the president. Therefore, I decided I had to try to alert the president *myself*. But how?

I knew that a personal meeting with the president was impossible. I was one echelon down, and both McFarlane and Don Regan would have opposed it. My conversation with the president's close friend in Congress had shown me that someone who wasn't a direct part of the foreign policy decision-making process simply couldn't understand the subtle process by which the president was misled. Nor could he have enough confidence in his command of the facts to give the president the double-barreled warning I was trying to send.

Further, I knew that the members of the foreign policy cabinet would be reluctant to criticize their colleagues. The "Reaganite" foreign policy cabinet members would urge that specific issues be brought to the president in an NSC meeting. But they seemed unwilling to complain about the essential breakdown of the NSC decision-making process the State Department's maneuvers caused.

I decided. There was only one way for me to reach the president: a personal letter.

I would include enough factual detail to document my warning that the State Department repeatedly attempted to end-run the president on Central America issues. And I would offer a concise proposal for a counterterrorist strategy.

First, I compiled a detailed chronology of the policy history on Central America. Next, I gathered together key documents showing the breakdown of the NSC process. Ben Elliott used his superb writing skills to help me reduce the letter to twelve pages.

How was I going to get it into President Reagan's hands? Here I was with a presidential commission, in an office just across the way from the West Wing, not being able to deliver an important warning to the president for whom I worked. I knew that the only way my letter would get read by President Reagan was for someone he trusted to give it to him.

On August 5, 1985, I went to see another of President Reagan's longtime friends, who knew me, my work, and the foreign policy scene. He listened to my concerns, then read the letter.

"Yes," he said, "I think it's important that the president read this, and I might take it to him during his vacation this August. But first I'd like you to show it to Bill Casey. I'd like to know if Bill agrees that you've presented the facts correctly."

It was sheer luck that the president's friend was in town and that I could get an appointment to see him. I called Casey and asked if I could come out to see him. "Sure," he said, "come on out right now."

Half an hour later I was sitting in Casey's office at CIA headquarters admiring the spectacular view of the Potomac River. I explained why I had written the letter and said I was fully prepared to be fired by McFarlane as the price of the president reading it. And I told him our mutual friend wanted his opinion on whether it was factually accurate.

With his usual mock gruffness, he handed me a stack of reports and said, "I want to get your views while you're out here, and I don't want to see the taxpayers lose fifteen minutes of your time by letting you just sit here while I read this."

So we both did our reading. He picked up a pencil and began making a few editorial changes. After ten minutes Casey looked up and said, "This is first-rate. And the facts are correct."

He then picked up the telephone and asked Betty Murphy to track down the president's friend. A few seconds later she had him on the line. "This is excellent," Casey told him, "and the facts track with my recollections."

I drove down the parkway and back to my office, where Judy typed the few editorial changes Casey had suggested.

The next morning, August 6, I gave the letter to the president's friend. He said that he would give it to President Reagan at his ranch later in August when he would have time to reflect on it and also to share it with the First Lady.

I was very happy. That night as I left for a vacation with my family, I felt I had done something useful for my country.

When I returned to Washington in late August, it took me a few weeks to catch up with the president's friend. That should have been my first clue.

"Constantine," he said in a noticeably subdued voice, "Poindexter came to see me, and McFarlane also talked with me. They knew you'd given me a document. And they said, 'If this is something for the president, *we'll* give it to him; you can give it to us.' I did not give it to the president, and instead urge that you give it to McFarlane for transmittal."

I was surprised and saddened. I knew the August vacation was one of the best opportunities for the president to read and think about a long document like my letter. All I could say was, "I can understand why you changed your mind once McFarlane and Poindexter talked to you. Unfortunately, I've seen too much devious behavior by McFarlane and Poindexter. I don't believe they would really give my letter to the president—that's why I did not send it to them for transmittal. My guess is that McFarlane and Poindexter would simply take this letter, make it disappear, and then tell both you and me that the president had received and read it."

He said quietly, "Sorry it didn't work out." And then, almost as an afterthought, he added, "How did they find out?"

"Thinking back," I replied, "I remember seeing Wilma Hall talking to your secretary at a White House reception in early August. Maybe your secretary just casually mentioned to Wilma that I had been over to see you a few times and had left you a document marked 'personal.' Or perhaps all the NSC computer typewriters are bugged. I really don't know how they found out.''

So there it was. After four years on Latin America, I had been "moved up." Of the many questions that flooded my mind, one was, "Now what?''

PART THREE

"BROADER RESPONSIBILITIES"

9

ANGOLA

Shortly after my "move up" in July 1985, I had a talk with Bill Clark. "When I come back from vacation," I joked, "I'll probably find they've stuck me in a closet-sized office in the deepest dungeon in the EOB, with a phone to be installed *mañana.*"

McFarlane did exclude me from the morning senior NSC staff meetings, but he left my rank as special assistant to the president and White House mess privileges. He probably realized that having told President Reagan I had been "moved up," it would have been unwise to initiate the process to rescind my presidential commission.

One of the issues I began to work on was Angola.

At the July luncheon with the senators I had mentioned the immense opportunity presented to the free world by the four hundred thousand resistance fighters who were opposing pro-Soviet dictatorships, not only in Nicaragua but also in Afghanistan, Ethiopia, Mozambique, Angola, and Cambodia.

It had been my view for years that with adequate political and financial support those movements could restore pro-Western, moderate governments. The positive results, would include an immeasurably better life for the people in those countries; real peace in the regions and a reduction in terrorism because those six countries would no longer be accomplices of the Soviet bloc.

Senator Steven Symms (R.-Idaho) was one of those present at the luncheon. At that time he was leading the effort to repeal the 1976 "Clark

231

amendment,'' which had prohibited the United States from providing any form of support to pro-Western groups in Angola.

Some background may be in order here.

Angola and Mozambique had been colonies of Portugal and were among the very last in Africa to attain independence. In late 1974 and 1975, as Portugal's communist movement with immense Soviet covert aid (in violation of the 1972 U.S.-Soviet agreement on "rules of detente") nearly took power there, the communist anticolonial armed groups in Angola and Mozambique received ever-increasing military and covert aid from the Soviet bloc. In Angola and Mozambique there were competing pro-Western armed anticolonial groups, but they needed free world help.

The Alvor agreement of January 1975 specified that Portugal would grant Angola independence in November, and that Portugal, the communist movement, and the pro-Western independence movement would *each* provide eight thousand troops to monitor a free election. Unfortunately, the Soviet Union had begun moving Cuban military advisers and increased amounts of weapons into Angola starting in late 1974. Despite the Alvor Agreement, this continued and increased in early 1975.

At the same time—the spring of 1975—the North Vietnamese invaded South Vietnam. This was a violation of both the 1973 "peace treaty" and international law. In 1973 Nixon and Kissinger had promised immediate U.S. military assistance in the event of a North Vietnamese attack. They did so in order to persuade South Vietnam to sign the seriously defective 1973 "peace treaty," which had left 120,000 North Vietnamese communist troops *on the territory* of South Vietnam. But the United States ignored North Vietnam's illegal infiltration of 30,000 additional troops, and in the spring of 1975, as North Vietnam invaded, the Ford administration did not use its air power to help South Vietnam. This U.S. passivity and South Vietnamese tactical military errors created panic.

In two short months all this unraveled, the combined success of the South Vietnamese and U.S. forces who together had virtually defeated the communist-initiated guerrilla war from 1959 to the withdrawal of U.S. troops by 1971. By the end of April 1975 communists were in full control of South Vietnam, Cambodia, and Laos and were beginning the massive repression and brutality that in only three years would kill between two and three million civilians.

Emboldened, the Soviet bloc then stepped up the movement of military equipment and personnel to help the communist guerrillas of Angola and Mozambique.

"The massive Soviet military supplies to the [communist] MPLA reached Angola in March and April [1975]," wrote Professor Jiri Valenta in 1978, "several months before U.S. shipments of military supplies began to reach the [pro-Western] FNLA through Zaire." In September 1975 *The New York Times* belatedly reported that one hundred tons of arms had been flown to bases of the communist MPLA *in April*, while Soviet, Yugoslav, and other ships arrived full of heavy weapons. Secretary of State Henry Kissinger testified to Congress in 1976 that Zaire and Zambia requested "assistance from the U.S. in preventing the USSR and Cuba from imposing a solution in Angola."

While the Soviet Union and Cuba were sharply increasing military support to the communist forces, Congress began debating whether it should continue or cut off the $30 million in U.S. covert aid that the United States had begun providing the pro-Western armed groups—in the summer of 1975. That aid could help them establish a noncommunist postcolonial government.

In August 1975 Cuban generals arrived in Angola and later in August the first of more than fifteen thousand Cuban combat troops. At the same time Moscow flew into Angola rocket launchers, artillery, mortars, armored personnel carriers, tanks—all to be used by the Cuban troops fighting with the communist Angolan group.

Dr. Jackson Wheeler, an expert on the freedom fighter movements, describes what happened next.

> On October 23, 1975, a mechanized force of some 2,000 men, comprised of UNITA and FNLA guerrillas, Portuguese Angolans, and regular South African Defense Forces crossed into Angola, from Namibia (controlled by South Africa) and began to move rapidly north. Within days, four or five more Cuban troopships had left Cuba for Luanda, and by November 7, a troop airlift had begun from Holguin in eastern Cuba to Luanda [Angola's capital]—initially with Cuban Bristol Britannias refueling in Barbados and Bissau, and later with Soviet-supplied Aeroflot IL-62s, refueling in either Bissau or Conakry.
>
> By November 5, Cubans had fallen back from Benguela and Lobito, while the South African-assisted column had moved north of Nova Lisboa (over 500 miles in less than two weeks) and was on the outskirts of Nova Redondo (Ngunza). By November 11, MPLA-controlled territory had been reduced to a thin slice of the country—Luanda, and from the area around Luanda extending eastward.

November 11 had been declared (at Alvor) Angolan Independence Day, and the Portuguese government was determined to turn governmental authority over to whoever controlled the capital of Luanda on that day. In addition to Cuba and the Soviet Union, the MPLA's declaration of legitimacy in Luanda received immediate diplomatic recognition from seven Soviet-aligned African nations (Tanzania, Congo-Brazzaville, Mali, Guinea, Mozambique, Ethiopia, and Algeria); North Vietnam; the Soviet-bloc countries of Eastern Europe; and Brazil.

The South African intervention in late October was subsequently used by Moscow and Havana as post facto rationalization for their invasion of Angola. The semiofficial Cuban version of events was written by a Colombian author close to Castro, Gabriel García Márquez, who dubbed the main invasion "Operación Carlota," and claimed it was not initiated until early November. . . .

On December 19, 1975, the Democratic-controlled Senate passed the Clark amendment, which called for the cut-off of American covert aid to pro-Western armed groups in Angola. A month later the Democratic majority in the House approved this measure. Not long after that South Africa withdrew its small force of 2,000—compared with 15,000 to 18,000 Cuban troops in Angola. Within a matter of months the communists controlled both Angola and Mozambique.

What happened to the eight million people of Angola and the fourteen million of Mozambique foreshadowed the fate in store for the tens of millions in southern Africa if the communists succeed in taking over the entire region: soon there were severe shortages of food and other staples—though not of course for the privileged Party elite, or the secret police, or the military and government bureaucracy. Communist repression in Angola meant that many died and thousands were locked up in detention camps. In Mozambique communist repression was even worse. There, the estimates of deaths reached 75,000 and 200,000 to 300,000 in prison camps reported to be even harsher than those of Angola.

The new communist governments immediately began to cooperate with the rest of the Soviet bloc. They offered a land base for pro-Soviet terrorist groups—such as the Southwest Africa Peoples Organization (SWAPO) aimed at Namibia or the African National Congress (ANC)—targeted against South Africa. Angola and Mozambique permitted guerrilla and terrorist groups to receive weapons and training from Soviet-bloc and Cuban personnel for repeated attacks on Zaire and other independent

African countries during the late 1970s. It was at this point that President Carter publicly accused Cuba of providing terrorist training in Angola. Castro responded by calling Carter "a liar."

That the U.S. Congress had made a tragic mistake in 1976 was demonstrated by the years of misery that followed the communist takeovers in Angola and Mozambique. In Angola the repression and failure of the communists' economic programs meant that more people turned to pro-Western black nationalist groups, such as the Union for the Total Independence of Angola, or UNITA.

By 1985 UNITA controlled about 40 percent of Angola and fielded more than fifty thousand armed insurgents. UNITA faced off against a demoralized communist government, which was dependent on the U.S.-owned Chevron Oil Company for 60 percent of its income. Ironically, the Angolan government used this revenue provided by the American oil company to pay Fidel Castro an estimated *$800 million* a year (in Western currency, no less); that was Castro's bill for the services of his Cuban intervention forces. The battered Angolan communist army of about 75,000 was on the ropes. Only the 40,000 Cuban troops kept the communist regime in power.

In Mozambique the regime was even worse. There, the National Resistance of Mozambique, or RENAMO, was a pro-Western, armed black nationalist group, numbering about 30,000 in 1985. The communist government of Mozambique has been responsible for mass repression and starvation and is dependent on Soviet-bloc and Cuban secret police (and other personnel). Despite the more than $2 billion worth of weapons provided by the Soviet bloc, the secret police with their Gestapo tactics, and all those Cuban troops, the tide of pro-Western freedom fighters kept rising in both countries. And that was why in the summer of 1985 the U.S. Congress began to consider the repeal of the Clark amendment.

Senator Symms had taken the lead in the Senate, and Congressmen Jack Kemp, Trent Lott (R.-Miss.), and Claude Pepper (D.-Fla.) were effective in persuading the House.

Another major factor was the landslide reelection of Ronald Reagan and his ringing endorsement of the freedom fighter movements in his 1985 State of the Union address which would come to be called the "Reagan doctrine." In late 1985 the Republican Senate repealed the Clark amendment, and the Democratic House followed.

But this had little impact on the State Department. During the congressional debates, State had opposed the repeal of the Clark amendment, and McFarlane apparently went along. For years the State

Department had pursued a policy of trying to "wean" Angola and Mozambique away from the Soviet bloc through economic aid, diplomatic contacts, and negotiations. The State Department even refused to classify Angola and Mozambique as communist: that would have prevented the United States from providing tens of millions of dollars in economic aid, such as credits and U.S.-backed loans.

During the first Reagan administration, the State Department had participated in four years of negotiations with the Angolan government and South Africa. These negotiations sought an exchange: the withdrawal of all Cuban troops from Angola for the withdrawal of South Africa from Namibia. But this diplomacy had been unsuccessful year after year and was based on three fundamentally incorrect premises.

The first was that as part of such a settlement Castro would actually withdraw his troops. The Cuban dictator repeatedly said that Cuban troops would leave Angola only when South Africa was "liberated"—by which he meant when it was under communist rule.

The second incorrect premise was that the Angolan communist regime wanted to move away from the Soviet bloc. There were no significant Angolan actions in that direction. Naturally, Angola wanted to string the State Department along in order to get Western economic aid and halt free world help for UNITA.

The final premise was that there could be a fair and impartial *UN-supervised* election in Namibia after a South African withdrawal. But this was unlikely because the UN General Assembly had made the mistake of declaring the pro-Soviet terrorist group SWAPO the "sole and authentic representative of the Namibian people." By this resolution the UN demonstrated its bias toward the pro-Soviet groups that were competing with prodemocratic groups in Namibia. Given that about 100 of 160 UN-member governments are dictatorships, the UN is an unlikely guarantor of fair, democratic elections for Namibia.

In late July 1985 I had a visit from several congressional staff members. They said that the senators they worked for believed the Senate's repeal of the Clark amendment finally offered President Reagan the opportunity to jettison this failed State Department policy. But how could the senators bring this issue to the president?

"In my opinion," I answered, "the best way to get the president to reconsider the State Department's current policy is for your senators to write a factual criticism of the current policy, then present an alternative pro-Western policy. When this is written, a group of senators should first send it to Secretary Shultz and ask to meet with him for a discussion. But," I warned them, "most likely Shultz will have Chester Crocker [the assistant secretary of state for Africa] send back a letter explaining that the current policy is fine, thank you!"

Should their senators send letters to McFarlane? Isn't it the NSC adviser's job, they asked, to bring major opportunities—like that opened up by the repeal of the Clark amendment—to the attention of the president and the entire NSC for consideration?

"Yes," I replied, "the NSC adviser *should* do that. But if you send him the same letter you send Shultz, his senior director for Africa, who just happens to be a career official, will most probably send it to the State Department, and you'll simply get the same reply."

I explained that any member of the foreign policy cabinet has the right to request that an issue he considers urgent be discussed with the president at an NSC meeting. First, he would ask McFarlane to schedule such a meeting. If McFarlane refused, he could go right to the president, and the president could then *tell* McFarlane to schedule an NSC meeting on this topic.

"Now that Bill Clark and Jeane Kirkpatrick have left the administration," I continued, "the two remaining NSC principals who would understand this issue are Bill Casey and Secretary Weinberger. Since Weinberger has to fight so many battles with Shultz on defense and arms control issues, he seems to me unwilling to take this kind of initiative. He already has his hands full, and this seems to fall outside those directly military-related matters. So the person who could—and I believe would— request this NSC meeting is Bill Casey."

The next question surprised me. "Would you be willing to write a draft of such a pro-Western strategy paper?" They offered to provide some unclassified background information on each of the countries, along with papers provided to Congress by the State Department justifying its current policy.

I hesitated. I was in the middle of the very intense process of reviewing all my Latin American files and writing my letter to the president. And my letter was taking longer than I expected, partly because I was trying to make it as short and readable as possible.

But since I had been moved up, this certainly qualified as a "key foreign policy issue." So I agreed to write a draft strategy paper. But I said I would do this at home during the weekends. I would not look at *any* classified information: I wanted it to be a draft that could be easily and widely circulated by the senators.

In early August 1985 I finished a five-page draft and gave it to Margaret Calhoun of Senator Symms's staff.

The first section summarized my proposal for a new "pro-Western strategy":

> In January 1985, President Reagan declared, in his State of the Union address, that "the U.S. should and will support those fighting for their freedom . . . from Afghanistan to Nicaragua. . . ." The Congress has now lifted the Clark amendment restrictions, which had prevented U.S. paramilitary assistance to the pro-Western armed resistance movements in Africa, and this offers a major opportunity for a new policy with the following mutually reenforcing objectives:
>
> 1. *Angola*—shift to a U.S. policy of support for the pro-Western armed resistance movement of UNITA and its goals of a "National Unity government" with the least hard-core communist elements of the current regime, fair elections and the removal of the Cuban/Soviet-bloc personnel.
> 2. *Mozambique*—shift to a U.S. policy of full support for the pro-Western armed resistance, RENAMO, and work with friendly governments to bring about a "National Unity" coalition between RENAMO and the least pro-Soviet elements of the current communist government.
> 3. *Namibia*—help the prodemocratic Namibian political groups to organize so that they can compete effectively in genuinely democratic elections to be held under supervision of an international commission of genuinely democratic countries—not the United Nations, which has a conflict of interest, since it has already recognized the communist SWAPO guerrilla organization as "the sole and authentic representative of the Namibian people."
> 4. *South Africa*—encourage peaceful evolution to multiracial democracy from the apartheid system while also assuring that the communist-led violent opposition groups are unable to bring a hostile, anti-Western repressive dictatorship to power in the name of equal rights for all.

When I returned from vacation in late August, I was pleased to learn that a group of Republican senators had indeed sent Secretary Shultz a virtually identical strategy paper. A few weeks later they received a short note from him telling them that the current U.S. policy *was* "pro-Western," and it was working just fine, thank you.

Toward the end of September I asked to see Bill Casey. We met on one of his frequent White House visits. He asked me to drive with him in his limousine to National Airport, since he was leaving on a trip. During the fifteen-minute drive, I gave him a copy of the senators' letter to Shultz, along with their proposed pro-Western strategy, and a copy of Shultz's reply. I told Casey about the growing support for the bipartisan bill to aid freedom fighters, including those in Angola and Mozambique, which Congressmen Jack Kemp and Claude Pepper had introduced.

"It seems to me," I said, "that now is the right time for the president to hear a debate at an NSC meeting, change our policy toward Angola and Mozambique, and start supporting UNITA and RENAMO." I also explained why I believed that McFarlane would not bring this opportunity before the president.

Casey asked a few questions, quickly skimmed the strategy paper, and put it in his briefcase. He said a cheery good-bye as he dashed for his airplane. On my way back to the White House, I realized that Casey hadn't told me what he would do. Nonetheless, I was optimistic. There was something about Bill Casey that always made me feel that way.

In early August I had also been visited by *another* congressional staff member. He said that his boss and several other Republican congressmen—all strong supporters of the president—were deeply distressed by my removal from Latin American responsibilities. These congressmen felt this typified the growing chasm between Reagan's foreign policy decisions, as reflected in his sensible public statements, and the actions of the State Department. He told me that these members of Congress wanted to communicate their concerns to the president. "Can you help?" he asked.

"Yes, but since we all work in quite distinct 'compartments,' the factual illustrations I know about in detail are limited to Latin America, South Africa, and a few items on strategic arms control issues. When you've done a draft based on your sources of information, I'll be glad to review and comment on it."

The congressmen produced a very good draft by mid-September and, on October 22, 1985, sent their letter to President Reagan. One major focus was their suggestion for a new pro-Western strategy in Angola and Mozambique. They pointed out that the September 1985 visit to the White House of the communist dictator of Mozambique had produced no visible change in that country's pro-Soviet orientation.

Bentley Elliott read a copy of their letter to the president and joked,

"Constantine, I see you're determined to get *your* letter to President Reagan one way or another."

I laughed but said, "The congressional letter does tell the president that we don't have a real strategy against subversive aggression and terrorism. It also tells him, candidly, how the problems in the NSC process are preventing him from getting the information he needs in order to know what's really going on. Besides, the Reaganite foreign policy experts in the subcabinet are being removed or shunted aside, out of the real policy jobs. He has to be told about that, too. My question is, will Don Regan let the president see this letter?"

In the letter, the Republican congressmen reminded President Reagan about the facts in Mozambique. They also quoted the 1984 Republican party platform: "The tripartite axis of the Soviet Union, Cuba, and Libya has unleashed privation and war upon the [African] continent. We are committed to democracy in Africa and to the economic development that assures it will flourish." They also quoted the president to the president: "We must have the same solidarity with those who struggle for democracy as our adversaries do with those who would impose communist dictatorship."

They summarized the facts of the Mozambique government's brutality and covert aggression: "There are currently 20,000 Soviet-bloc troops and advisers in Mozambique, supplied with about one billion dollars in Soviet arms. President Machel (of Mozambique) signed a new package of agreements with the Soviet Union on August 27, three weeks before you met him in the White House." The State Department, they went on, was supporting military aid to help Mozambique defeat the pro-Western RENAMO resistance.

The letter then summarized, in words well chosen to appeal to Ronald Reagan's core values, their critique of the Reagan administration's policy toward Angola and Mozambique:

"We do not believe that this is your policy. It is entirely inconsistent with American values and with your expressed policy of support for freedom fighters. It would never have the support of the American people, and it is doomed to failure. What is true in Nicaragua is true in Angola and true in Mozambique: the only way to contain, reform, or remove communist regimes is to support the freedom fighters who need our help. In all three nations people are fighting to gain objectives that we support—negotiations leading to genuinely free elections."

Clearly they had taken their best shot. It was hard-hitting, and it was clean. But would it land? They received no immediate response from

President Reagan, and I began to doubt that he ever saw their letter. (When the Iran-contra matter became public a year later, these congressmen at least knew they had tried their best to warn Reagan about the lack of a fair NSC process.)

In mid-October Shultz was revealed as being totally opposed to aid to UNITA as well as to RENAMO—despite President Reagan's public endorsements of the freedom fighter movements.

As a result of the bipartisan Pepper-Kemp bill to provide nonmilitary aid to UNITA, the Republican House leaders had joined their Senate colleagues in urging Shultz to change State's failed and misguided policy. Shultz then wrote a letter to House Republican leader Robert Michel, in which he said:

"I understand that Congressmen Pepper and Kemp have introduced legislation which would provide $27 million in nonlethal assistance to Dr. Savimbi's movement, UNITA, in Angola. . . . The suggested legislation should be opposed. . . ."

On October 18, 1985, House Republican leader Michel responded to Shultz with a forceful letter. In view of the thirty-five thousand Cuban troops in Angola and the $2 billion in Soviet military aid to the communist regime, U.S. support for UNITA was "not only a geostrategic but a moral necessity." If the Cubans were willing to negotiate, Michel wrote, it was because of the pressure of Savimbi's popular forces. "I cannot see how," he wrote, "we can argue that aid to the democratic forces in Nicaragua helps the chance of negotiations while aid to UNITA somehow damages the negotiating process." Shultz himself had recently given a speech about freedom fighters in Nicaragua, Cambodia, Afghanistan, and Angola in which he had said, "There should not be any doubt of whose side we are on." Michel commented: "It is my belief that what Jack Kemp and Claude Pepper are proposing to do in sending aid to Dr. Savimbi's forces can leave no doubt whatever whose side we are on."

Shultz's letter to Republican leader Michel opposing the Pepper-Kemp bill to aid UNITA was also given to Saul Singer, a new congressional aide to Congressman Dan Burton (R.-Ind.). A reporter who'd heard that the letter was sharply at variance with the president's views asked Singer about it. And Singer, in turn, asked a staff member who worked for Congressman Michel if he should share the letter with the reporter. The answer was "yes." So Saul Singer gave Shultz's unclassified letter to a *Washington Times* reporter. The result was a headline story, on October 23, 1985.

SHULTZ WORKS AGAINST BILL TO AID UNITA ANTI-MARXISTS

Secretary of State George Shultz is trying to defeat proposed legislation to provide $27 million in humanitarian aid to anticommunist rebels fighting the government of Angola. . . .

That same day the six Democratic members of the House Subcommittee on Africa—Congressmen Wolpe (chairman), Crockett, Solarz, Berman, Weiss, and Garcia—sent a letter of alarm to their colleagues:

"Any U.S. aid to UNITA would ally us with South Africa in its regional aggression and effectively undermine our ability to pressure South Africa to dismantle its internal system of apartheid. . . ."

Then these congressmen demonstrated a most remarkable ability to turn the facts of history upside down. Instead of recalling the Soviet-bloc and Cuban military aid to the communist Angolan faction had accelerated in late 1974, that the communist Angolan faction broke the agreement for free elections, and that thousands of Cuban troops and tons of Soviet weapons were in and moving to Angola weeks *before* the United States aided the pro-Western independence movements and months before South Africa moved troops there, these six Democratic congressmen wrote to their colleagues: "We do not have to guess at the consequences of U.S. aid to UNITA. When the U.S. joined South Africa in providing military and other assistance to UNITA in 1975, it resulted in a vast expansion of the Soviet and Cuban military presence and the nadir of U.S. prestige in Africa. That is why Congress ended the aid program in early 1976."

At this same time four former Reagan ambassadors decided to break their silence and tell the American public how they had experienced the State Department's undermining of President Reagan's foreign policy.

The Heritage Foundation held a symposium that featured former ambassadors Evan Galbraith (U.S. ambassador to France 1981–85), Charles Lichenstein (deputy ambassador to the UN 1981–85), David Funderburk (U.S. ambassador to Rumania 1981–84), and Curtin Winsor (U.S. ambassador to Costa Rica 1982–85). Their public criticisms were published in the *Washington Times* and the conservative weekly *Human Events*, as well as in a Heritage Foundation booklet. One focus of their criticism of Secretary Shultz was the failed policy in Angola and Mozambique. I believed their remarks made at the symposium and the attendant publicity would help to set the historical record straight. But I still wondered: Would the issue of aid to UNITA be brought to the president? Would there be an NSC meeting?

* * *

During my time at the White House, some of the toughest battles were fought over words. The president's speeches were often the subjects of fierce contention. When, for example, the president enunciated the "Reagan doctrine"—a pledge of U.S. support for democratic freedom fighters everywhere—in the draft of his 1985 State of the Union address, the State Department fought to delete the passage or water it down. But the president was enthusiastic about it, and it stayed.

Similarly, in May 1984 the president was to give his televised speech on Central America. A State Department staffer who had been sent over to "help improve" the text suggested that we strike out, as offensive to Mexico, the sentence "This communist subversion poses the threat that a hundred million people from Panama to the open border on our South could come under the control of pro-Soviet regimes."

The president liked it, and the speech writers and I liked it, so we declined to delete it. But Shultz bustled over to the Oval Office and came out to say that President Reagan agreed to remove it. So I went to Dick Darman, the speech writers' point of contact with Jim Baker, and persuaded him that it should be restored. Armed with Darman's signed statement in agreement, I went to McFarlane and urged him to have the president reconsider. McFarlane was uncomfortable as always about opposing Shultz, but he did the right thing. The dramatic warning went back into the speech and was repeated in later speeches by the president.

But one of the biggest behind-the-scenes battles was waged in October 1985 over the president's annual speech to the UN General Assembly. The internal struggle centered on the Reagan doctrine of supporting freedom fighters in such areas of conflict as Angola. Few outsiders could have appreciated the importance of subtle verbal formulations, but we did, and the State Department did. A few differences of phrase can have enormous meaning in the world of events.

The president's speech writers knew this would be one of his most important statements on foreign policy, and they had worked long and hard to prepare a draft that would reflect the policies and priorities of the man they knew so well and with whom they worked closely.

Some weeks earlier Ben Elliott had asked for my ideas (and a suggested text) on U.S.-Soviet relations and on the "regional conflict issues" that would be major focal points of the speech. Regarding U.S.-Soviet relations, I suggested the president make three basic points about strategic arms control: that reductions in offensive weapons be negotiated in their own terms on the basis of reciprocity—therefore, strategic defense should not be traded away to obtain offensive cuts; that the United States emphasize it had continued seeking reciprocal arms reductions in good faith despite the Soviets having walked out of the talks in 1983; and that any agreement must include an effective verification system.

To my near astonishment, the first point, though fought by State, was included in the speech.

My suggested text on "regional conflicts" made clear that nearly *all* these conflicts had been caused by Soviet-bloc aggression, whether direct or indirect. And it also pointed out that in five of these countries the resulting governments were illegitimate: Afghanistan; Cambodia (due to external invasion); Angola; Mozambique; and Nicaragua (due to communist seizures of power in violation of international agreements). Finally, as a direct consequence, the armed resistance movements in those countries could and should be given U.S. support; they were seeking to restore national independence, defeat external aggression, and offer the promise of far better government. Ben Elliott put these thoughts into ringing prose, and with this text as part of the first draft, they became a further explanation of the "Reagan doctrine."

The speech was too sensible. Something was bound to go wrong. It did.

After this first draft had circulated to the foreign policy leadership for comments, McFarlane handed the speech writers a specific text on this issue. It had obviously come from the State Department: it carried State's patented formula for ill-conceived political settlements.

The State Department would have President Reagan propose a "three-phase regional peace process." The first phase would be a cease-fire and negotiations among the warring parties in each country. But I believed the communist regimes might use the cease-fire to regroup and then unilaterally violate it; no Western journalists would know, while those same governments could see to it that the journalists saw evidence, real or fabricated, of violations by the freedom fighters. Further, this step would most likely lead some in the West to argue for suspending military aid to the armed resistance movements during the cease-fires in order to "help the negotiations along."

According to the second phase, "once the negotiations take hold . . . the U.S. and the Soviet Union should sit down together for a separate set of talks. . . . The primary task is to promote this goal: eliminating the foreign military presence and the flow of outside arms." The grave risk in this seemingly balanced formulation had been revealed by the negotiating record to date. The Soviet Union might offer, or even actually remove some Soviet-bloc troops in the *future* but would demand the *immediate* end of all military aid to the armed resistance. The text, moreover, made no provision for verified, simultaneous, and reciprocal actions on these two issues.

As the third phase, State proposed that "we could move on to . . . welcoming each country back into the world economy. . . ." The trouble with this idea was that is assumed the *current* communist regimes would remain in power. It promised economic aid when *those regimes* had brought about "national reconciliation," which, in effect, told the freedom fighters they would not win.

This three-part plan again revealed State's incompetence and shallow economic determinism. Shultz and his top foreign service staff were underestimating communist cunning again and trying to have Ronald Reagan endorse an extension of their failed effort in Angola and Mozambique. This involved "buying out" or "weaning away" pro-Soviet regimes by establishing a process which would lead to the abandonment of the freedom fighters *and* promising U.S. (taxpayers') money after that had been accomplished. In a word, appalling.

I said that what was needed in the president's speech was a clear statement of U.S. objectives for genuine settlements: verified agreements assuring the immediate and permanent withdrawal from each country of all Soviet-bloc military/secret police and other personnel; self determination; and a new, independent transitional regimes leading to a democratically elected governments. But how to get this into the speech? I knew only Casey or Weinberger would understand and be willing to take this issue to the president. Also McFarlane and Shultz seemed so determined to have this self-defeating scheme endorsed by the president that any changes anyone else suggested would have to blend in with State's three-part plan.

Ben and I noticed that the State Department draft had been willing to leave in a few paragraphs of tough anti-Soviet rhetoric. This struck me as an obvious ploy to make President Reagan believe the plan was based on realism—the same tactic I had seen Shultz use, over and over again, both in his public speeches and in his discussions with the president. Talk tough, but act as the State Department bureaucracy suggests. McFarlane and Shultz must have felt pretty confident about this "plan," because several national columnists had already published leaks heralding the "regional plan" as the centerpiece of the president's coming UN speech.

The presidential speech writers had made one attempt to change this section, perhaps hoping that this single page out of twenty would slip by McFarlane and Shultz. They knew the president would favor their text. But McFarlane had caught them and demanded that the State Department plan be reinserted.

So, once again, I called and asked to see Bill Casey. He suggested I come out to CIA headquarters. We met for nearly an hour on October 15, and I gave him a copy of the State Department's three-part "regional peace plan." He immediately saw its subtlety—and flaws. I gave him my suggested text to improve it, and he said he would try to change the second draft when it came around to him.

I also gave him a copy of my one-page (suggested) speech text on strategic arms control and SDI. I told Bill Casey that with the Geneva summit coming up in November, my guess was the Soviets, as a bargaining ploy, were publicly insisting there could be no *research* on SDI. This unenforceable prohibition was obviously a Soviet bargaining ploy so they could "compromise." And the State Department was already leaking hints that SDI deployment would be discussed "later." Therefore, it seemed to me that the likely "compromise" in the wind was that research *and* laboratory testing of SDI would be permitted, but there would be no realistic testing and no deployment.

I told Casey I believed that Shultz was once again being misled by the State bureaucracy and in turn misleading the president by saying on national television that of course State agreed with the "broad interpretation" of SDI testing permitted by the 1972 ABM treaty, but "for the time being" the administration would act on the basis of the restrictive interpretation. The effect, I suspected, would be to limit SDI research with virtually no testing and absolutely no deployment for a number of years.

"Bill," I said, "he's doing it *again*. These two ploys show he's *still* manipulating and evading the NSC process. It's just like that phony election-eve treaty last October.

"Is this the same George Shultz who promised that this year he was going to work in a fair way with his cabinet colleagues? I think President Reagan needs to see my letter. If he read that, I think he'd fix the foreign policy process one way or the other—either by changing people, or by requiring them to work in a fair and orderly way."

Then I took a big step. I said, "Would *you* give it to him? I'm not asking you to endorse it. And I recognize that the likely consequence will be my removal from the NSC. But if that happens, I'll leave government knowing that my warning was read by the top man."

Casey was sitting behind his big desk, fiddling with a paper clip while I spoke. He listened intently and thought for some moments. Then he said, "Your letter *should* reach the president; it's important. But I can't do it. I'm a fellow member of the same cabinet with two people the letter criticizes. And you work for NSC, not for me. Sorry, Constantine, but you must know other friends of the president who'd be able to give it to him."*

Six days later I received a copy of the final draft of the president's UN speech. I could see that while there had been some improvement in the formula for the "regional peace process," State had still kept the essence of its misguided approach. Therefore, unless changed, the president's speech would in combination with State Department diplomacy undermine his own oft stated objectives for the success of the freedom fighters in the five countries.

I called Casey's office and said it was urgent that I see him. Betty Murphy checked and called back to tell me he would be in his White House office for lunch from noon to 1:00 P.M. and then would be seeing the president. She said I could see Casey at noon.

It was then about 11:00 A.M. After my "move up," I had been assigned an excellent temporary secretary, Mrs. Laurie Chipperfield, but I couldn't dictate this sensitive new text for the speech to her: she shared a word processor location with two other secretaries, one of whom worked for a career government employee who took State's side on almost all issues.

I had an idea. I went to Bill Casey's White House office, which was located near mine in the Old Executive Office Building. I told his secretary that I had an urgent item to give her boss that I would like to dictate to her if she could take the time. She readily agreed to do so. We finished the first draft at noon—just as Casey and his security guards came in.

"Well," said the CIA director by way of introduction, "don't you agree that the three-part plan is okay now? They did put in a few of the changes that I suggested."

I said, "It's better, but still opens the door to defective political settlements in Nicaragua and Afghanistan that won't meet the president's objectives."

* In July 1987 the columnists Evans and Novak reported that in November 1986 Bill Casey wrote his own letter to the president calling for Shultz's removal since the State Department was leaking reports to protect itself. An informed person told me after this fact became public that in the spirit of honesty and candor, Casey sent Shultz a courtesy copy of this letter to the president.

After I'd pointed out the problems in the text, Casey said a bit roughly, "You're right. If this is so clever that it can even get by me, I understand how the president can miss it in a quick reading of twenty pages. Do you have a way of fixing it?"

I gave him the new page I had dictated to his secretary and offered to go down to get his lunch so he could revise my text with her while he wrote his own memo to the president on this section of the speech.

"Good idea," he said.

Twenty-five minutes later, when I came up from the cafeteria of the Old Executive Office Building with his luncheon tray, Casey asked me to read his memo to the president. As always, when Casey wrote something it was concise and effective. He presented his suggested changes and kept to the three-part structure of the plan.

A few hours later I got a call from the speech writers. They were elated: President Reagan had handed McFarlane the Casey text and said, "I want this text in the speech exactly as written here."

It had happened again: the president, with a little help from his (true) friends, was able to rescue and reaffirm his own sensible policy. (Unfortunately, as events in Nicaragua and Afghanistan showed, State ignored the president's formulation and continued pushing its approach in regional diplomacy!)

In early November I met Frank Shakespeare, the new U.S. ambassador to Portugal, at a White House reception. With a distinguished bearing and good humor, Shakespeare always conveyed a sense of purposeful energy. He had been president of a major communications company, head of the U.S. Information Agency in a previous administration, and chairman of the Board for International Broadcasting. He was one of the Republican leaders who really understood the importance of political ideas and the immense value of systematic efforts to tell the truth about democracy and communism. Because of our shared interests, we had met from time to time during the Reagan administration. Our last conversation had been an elegant breakfast meeting at a downtown hotel where a number of individuals, including some from the Congress, had discussed the prospects for aiding UNITA after the Clark prohibition had been repealed.

Now at the November White House reception Shakespeare came over to me, said a cheerful hello, and then lowered his voice and asked: "Has the president had a chance to decide whether UNITA will get some help from us?"

My reply was candid: "Frank, I've heard rumors that there has been an NSC meeting in which President Reagan has decided to initiate support—including military material—to UNITA. I've done what I could to bring this issue to the president. I'm not certain whether these rumors are true. Since Bill Casey hasn't told me, I haven't asked him directly since I don't have an operational 'need to know.' *You* might ask Bill since this may bear on U.S. relations with Portugal."

Shakespeare replied: "Well, it sounds as though things are moving in a sensible direction. I'll try to find out."

My uncertainty about this decision ended in a most unusual way. After President Reagan returned to Washington from the November 1985 U.S.-Soviet summit meeting in Geneva, he met with a group of journalists and in the course of an extended discussion of foreign policy issues told them that he had decided to provide military aid to UNITA. This was promptly published. One of my colleagues joked, "It looked like the president wanted to scoop *The Washington Post* by revealing this himself!"

I was pleased that President Reagan had made this decision. It represented an important step toward a more effective and coherent pro-Western strategy. In September 1986, when Congressman Hamilton, the Democratic chairman of the House Intelligence Committee (and in 1987 co-chairman of the joint investigating committee on the Iran issue), tried to obtain a vote to prohibit this aid, the president's policy was sustained by 220 to 187. This was a significant sign of bipartisan political support for Reagan's decision to help the freedom fighters in Angola.

10

IN SEARCH OF A COUNTERTERRORISM STRATEGY

It was about 9:00 A.M. on a Sunday morning when I answered the unexpected telephone call. A friendly voice said: "Hello, Constantine, this is the vice president. I understand you talked to my son Jeb, and you have some interesting ideas about a strategy against terrorism."

I was pleased that Jeb Bush had followed through *and* surprised to be getting this call.

"Yes, Mr. Vice President," I said. "I enjoyed meeting Jeb, and I do have some practical suggestions which I believe would be of interest to you."

With his customary chipper cordiality, the vice president said, "Well, great! Why don't you give me your suggestions now?"

Surprised by this request, I said, "The general concept isn't classified—in fact, I even wrote about it in *The New York Times* some years ago—but the specifics I'd like to discuss with you are, at the very least, sensitive. We wouldn't want our enemies to know about them. I don't know about *my* telephone, but I'd say the KGB isn't doing its job if it isn't trying to listen to *your* telephone, Mr. Vice President."

"Well, yes," he replied, "it might be better if we meet in person. I'll have my office set it up for this week." The meeting was arranged for ten o'clock the morning of February 12, 1986.

President Reagan had designated Vice President Bush to chair a governmentwide task force to come up with measures to combat terrorism. His group had been working at it for six months. I had been trying for five years to persuade administration leaders to formulate a counterstrategy that went beyond rhetoric, defensive measures, and reaction to the next episode. Now I would have a chance to provide my ideas to the right person. My hopes rose, but my previous experiences with Bush made me wonder: Would he understand? And would he take action?

A July 1986 article by Judith Miller in *The New York Times Magazine* described a terrorist attack in Ankara, Turkey:

> Gabriel, age 20, glanced to one side of Neve Shalom [Oasis of Peace] Synagogue and saw the terrorist standing in the doorway.
>
> The terrorist looked about as old as Gabriel. He wore sunglasses and was dressed in black.
>
> Gabriel blinked. The terrorist opened fire. Gabriel, who was seated next to his father near the front of the temple, dropped to the floor and hid under a bench. As the terrorist sprayed the synagogue with machine gun fire, Gabriel felt his father slump down next to him, his face turned away.
>
> Gabriel played dead as the deafening sound of machine gun fire echoed through the vast, newly renovated synagogue. Bodies fell around him. Screams and moans of the worshipers gave way to the voices of the two terrorists yelling instructions at each another in a language Gabriel thought was Arabic. He felt wet and glanced down at his clothes. He was lying in blood.
>
> He lay there, motionless, as the terrorists circled the room, firing more bullets into the bodies to ensure that the Jews were dead. The terrorist approached his bench. The man in black sprinkled something on his father's leg—a clear fluid that smelled faintly of gasoline.
>
> The terrorist struck a match and set Gabriel's father's leg on fire. "I realized my father was dead when his leg was burning, but he didn't move," Gabriel said.

Even this poignant account by a young survivor can only suggest the fear and horror caused by each terrorist assault. And there have been thousands of them since Ronald Reagan took office.

When President Reagan was inaugurated in 1981, it seemed that at last someone in a position of great power was going to *do* something about terrorism. Even Iran appeared to think so: on Inauguration Day, the so-called independent group of Iranian students released the fifty-two hostages who had been held in captivity in the U.S. embassy for 444 days.

A few days later, when the president welcomed the hostages home, he issued a warning: "Let terrorists know that if they strike against our

citizens anywhere in the world, there will be swift and sure retribution.''
All of us who had worked in the Reagan campaign were as heartened by
this statement as by the release of the hostages. And we expected the new
administration to come up with a counterstrategy against terrorism, one
that over time would show results. For that was clearly needed.

Starting in November 1980 I made a series of efforts proposing a prudent,
ethical, legal, and politically sustainable counterstrategy. The administration's failure to produce such a counterstrategy proved to be one of my
greatest frustrations in the five years I served under Ronald Reagan.

The West has been to slow to respond because no single terrorist
incident, however bloody, seems to pose a major international threat. With
exceptions, the usual Western response has been to react to each incident
separately, to negotiate for hostages, in some cases to capture and punish
the perpetrators, but on the whole to drop the subject as soon as the latest
kidnapping, hijacking, or bombing subsides from the front pages.

Is the problem really that serious? Aren't all these acts, deplorable as
they may be, finally unconnected and of less than global importance? The
public can be excused for thinking so, but this is a mistake all the same,
and is one mistake that many leaders have been tacitly making, too, in
spite of much sincere antiterrorist rhetoric.

The short answer is that with a few exceptions, such as Iranian actions,
most terrorist assaults are not ''isolated.'' They belong to a continuum of
subversive tactics used by the Soviet Union and its accomplices in the
indirect war they have been waging against the free world since 1944.
These tactics include propaganda, disinformation, political organization,
communist penetrations of key institutions, terrorism, guerrilla warfare,
and the use of Cuban and other Soviet-ally troops. And these tactics
add up.

One analysis concluded that in the decade from 1976 to 1986, about
forty thousand people—*all* in free world countries—had been killed and
injured by terrorist attacks. The Rand Corporation, using a narrower
definition of terrorist actions, has also noted an overall increase in the
number of such acts since the late 1960s. During the Reagan years the
annual number of terrorist attacks rose from about five hundred during
the first three years to six hundred in 1984 and eight hundred in 1985.
Virtually all terrorist attacks were against free world victims. The U.S.
government estimates that from 1981 to 1985 such attacks killed and
wounded about 660 American civilian and military personnel.

In her 1981 book *The Terror Network*, American journalist Claire
Sterling called the public's attention to what Western intelligence services

had already known: the Soviets and their allies both promote and profit by terrorism. She quotes Yuri Zhukov, a high Soviet official, who after a perfunctory condemnation of terrorism gives the Soviet line: "It's odd that all the armed violence is happening in the West. Fortunately for the East, the terrorist phenomenon does not exist there, inasmuch as our political situation is more healthy."

In late 1980 the British author Robert Moss wrote an important article in *The New York Times* entitled "Terror: A Soviet Export." He cited a recent U.S. government conclusion that Soviet covert action provides "roughly $200 million a year . . . giving arms, military training, funds, and operational intelligence to organizations that often engage in terrorist acts against Western countries and nations whose governments are generally friendly to the West."

In his 1987 book *Terrorism*, historian Walter Laqueur writes: "Official soviet spokesmen have always condemned terrorism. . . . Yet, at the same time, the Soviet Union has provided arms, financial aid, military training, and, on occasion, political support to various terrorist groups. . . . Furthermore, it has closely cooperated with the countries which have been the main sponsors of international terrrorism, Libya and Syria".

Judith Miller, in her article on the Ankara synagogue bombing, said the raid was carried out with "clearly marked communist weapons found at the synagogue and sites of other terrorist attacks in Turkey" and concluded that the direct sponsors of these attacks were most likely Syria, Libya, and Iran.

Among my writings on this subject is an article entitled "Radicalism Abroad," published in *The New York Times* in June 1980. There I defined three components of the terrorist network: the Soviet Union, which provided weapons, training, and intelligence information; anti-Western governments, such as Cuba, Libya, and Syria, which provide money, weapons, and, most important, protected territory for terrorist training camps and headquarters; and the "stateless" terrorist organizations, which carry out specific attacks.

This "destabilization coalition" was conducting an "invisible war," I wrote, which threatened the free world with hostile control of Central America, Mexico, and the Middle East oil states and, by that means, the neutralization of Western Europe and Japan.

Too few Western leaders, career government officials, and members of the media and opinion-forming elites understood this form of warfare. So in November of 1980 I convened a small group of experts to outline a practical counterstrategy. My own brief sketch of the threat to friendly countries looked like this:

Subversive Aggression/Terrorism Against U.S. Interests in Three Strategic Arenas

Experts have disagreed about the extent of Soviet control and direction of each and every anti-Western terrorist or guerrilla group. However, the following construct offers a perspective on the nature of the political-paramilitary war being fought against U.S. interests by hostile groups which agree on targets for destabilization and cooperate with each other in various degrees.

TARGET COUNTRIES	DESTABILIZATION COALITION
Latin America	
Colombia	Cuba
Venezuela	Regional communist/guerrilla groups
Central America	USSR
Panama	Palestinian terrorists/Libya
Belize	
Mexico*	
Middle East	
Israel	USSR
Egypt	Pro-Soviet regimes (South Yemen,
Iran (post-Khomeini)	Syria)
Oman	Cuba
North Yemen	Palestinian guerrillas
Persian Gulf regimes	Libya
Saudi Arabia*	
Africa	
Zaire	USSR
Morocco	Cuba
Sudan	Libya
Namibia	Pro-Soviet regimes (Ethiopia, Angola,
South Africa*	Mozambique)
	Regional guerrillas/communist groups
	(SWAPO)

Designates the main strategic target, November 1980

Seven years later, after five years of experience within the government, I would make only small changes in this schematic description.

During the five years before 1980, this subversive aggression, including heavy support for terrorism, had resulted in the establishment of ten new pro-Soviet dictatorships on three continents. But from 1981 to 1987 none of the target countries fell and no new pro-Soviet regimes were created. Unfortunately, the destabilization coalition still exists, and the target countries, along with the three main strategic targets—Mexico, Saudi Arabia, and South Africa—remain vulnerable.

Up to early 1988, the Reagan administration has a mixed record in dealing with this form of warfare: no additional losses, but no major victories. And this violent indirect aggression continues to claim many lives in free world countries. Except in Central America, the Reagan administration has failed, year after year, to come to grips systematically with aggression-through-armed subversion and to design a counterstrategy.

True, strong antiterrorist rhetoric has been stepped up, with Secretary of State Shultz taking the lead in late 1984. The administration *has* taken important defensive measures that were needed to improve intelligence collection, to share information with friendly governments, and to protect government installations at home and abroad. With each new terrorist episode, "crisis management" facilities have been improved. All necessary—but not sufficient to make progress against the continuing threat.

What follows is the story of my repeated efforts to "jump start" the decision-making process so that those with real power could begin policy discussions that would result in a presidential choice of counterstrategy. Soviet-supported subversive aggression and terrorism is exactly the kind of issue that requires action by the president, acting through the National Security Council. It is the type of threat that evades the unique responsibility of State, Defense, or CIA but requires all three to work together effectively. If the NSC staff does not take the lead to formulate a counterstrategy, none is likely.

In December 1980 members of my informal group gave a copy of the two-page suggested counterstrategy to their personal friends, who included NSC adviser Richard Allen, Secretary of State Alexander Haig, Secretary of Defense Caspar Weinberger, and CIA Director William Casey. It seemed to me that little happened. Most likely these busy men, facing other urgent pressures in their new cabinet posts, smiled graciously to the personal friends who handed the proposal to them, tucked it in some safe place as *must* reading, and turned back to their crowded schedules.

Those who actually read it probably agreed with its thrust and felt that what they were already doing was heading in that direction. Haig, for example, may have felt that his strong speeches opposing terrorism, together with his having a "counterterrorism coordinator" at the State Department, meant the problem was being "worked."

When I entered the administration later in 1981, I was immediately plunged into the intensive seven-week interagency process to propose U.S. policy toward Central America and Cuba. That, and other tasks associated with my new responsibilities at CIA, took all my time.

But in January 1982, when Judge Clark became NSC adviser, I thought this offered the NSC, under Clark's leadership, the chance to start an interagency effort that could propose a counterstrategy to the president. I then gave my November 1980 paper to Bill Casey and asked him to pass it along to Bill Clark with a recommendation that the NSC act. I remember Casey's reply: "Constantine, this is the third time I've received this document. Once it came to me from Leo Cherne [an old friend of Casey's, vice chairman of the president's Foreign Intelligence Advisory Board.] Then you gave it to me when we were discussing your coming to work here. And now you want me to give it to Bill Clark! That's okay, but I should wait a few months until he is settled in his new job."

I waited two months, then gave my 1980 proposal to Ron Mann, saying, "I think Bill Clark would react positively to this. He might even be willing to have the NSC task the agencies to develop a counterstrategy."

"Yes," Ron said, "Clark would be interested, but he's swamped with work, and would most likely turn this over to his deputy, McFarlane. And Bud would probably just say, 'The State Department counterterrorism office is handling this.' McFarlane is an old buddy of Haig's, and would want to make sure that Haig remains 'in charge' on this issue."

Then Ron showed me the first NSDD issued by the new Clark-McFarlane team: "As you see, this formalizes the system Haig began last year [1981] of having the State Department chair all the interagency meetings on foreign policy below the presidential-NSC level. McFarlane persuaded Clark to do this, because McFarlane believes the career bureaucracy—especially at State—knows best. So he probably wouldn't want the NSC to push for action on the terrorism issue in the strategic way you have in mind."

*   *   *

In April 1983 a small truck loaded with explosives was driven into the front door of the U.S. embassy in Beirut, Lebanon. This terrorist attack killed sixty-six persons, including my counterpart, Robert Ames, the national intelligence officer for the Middle East, who was visiting our embassy there.

I remembered the cold, rainy day in April 1983 when I drove out to Andrews Air Force Base with Herb Myer and other CIA, State, and Defense officials receiving the bodies of the victims. We were in a huge aircraft hangar decorated with large American flags, a small dais, with red, white, and blue bunting and black crepe, and row on row of flag-covered coffins. The usually upbeat Bill Casey was sadder than I had ever seen him.

To some of us it seemed as if the bad days of the Carter years were returning. We recalled 1979, when mobs organized by Qaddafi burned down the U.S. embassy in Libya, when terrorists took the U.S. ambassador prisoner in communist Afghanistan, where he was then killed during a "rescue." We also recalled when leftist radical mobs stormed the U.S. embassy in Pakistan, all of this *in addition to* the hostage crisis in Iran.

This tragedy led me to make another try at influencing the formulation of a clear antiterrorism policy.

First, I asked a friend at the White House to get me a copy of President Reagan's 1981 speech pledging "swift and sure retribution" against terrorist attacks. Then I took that speech to Casey, saying, "There needs to be a careful analysis of which terrorist groups and governments did this. Next, using lawful means, the United States and our allies should act against the perpetrators. It seems to me that it's ethical to hold all armed units of the terrorist organizations involved accountable. I don't go along with counteractions like bombing or shelling the zones from which the terrorists operate if this risks killing and wounding civilians living there. Unless there's effective retribution, I believe we'll see more attacks like this."

Casey was somber. As he listened he took a copy of the president's speech and read it. I continued, "At the risk of playing the same tune too often, I repeat: we don't have a counterstrategy, but we could move ahead and formulate one."

Casey scowled. "We *are* doing a number of things, so everyone thinks we're making progress. But you're right: we don't have a real counterstrategy yet. Do you have a copy of that two-page document you kept pestering me with last year?"

I did and gave it to him, commenting, "I've been concerned about this problem of indirect warfare for years, and I'd be pleased to help in any way."

Casey simply said, "You have your hands full with Latin America."

Only after I'd arrived at the NSC in October 1983 did I learn that a careful analysis had revealed which terrorist organizations and governments had joined in blowing up our Beirut embassy. This investigation had been completed in the summer of 1983, but apparently no action was taken. Later, in public statements, Secretary of Defense Weinberger would identify Palestinian terrorist groups along with Syria and Iran.

On Sunday morning, October 23, 1983, when the White House operator told me about the killing of 247 marines by a terrorist truck bomb, my first reaction was deep sadness; then I said a prayer. I told myself: "I have to try again after Grenada."

In December 1983 terrorists blew up part of the U.S. and French embassies in Kuwait. They also tried to kill the leaders of the Kuwaiti government, hoping to install a radical pro-Soviet government in that oil-rich minicountry. Obviously the terrorists and their patrons were not at all deterred by strong administration rhetoric on this topic.

I resolved to try even harder to put my materials into the hands of someone who could get things moving. I didn't have to wait very long for an opportunity.

In February 1984 I spent ten days traveling with Secretary Shultz. As we flew on his airplane from Central America to Venezuela, then to Rio de Janeiro, Brazil, and on to Barbados, Shultz would ask us to have an informal chat with him about the issues he would face at our next stop. Toward the end of the trip, as we approached Barbados to meet with all the prime ministers of the eastern Caribbean democracies, I told Shultz about some of the Libyan activities to foment subversion and terrorism in that region. He was surprised.

At lunch I asked one of the Caribbean prime ministers whether he could tell Secretary Shultz what the Libyans were doing in his country. This led first one and then several others to describe the hostile activities of the Libyans and North Koreans in their countries, in addition to the subversive actions of Cuba and the Soviet bloc. I could see this too surprised Shultz and made an impression on him.

I had taken my counterstrategy paper along on the trip, hoping that during the five-hour flight back from Grenada, our last stop, Shultz would be able to give me fifteen minutes on this topic.

On the long trip home, after we had been airborne about half an hour,

I took two copies of my 1980 paper on a counterstrategy and my *New York Times* op-ed page article. I went forward toward the secretary's portion of the aircraft and gave them to Shultz's executive assistant.

"Please tell Secretary Shultz," I said politely, "that I'd like to discuss these ideas with him for no longer than ten to fifteen minutes. I've heard that he's been getting more concerned about the terrorism problem lately, and I believe he'd be interested in reading this and talking with me for a few minutes."

The executive aide said amiably, "Fine. I'll give this to the secretary, and we'll let you know when you can come forward."

Just to be sure that Tony Motley wouldn't think I was intending to talk to Shultz about Latin America without him, I also gave Tony a copy of the three pages and told him of my request. That was a calculated risk, as I knew full well that Motley wanted me to have as little contact with Shultz as possible. But I thought that if I didn't tell Motley what I was doing, he would see me on Shultz's part of the aircraft and start to worry. Then he might secretly tell the executive assistant to dump my paper.

One hour passed. Then another. I went up front and said to the executive assistant, "When will I have the chance for ten minutes with Secretary Shultz?"

With practiced smoothness he smiled and said, "I'm sure it won't be long now."

Another hour went by. I could see that Shultz was spending a good deal of the time meeting with some of the twenty or more journalists who had come along on the trip. After yet *another* hour, I went up to the executive assistant and said, "If you'd give Shultz my short paper, I really believe he'd find it useful to spend ten minutes talking with me about how to start cutting back the terrorist menace."

This time there was no smile. The executive assistant said, "I'll call you."

Shortly before we landed at Andrews Air Force Base, Shultz came back to the section of the plane where I was sitting. Was he coming to tell me something personally? No, he was coming back to thank each of us for our work during the trip. It was a thoughtful gesture. Because I had the strong impression he never received my document, I decided to give him another copy.

"Mr. Secretary," I said, "these two pages outline a possible counterstrategy against terrorism. I hope you might have ten minutes to discuss this with me."

He took the document with no indication that the executive assistant had given him my earlier copy. I felt myself growing angry at Shultz's aide. It seemed to me that he had failed to do his job in passing my request and document along to Shultz.

Shultz then said, "Perhaps we'll be able to chat about this in Washington."

My secretary called to follow up, but Shultz never found the time to meet with me. This was months before his anger at me in June 1984.

A few days after this trip I wrote McFarlane a memo (unclassified) entitled "Countering State-Supported Terrorism." I simply refused to give up without more of an effort.

This nine-page memo summarized my sense of the threat and a counterstrategy. It discussed potential vulnerabilities in a number of regions and requested that McFarlane convene the NSC's senior directors for the world's five geographic regions for a discussion "where we would have the time for an in-depth exchange of views."

I included a diagram indicating what published data suggested about the countries in each of the world's five regions where the elements of the destabilization coalition were taking hostile action. I did this because I had noticed that the tight regional organization of the U.S. government in foreign policy meant that Middle Eastern analysts who might know about PLO activities in their region tended not to know about PLO activities in Latin America. By the same token, the staff working on Latin America tended to be unaware of hostile actions by extraregional terrorist groups like the PLO. The same had applied to Libyan and North Korean hostile actions in Latin America. In fact, a number of the stateless terrorist organizations were killing people thousands of miles from their home regions with the support of Soviet-bloc and terrorist-partner governments, such as Syria, Libya, North Korea, Nicaragua, and Cuba. This global threat to friendly governments, I suggested to McFarlane, required us to synthesize the available information for a global counterstrategy.

I also said we needed preventive action in several vulnerable countries where it seemed we were being too complacent, such as the Philippines. The situation in that country so worried me that I described it in my February 1984 memo—nearly two years before our government seemed to perceive the crisis there—as "a potential combination of 1979 Nicaragua and Iran."

Indeed, it seemed to me that this friendly, strategically important country of fifty million faced great danger. In 1981, when Michael Armacost became ambassador to the Philippines, I had urged him to undertake a major program to encourage and support the democratic groups that were opposed both by the Marcos regime and the communist-guerrilla apparatus. My view was that a political transition was likely in the next years. While maintaining normal relations with the friendly Philippine government and not working to destabilize it, the United States could simultaneously provide open but discreet help to the genuinely democratic opposition. Further, we could urge the democratic groups to use nonviolent means and avoid the mistake of making any type of an alliance with the communist opposition.

After the murder in August 1983 of Aquino, the leader of the democratic opposition, I became concerned that the communists would repeat their success in Nicaragua by using the understandable outrage of the genuine democrats as the basis for proposing and *leading* a unified anti-Marcos coalition.

My memo to McFarlane described a scenario we should avoid: The Philippines "could combine the speed of collapse seen in 1979 Iran (when the shah's regime moved from control to flight in eleven months) with the mistake made by the . . . genuine democrats in 1979 Nicaragua—thinking anything was better than the dictator they wanted to remove, they joined in coalition with the Marxist-Leninist left."

Naturally I told the other NSC senior directors about my memo and explained that I had not "coordinated" my discussion of countries in their region with them because I wanted this to reflect one observer's concerns, based only on published information, and to provide a basis for an in-depth discussion among all of us where we would use the full range of classified and other information we each had. But for now the purpose of my "think piece" was to stimulate McFarlane into taking some time for a discussion about a foreign policy strategy. Most of my colleagues assured me that they hoped my paper would lead to the discussion I had requested. I hoped they were right.

What happened? I waited weeks—knowing the enormous demands on the national security adviser's reading time—but still had heard nothing. So, in mid-March 1984, I briefly described my memo at a senior staff meeting and said, "Bud, I sent you this memo on February 24, because I believe you and the regional senior directors could have a useful discussion." McFarlane simply looked at me. So I asked, "Did you receive and have a chance to read my memo?" With no trace of emotion, or hint of his opinion, he said, "Yes." Nothing more.

I also gave a copy to Donald Fortier, who had recently been promoted to McFarlane's second deputy after Poindexter, and who seemed to be charged with thinking ahead on issues. Fortier and I discussed the matter over breakfast one morning. He was always cordial, easy to talk with, and apparently interested in ideas and information. His expertise was in nuclear proliferation issues, and he said these questions of terrorism and subversive aggression were somewhat new to him at the time.

I said, "Don, I think it would be worth McFarlane's time to spend one hour with the regional senior directors to start the process of developing a counterstrategy. The administration is more than three years old, and all we're getting is more rhetoric and higher walls around our embassies. If you're going to be in charge, I will be willing to help in any way."

Don, in his usual low-key way, replied, "I hope we do something on this, and I would welcome your help if you can spare time from the Central American crisis."

The months of 1984 went by. I never heard from McFarlane, Poindexter, or Fortier about this matter. I hoped somebody was working on the issue and that I was simply uninformed. But my guess was that this was the type of problem that everyone intends to work on "tomorrow," but, as they say, "the urgent always preempts the important."

During 1984 Congress passed several new laws on terrorism, with strong leadership from the executive branch. McFarlane and Poindexter did seem to work with Fortier and North on what I would call the very important "police" and defensive aspects of counterterrorism, such as the "1984 Act to Combat International Terrorism," which authorized the payment of up to $500,000 in reward money for information about cases of domestic and international terrorism. New legislation also gave the federal government the authority to prosecute anyone who destroyed an American aircraft outside the United States, if that person enters the territory of the United States.

And in late 1984 the press also carried reports that a new National Security Decision Directive had been issued by President Reagan to strengthen defenses against terrorism. These actions were fine, as far as they went. But they were all defensive.

After the reelection in 1984, I decided to try again. Using one legal-sized page, I summarized "two foreign policy futures" if the second-term Reagan administration pursued "accommodationism," as preferred by the State Department, or "realism," reflecting—I believed—the views of Reagan, Casey, Kirkpatrick, and Weinberger. For the issue of subversive aggression-terrorism, I defined the accommodationist approach to include "main emphasis on . . . negotiations which leave the pro-Soviet dictatorships in power, such as Angola, Mozambique, and Nicaragua'' and ''definition and treatment of international terrorist attacks on the U.S. as a series of disconnected episodes.'' I then summarized the ''likely results,'' including ''increased terrorist attacks on the U.S. presence in key Soviet-bloc target areas.''

McFarlane and I were scheduled to meet (in December of 1984) and discuss my three foreign policy suggestions for the second term, and when we did I gave him a copy of the ''accommodationism-realism'' proposal. He held my one-page overview in his hands and looked at it quickly. When I saw him set his jaws, I knew the reaction was not good (though I could never understand why he should be angry with my effort to propose practical ideas). From that point on McFarlane neither asked questions nor discussed the matter with me.

Later that same month I had discussions with Casey, Meese, Clark, and Kirkpatrick. All seemed to agree, in principle, that a high priority during the second term should be to launch a counterstrategy. But events then intervened—the ''Battle of the Ambassadors''—and in early January 1985 the nearly simultaneous announcements that Michael Deaver and Bill Clark would be leaving the Reagan administration in the spring of 1985, soon to be followed by Jeane Kirkpatrick.

In November 1984 I had also asked Craig Fuller, chief of staff to Vice President Bush, for a chance to speak with the vice president for about twenty to thirty minutes on this issue and on the ''coalition for democracy'' idea. Since the vice president had lunch alone with the president every week, I thought if Bush agreed that we needed a counterstrategy, he might be willing to suggest this idea to the president or even just nudge McFarlane in that direction. When Craig said he'd do what he could, my hopes rose.

Unfortunately it would be another fourteen months before I had the chance to make this presentation to the vice president.

As always, I was very busy—we all were—as the months passed in 1985. I saw very little of Ollie North after January 1985. However, since he seemed to be the person McFarlane and Poindexter used to coordinate paramilitary activities, including preparation for dealing with the next terrorist episode, I had given Ollie my 1980 materials and my February 1984 memo to McFarlane.

At times in late 1983 and early 1984, we had discussed this topic at some of our White House breakfasts. But I noticed that Ollie, perhaps as would be expected of a marine officer, was much more interested in the immediate tactical response issues—such as how to use U.S. Special Forces in the rescue of U.S. citizens. He showed little interest in or feeling for the *strategic* dimension of counterterrorism. For example, Ollie didn't seem to understand that the threats posed to friendly regional countries by Cuba, Libya, Syria, or Iran gave our allies even more reason to cooperate with us on a counterstrategy.

By early June 1985 I had concluded that McFarlane and Shultz would never make progress on this issue unless they were pushed to do so by the president. That is when Dana Rohrabacher arranged for me to meet with a congressional leader whom the president liked and respected. Dana said, "If you can convince him, he can call the president, outline the idea, and suggest that McFarlane be asked to come up with a counter-strategy over the next weeks. I suggest you meet with him." Despite genuine interest, this individual—as mentioned earlier—seemed unwilling to call the president with this idea—and I could understand his reluctance.

Then the June 1985 TWA hijacking moved me to write another memo to McFarlane a week after the event. Repeating my suggestion that the administration develop a counterstrategy, I proposed that Vice President Bush be placed in charge of an interagency effort. There was no reply. But in early July the president designated Vice President Bush to lead an interagency "task force on combatting terrorism," which was to report in February 1986. Pleased, I suggested to McFarlane that the vice president's effort include but go beyond our usual ad hoc response and come up with something new and *effective*. I offered my help on this to McFarlane and to Vice President Bush's office.

Whatever hopes I may have had were diminished when I read the roster of the task force. A retired naval admiral was named executive director, and the entire staff consisted of foreign service officers and military personnel. The senior NSC representative was John Poindexter, and Oliver North was the day-to-day NSC participant. This and what I learned about the definition of their tasks, made me wonder whether the vice president's effort was likely to get beyond military tactics and bureaucratic issues, which only focused on dealing with specific terrorist episodes. But I reserved judgment. Still, I could sense something *ticking*.

During 1985 Bill Casey had given a number of excellent speeches and written several articles about subversive aggression and terrorism. These speeches defined the threats, presented some of the evidence, and were reflected in the landmark speech on terrorism given by President Reagan on July 8, 1985.

But the administration did not follow up these good analyses of the terrorist threat with equally good ideas about how to counter it. So my August 6, 1985, letter to President Reagan not only warned him about the threat to his Central America policy posed by the lack of a fair NSC process, but also outlined a practical counterstrategy:

> Your July 8, 1985, speech to the American Bar Association outlined much of the problem. Based upon the overwhelming evidence we have, you pointed out that there are three reinforcing components to this threat: the Soviet-bloc countries; the terrorist partner governments, such as Nicaragua, Libya, Cuba; and the main terrorist organizations, some of which attack in several geographic regions.
>
> In addition to intelligence and police-type actions needed to deter and deal with the specific episodes of terrorism, the following are, I believe, the elements of a successful strategy:
>
> • *Political and communications actions*—to affirm democratic values; tell the truth about the U.S. and other democracies; counter hostile propaganda; tell the truth about the repression, poverty, and elitism of communist governments; and strengthen moderate leaders and institutions.
> • *Containment*—timely identification of vulnerable target countries and the competent use of U.S. and allied resources to help defeat efforts by pro-Soviet groups to take power.
> • *Pro-Western restoration*—U.S. help to reasonable and effective indigenous groups in cooperation with neighboring governments to bring about pro-Western governments replacing terrorist-partner and recent pro-Soviet regimes.
>
> This strategy does *not* involve any deployment of U.S. combat forces to the territory of any of these countries because with prudent foresight, we would be acting in time to help pro-Western groups and governments achieve our shared objectives.

My hope was that if the president had read my letter at the ranch in August, he might have talked with McFarlane and Bush to assure that the vice president's task force would also include the strategic dimension. But my letter did not reach the president in the summer of 1985.

And then terrorists struck again. And again. And again.

On August 8 a car bomb killed or wounded twenty-two Americans and Germans at a U.S. airbase in West Germany.

In Rome on September 16 terrorists used hand grenades to kill or wound thirty-eight, including nine Americans, in a popular tourist restaurant.

Then, in October 1985, Palestinian terrorists hijacked the Italian cruise ship *Achille Lauro*, shot a crippled, elderly American tourist, and threw his body overboard, while threatening to blow up the entire ship.

Using a combination of superb intelligence and excellent tactics, President Reagan ordered U.S. Navy aircraft to capture the terrorists' getaway airplane.

When that happened the entire country—and free world—cheered. But crisis management was not followed by any observable "swift and sure retribution," against either the terrorist organization or its government sponsors.

In early December McFarlane suddenly resigned as NSC adviser. He called the entire NSC staff together—about one hundred people—in the ornate Indian Treaty Room of the Old Executive Office Building. (I had gotten the word late and was already at lunch in the White House mess with Benjamin Huberman, who knew Poindexter and told me that Poindexter was about to become the NSC adviser.)

I was told that McFarlane made an emotional departure statement. But he regained his composure quickly and only minutes later was able to join President Reagan in the White House press room, where his resignation and Admiral Poindexter's promotion were announced. The next time I saw McFarlane was two weeks later at the annual White House Christmas festivities for the cabinet members and senior White House staff. He looked cheerful in a colorful plaid vest and was dancing happily with his wife.

Christmas is a time for reconciliation, and as I was dancing with my wife I twice looked directly at McFarlane and said a cordial "hello." He looked right through me; perhaps he had not heard me.

But the White House speech writers had told me that McFarlane had picked up Shultz's petty practice of snubbing staff members who were deemed a "problem." Ben Elliott and another presidential speechwriter, Peggy Noonan, told me that at the recent U.S.-Soviet summit in Geneva, McFarlane and Shultz had refused to speak with them or even acknowledge them on Air Force One, in a Geneva hotel elevator, and on other occasions. When Ben and Peggy told me this, I thought: What an odd way to act while on a peace mission. Ronald Reagan would certainly disapprove if he knew about this behavior.

The holiday season had already seen too much terrorism: just before Thanksgiving, a terrorist bomb had exploded in a U.S. military shopping mall in Frankfurt, Germany, severely wounding thirty-two people, including twenty-three Americans. The day before that an Egyptian airplane was skyjacked, landed in Malta, and during the armed rescue sixty people died, including one American. These and other events had caused me again to check into what the vice president's task force was doing. Everything I learned indicated it was still totally focused on police, intelligence, judicial, and organizational issues. It wasn't even considering a counterstrategy. I was disappointed but not surprised. What more could I do? I wondered.

At the White House Christmas party, Nancy and I were on the receiving line just in front of Donald Regan and his wife. Should I say something to him? . . . No, it was the wrong time and too far out of his ken. Nancy and I shook hands with President and Mrs. Reagan—both were very cordial standing in front of the beautiful Christmas tree. Reagan said, "Merry Christmas, Constantine," as we four posed for a photo together. Later, as Nancy and I were helping ourselves at the elegant buffet in the State Dining Room, I looked across the room and saw Craig and Karen Fuller. Since Karen worked as Pat Buchanan's secretary, I had seen a good deal of her in recent months and respected her cordial professionalism. Now and then I would remind Karen of my languishing request to speak to the vice president, and she would good-naturedly promise to mention it to Craig.

Determined to make one last try to see the vice president, I walked over to them. "Merry Christmas! Nice to see you both. . . . Craig," I said, "I don't like to bring up work, but I believe the vice president would be interested in spending fifteen minutes to hear my suggestion for a counterstrategy against terrorism. Over a period of months, with competent implementation, it could reduce terrorist violence against us and our friends. It's some months since I first made the request, and now the vice president has the responsibility for leadership on this issue."

Craig said, "I'll do my best."

A few days later, on December 27, 1985, two terrorist groups armed with automatic weapons and hand grenades simultaneously attacked civilian airports in Rome and Vienna. The 132 people dead and wounded included 7 Americans, one of them an eleven-year-old girl on her way home for Christmas vacation. The photos of the victims' shattered bodies added to the mounting national outrage. The year 1985 ended with 103

Americans wounded and killed in international terrorist attacks and 6 American citizens held hostage in Lebanon.

Two weeks after the Rome and Vienna attacks I was in Europe for a series of public diplomacy briefings on a range of issues. Ambassador Faith Whittlesey had invited several of her fellow U.S. ambassadors for an informal discussion on public diplomacy and asked me to join them in Berne, Switzerland. The purpose was to look ahead to the 1986 international political events and the likely timing of major Soviet-bloc and communist propaganda offensives: SDI/arms control; Central America; South Africa; the Philippines; and terrorism.

I brought along for the U.S. ambassadors in Europe a brief synthesis of President Reagan's policy statements on these issues, a list of likely future events related to each issue, and possible themes for public diplomacy by our embassies in Western Europe. Also, for each of the seven U.S. ambassadors I would be meeting, I brought a packet of unclassified, relevant U.S. government information publications, speeches by the president and secretary of state, and the just issued report by President Reagan on twenty-five years of Soviet violations of many arms control agreements.

It was a special pleasure to see Ambassador Faith Whittlesey again. She had performed loyally—and brilliantly—as the president's director of public liaison on all major issues, foreign and domestic. She and her staff reached leaders and the grass roots effectively to make the case for the administration's policies: holding public briefings, publishing an incisive *White House Digest*, and building a superb team that included such skilled political strategists and communicators as Morton Blackwell and Robert Reilly. But for reasons I never fully understood, Michael Deaver seemed to view Whittlesey as "controversial" instead of a great asset to the president. In 1985 she accepted an offer to return to her previous post as ambassador to Switzerland. There she used her enormous energy and talent to deepen cooperation and counter the attempts of communist propaganda to mislead our friends in Europe. What made her all the more remarkable was that she had accomplished so much while also providing a loving home for her three children after having been widowed at the age of thirty-three.

In Switzerland there were five of us who spent about two days exchanging ideas about how United States public diplomacy could be more effective during 1986: U.S. Ambassador to Luxembourg Jeane Gerard; U.S. Ambassador to Portugal Frank Shakespeare (now ambassador to the Vatican); Ambassador Whittlesey; Robert Reilly, whom she persuaded to leave his

White House job and become the counselor for public diplomacy; and myself. After our working meetings, we had the chance for good conversations as we shared lunch and dinner at the ambassador's residence. It was my first visit to Switzerland during the winter. I was taken with the beauty of the snow-covered landscape and the charming old quarter of Berne. From my hotel I could see the blue-green Aare River surging below the city walls.

After productive discussions, I continued on my mission and stopped in Italy, France, and Portugal.

In Rome it was a pleasure to see Ambassador William Wilson and his charming wife, who were old friends of the president and First Lady and who had represented the United States at the Vatican for nearly four years. I had met Ambassador Wilson a number of times during his visits to the White House, and after my "move up" I had sent him some preliminary ideas for efforts to inform the leadership of the Roman Catholic church about several key foreign policy issues. Ambassador Wilson and his staff had the opportunity for dialogue with the governing authorities of the Catholic church as well as with the leadership of the many seminaries and advanced educational institutes that trained the members of the major religious orders. In addition, they met with the national representatives to the Vatican of more than sixty different countries. The potential for better understanding by sharing our information and point of view were very great.

While in Rome I had excellent conversations with Ambassador Max Rabb, the president's envoy to Italy. He had been the intended target of several terrorist attacks, which fortunately had been prevented through good intelligence warning. In the preceding decade the Red Brigades, the pro-Soviet terrorists in Italy, had killed thousands of people. They were now finally becoming less active, thanks to the effective counteractions of the Italian government. And Rabb had helped facilitate better cooperation between Italy and the United States on a number of issues, including the prevention of terrorism.

One of Ambassador Rabb's daughters was a neighbor of mine in Washington. My wife and I had become friendly with her, her husband, and their children. Rabb's grandson and my son were about the same age and had often played together. The ambassador had served in the Eisenhower White House and was always very cordial when we had met, even briefly, in Washington.

I had heard that Ambassador Rabb had a very good relationship with George Shultz. For all these reasons, in our private conversation I brought up as a personal issue the need for a U.S. counterstrategy against terrorism.

"Mr. Ambassador," I said, "you've seen what terrorism has done here in Italy for years. You played an important role in the *Achille Lauro* crisis last October, and only days ago you consoled the families of the people killed at the airport here. Our government is making progress in some important aspects of defense against terrorism, but we have still not formulated a real counterstrategy against terrorism. You're on good terms with Secretary Shultz. Here's a two-page proposal I wrote in 1980, which I believe could be the basis for a sensible counterstrategy. When you next see him, would you please suggest to Secretary Shultz that we need to move beyond simply dealing with each new episode as it happens?"

I realized this was an unusual, perhaps even impertinent suggestion. But I was counting on Ambassador Rabb's goodwill and knowledge of the Washington scene to help him understand that I was only trying to be helpful to the Reagan administration—and my country.

He looked at my proposal, said it was "interesting," and asked a few questions. He said he would think about what he could do about this "when I'm next in Washington."

He added that Deputy Secretary of State Kenneth Dam would be visiting him the next day: "Maybe I'll mention this to him and urge that he and Shultz talk with you."

"Thanks," I replied, "but I've tried that without success. How about leaving my name out, and simply talking about the urgent need for a counterstrategy and giving him the document."

Ambassador Rabb gave me the look of wisdom that comes with experience. "I understand. I'll do what I can."

My hope was that Ambassador Rabb would be willing to discuss the matter informally with Shultz on his next Washington visit. But I also understood he had made no firm commitments.

On the eve of this conversation, I had dinner at the Cafe de Paris on the Via Veneto. I was struck by how empty it was.

"Business is a little slow tonight," I remarked to my waiter as I paid the bill.

"Yes"—he nodded—"it's been slow for months. Ever since the terrorists bombed us and killed all those American tourists."

I'd forgotten that attack. But this made the third site of a terrorist attack I'd visited that day. I'd awakened in Vienna and checked in at the airport, where terrorists had murdered several people a few days earlier, on

December 27. Then I'd flown to Rome, whose airport had been struck simultaneously.

After returning to Washington in late January 1986, I again called the vice president's office and repeated my request for a brief meeting with him on terrorism. By now his task force on combatting terrorism had spent nearly six months working on the issue. While both Poindexter and North knew of my strong interest in the subject, neither ever talked to me about the work of the task force.

Concerned by the lack of discernible progress on one hand, and the increase in terrorism on the other, I decided to find out how the work was coming. I asked to see a copy of the draft report, which was due the next month.

I was given a copy of the *un*classified draft. The classified version, I was informed, was on "extra close hold." However, I was assured that the overall policy content of the two versions of the report was the same—the classified report merely included sensitive "details."

I read the draft with great care. I realized it did a thorough job in delineating the legal and bureaucratic aspects of counterterrorism. It also proposed a number of practical actions to improve what I call the defensive and intelligence preparations for dealing with terrorist attacks. Further, it urged: "A full-time NSC position with support staff as necessary to strengthen coordination of our program."

Aha! As soon as I read that, I knew Oliver North would persuade Poindexter and the vice president that he was the right man for the job— he did.

I called Craig Fuller and reminded him of the request to meet with the vice president that I'd made at the Christmas party. No reply.

In Florida to give speeches in late January 1986, I had a delightful discussion with Jorge and Irma Mas about the success of Radio Martí (the idea he had first proposed in 1980), the situation in Central America, and the current activities of the Cuban/American National Foundation. I also expressed my sadness at the continuing wave of terrorist attacks and added that I'd been trying to see Vice President Bush on this issue for some months.

Jorge replied, "We work very closely with Jeb Bush, one of the vice president's sons. He's a terrific fellow, and really understands foreign policy. If you agree, I'll try to get you both together at my house." *Naturally* I agreed.

That weekend Jorge invited Jeb Bush and me to his home. He

introduced us, stayed for a few minutes, then left us to chat alone. We sat on a veranda next to the swimming pool.

Jeb Bush is a leader in the Florida Republican party. He speaks fluent Spanish and has a strong interest in Latin America. I had heard him speak on Central America a few times, so I opened the conversation by complimenting him on his effectiveness in both English and Spanish. He returned the compliment by saying he had heard many good things about me, and that he was delighted to meet me.

I told him that his father had a chance to help the Reagan administration finally define and carry out a counterstrategy against terrorism. I mentioned my disappointment with the unclassified draft report of the task force, and I gave him a copy of my 1980 proposal. I discussed how the vice president could still take the lead in this direction since he had another month before his report was due. As I recall it, Jeb said, "I agree with you that this is important. I'll talk to my father and suggest he see you."

It was early the next Sunday morning in Washington, when my telephone rang. Jeb Bush had not let me down—it was Vice President Bush! Our meeting was arranged for ten o'clock in the morning on February 12, 1986. I didn't know if others would be present, but I thought that was likely, so I made six copies of a short briefing packet.

The meeting was in the vice president's office in the West Wing of the White House. I arrived some minutes early, and his secretary asked me to wait in the West Lobby. A few minutes after I had sat down, a short middle-aged gentleman came in and introduced himself as Admiral Holloway, "executive director of the vice president's task force on combatting terrorism."

I later learned that Admiral Holloway was a friend of Poindexter's. As chief of naval operations he had been Poindexter's boss a few years back. Admiral Holloway began a pleasant conversation with me. "I'm looking forward to your presentation," he said. Just then the vice president's secretary came out and asked the admiral to step into the office for a few minutes.

For once I let my hopes rise. This meeting might be the start of something we badly needed. The vice president had a good relationship with Reagan, and he had the personal attributes of vigor, openness, and political instinct, which could help him break through the old ways of thinking about terrorism. He also was seen by the government agencies as a possible future president, and this added to both his authority and his ability to provide real leadership on a complex political-legal-security issue such as terrorism. After all, he was the *vice president*.

As a matter of course, I had sent Poindexter a memo telling him of this meeting and attaching the briefing packet I would give Bush. That memo also recommended that Poindexter meet with me for a discussion of the same topic. Perhaps the combination of the vice president's interest and Poindexter's desire to perform well in his new job could move the NSC, finally, to propose a counterterrorism strategy for decision by the president.

As I entertained these thoughts, Admiral Holloway returned to the West Lobby. I expected him to continue our conversation of a few minutes before. Instead, he picked up one of the newpapers from the antique coffee table and began reading.

Strange, I thought. He seems suddenly to have lost interest in talking with me.

A few more minutes, and we were told, "The vice president is ready." We walked into the impressive West Wing office. The vice president came forward and greeted me warmly. A photographer busily took photos. Then Bush motioned me to a comfortable chair next to him and said he presumed I knew the other individuals who would be joining us: from the NSC, Lieutenant Colonel Oliver North; Lieutenant Colonel Samuel Watson and Mr. Donald Gregg, both of Bush's personal staff; and Admiral Holloway. I said hello, gave the vice president a copy of the briefing packet, then stood up and gave one to each of the others.

A warm fire was crackling in the fireplace. I mentally recalled August 1984, when I had briefed Vice President Bush just before flying with him to Ecuador. This time I began my briefing by saying, essentially, what I had attempted to tell President Reagan in my August 1985 letter. I explained that the vice president's unclassified draft report was fine in dealing with some very important aspects of the terrorism problem, but that in my view it failed to define the threat correctly in terms of international political realities: it completely omitted the key facts of linkages among the Soviet bloc, terrorist governments, and terrorist groups. It also failed to address the need for a counterstrategy to help friendly governments defeat this indirect aggression.

I described the current threat posed by the "destabilization coalition" against geopolitically vital target countries. Then I suggested a counterstrategy, in broad terms, and gave specific examples of actions to be taken that I believed could, over time, reduce the threat from the terrorist organizations. These actions, which were summarized on one page, seemed to interest the vice president. He asked a number of questions.

Then he and I had a friendly and, I thought, stimulating colloquy for another thirty minutes. The meeting ended about an hour after it had begun.

Had it gone well? Vice President Bush had *seemed* very interested. He had asked some sensible questions about the feasibility of some of my practical suggestions. But none of the others had said *anything*—not even Ollie, who was always articulate.

As we were leaving the vice president's outer office, I noticed the continuing silence of the other participants. Usually after this type of briefing there would be at least a pro forma comment—"that was interesting" or "I have some questions and would like to discuss this further with you." But this time *no one said anything to me* or to one another.

I turned to Admiral Holloway and said, "If this conversation has opened any new directions and I can help, I'm available. Just let me know."

He barely looked at me—where had his charm gone all of a sudden? "Fine," he grunted.

A few days later I received Poindexter's answer to my memo. After my suggestion that he and I speak, he had checked "disapproved." Then he wrote in his neat handwriting something like Your ideas are overtaken by events and not useful. We are doing the right things now. (In November 1986 I would learn about the military sales to Iran. Is that what he meant?)

That was my answer. Poindexter would not have been so direct unless he had known that the vice president had no further interest in any of the suggestions he had heard. Clearly the vice president was simply going to "go along" with the recommendations of the task force as they were. If Mr. Bush had felt even a glimmer of interest in taking the offensive against terrorism through a counterstrategy while I was meeting with him, Poindexter's note to me made it obvious that the "task force to combat terrorism" would be content to stick with the reactive approach contained in its draft report.

This was even more surprising in view of the way the vice president described his assignment in the final report: "When President Reagan asked our task force to review the nation's program to combat terrorism, it was not primarily a mandate to correct specific deficiencies, but one to reassess U.S. priorities and policies." Yes, but . . .

At the end of February 1986 the vice president issued his public report and personally signed this introduction:

Our Task Force was briefed by more than 25 government agencies, visited 14 operations centers to observe our capability firsthand, met with over 100 statesmen, military officers, scholars and law enforcement officials, and traveled to embassies and military commands throughout the world where discussions with both U.S. and foreign officials were conducted.

I personally met with many members of Congress, airline chief executive officers, media executives, and former cabinet officials and diplomats.

Our conclusion: the U.S. policy and program to combat terrorism is tough and resolute. We firmly oppose terrorism in all forms and wherever it takes place. We are prepared to act in concert with other nations or alone to prevent or respond to terrorist acts. *We will make no concessions to terrorists.* At the same time, we will use every available resource to gain the safe return of American citizens who are held hostage.

Our national program is well-conceived and working.

The United States currently has in place antiterrorism activities in virtually every federal department and agency. Specific agencies have been assigned to respond to any threat or attack directed at our citizens whether on foreign soil, here at home, in the air or at sea. [emphasis added]

After I had put all the pieces together, I wondered if my meeting with the vice president had been a political courtesy to show the Cuban American friends of Jeb Bush that Reaganites could get a hearing.

Never would I have dreamed that on January 17, 1986, Vice President Bush, John Poindexter, and Don Regan had met with President Reagan and given him Oliver North's memo proposing the sale of U.S. weapons to Iran in the hope that this would open a new relationship and obtain Iranian help to bring about the release of U.S. hostages in Lebanon. Instead of a counterstrategy, the administration had decided to appease one of the most violent sponsors of terrorism.

I didn't know of this until it became public in November 1986. But the previous February [1986], I had been able to see that my discussion with the vice president and the people he had chosen as the leaders in the fight against terrorism—including Oliver North, who would be named the new NSC counterterrorism coordinator—had produced no movement toward a real counterstrategy.

In March of 1986 I told my wife that I felt it was time to seriously consider leaving the Reagan administration. The wall around the president seemed impenetrable. And now, I said to Nancy, "Bush was in charge of this task force on terrorism. Is it the prototype of a Bush presidency? The entire staff were career government officials who couldn't look beyond the bureaucratic and defensive side of counterterrorism. And when Bush finally took the time to hear a practical strategic concept, he ignored it. With President Reagan," I said heatedly, "if you can get the foreign policy issue to him, he'll make a good decision eighty percent of the time."

With Poindexter as NSC adviser, I told Nancy, there seemed to be little or no chance that any of my international political ideas would get a hearing. In September of 1985, when the Panamanian military strongman, General Noriega, had illegally coerced the elected president of Panama into resigning, it was the first step back from democracy in Latin America. The sub-cabinet officials on Latin America seemed to do nothing. Then, I wrote a plan for the United States to use peaceful political and economic means to help Panamanians restore their constitutional system. I told Poindexter that this was important in demonstrating President Reagan's commitment to democracy, and I had warned that a Noriega-led military regime in Panama would make it far more vulnerable to destabilization and ultimate takeover by radical pro-Cuban/Soviet elements. I tried unsuccessfully for months to get this issue before President Reagan.

"Well," Nancy told me calmly, "you know it's alway frustrating to try to make new things happen in foreign policy. There's really no change since your 'move up' in how you have to work to get results. When you were senior director for Latin America and McFarlane and Poindexter were going along with the State Department, if you wanted to get something big to Reagan you had to go to other members of the cabinet. It's the same now. But I don't think you should stay on unless you feel able to accomplish something useful for the country."

Soon after that I put the same thought to a friend, Herbert Myer, who had worked at *Fortune* magazine until Bill Casey asked him to come to the CIA. Herb and I had been fellow "outsiders" there, and neighbors as well. "Should I stay?" I asked.

Herb was direct: "No. You should get out. It's ridiculous for you to have to maneuver around just because Poindexter doesn't want to think in strategic terms. This whole phony promotion was an insult to you, *and* to the president."

Herb's advice, on top of recent events, nudged me to make a private decision: I would stay and try to help the president win the coming congressional votes on aid to the Nicaraguan freedom fighters. Then I'd leave the Reagan administration.

11

"YOUR TOUR OF DUTY HAS BEEN COMPLETED"

The way I left the Reagan administration turned out to be one of those times when my life read as if it were following a script—and a pretty dramatic one at that. My "final battle" on behalf of President Reagan involved his Central American policy. Irony of ironies, I was trying yet again to save it from the State Department at the same time others were working to remove me from the National Security Council staff.

And, once again, in regard to the president's policy, it was a question of heading the "bad guys" off at the pass. This time, in the spring of 1986, the outcome hinged not on a team effort by some members of the foreign policy cabinet, but on a single congressman, a longtime friend and admirer of Ronald Reagan. Would he be able to get a warning about a destructive and important document to the president in time? And if he did, would Ronald Reagan recognize the danger and convene the first NSC meeting on Central America in many months?

A little recent background will help explain the dramatic but hidden battles of the spring of 1986. In April 1985, right after the House had voted down contra aid, Nicaragua's communist strongman, Daniel Ortega, made a tactical error: he flew to Moscow for a widely publicized official visit, complete with all the public symbolism of Soviet-Nicaraguan friendship and the signing of new agreements.

This turned out to be highly embarrassing to such House Democratic leaders as Tip O'Neill. The administration, on the other hand, pointed out

277

that Ortega's mission to Moscow only underlined the need for true democracy in Nicaragua, and as a result of the flap, in the summer of 1985 Congress voted $27 million in *non*military aid to the contras.

Congress made it clear, however, that neither Defense nor the CIA was to administer this aid by adding the now famous third Boland amendment.

At about the same time, Elliott Abrams was confirmed by the Senate as the new assistant secretary of state for Latin America, taking office in July of 1985, just as I was being moved up—and out of responsibility for Latin America. One of his first jobs was to administer, with the help of a small staff, that $27 million in "humanitarian assistance."

During several long conversations as Abrams was preparing for his confirmation hearings, he told me he fully supported the president's policy in Central America and would not do what his predecessors had done. I told Abrams about the president's actions to establish his Central and Latin American policy and keep it on track. I showed him National Security Decision Directives on Central America going back to 1981 that clearly defined this policy.

Abrams then told me something very revealing about the State Department's view of presidential orders: "You know, Constantine, when I was informing myself about Latin America, one of the first things I asked to see were the presidential decision directives from this administration. But nobody at State knew where to find copies for me!"

"That says it all," I said, nodding. His story, I continued, reminded me of Jackie Tillman's account of calling Motley to protest an action that violated a written presidential directive. When she read him the directive over the secure phone, he started to say, "But that is only what the pres—" She said he stopped in midsentence, realizing he was talking to "someone who believed that the president's decisions govern the entire executive branch— even the State Department."

"Year after year," I went on, "the State Department has done too little to provide leaders in the Latin American countries with the facts about Central America. Meanwhile, the Soviet-bloc, Cuban, Nicaraguan, and internal communist propaganda organizations spread lies and spend enormous resources. You could take the lead and carry out the president's directives to get the full truth about Central America to Latin America and Western Europe, and to make extra efforts to persuade Mexico to change its pro-Sandinista policy. And this might persuade Venezuela, Colombia, and Panama to stop going along with the phony peace treaties Mexico keeps writing. In the next weeks it would also be a good idea to prevent Mexico from adding Peru, Brazil,

Argentina, and Uruguay to the 'Contadora group' that Mexico consistently misleads.

"If the U.S. would make a real effort before the December 1985 OAS meeting of foreign ministers, Bill Middendorf and I think we could persuade the majority of members to agree on two simple resolutions. First, Nicaragua is obligated to implement democracy and has not yet done so. Second, Nicaragua has committed aggression through armed subversion against OAS members since the autumn of 1979. We had irrefutable public proof of that, and El Salvador, Honduras, and Costa Rica have also all documented the fact that it's Nicaragua that *initiated* cross-border paramilitary actions against all three of them. And this was *long before* the U.S. provided any help to the armed resistance opposing the Sandinistas."

Abrams said he agreed with all of these ideas: "I hope to do much more along those lines than has been done in the last few years."

I gave him copies of several one-page, unclassified point papers that presented our legal and factual case, plus copies of various public diplomacy and action plans we'd done at the NSC, some of which we had privately given to Motley in the hope he might implement them if we were not seen to be pushing him.

Then Abrams asked me for suggestions about competent people for the five deputy assistant secretary positions in his bureau. I suggested several foreign service officers and about five very competent nongovernment Latin America experts who also supported President Reagan's policy.

Soon after his Senate confirmation, Abrams made his decision on personnel. He kept James Michael, whom Enders had brought into Latin America from State's legal office and who had participated in every tricky maneuver. Motley had promoted Michael to the top deputy position, and Abrams kept him there. None of the outside Latin American experts was hired.

I vividly remember my conversation with Abrams on July 15, 1985. We had both been invited to a big White House reception for the Diplomatic Corps. My wife and I arrived after most guests had taken their seats on the south lawn to listen to an outdoor musical program. I noticed Elliott leaning against a tree, with his jacket off. Nancy and I joined him in the shade. I said a cheerful hello and congratulated him on his recent Senate confirmation.

Then, as the band paused for an intermission, I said, "Elliott, I'm sure you've heard about my so-called move up and out of responsibility for Latin America. I consider it too bad, since I'd been looking forward to working with you. I've had over twenty years of work on Latin America and the last six years of intense work on Central America, and I'm more than happy to help you, privately and informally, at any time.'' He said something vague.

That reaction made me realize I wouldn't be seeing much of Elliott Abrams. I decided I'd better give him a warning right away that I'd been planning to deliver only after he'd worked with Oliver North for a while. I felt I had to say it now, as the three of us stood on the south lawn of the White House.

"I want to tell you my opinions about Ollie's work," I said. "He's a dedicated, hardworking man, and he's been given more and more power by McFarlane and Poindexter. Unfortunately, Ollie doesn't know what he doesn't know about international politics. He also wants to control and run everything he gets involved with, and he thinks he can do mostly everything all by himself. It took me almost a year to understand that Ollie has a habit of giving his colleagues misleading information, even about important matters, not just the self-important boasting and name dropping some of us at the NSC have come to know well. His style is to preempt people, to 'make things happen' his way. I urge you, never take *any* important action based solely on what Ollie tells you. If he says he has an intelligence report about some coming danger that has to be stopped, check it out yourself with CIA. If he claims to have intercepts, get your own copies. I'd advise you to work closely with people like Fred Ikle at Defense, the national intelligence officer for Latin America at CIA, and the regional NSC staff—especially Jacqueline Tillman, who has good political judgment—as well as Ollie."

Abrams simply said, "Oh." He asked no questions, and it was clear he wasn't interested in continuing the conversation. Nancy and I said, "Good luck," and walked off. I commented to her that Elliott seemed quite distant, which surprised me, as I was only trying to be helpful.

Nancy shook her head. "Don't you see, Constantine? He didn't understand you, and he doesn't believe you about Ollie North."

Events again proved Nancy right—on all counts.

In September 1985 I wrote a public diplomacy plan intended to energize the U.S. government into communicating the truth about Central America to all thirty-two Latin American countries. The simple idea was to start a program of visits and briefings by U.S. officials in October and November so that at the December foreign ministers meeting a majority of the OAS members would tell the world that the Sandinistas had not yet implemented democracy and were continuing their aggression through armed subversion against their neighbors. This would be politically important in the Western Hemisphere and in Westen Europe and would also help support the administration's Central America policy with Congress during the debates and expected close vote of early 1986.

The NSC sent this suggestion to State, but week after week passed and there was no action. The new ambassador to the OAS, Richard McCormack, one of the few remaining Reagan policy appointees at State, also agreed with this plan. So did another Reagan appointee, Otto Reich, the special ambassador for public diplomacy. Both could do some things on their own, but only Abrams could order the U.S. ambassadors to participate in a systematic and comprehensive effort, since "the line of authority," as Secretary Shultz often reminded the ambassadors, went from the president to Shultz to the regional assistant secretary and then to U.S. embassies abroad.

By mid-October 1985 time was slipping away, and I judged that the Cubans and Nicaraguans would be preparing to spring some diplomatic surprises, using all their resources to prepare the groundwork. So I called Abrams's office and arranged for him to meet with Ambassador McCormack, Ambassador Reich, and me to discuss implementing the agreed-upon communications plan. We arrived at the appointed time and were told he would be with us "in a few minutes." Forty minutes passed, and a journalist emerged who had obviously been effective at keeping Abrams talking. But then Abrams told the three of us he had another appointment and had to leave. We all tried to reschedule our discussion, but it did not happen.

An NSC colleague, the most senior NSC person on public diplomacy issues, tried to push for implementation of the plan. Nothing was done. By mid-November the State Latin American bureau began to justify its passivity by saying that this would be a "routine meeting of the OAS." I countered by saying, "Whatever the formal agenda, whenever all the foreign ministers of the Western Hemisphere meet, it is intrinsically a political opportunity for both sides, and we should prepare to use it."

As it turned out, the Cubans, Nicaraguans, and Mexicans were good and ready to use the December 1985 OAS meeting against the United States. First, there was an effort to reinstate Cuba as a full OAS member. Second, Nicaragua, with Mexican support, tried to get a vote condemning the United States for having imposed economic sanctions in the spring of 1985. Only extraordinary last-minute efforts by Abrams, McCormack and the U.S. delegation prevented these two resolutions from passing.

What could not be prevented was a unique meeting of an international group founded by Mexico that *includes* Cuba but *excludes* the United States. Virtually all the OAS foreign ministers were flown directly from the OAS meeting to another place, where, with Cuba in the chair, they discussed the hemisphere's "economic and social problems," especially the burden of debt owed to "imperialist" banks. All of this was aimed at separating Latin America from the United States.

Since 1981 I had been trying to help my State Department colleagues understand the political front of the indirect war that was being waged in Central America. One of the main difficulties they had was in grasping that it took place in three different arenas simultaneously: the target countries in Latin America and the whole Latin American region; the broader group of democratic countries worldwide and the main international organizations (such as the OAS and United Nations); and the United States domestic political system, with Congress as the focal point.

The communist strategy of indirect warfare—repeated in many previous victories—was to isolate the target government or governments (El Salvador or Guatemala, say) from regional, Western international, and, especially, U.S. support. And they attempted to do this by a relentless process of propaganda, deception, and diplomatic cunning, all of which was aimed at removing the legitimacy of the target governments in the eyes of the democratic world.

This concept of three arenas required those of us in the U.S. government to look ahead at least a year, anticipate the opportunities and risks in each arena, and then use our immense political and diplomatic resources to help our friends. We needed to plan and carry out political, diplomatic, and communications efforts to help build coalitions of support for the friendly target governments in the region (that is why the OAS meetings were so important) among the leading democracies and within the U.S. Congress. But whenever I would write up practical action steps to do this and give it to State or to McFarlane and Poindexter, they were never willing to use the president's authority to make something like this actually happen, even though he had issued general orders to do this.

In 1986 the major battle in Congress over Central America would again focus on the president's request that Congress approve funds to provide military support to the contras. Poindexter, now the NSC adviser, continued to work mainly with Oliver North and my successor Ray Burghardt in devising a plan to win the vote. For the third year in a row, I tried to be helpful by drafting (on one legal-size page) a plan of proposed actions for each of the twelve weeks until the time the vote was expected, the week of March 17–21, 1986. This plan suggested a series of activities and called for the president to go on television the week before the vote. I gave copies of this suggested plan to Oliver North, Ray Burghardt, Walt Raymond (the senior NSC public diplomacy person), Jacqueline Tillman, Otto Reich, and Richard McCormack. I also sent a copy to Elliott Abrams.

Since providing information to Congress in support of the president's policy was a "communications" issue, it was perfectly appropriate for me, under my new mandate, to propose this plan. But it seemed that North, Ray Burghardt, and Don Fortier would essentially be shaping the proposed strategy for Poindexter.

In late January I discovered that the State Department had written up its own plan and made a major mistake. As if driven by an unseen bureaucratic force, this involved another tilt toward Mexico.

The annual summit between President Reagan and President de la Madrid of Mexico took place on January 3, 1986. Just as before other U.S.-Mexican summit meetings, there were various news "leaks" from "informed sources" in the Mexican government suggesting that Mexico would become less active in Central America in order to concentrate more on "solving its internal economic crisis." Then, at the U.S.-Mexican summit, President Reagan once again offered significant economic help.

Only nine days afterward the Mexican foreign ministry—repeating its pattern of destructive activism on Central America after Mexico had obtained additional economic benefits from the United States—announced the "Carabellada Declaration" on Central America. This repeated the main elements of every Mexican "peace initiative," and all the defective Mexican-drafted Contadora treaties for Central America, including the immediate cessation of outside military aid to the Nicaraguan armed resistance and to the governments of Central America, with a promise (*another* promise) that the Sandinista regime would eventually take steps toward political pluralism. Most important, this Carabellada Declaration declared that the negotiating process "must result in the prompt signing of the Contadora Act for Peace and Cooperation"—the very flawed Mexican drafted treaty that the four friendly Central American countries had repeatedly rejected.

Mexico persuaded the other seven Contadora foreign ministers to sign this document, then took it to the inauguration of the newly elected president of Guatemala on January 14, 1986. This inauguration marked a major step forward for Guatemala. It was a victory for the forces of democracy in Guatemala and all of Central America, and it proved again that President Reagan's prodemocratic policy for the region was in tune with what the people in Central America really wanted.

Instead of letting this hopeful transition in Guatemala be the focus of the inaugural festivities, Mexico used the gathering of democratic presidents from all of Latin America as a propaganda platform to try to obtain additional endorsements for its destructive political settlement in Central America. Mexico successfully leaned on the new president of Guatemala to sign, and the Sandinistas were obviously eager to endorse the Carabellada Declaration. As a result, among the five Central American and eight Contadora mediating countries, Mexico succeeded in lining up ten against three—Costa Rica, Honduras, and El Salvador, whose leaders understood that this declaration in fact was a threat to democracy. Mexico then led a group of foreign ministers to Europe, where they obtained the endorsement of the European Economic Community.

On January 22, 1986, Congressman Michael Barnes, an articulate opponent of administration policy on Central America, and chairman of the House Foreign Affairs Subcommittee on the Western Hemisphere, endorsed this document. He sent it, along with a letter, to President Reagan and also sent copies to *all* members of the House and Senate.

When Barnes's letter to the president crossed my desk in late January, I immediately sent copies to Elliott Abrams, Richard McCormack, the NSC Latin American group, and Oliver North. I warned them that this letter suggested, to me, that the congressional Democrats would use the Carabellada Declaration as a major argument against aid to the freedom fighters. As in the Barnes letter, they would contend that "the Latin American countries"*also* oppose U.S. aid to the contras. Therefore, the State Department should mount a major diplomatic effort to obtain a counterdeclaration or clarification from a number of Latin American countries (as I had been suggesting in both the September 1985 and January 3, 1986, public diplomacy plans). There was no response.

In late January of 1986, only a few days later, I was shocked to read the State Department Latin American bureau's plan for "winning" the contra vote. Despite the new Mexican diplomatic activism against aid to the contras, the State Department plan called for Shultz to invite Mexico and the other seven Contadora foreign ministers *to Washington* on February 10 and *again* a week or so before the House vote.

I could hardly believe my eyes when I read this State Department document! I called to request an appointment with Abrams, who had assured me in the spring of 1985 that he would not fall into the Mexican trap of endorsing a false political settlement. After several days of delay his secretary told mine, "Mr. Abrams cannot meet with Dr. Menges, and will send him a letter explaining why."

Later, a senior State Department official told me that he had warned Abrams about the negative impact of this plan: "Elliott became very angry. He said, 'We have thought about this carefully. Shultz is going to invite Mexico and the others, and you keep out of it!' "

Once I heard that, I knew the Latin American bureau was still determined to go in the wrong direction and that they had persuaded Abrams to go along. Burghardt and North were clearly going along, too—they also had copies of the same State Department plan—so there was only one thing for me to do. I called Bill Casey on the secure telephone. I told him what State was planning, stressing that it would be a political setback for the president and that he should warn Shultz. Casey, who sounded pressed for time, simply said, "I'll have some of my people look into it." I also told Ikle and asked him to use his influence with Abrams to explain why this was a mistake.

As planned, Mexico and the other seven Contadora foreign ministers met with Shultz and Abrams on February 10, 1986. The next day's headline in *The Washington Post* was LATINS URGE U.S. TO HALT CONTRA AID. This same story also reported that "31 swing vote members of Congress expressed essentially the same position in a request to President Reagan last week . . . [and in another] letter to Reagan, 9 liberal Democratic senators yesterday said that the Carabellada Declaration initiative made this 'a particularly bad time' to request new aid for the Contras . . . it was signed by Senators Tom Harkin of Iowa, Claiborne Pell of Rhode Island, Christopher J. Dodd of Connecticut, Gary Hart of Colorado, Paul Simon of Illinois, Alan Cranston of California, Edward M. Kennedy, John F. Kerry of Massachusetts, and Patrick J. Leahy of Vermont."

Obviously the opponents of contra aid had their own plan to win the vote, and one element was these letters from forty Democratic senators and congressmen intended to discourage the administration from even requesting this military aid. The eight visiting foreign ministers from Mexico and the other Contadora countries were interviewed in the local and regional media, expressing their views against aid to the contras.

Following this negative public relations bombshell, Bill Casey became noticeably more interested in my concerns about the impact still to come from State's *plan for a return visit from the same eight countries—just before the vote in Congress.* Since Poindexter would go along with North and Burghardt, who were seemingly agreeing with State on this, there seemed little chance of getting an NSC meeting. I offered to draft a memo from Casey to Shultz summarizing the negative actions of Mexico and explaining why State would be making a major mistake by inviting Mexico and the other Contadora countries back just before the crucial vote in the House.

I then gave Casey a copy of the State Department plan. He was stunned. My draft memo also proposed a "constuctive diplomatic plan" to build a positive coalition among about fifteen to twenty Latin American countries to counterbalance the efforts of Mexico, Cuba, and Nicaragua.

In late February 1986 I met Casey and Judge William Clark at the Metropolitan Club. Briefly we discussed the misguided actions of the State Department on Central America, southern Africa, and in the strategic arms control negotiations. Later Casey redrafted my memo and sent his version to Shultz. Apparently that got results, because the State Department canceled its invitation for Mexico and the Contadora countries to return to Washington just before the contra vote.

During my brief chat with Casey and Clark, and later in a much longer discussion with Casey, I made the point that the president could win the contra vote if we learned from and avoided the mistakes of 1984 and 1985. This meant the State Department had to stop doing things like inviting the Mexican-led Contadora group to Washington and finally use its enormous resources in Washington and abroad in a systematic and coherent effort that matched Shultz's strong rhetoric. It also meant that the State Department, Poindexter, and the White House legislative staff had to stand firm for a "yes" or "no" vote.

Congressman Kemp and virtually all the leading House Republicans were telling the administration that this was the best way to obtain the 48 of the 253 Democratic votes needed to win. Finally I reminded Casey of my belief that had the president given a television speech on Central America in April 1985, we most likely would have won the vote. I urged Casey to raise the need for a speech with Don Regan—and if necessary the president. I told Casey that Poindexter was not likely to push hard on this if Don Regan was dubious, as he seemed to be. In our long conversation on this same topic, Casey said maybe he should send a letter making these points to his cabinet colleagues.

"Only someone like you who works on this full-time can keep the chronology and facts clearly in mind enough to see the patterns and suggest the lessons for the next round of efforts to win the vote," Casey said to me.

I agreed, saying, "The constant turnover in legislative liaison staff at State and the White House has made it hard for people there to have a sense for the political process on this issue. Besides, Elliott Abrams is new; this is his first time. Unfortunately he's kept Jim Michael as his top deputy, and Michael continually comes up with bad ideas on contra aid."

I offered to write a first draft of such a letter from him to his colleagues in the foreign policy cabinet. "That would be a help," Casey said.

I gave him a draft in mid-February, but I think he decided not to send it. However, shortly after this discussion I got a call from Casey's secretary, asking if I had a copy of "that sensitive letter you wrote in August 1985. The director would like to have a copy at once. May I send a courier to pick it up?" My hopes rose. Did this mean that Casey was now willing to take my letter to the president? Or was he going to use my factual summary to brief the president, maybe even to write his own letter? I said, "Certainly. I'll give a sealed envelope containing the item to your courier. Do you know why the director wants this?"

Betty Murphy replied cordially, "No, I'm just following orders to get a copy from you."

Some days later I would learn that a close friend of Casey and President Reagan had decided to write his own letter to the president. Apparently Casey gave him a copy of my letter in order to help him weave the facts together succinctly. The president's friend also wanted to warn the president about several foreign policy issues and problems with the foreign policy decision-making process.

I never saw that letter, but I was told it had been submitted to the president—but through Poindexter. This surprised me because the president's friend certainly had the ability to give the letter directly to Reagan. I later told this person that, unfortunately, I did not trust Poindexter to give his letter to the president, even if Poindexter had assured him he would do so. I admired this individual and respected his effort, but I felt that just like the president, he was too trusting. Did his letter ever get through? Only he, the president, and history could tell us. But I'd guess not, partly because I saw no change in how things were functioning. Two months later, when I again asked the president's friend whether it had reached "the coach" (our code term on the open phone line), he told me Poindexter had decided to "staff" this letter before giving it to President Reagan, a process that could stretch into months.

The days went by, and the crucial House vote was approaching. Our best estimate was that it would be in the third week in March. Although Casey had persuaded Shultz to scrap the return of Mexico and the other seven Contadora countries just before the vote, the State Department did not mount a diplomatic campaign seeking to persuade a majority of OAS members to affirm Nicaragua's continuing obligation to establish democracy and terminate its armed subversion.

In the second week of March, I had dinner with a friend and senior White House staffer who told me Poindexter was going to remove me as soon as the contra vote was won. He said, "Poindexter feels it is time for you to go, but he doesn't want to rock the boat until the vote is won."

I told my friend, "I guess it means Poindexter now feels he's close enough to Don Regan that he doesn't have to worry about any reaction from the Republicans in Congress. The funny thing is, he has the same timetable in mind as I do. Because if the freedom fighters vote is won, I'll feel I've done my best for five tough years, and I'll be ready to leave. But I don't want to be pushed out until that vote is won. Should I try to see Poindexter and make a deal?"

My friend grimaced: "Oh, no! You can't let anyone know you heard this. That would compromise the person who told me."

On March 12 Jack Kemp, chairman of the House Republican Conference, invited Elliott Abrams and me to come up to Capitol Hill and brief most of the 182 Republican members of the House. I was pleased to see that Abrams had brought with him excellent briefing material for each one of the Republican congressmen. That was a real step forward.

After Abrams's strong briefing, I gave mine, which consisted of the reasons to vote aid for the contras, plus the five main arguments against aid, along with answers to each. House Republican leader Robert Michel was so enthusiastic about my talk that he and Kemp asked me to write up a two-page version immediately. I did, and they gave it to every Republican House member. (Bob Michel wrote President Reagan a letter complimenting my briefing. Could it be that a White House friend helped prompt that letter as a way of suggesting to Poindexter that it would be risky to remove me?)

The vote was now scheduled for Wednesday, March 20, 1986. On the Monday before, Jack Kemp again urged the administration to insist on a "yes" or "no" vote and not to enter into a complicated compromise that would let the Democrats confuse the issue. With authorization from Poindexter, I was working in the House Republicans' tactical office headed by Congressman Trent Lott, just next door to the floor of the

House chamber, helping Dan Fisk, Frank Gregorsky, and other able staffers assemble a collection of about 40 one-page fact sheets on all the issues about Central America and Nicaragua that were likely to come up in the debate. Then, as we watched the intense and dramatic House debate on closed-circuit television, staff members would give relevant information to congressmen on the floor or the congressmen would come directly to us with their questions. This was a welcome contrast to the total lack of preparation in 1983.

Later that afternoon I was scheduled by the White House media office to give about six radio interviews to stations around the country. This could be done from any telephone, but I needed to have a quiet corner, so I asked Congressman Lott's secretary where I could find a room that wasn't noisy. She directed me to the large anteroom adjoining Bob Michel's Capitol office. I walked down the ornate hallways of the Capitol and opened the door.

The scene was like an oil painting. There sat Fawn Hall, typing away. Next to her was Oliver North dictating a memo, and to my right as I viewed the tableau, and apparently waiting for the copy, were Abrams, Don Fortier, and Don Regan's top legislative strategist. They were as surprised to see me as I was to see them.

I said a friendly "hello" and, as I recall, teased Fawn about not even getting a chance to get away from the word processor when she was visiting Capitol Hill. The I asked Ollie, "Are you writing the language for a compromise with the Democrats?" When he said yes, I added, "In my judgment this is a mistake. I believe Kemp and the other Republican leaders are correct—this should be a straight yes-or-no vote, to put the Democrats in Congress on record. A murky compromise will give some of the Democratic congressmen a pretext for voting against the president by saying the administration compromise didn't go far enough."

Ollie, whom I hadn't really talked to in months, got angry. "Well, we're still some votes short. And *we* all think this compromise is needed. What's more, Poindexter agrees. If this vote is lost, it's me and my marines who will have to go down and fight in Nicaragua. So I want to win this vote even more than you do."

I asked if I could read the compromise. "Sure," Ollie replied, "it's coming out of the printer now. Fawn, give Constantine a copy."

I read it and saw, somewhat to my surprise, that Ollie didn't seem to have gotten any wiser politically. This 1986 compromise stipulated that if the Sandinistas did three things (lifted the state of emergency; declared a cease-fire; and negotiated with the internal opposition), the administration would suspend aid to the armed resistance. But those three things could easily be simulated by the Sandinistas, and it would take many months and still be hard to *prove* they were faking.

So I said to Ollie and the group, "In my judgment, on this particular vote, any compromise is a mistake. But if you're going to have a compromise, you should specify certain additional actions that the Sandinistas would have to take, which we could independently verify." I recited them quickly (terminating all further importation of weapons; ending military support to communist guerrillas; closing the communist guerrillas' radio command centers in Nicaragua; Sandinista reaffirmation of their 1979 obligation to implement democracy; removing all Soviet bloc, Cuban, Libyan, and PLO operatives).

There was a dead silence. Obviously they had all made up their minds already. Discreetly I telephoned Casey, hoping he would call Poindexter—but Casey was away. So I began my radio interviews.

The next morning, as I was starting back to Congress for the second day of the debate, Poindexter's office called me with a curt message: "Stay off Capitol Hill for this vote." I asked why. "Poindexter's orders."

On Wednesday afternoon, March 20, 1986, I was at the White House with Ben Elliott, Peggy Noonan, and Dana Rohrabacher watching the final House debate on television. Tip O'Neill concluded the heated floor debate by giving his final reason for voting against President Reagan. He told the House that the foreign ministers of the most important Latin American countries all had visited Washington the previous month, and they too opposed U.S. aid for the contras. Then, with a dramatic flourish, Speaker O'Neill slowly named those Contadora countries: Mexico, Brazil, Argentina, Peru, Venezuela, Colombia, Uruguay, and Panama.

We watched with dismay as the president lost the vote.

The next day I sent Poindexter a memo entitled "Actions to Win the Freedom Fighter Vote." In it I told Poindexter I believed that with the systematic steps I was proposing, the president could still win the House's second vote, which Tip O'Neill had promised. I suggested to Poindexter that he work with Dole, Lugar, and other Republican Senate leaders to add six additional conditions to the compromise in the Republican-controlled Senate. My reasoning was that if the Republican Senate added my six requirements for the Sandinista regime, there was a chance that the final House-Senate compromise would keep six of the nine conditions and thus be realistic enough. But merely transferring to the Senate bill the totally inadequate and self-defeating compromise that

Poindexter, North, and the others had already agreed upon to the Senate bill meant that the House Democrats would likely weaken it even further in the final legislative bargaining (as had happened repeatedly since the first Boland amendment of 1982).

My memo also proposed public diplomacy actions in the region—to reassure friendly countries, build a supportive coalition of Latin countries, and persuade Mexico to modify its destructive activities. For the Congress and the U.S. public, I suggested increased communications efforts and repeated one simple idea I had often proposed before, assigning about eight to ten knowledgeable subcabinet officials who would each be responsible for providing information to about ten congressmen who were possible "swing votes" for the president. Over the next weeks each subcabinet person could offer to brief each of his or her assigned congressmen and be continuously available to answer their questions.

My memo to Poindexter also warned that we could expect the Soviet bloc and Cuba to increase military aid to the Sandinistas and "encourage every military effort to hammer at the freedom fighters while their hopes and morale are low due to the negative House vote."

I had no reaction from Poindexter or any of my colleagues to whom I sent copies. Not a word. A few days later the Sandinistas sprang to action. They sent invading troops across an international border in the hope of destroying several of the main contra base camps. This was a major military attack, involving thousands of Sandinista troops, with an additional five to ten thousand troops being moved into position for a potential follow-up. Obviously the communist Sandinistas hoped to finish off the contras before the House could vote again.

Ben Elliott proposed that the president call Congress back from its Easter recess and use the bold Nicaraguan military invasion of Honduras to dramatize the communist threat and thus help win a second vote. I am told that Pat Buchanan took the idea to Poindexter and Don Regan. Unfortunately, neither was willing to propose it to the president or urge an NSC meeting to discuss it. However, the administration did quickly provide U.S. helicopters to transport friendly troops to the border region, where they mopped up after the freedom fighters had inflicted heavy casualties on the invading Sandinista troops.

At just this crucial time, late March 1986, at the suggestion of the State Department and with the agreement of Poindexter, the president appointed retired foreign service officer Philip Habib as the new special presidential envoy for Central America. Habib had originally been one of the mentors of Michael Armacost, who now was under secretary for political affairs. Habib had held this same top policy job at State from 1976 to 1978—three years of setbacks for the free world.

In 1981 Habib had come out of retirement to serve as special envoy in the Lebanon crisis. I am told that in the spring of 1983 Habib assured Shultz that if Israel signed an agreement with Syria and withdrew its troops from southern Lebanon, Syria would do likewise, and peace would follow. Israel signed and withdrew its troops; but Syria did not, and much more violence followed instead.

Somehow this record of negotiating experience suggested to the State Department that Habib was the right person to become special envoy to the Philippines in late 1985 when the United States finally realized that the Marcos regime was in crisis. As it turned out, Marcos was the architect of his own demise: it was Mrs. Corazon Aquino and the Philippine people who brought about the democratic transition.

Now, in early April 1986, Habib was the new special presidential envoy to Central America. He did not know much about the region, and his other assignments clearly meant he had not been able to follow the details of Central American political or diplomatic events during the last few years.

When I heard about the Habib appointment, I wondered if President Reagan, or even Secretary Shultz, had the vaguest idea of the track record of this friendly, hardworking negotiator. Did they know that in 1979, after the Grenada communist coup in March and the Sandinista victory in July, he had served as senior adviser to Carter's secretary of state? I remembered that in July 1979, after the Sandinista victory, I met with Habib, both before and after his trip, to assess events in the Caribbean region. My recollection is that Habib dismissed my concerns that Sandinista-led Nicaragua would become a second Cuba. On his return Habib reportedly counseled the Carter administration to take a few preventive actions, but not to worry much about either Nicaragua or Grenada.

Now, in the spring of 1987, I decided it might be useful to Habib if I provided him with some information about Central America, including the president's policy favoring a genuine but opposing a defective political settlement. So on April 17 I was ushered into his State Department office. Habib seemed cordial and relaxed. I opened our conversation by saying, "Thanks for taking the time to see me. You may recall that the last time we met in the State Department was in the summer of 1979. You were assessing the impact of the new regimes in Grenada and Nicaragua for Secretary Vance and President Carter."

He smiled and said, "Yes, I do seem to remember that we chatted then. What's on your mind today?"

Briefly I mentioned that I had been working in the Reagan administration at CIA and NSC on Central America since 1981. Then I handed Ambassador Habib a briefing packet with a one-page outline and five attached tabs. These explained the president's policy and the pitfalls it faced.

Habib listened, glancing at each document as I described its contents. Then he said, "This is helpful. But you should know that Secretary Shultz made it clear in asking me to take this assignment that he of course wanted what you call a 'genuine political settlement' and that he fully supports the objectives of President Reagan."

"That's good news," I said. "But as somebody who has been involved with this issue daily for nearly five years, I can tell you that on more than one occasion the Department of State attempted to bring about political settlements which were contrary to the essential goal of President Reagan, which is that Nicaragua be a real democracy as agreed with the OAS in 1979."

"I don't know what you're talking about!" Habib shot back angrily. "Neither Shultz nor the State Department would act against the orders of the president."

"I would have thought that, too, except for my direct observation of a number of cases where the State Department tried. It was only stopped when President Reagan did so personally, by telling Shultz in essence: No, George, I don't want to do that. I want to remain with my policy."

My intention and hope had been to tell Habib one or two of these stories, very briefly, so he wouldn't wind up making the same mistake as his predecessor. But Habib wanted to end the discussion.

"As you know," he said, "I'm leaving for Central America tomorrow and have to prepare. My secretary has just told me my next appointment has arrived. You don't have to worry so much about the State Department. My job is to help Shultz and the president obtain a good settlement."

As I walked out of Habib's office, whom did I see waiting for him but William Walker, the career foreign service officer serving as deputy assistant secretary for Central America. Walker and I had seen each other at various public diplomacy meetings since he began the new job in the summer of 1985, but we had never talked. Someone who had served with Walker in his previous posting in Bolivia had described him to me as "one of the most left-wing foreign service officers." I never took such characterizations at face value. I had looked forward to chatting with Walker so I could draw my own conclusions. But he seemed to avoid me, and the months passed without our ever having a real conversation.

Today Walker seemed startled to see me. He said, "Constantine, I might have known you'd try to see Habib." It sounded as though Walker were concerned that I might have infected Habib with a dose of information about President Reagan's policy. All I could think of to say was, "Good morning."

Habib was planning to meet with the Central American leaders from April 18–28, 1986. There was a calendar of coming diplomatic events— mostly set by Mexico—that included the following:

- *May 8*, the inauguration of Oscar Arias Sanchez as the new president of Costa Rica (the oldest democracy in Central America); Arias had already told a U.S. television interviewer that he opposed U.S. military aid to the contras. Clearly Mexico would use this gathering of heads of state to propagandize for its phony treaty.
- *May 16*, the eight Contadora countries were to meet, and Mexico would probably urge more political and perhaps economic pressure on the four Central America democracies, pushing them to sign the phony treaty.
- *May 18–19*, the five Central American leaders would meet, and the likelihood was that Nicaragua, Guatemala, and now Costa Rica would try to pressure El Salvador and Honduras into signing the Contadora treaty.
- *June 6*, the eight Contadora countries and five Central American countries would meet with the likelihood that *eleven* (eight Contadora plus three Central American) of them would try to pressure El Salvador and Honduras to sign the defective Contadora treaty.

Speaker O'Neill had scheduled the promised second vote on contra aid to *follow* the expected treaty signing on June 6, 1986. Congressional Democrats who opposed aid to the contras obviously hoped to use the signed Central American "peace treaty" as the reason why aid to the armed resistance was no longer necessary or appropriate. They could say, "Let's give the peace treaty a chance to work." I had explained this to Habib. Yet the State Department seemed not to understand this. I was far more surprised that Ray Burghardt, Oliver North, and John Poindexter, who had all seen this same pattern in 1984 and 1985, still could not recognize, understand, or counter it in 1986.

In this political context it would be essential that Habib make clear to the four friendly Central American leaders he'd be meeting with that President Reagan was standing firm for a genuine settlement and would not want them to sign a false treaty. But did Habib do so?

A few days after my talk with Habib, Saul Singer, who worked for congressman Dan Burton, showed me an unclassified letter Habib had sent to three Democratic congressmen on April 11, 1986. It showed me why Habib had gotten so angry during our conversation. I had already been too late! This now infamous "Habib letter" had violated a key element of President Reagan's policy: it said that the United States would interpret the provisions of the draft Contadora treaty "as requiring a cessation of support of irregular forces . . . from the *date of signature."*
Once again the State Department had decided to pursue its own policy, even though President Reagan had made clear over and over again that U.S. aid to the Nicaraguan armed resistance would end *simultaneously* with the establishment of real democracy in Nicaragua and the verified termination of its aggression.

Habib had written his letter to Democratic Congressmen Barnes, Richardson, and Slattery. From their offices it had circulated quickly to Central America and was being touted by the Mexicans as proof that the Reagan administration was ready to endorse the signing of the draft peace treaty on June 6.

During the Easter congressional recess, House Speaker O'Neill had led a delegation of congressmen to several South American Contadora countries, where it was reported that they repeatedly lobbied the heads of state *against* President Reagan's Central American policy, in particular against aid to the contras. The U.S. ambassador in Argentina was shocked by the partisan behavior of these visiting congressmen during their meeting with that country's president. He described these actions in a cable that leaked to the press.

At the same time, Congressman Barnes and other congressional Democrats went to Panama, where they reportedly lobbied against President Reagan's policy with the Contadora and Central American leaders who were meeting there. I wondered if it ever occurred before in American history that members of one political party conducted their own foreign diplomacy opposing their president *while they were on tax-funded visits in foreign countries.*

All these events suggested, at the least, implicit tactical coordination among some congressional Democrats opposed to contra aid, and the Mexicans—both wanting a signed political settlement by June 6, 1986. Fortunately for the president and his policy, Jack Kemp understood what was happening. He and Congressman Dan Burton urged the House Republican leadership to invite Ambassador Habib to meet with them as soon as he returned from his Central American trip.

On April 29, 1986, House Republican leader Rober Michel, along with Congressmen Kemp, Burton, Cheney, and Hyde, spent an hour with Mr. Habib. As I heard it from Kemp himself shortly afterward, they were shocked by Habib's statements. Kemp told me, "Habib argued vigorously for a treaty to be signed by June 6, and, just as in his letter, he seemed not to understand that if aid to the contras were cut off first, there would be absolutely no chance of Nicaragua having real democracy. Furthermore, he doesn't understand the political war inside Nicaragua. He kept saying that even if Congress provided the aid requested by the president, 'the contras have no chance of winning.' "

Habib's attitude and judgments were definitely bad news. But the fact that Republican congressional leadership had heard this, and debated him themselves, was good news. Now the question was how to let the president know that the State Department was up to its old tricks? And how to do this in time to stop the steamroller that was building toward a false treaty on June 6?

There were two immediate difficulties. First, the president would be traveling to the economic summit of the seven industrial democracies in Tokyo from April 30 to May 9, 1986. Shultz, Poindexter, and Don Regan would be along with him. Second, Bill Casey would also be out of the country. Further, Casey and Secretary Weinberger were currently preoccupied with measures to prevent more Libyan terrorist attacks in the aftermath of our April 15, 1986, retaliatory bombing strike.

At the NSC Jacqueline Tillman tried to warn Poindexter about the implications of the Habib letter. Before Tillman could get Poindexter's attention on this, he was off to the economic summit with the president.

Air Force One was barely out of sight when my secretary got a call for me from retired Navy Captain Rodney McDaniel, Poindexter's right-hand man. He wanted to invite me to breakfast in the White House mess.

Terrific, I thought. Now that the NSC was a bit more quiet, I figured, he probably wanted to continue the discussion I'd initiated some months ago about a counterterrorism strategy. As usual, I was thinking positively.

Later that afternoon, however, I got a call from an aide to a Republican senator, who asked, "Have you heard the news?"

"What news?" I said.

He replied, "The State Department is so overjoyed about it that some people over there have been telling their Democratic friends in Congress, and word has even filtered over to this side of the aisle."

"What is it?"

After a pause for effect, he said, "Poindexter's navy buddy McDaniel is going to have breakfast with you so he can tell you 'your tour of duty at the NSC has ended.' Their plan is to remove you while the president is at the economic summit."

"Well," I said, startled by the news, "I guess I should consider it some kind of badge of honor that Poindexter is so concerned about congressional opposition to his removing me that he has to wait till the president is out of town and do it in a sneaky way."

The caller went on to say, "My senator is going to call McDaniel to find out if the story is true and, if so, to tell him and Poindexter not to do anything until the president is back in town."

Later that evening the same man called me at home and said his senator had talked to McDaniel, who had confirmed that the purpose of his breakfast with me was to inform me that my "tour of duty with NSC staff has been completed." McDaniel also told the senator that Poindexter, and not the Republicans in Congress, managed the NSC staff, a report of McDaniel's assertiveness that surprised me. Then the senator's aide told me that several senators were calling Poindexter in Tokyo to protest and to urge that he take no action until President Reagan returned to Washington. They wanted to be sure that the president knew about this before Poindexter made a final decision.

The next day, April 30, 1986, something happened that buoyed me. Thirty-one members of Congress, including thirteen senators and eighteen representatives, sent a letter to Admiral Poindexter. Their letter, which took a very constructive approach, delivered a clear message:

> As conservative Republican Members of the House and Senate, we sincerely appreciate the efforts you have made to forge stronger ties with the President's supporters on Capitol Hill.
>
> We believe it essential that a President of either party have at a senior level of the NSC staff competent foreign policy experts who share the President's political values and are independent of the career bureaucracies.
>
> Unfortunately, the NSC senior staff [today] is one in which career

government personnel (mainly State Department Foreign Service Officers) have the senior responsibility for the Soviet Union, Europe, the Middle East, Africa, Latin America and Asia—in fact, all parts of the world. Dr. Constantine Menges and Mr. Kenneth deGraffenreid are among the only Reagan appointees left on the senior staff.

We would urge that you remedy the current imbalance by appointing to the NSC senior staff more experts from outside the career government bureaucracies who combine foreign policy competence with proven support for President Reagan and his foreign policy principles and policies. We can assure you that such a shift would be both welcome and most appreciated by the President's strongest supporters in the Congress.

I was honored that these members of Congress had taken the time to write Poindexter on my behalf. And I was especially grateful to Congressman Dan Burton and his staffer, Saul Singer, and to Senator James McClure and his assistant, Jade West, for having taken the lead in writing this letter. I understood that these congressmen were interested in my situation, but more important they worried that unless the senior NSC staff had enough people who were competent, independent of the career bureaucracies, and supportive of the president, real power in foreign policy could not be exercised by the elected chief executive.

While this letter was in transit, I was told that my former colleague, Chris Lehman, who understood exactly why Poindexter wanted only career officials at the NSC, spoke at a Metropolitan Club luncheon of John Carbough's informal discussion group and urged the participants— all Reagan supporters—to mount a "campaign" to prevent my removal without the explicit knowledge and approval of the president.

I welcomed this battle because I thought that even if I were removed, it might at least alert the president that he needed more Reagan foreign policy experts in his administration. Our ranks hadn't just dwindled, they had been decimated. The previous January, a few weeks after his appointment as NSC adviser, John Poindexter had "reached out" to a number of conservative leaders and asked them to suggest competent, Republican foreign policy experts for his NSC staff. One of these, also a longtime friend of President Reagan, was pleased by Poindexter's overture and discreetly asked me to help compile a list of competent experts. I remembered writing the first draft while flying down to Miami at the end of January and then giving the home-typed list to this individual's associate in early February. My suggestion to him was that with the normal rotation of career government staff during the summer, Poindexter had five months to recruit competent people and arrange for the changes to occur in a dignified and considerate way. That way whichever career employees were replaced could leave on a "normal rotation" basis rather than being suddenly "expelled" back to their career agencies. But Poindexter did not hire any Reagan experts from outside the career agencies.

More important, I welcomed the May 1986 effort to keep me from being removed immediately because I felt that events were again building toward a false treaty, and that the president would *then* lose the contra aid vote. I wanted to stay long enough to see that vote won, at last.

And then an entirely different circumstance intervened. The morning after this news reached me, I was bending over to tie my shoelace when I heard a snap in my lower back. Instantly I felt great pain. First I tried to treat it with heating pads and by lying flat, but then I followed my doctor's advice and went to an orthopedist. This doctor took X rays and after studying them prescribed at least eight days "of rest with regular back exercises." The orthopedist urged me to take this seriously and said I should not be sitting at a desk.

In the first days of May I was stuck at home with my heating pad. As President Reagan returned from abroad, a mutual friend told me that Bill Clark had been trying to persuade Poindexter not to remove me. But Poindexter was adamant. Clark himself told me that Poindexter had said the president would be informed *before* there was any final decision to remove me.

On May 9, the day Poindexter returned from Tokyo, I sent him a personal letter. I mentioned the rumors about his wanting to remove me and said they'd given me the idea it might be a good time for me to come in and discuss my NSC future with him. I made it clear that if he decided to remove me from the NSC, I would not accept any offer to continue working elsewhere in the federal government but would return to private life.

To that letter I attached copies of a May 5 editorial and cartoon from the *Washington Times* protesting my rumored dismissal. The cartoon showed a wrapped bundle being carried out the back door of the White House *by mice,* and the caption read, "When the President's Away . . . The White House and State Department Accommodationists Will Play." The bundle they were carrying was labeled "Menges." (My young son asked, "Why are the mice carrying you?")

The accompanying editorial read:

With the boss out of town, what better time to knock off an old enemy? . . .

If you wanted to see what Mr. Reagan was going to do before he did it, you could read Mr. Menges. It was long before Mr. Reagan made his famous "Star Wars" speech that Mr. Menges wrote, in October 1978, of the need for a strategic defense. Mr. Menges also gave plenty of warning about the true nature of the Sandinistas, spelling it all out before the Sandinistas even took charge.

Congressional Republicans want Mr. Menges to stay, and word is that their discontent will be made known to the President.

I was told that several congressmen had talked with Poindexter in Tokyo and protested the rumored action.

While this was going on in Washington, Vice President Bush traveled to Costa Rica on May 8 to represent the United States at the inauguration of the newly elected president. This was an important trip because the new Costa Rican president, Oscar Arias Sanchez, had declared that he opposed U.S. aid to the Nicaraguan armed resistance. That remark had been welcomed by the congressional Democrats who opposed aid to the contras. If I had been helping to brief Vice President Bush for this trip, I probably would have tried to urge him to reaffirm the president's Central American policy with each head of state he met. I would also have urged him *not* to endorse the Habib letter.

But Vice President Bush, believing the State Department, unintentionally added to the Mexican momentum for a false treaty by stating publicly in Costa Rica, "The terms of the letter sent to Congress . . . by Ronald Reagan's personal envoy in the Central American crisis, Philip Habib, are endorsed at the highest level of my government" (FBIS, VI, 12 May 1986, p. A1).

On May 10, 1986, I wrote Poindexter my last memo as a member of the Reagan administration. I reviewed the misfortunes that had followed since the Mexican-inspired Carabellada Declaration of January 12, 1986, and warned of coming events that could culminate in a defective treaty on June 6, a treaty that could still be avoided. After recommending eight specific actions, I also attached a copy of the April 11, 1986, Habib letter.

There was no reply of any kind from Poindexter, North, or Burghardt, all of whom were sent copies.

On Sunday, May 11, Bill Casey returned from his trip, and I went over to his home that evening. I gave him a copy of my unclassified "final memo" to Poindexter and told him he would recognize the proposed action steps from my memos of January, February, and March. I told

Casey the president could win the vote if the administration really tried *and* if there were no false political settlement on June 6. I urged Casey to seek an NSC meeting to bring the president up-to-date and have him repudiate the "Habib letter," which was being used by Mexico.

I also brought Casey up-to-date on my personal situation, giving him copies of the *Times* editorial and cartoon. When he saw the cartoon he laughed, and said I was welcome anytime to come back to the CIA. I thanked Casey, but I told him what I'd written to Poindexter: if my time at the NSC were up, I *would* resign from the federal government.

Casey was concerned about everything I'd told him, but he didn't say whether or not he'd try to get an NSC meeting with the president. Meanwhile, Jack Kemp said the House Republican leaders had to alert the president about the implications of the Habib letter and about the depth of Habib's misunderstanding of U.S. policy.

Kemp then made an important and courageous decision. On Tuesday, May 12, 1986, he took a copy of the Habib letter along to the Republican leaders' meeting with President Reagan in the Cabinet Room. At the end of the regular discussion, Kemp reached across the table and gave President Reagan a copy of the Habib letter and asked, "Mr. President, does this letter from your special envoy correctly reflect your Central American policy?"

There was a hush as President Reagan read the letter and then said with obvious determination, "Absolutely not!" He then went on to reiterate his policy.

I am told that Poindexter was startled by the question and that Shultz became visibly angry after the president's response. Looking at Kemp, Shultz said, "Of course, negotiations are part of our policy." Kemp replied that everyone favored negotiations but the Habib letter seemed to show the State Department was not pursuing the president's negotiating *objectives*. He urged Reagan to convene an NSC meeting so that he could be informed of the international and State Department pressures being exerted for an inadequate treaty in order to prevent it.

That same day political columnists Rowland Evans and Robert Novak tried to alert the president by publishing in *The Washington Post* a column entitled, "A Box Called Contadora," which started with these words: "Angry voices were raised when House Republican leaders told Ambassador Philip Habib behind closed doors April 29 that his pursuit of the Contadora process was a sellout of the contras and could make the U.S. hostage to phantom Sandinista 'reforms.' "

The next morning, Wednesday, May 14, 1986, Senator Jesse Helms, chairman of the Latin American subcommittee of the Senate Foreign Relations Committee, personally gave President Reagan a letter to alert him to the situation. Later, Senator Helms told me that when President Reagan read his brief letter (which warned about the Habib letter and suggested four steps to prevent a false treaty), the president said he was now aware of the problem and "would take care of it."

That same day the *Washington Times* carried a story describing the House Republican leaders' concerns about the dangers of a "phony treaty," which resulted from their meeting with Ambassador Habib. Jack Kemp was quoted as stating that Mr. Habib "is saying one thing, and the President is saying another."

Also on that day the *Washington Times* ran another editorial about my personal situation, which it entitled "Selling Out the President."

> Constantine Menges goes back to work today, contrary to the best-laid plans of mice and men. He was to have been bagged during the president's trip to the Orient, possibly to spare Mr. Reagan the pain of seeing one of his brightest, most loyal supporters stabbed in the back, but Mr. Menges managed to wriggle clear of his assassins until the president's return.
>
> With the aid to the Nicaraguan resistance still in doubt, the president needs this man's skills acutely. . . .
>
> If Mr. Menges's enemies succeed, Mr. Reagan will leave office with Communist governments firmly in place in Nicaragua and Afghanistan. . . . By his stubborn advocacy of the president's policies, Constantine Menges has done his part to prevent such a calamity, making bitter enemies thereby. Ronald Reagan should not count himself among them.

Seeing my name in print so prominently was quite a new experience for me. On May 4 former UN Ambassador Kirkpatrick had published the first warning that the State Department seemed to be abetting negotiations in both Central America *and* Afghanistan that would produce settlements contrary to the president's policy. On May 12 Senator Gordon Humphrey published an op-ed piece entitled "Fears of an Afghan Sellout" in the *Washington Times*. He said:

> The president has been badly served by the State Department, which has given its blessing to these negotiations that do not meet the criteria he laid down in his speech to the United Nations and which in December reversed the previous U.S. position by offering to act as a "guarantor" of a settlement the final terms of which are still unknown.

I took copies of these articles to Bill Casey and told him it seemed to me that Senator Humphrey was correct: although Casey had helped the president to define a sensible negotiating approach in the October 1985 speech to the United Nations, the State Department seemed to be proceeding along the lines of its formula—*which the president had rejected.*

Meanwhile Dr. Fred Ikle, under secretary of defense, released a public report entitled "Prospects for Containment of Nicaragua's Government." The report asked one basic question: If the proposed Contadora treaty were signed by all five Central American governments, and the Sandinista regime remained, what would be the cost and likelihood of containing it? This report summarized the systematic communist violations of four post–World War II peace agreements. It then said that if communist Nicaragua acted in the future as it had since 1979, containment could only work if Honduras and Costa Rica "permit the stationing of sizeable numbers of U.S. and/or allied troops in their territory" and "agree to embarking on a massive restructuring of their armed forces." Then, to reduce and ultimately cut the flow of Nicaraguan military aid to the regional communist guerrillas, the report estimated a first-year cost for air, land, and sea surveillance and interdiction of about *$8.7 billion* with annual costs of about *$9 billion* and the commitment of one hundred thousand troops in the countries bordering Nicaragua. The Defense Department report concluded that "even with a major commitment of the U.S. and its allies . . . containment . . . likely would only be partially effective."

This report represented the first time some of the consequences of a false treaty had been clearly spelled out, and the reaction was sharp and dramatic. The congressional Democrats opposing the administration's policy denounced it, but that was to be expected. What was unprecedented was the statement by Under Secretary of State Michael Armacost, who dismissed the report as unofficial and unauthorized. Under Secretary of Defense Ikle stated that it was an official statement of the U.S. government that had been cleared by an interagency committee that had included the State Department. I wondered whether Habib would need to be diverted from Central America to arrange a peace treaty between State and Defense!

While all this was swirling about, I asked for an appointment to see Admiral Poindexter. I wanted to discuss all these rumors regarding my apparently imminent dismissal—but Poindexter didn't answer my letter or my request for a meeting.

In the hallway I ran into Ollie North, whom I hadn't seen in months.

"Constantine, those reports about your leaving are bad news," he said with what looked like a perfectly sincere expression. "I want you to know that I'm using all my influence with Poindexter to tell him the NSC needs a strategic thinker like you."

That sounded great, but by this point I knew Ollie well enough to know that he would tell me the same thing even if he was doing *nothing* on my behalf. So I simply said, "Thanks for your interest." I changed the subject by telling him about Kemp's action, and I urged him to encourage Poindexter to hold an NSC meeting.

A few days after this talk with North, a mutual friend on the White House staff told me he had asked Ollie to use his influence with Poindexter to keep me on. North had said to him, "I think it's time for Constantine to return to being a private citizen and scholar. He can do more good for the cause from the outside, because there are so few people who speak and write as effectively as he does."

On Friday, May 16, 1986, there was an NSC meeting, and once again President Reagan saved his own policy. He rejected the Habib approach. A new NSDD was written that reaffirmed his standing policy and ordered several actions. The result: the political momentum in Central America for a false treaty slowed and then stopped.

(After this NSC meeting a State Department official is reported to have told *The New York Times*, "on background," that Habib's letter was an "unauthorized" departure from policy. The grapevine said Habib responded by telling the press on background that the Latin America bureau had not merely approved the so-called Habib letter, but had actually *written* it.)

On June 6 the four democratic Central American countries once again rejected the defective treaty drafted by Mexico. The White House took the lead in a major effort to provide information to Congress. On June 24 the president gave a superb speech about Central America on national television. The next day the House of Representatives voted (221–209) to provide $100 million in military and other support to the freedom fighters of Nicaragua. This was a major positive step for the cause of democracy and peace since the Republican-controlled Senate was with the president on this issue.

On the same day the president again saved his own policy (May 16), I was sent two brief notes from the NSC administrative staff. The first, from NSC Executive Secretary Rodney McDaniel, was two lines long: "Dear Dr. Menges: Your tour of duty with the National Security Council Staff has been completed."

The second was from the NSC administrative assistant. It instructed me to turn in my building pass, beeper, and parking permit—"immediately"—and to vacate my NSC office.

And then, a few minutes after 5:00 P.M. on the same day I received my notice to vacate, the NSC administrative assistant sent a crew of workers to "secure" my office by changing the locks and the combination to the safe. (The next week this was rescinded, and I was given some weeks to go through my files and have an orderly departure.)

On Sunday, May 16, I met with Ambassador William Wilson, an old friend of the president's and a fellow Californian. Since the ambassador was going to be meeting with the president the very next day, I asked him to tell Mr. Reagan that Poindexter was in the process of removing me. I told Ambassador Wilson that Poindexter had assured Judge Clark that the president would be told in *advance* of my actual removal. I added that I simply didn't believe this had yet occurred.

That Monday afternoon after his meeting with the president, Ambassador Wilson told me that Poindexter and Don Regan had also been in the meeting, so he only got to mention my situation at the end, as he and the president were walking together toward the door of the Oval Office.

"Was there any reaction?" I asked.

"Yes," said Bill Wilson. "The president looked totally surprised and said he hadn't known about this."

PART FOUR

REFLECTIONS

12

THE LESSONS NOT LEARNED

My last day with the Reagan administration was July 4, 1986—just days after the House of Representatives voted in favor of President Reagan's request for $100 million to help the armed resistance of Nicaragua. That event made me much more hopeful and optimistic about the future in Central America and Mexico. At least in this part of the world, right on our southern border, the United States would be able to help its friends defeat communism and thereby have real peace and the opportunity for democracy and prosperity.

I felt a sense of satisfaction with my five years of public service. I had done my best for my country. And I had helped assure that the foreign policy decisions of President Reagan were not undermined or countered by those in the administration who thought their foreign policy was better for the country than the president's. Again the false political treaty had been stopped—this time thanks to Jack Kemp and the president's good instincts. This was the *seventh* time I had been the catalyst to bring this misguided maneuvering to Reagan's attention. Despite the combined efforts of the State Department, the isolationist Democrats in Congress, the Mexicans misleading the Contadora seven, and the pressures on the Central Americans from Cuba and Nicaragua, once Reagan again reaffirmed his support for real democracy in Nicaragua there was an end to the political momentum that had been building for the defective treaty.

Since the Democrats in Congress did not have the pretext of that Central America treaty in early June 1986, they had to vote yes or no on aid to the Nicaraguan freedom fighters. Fortunately enough Democratic congressmen voted to support their president and stop the Soviet-backed communist regime in Nicaragua sooner rather than later. This is exactly what Chris Lehman and I, along with Jack Kemp and other Republican congressmen, had told McFarlane and Poindexter would happen if they would only take firm action to stop State Department preemptive concessions from undermining Reagan's policy both in Central America and Congress.

I was pleased to be a private citizen again. My deep concern about the need to expose and encourage the reform of the subculture of deception and manipulation within the executive branch, which I experienced for five years, led me to begin writing this book in the summer of 1986.

At the same time I needed to earn a living and wanted to work on two foreign policy issues that I believed needed much more thought and attention and which had interested me for many years: transitions to democracy abroad and how the United States can encourage and support the success of democratic institutions; and the impact on the U.S.-Soviet global balance of the success or defeat of the freedom fighter movements. I wrote two proposals for books on these issues.

Naturally I knew that it would take some time before either of these research proposals might receive funding from a foundation. And I also knew that I needed such foundation support because of the financial stringency faced by the few public policy research organizations in Washington that might welcome my affiliation. (I guessed that my foreign policy views would preclude most of the liberal think tanks from being interested in my skills.)

As a middle-income person from a family of modest means and without a university professorship, law practice, or business awaiting my return, I faced the future with some financial uncertainty. During my years at the White House, I had often felt that my standing up for the president and his policy might well cost me my job any day (and it did, but it took longer than I expected). For that reason my family had saved for this "rainy transition." And my talented wife, a social worker in the prevention of child abuse, provided some income through her part-time work.

As matters turned out, I was fortunate in almost immediately having the opportunity to do analytic writing on foreign policy part-time for a small think tank. My former White House colleague Donald Eberle was executive director of the Fund for an American Renaissance. He had established a pleasant and collegial place to work. Then during the first months of 1987 I worked full time to write and complete this book.

In mid-1987 at the invitation of Christopher DeMuth, the new president of the American Enterprise Institute, I joined their foreign policy program headed by Ambassador Jeane Kirkpatrick. I was very happy to be working with Jeane again, as well as with other new arrivals—Allan Gerson, Joshua Muravchik, Richard Perle, and Alan Keyes—who joined AEI's group of first-rate scholars and thinkers. And I felt extremely fortunate that the Bradley Foundation had decided to support a program of foreign policy studies that would give me the opportunity to write both books I had outlined in my proposals.

In November 1986 the central issue of this book—how the president can truly govern in foreign policy—was raised in the most public and dramatic fashion by two events: the Iran-contra affair and the Arias "peace plan" for Central America.

IRAN-CONTRA

In early October 1986 Patricia Ellis, a producer with the *MacNeil-Lehrer NewsHour,* called and asked if I would appear that evening to discuss the capture of an American citizen shot down while delivering arms to the armed resistance inside Nicaragua. I was pleased to be called because I felt it important for the media to have some balance in their commentary on foreign policy. And before the Sandinista takeover, the *MacNeil-Lehrer NewsHour* was one of the few TV programs willing to give me a chance to express my view that this was a communist movement that would establish a second Cuba.

"Pat," I said, "I'd be willing to come on the program. Can you tell me a little more about the facts?"

After getting her information I checked the newspapers and then called Oliver North. I assumed that as the liaison between the NSC and the contras since 1983 he would know something about this private air support operation and might be able to give me some helpful background.

Like nearly everyone else in the executive branch working on these issues, I knew that the contras were North's account—he made that very clear. We knew that Ollie was the contact point between the U.S. government and the leadership of the Nicaraguan resistance—and we assumed he used his enormous energy to keep their morale up and help them understand that ultimately President Reagan would be able to persuade enough Democrats in Congress to vote for full military aid.

Fawn Hall answered the phone.

"Hello, Fawn," I said. "This is a voice from the past."

Friendly and efficient as always, Fawn said, "Constantine, Ollie isn't here, but his deputy, [Lieutenant Colonel] Bob Earle, can tell you about the airplane that was shot down."

I had met Bob Earle in June when saying good-bye to Ollie. Both Ollie's deputies in the new counterterrorism unit were military officers. Bob Earle got on the phone and told me this was a "private resupply effort having no connection to the United States government."

That night on *MacNeil-Lehrer* I explained that this aircraft had likely been part of a private operation to help the Nicaraguan armed resistance. I guessed it was financed by donations from people and foreign governments that understood how a communist Central America and Mexico would damage our security and therefore endanger them also. My debating partner was adamant that this looked like a typical U.S. covert operation: he noted that all the aircraft crew had formerly been in the U.S. military. He went on to repeat the charge that helping the contras was illegal and an act of war.

I replied that it was communist Nicaragua that had initiated aggression against its neighbors in 1979; the contras had begun operating in 1982 and were a legitimate defensive countermeasure that fell within the right of self-defense provided for in article 51 of the UN charter.

I added what I thought was a telling point: since documents suggested the unfortunate crew members who had died were connected with the Southern Air Transport Company, this could not possibly be a CIA operation. Any CIA person would know that Southern Air Transport had long ago been a CIA company and had been publicly identified as such. It had been sold to private owners in the mid-1970s. Therefore, I suggested no CIA operation would now use Southern Air Transport.

In early November a producer with ABC television news telephoned and asked me to comment on a wire story from Lebanon that Robert McFarlane had flown to Iran with weapons to exchange for hostages. He was also reported to have brought along a Bible and a cake. My first reaction was that it was a joke. My second that this was anti-American propaganda being published by some Lebanese faction. I said something like "It sounds very unlikely to me. I can't imagine President Reagan authorizing the shipment of weapons to Iran, and it seems almost inconceivable that McFarlane or anyone else would do this without presidential approval. All I can say is I hope it isn't true, and I'll be watching your news reports."

As we now know, it was true. On November 13 President Reagan confirmed the news reports in a television speech. On November 19 he was questioned at a press conference. After both those appearances I told Nancy, "I believe Reagan is telling us what he thinks to be true, but I don't think Poindexter is giving him the straight facts."

Nancy replied, "If I were Mrs. Reagan, I'd be very angry at seeing my husband so ill prepared for the press conference. I'd want to know what's really going on."

From the first days of November 1986, when the story of military sales to Iran was confirmed by administration sources, there was a bipartisan storm of outrage and concern. Could this president so opposed to terrorism and its sponsors and opposed to negotiations with terrorists have traded weapons for hostages? Was the president telling the truth when he said that this was not an arms-for-hostages deal? Rather, the administration explained initially that the military sales to Iran (both direct and those authorized through Israel) were for "one planeload of defensive weapons" that were part of a new political initiative aimed at exploring whether more normal relations could be restored with Iran. Administration sources also tried to paint this effort as possibly helping to end the long war between Iraq and Iran.

McFarlane published an op-ed article in *The Washington Post* that compared the administration's alleged political opening to Iran with the Nixon administration's opening to communist China. He said that a third country first proposed this in the spring of 1985, and that he felt President Reagan had made the right decision to pursue it starting in August 1985. As I read this and listened to the initial explanation from the administration, I had the same reaction as most leaders, citizens, and members of the media.

It might well have been a sensible idea to explore a political opening to Iran. But selling weapons as the first step? That seemed wrong. There was bipartisan consensus that if Iran defeated Iraq, it would accelerate its direct and indirect aggression against the fragile and vulnerable Persian Gulf oil states. If that resulted in hostile anti-Western, pro-Iranian regimes taking command of even more oil resources, it would only bring increased violence and death to the region, as had already been amply demonstrated by the situation in Iran since 1979.

Ironically, my August 6, 1985, letter to the president had used Iran as one example of the need for a counterstrategy. I had written the president: "The Soviet Union has wanted to dominate (Iran) since 1920. . . . While the Soviets are working very hard to 'turn' Iran, we are doing much too little to help the pro-Western Iranian groups prepare and organize for the opportunity to bring a moderate and friendly government to that country. This lack of timely and adequate help to pro-Western groups is repeated in nearly all the vulnerable countries." Since Islam and the West can and have coexisted for decades, while communism persecutes Islam (with brutality in Soviet Central Asia and Afghanistan), a competent *political* strategy could well bring normal relations in the *post*-Khomeini era.

It seemed evident from the facts that the shipment of weapons had been connected to the release of American hostages. Most Americans had agreed with the Administration's repeated statements that providing direct or indirect payments to terrorists or their sponsoring governments would only increase the risks to the millions of American citizens traveling and living abroad.

Knowing the people involved for the administration, my initial hunches were that the Iran military sale may have had a double purpose— promoting normalization and freeing American hostages—but that Poindexter and North had begun to focus on the tactical objective of getting the hostages out. Word was spread immediately by the State Department that Shultz had opposed this—and I believed it. (Many weeks later it became clear that Weinberger too had opposed this initiative.)

The issue of military sales to Iran by itself raised important questions about the judgment of Ronald Reagan and his administration. The media naturally probed for ever fuller disclosure, and there were questions about credibility and veracity, but it is likely that the issue would not have become a major scandal that threatened Reagan's presidency without a startling new revelation.

I had just returned from speaking on U.S.-Soviet relations at a University of Chicago program in which George Shultz and former CIA Director William Colby also participated. The next morning I attended the weekly breakfast hosted by Sam Dickens of the American Security Council. After the meeting I pointed out a new revelation to Sam Dickens in the morning press: Southern Air Transport had apparently been used to ship some of the weapons to Iran. That made me start wondering, and I said to Sam: "I hope this isn't so, but I wonder if North found a way to use some of the money from the Iran weapons sales to support the resistance in Nicaragua. If he linked two operations like that, it would be contrary to the need for compartmentation and secrecy. It would be hard to be sure that the Iranians wouldn't reveal this to the Soviets or even the Nicaraguans, since the Iranian government is helping the Sandinistas. And it would be a political bombshell that would hurt the president and the absolutely essential program of helping the Nicaraguan resistance.''

Sam looked at me and said quietly, ''I hope North didn't do *that*.''

I went to my office. Two hours later our next-door neighbors, Peter Flaherty and Ken Boehm, the dedicated and talented leaders of Citizens for Reagan, told us that Attorney General Meese was about to hold a White House press conference on the Iran military sales.

With his customary poise and fluency, Meese announced at that press conference on November 25, 1986 that the president had asked him to undertake a fact-finding investigation of the military sales to Iran. He and a small team had been working for several days. They had discovered that Admiral Poindexter and Lieutenant Colonel North of the NSC staff had known about and directed the diversion of money from the Iranian military sales to help the armed resistance in Nicaragua. Admiral Poindexter had resigned, and North had been dismissed.

That *was* a political bombshell for the administration. This new information set four investigations in motion. These captured the attention of political Washington, the media, and significant portions of the American public, especially during the televised congressional hearings held in the summer of 1987.

From the start the administration said that the president had not known about the diversion of monies to the Nicaraguan resistance. Naturally Nancy and my friends, along with many journalists, asked me what I thought. To Nancy and very close friends I said that I believed the president did not know, and that most likely this was North's idea. To the many members of the press who called I repeated my guess that the president did not know—I believed that he would never have permitted such an operation, since he would have understood it would endanger the political constituency in Congress for aiding the Nicaraguan resistance. But to the journalists I refused to comment, on the record or off, about the motivations or actions of my former NSC colleagues. I said that I would be looking at the facts and would write my own views in due time.

From the start of this revelation *by the administration,* I was deeply worried that the diversion would be used by the Democrats in Congress as an argument for disapproving further aid to the Nicaraguan resistance in 1987–88. My honest feeling—and a comment I made frequently in my media appearances and to journalists—is that "the president's policy in Central America, including support to the Nicaraguan resistance, has been correct and has been working. If some individuals acted improperly, they have to be held accountable, but it doesn't invalidate the policy." Sometimes I would go on to make a comparison: "Our Medicare program spends tens of billions annually. If some public officials or some doctors or some patients use Medicare benefits improperly, we don't call for the termination of this public program."

The investigations began. On the day of his dramatic disclosure, Attorney General Meese requested that an independent counsel (also called the "special prosecutor") examine the Iran-contra issues to determine whether criminal charges should be brought against any of the participants. That investigation continues. In December the Senate Select Committee on Intelligence held hearings behind closed doors. Poindexter and North refused to testify or comment then or until the summer of 1987, when they were granted immunity from prosecution for anything revealed during their testimony. They were exercising their constitutional rights against self-incrimination and their silence only spurred media interest. McFarlane, however, did voluntarily testify under oath during December.

Tragically, in December 1986, on the day before he was to appear before the Senate Select Committee on Intelligence, William Casey was rushed to Georgetown University Hospital. The medical announcement said that he had a cancerous brain tumor. I felt deep sadness and prayed for him.

I called Betty Murphy at CIA headquarters and asked: "How serious is it?"

"I can't tell you more than the newspapers," she replied, "but brain tumors are always serious."

"Would it be possible for me to bring a get-well note and a small box of chocolates by the hospital this evening, and perhaps chat with Bill before he has surgery in a few days?"

Betty promised to check.

Soon after, she called me at home and said: "Mrs. Casey says it's fine for you to come by, but she doesn't know if the director will be able to see you. CIA security knows you and is expecting your visit."

As I drove to the hospital I thought about the last time I had seen Bill Casey. Nancy and I were invited to a surprise birthday party for Arnaud de Borchgrave, which his lovely and charming wife, Alexandra, had arranged. Right after we had chatted with Jack and Joanna Kemp,

Sophia and Bill Casey came in. It was late October, just before the crisis began. Bill looked terrific and was having a wonderful time. I told him that he hadn't heard from me (except on one matter in September) because I knew how busy he was, and my rule was not to call government officials. He said something like "I'm always interested in what you have to say, so do send me your articles; I want to read them."

When the crisis broke I worried about its effects on the president, its implication for our foreign policy, and its consequences for Bill Casey. But my experience with him told me that he was too devoted to our institutions and too politically savvy about Congress to have agreed with or participated in such a diversion.

I walked down the hospital hallway hoping to be able to say a few words of friendship. The CIA security staff—always courteous and alert—told me, "Unfortunately, the director is sleeping now. He knew you were coming and thanks you. We'll give him your note and gift." After his operation I was told he was not receiving visitors; I would not see William Casey alive again.

The third investigation was the Tower Commission convened by the president to study the functioning of the NSC staff and document the facts about the Iran-contra activities. Its report was issued in February 1987 and included a great deal of documentary information from NSC memoranda as well as from the computerized professional office system (prof). This prof system permitted individuals to write highly classified as well as informal notes directly to each other. By using their office computer typewriters and code words, they believed that only the intended recipient could ever read that material.

It was a cold winter's day in February 1987 as I listened on television while the Tower Commission presented its report. It did not find that the president had known of the diversion. It did not propose major new legislation to change the NSC staff. It was highly critical of McFarlane and Poindexter's leadership. And among other findings, it said there had been much too little opportunity for a full hearing before the president made major decisions: "The National Security Adviser failed in his responsibility to see that an orderly process was observed," and "The NSC system will not work unless the President makes it work."

In early January 1987 the Senate and House both set up special committees to investigate the Iran-contra matter. Later these were merged into a single joint committee. Public testimony, nationally televised, began on May 5 and continued through August 3, with twenty-eight public witnesses providing more than 250 hours of testimony. All together the commission and its staff interviewed more than five hundred witnesses and reviewed more than three hundred thousand documents furnished by the executive branch (Iran-contra report, p. xv).*

On November 17, 1987, the select committees issued their final report. Nearly seven hundred pages long, it was divided into two sections: the majority report of the Democratic members and several Republicans and the minority report by eight Republican senators and congressmen. The majority report was critical of the administration and its officials, including the president, but on the central question of whether the president authorized the diversion of money to the contras, it accepted Poindexter's testimony that "he shielded the president from knowledge of the diversion" (Iran-contra Report, p. 21).

The report of the Republicans, while also critical of the administration and the key participants, had a very different tone. It said that "the mistakes of the Iran-contra affair were just that—mistakes in judgment and nothing more. There was no constitutional crisis, no systematic disrespect for the 'internal rule of law,' no grand conspiracy. . . ." On the central political issue, this Republican dissent said: "The evidence shows that the president did not know about the diversion. . . . This evidence includes a great deal more than just Poindexter's testimony. Poindexter was corroborated in different ways by the president's own diaries and by testimonies from North, Meese, Commander Paul Thompson (formerly the NSC's general counsel), and former White House Chief of Staff Donald Regan." This dissenting report also criticized the majority report, calling it "not a fair description of events, but an advocate's legal brief that arrays and selects so-called 'facts' to fit preconceived theories. Some of the resulting narrative is accurate. A great deal is overdrawn, speculative. . . ." (Minority Report, pp. 437–38.)

From my knowledge of the people and the NSC process, I had guessed correctly: the president had not been told. And that is precisely what I had tried to warn the president about in my August 6, 1985, letter. Reagan gave a speech after the end of the Iran-contra hearings and said exactly what I think any president would believe:

---

* Select Committee of the House and Senate, *Report of the Congressional Committees Investigating the Iran-Contra Affair*, Washington, D.C., 1987 (hereafter the majority report will be cited as Report, and the minority report as Minority Report, with page numbers).

The Admiral testified that he wanted to protect me; yet no President should ever be protected from the truth. No operation is so secret that it must be kept from the Commander in Chief. I had the right, the obligation, to make my own decision. (Ronald Reagan address to the nation, August 12, 1987)

THE ARIAS PLAN

Just days after the end of the televised Iran-contra hearings in August 1987, President Reagan faced a major foreign policy decision. George Shultz and Chief of Staff Howard Baker were most likely telling him that by doing as they suggested, he would make a political breakthrough for the administration and for the cause of democracy and peace in Central America.

But Jack Kemp was urgently trying to reach the president to warn him not to take Shultz's advice. Would Kemp get through? What would the president do?

To understand this fateful moment of decision, we need to go back a few months. In early January 1987 Frank Carlucci took over as the new NSC adviser. I was hopeful that his extensive foreign policy experience and his close relationship with Weinberger would help Carlucci restore a fair decision-making process. And since Carlucci had been deputy CIA director during the Carter administration and had seen the Sandinistas deceive the OAS, I hoped he and Weinberger would counterbalance Shultz on Central America.

In January 1987 Kemp had written the president a personal letter to warn him that "the 'neo-isolationists' in Congress and 'detentists' in the State Department think they see an opportunity now to pursue their own agenda, thus undermining the Reagan Doctrine and reversing your realistic approach to relations . . . [with] the Soviet Union." Specifically Kemp had warned Reagan about four potential setbacks: a long delay of SDI, unwise arms control agreements with the Soviets and "false settlements and sham agreements" in Central America, Afghanistan, and Angola.

I was able to give Kemp's letter to one of the president's friends who was willing and able to give it to Reagan. Not long after I chanced to be at a social function and spoke with Frank Carlucci and his lovely wife, Marsha, for a few moments as we were leaving.

"Congratulations, Frank," I said, "and good luck at a very difficult time for the administration."

Carlucci replied graciously: "Thanks, I'll need all the help I can get."
I went on, "I hope the president has had a chance to see Kemp's letter warning of four potential negative events that can be avoided."

"Yes," Carlucci responded, "Kemp's letter really got the president's attention."

Carlucci had asked a number of conservative leaders to recommend competent Reagan foreign policy experts, since he was going to be changing much of the NSC staff. He did receive suggestions—including some from me. Carlucci named General Colin Powell as his deputy and brought in mainly foreign service officers. However, for the senior Latin American position, Carlucci hired Dr. José Sorzano, who had served four years as Jeane Kirkpatrick's deputy at the United Nations. I hoped that Sorzano and Abrams, working with Ikle, Weinberger, Carlucci, and the president, could save Central America from the misguided initiatives of Shultz, Armacost, Habib, and the State Department's Latin American bureau.

I had a quick lunch with Sorzano in mid-January. In a few minutes I sketched out some of the stories about how the State Department had tried to countermand Reagan's policies. Then I said, "This has been stopped seven times, but I can predict that the State Department will try again this year. I don't know how or when, but Habib, Armacost, and their faction at State will be at it again. I urge you to rely on Jackie Tillman's good political instincts and experience with State. The key to stopping an end run by Shultz is to make sure the president has a chance to hear a fair and full debate—and that's up to you and Carlucci."

Sorzano replied, "From what Habib says to me, he seems to fully back the president's policies. I don't think there will be any repetition of the events you experienced."

I was dismayed at this naivete. But I realized Sorzano had been with Kirkpatrick at the United Nations and did not yet know the Washington subculture of deception. As he was getting up to conclude our brief lunch, I said, "Of course Shultz, Armacost, and Habib feel they're supporting the president's policy objectives. They mistakenly think their approach will do that. And they know you are a Cuban American, so Habib will highlight his toughness about communism when he talks with you."

In mid-February President Arias of Costa Rica unveiled his plan for Central America. After I had obtained a copy and studied it, I told Sorzano: "This is it! The Arias plan, I believe, is the instrument that will be used for this year's run at a false political settlement."

To my surprise, Sorzano said: "It looks mostly all right. Arias is talking about democracy in Nicaragua."

"Yes," I said, "the rhetorical goal of democracy in Nicaragua is there, and that's an improvement over the Contadora treaties drafted by Mexico. And it's even better than previous State Department proposals. But the Arias plan provides no way to bring that about, because its fatal flaw is that it would have the Nicaraguan armed resistance dismantled *today* in return for Sandinista promises to have democratic elections in 1990. The past eight years prove that the Sandinistas are willing to promise democracy any time it helps them get what they want, but they won't have genuine elections unless forced to by the success of the armed and unarmed democratic resistance."

Sorzano said: "Well, it's hard for us to speak against the Arias plan."

I replied: "The United States can praise the good intentions and democratic objectives of President Arias while telling him and our friends that the proposal needs significant changes in implementing procedures and timing."

I was very concerned because with Bill Casey gone from the administration and Frank Carlucci having been in private business when Shultz's unilateral initiatives had been stopped before (during 1983–86), Weinberger was the only cabinet-level person who would fully understand how the Arias plan might be used to undermine Reagan's policy. And I knew that Weinberger had to give first priority to the defense budget, sensible arms control, saving SDI, and managing a huge institution. In the summer of 1987 when this issue was breaking, Weinberger and Ikle were also preoccupied with the deployment of U.S. naval forces in the Persian Gulf.

After the Tower Commission reported in late February, I hoped Reagan would understand the problem he had had at the NSC during the tenure of McFarlane and Poindexter. But I worried that Shultz's influence and dominance would grow—first, because *this time* Shultz had been correct both in opposing military sales to Iran and in urging that the administration tell the full truth. But I guessed that the president did not understand how Shultz had so often since the spring of 1984 maneuvered unfairly to tilt the decision-making process his way. So I made another attempt in early March to have a friend of the president deliver my warning letter to him. No luck.

During these first months of 1987, I was writing intensively to complete this book. I had the good fortune to work with Mary Wallace, who retired after forty years as a secretary in the federal government and had the entrepreneurial idea of doing word processing to bring in extra income. Despite a physical handicap, Mary Wallace was always cheerful, considerate, and efficient. She was intrigued with the evolving story she was typing as she saw all its characters appear on the evening news reports. Then life imitated art. I learned that Habib was planning a trip to Central America, intending to persuade our friends there to endorse the Arias plan at their summit meeting scheduled for the end of June 1987.

Once again Congressman Jack Kemp came to Ronald Reagan's rescue. He wrote the president a letter telling him about Habib's impending trip and urging Reagan to be sure that the negotiating instructions were cleared by himself and the NSC. Kemp also urged Reagan to send the four democratic Central American presidents a letter somewhat along the lines of his September 1984 letter "defining a genuine political settlement and letting them know that if they enter into a false political settlement, they will have to live with the consequences." In a prophetic note Kemp closed his June 3, 1987 letter by telling Reagan that the Arias plan would mean "a false peace in Central America and a Congress unwilling to aid a democratic force that is being negotiated away."

As Mary Wallace typed these words she remarked: "This sounds like what you described last year."

"Another year, another phony peace plan," I said.

Now that I was a private citizen I could talk to the media. I happened to be with Nancy at an elegant black-tie dinner attended by Arnaud de Borchgrave and Robert Novak. So I told them about Kemp's letter to Reagan and why it was important. The *Washington Times* then published excerpts from Kemp's letter, leading—I heard—to an NSC review of the negotiating instructions. Then a Central American president was unable to see Habib, his mission was cut short, and the Central America summit planned for June 26–27 was postponed to August 6–7, 1987.

Not long after, I saw a senior administration official at a conference where we both spoke. He seemed confident that the defective Arias plan had been derailed. I replied: "No, Cuba, Nicaragua, Mexico, the isolationist Democrats in Congress, and Arias all will be pushing the four Central American presidents to sign at the August summit. So will Habib and the State Department. Unless you see to it that President Reagan sends the four democratic presidents a personal letter as he did three years ago, they won't know that he still stands solidly behind his policy. They'll fear he's been politically weakened by the Democrats winning control of the entire Congress and by the Iran-contra mess to the point where he won't feel able to stand by the freedom fighters and win another year of military aid. Our friends in Central America will be pressured to believe they can buy time by signing the Arias plan in August.''

The official looked at me and said confidently: "The Central Americans are too sensible to sign the Arias plan.''

By late July I had seen no sign that the administration was doing anything to make sure that the Central America summit would be constructive rather than destructive. Kemp also was concerned. But people I spoke with inside the administration seemed serenely confident that all would be well.

For one week in July Oliver North had held national attention as he testified before the Iran-contra committees. He had confounded the media's expectations. His effective testimony on behalf of the president's policy helped shift public opinion toward administration policy: it was one of the first times that many citizens had a chance to hear the administration's side on Central America.

On July 20 Jack Kemp made an important decision. He held a press conference on Capitol Hill and urged the administration to build on this new public understanding and immediately submit a proposal for $210 million in military and other aid for the Nicaraguan resistance over the next fiscal year, which would begin October 1, 1987. Kemp argued that this would save lives by shortening the civil war and would bring democracy more quickly. He urged the Reagan administration to press for an up-or-down vote *before* Congress began its summer recess in mid-August. There was no response and no action.

On Thursday, July 30, a friend from the *Washington Times* called. The newspaper's editorial board had hosted Frank Carlucci that day at an on-the-record luncheon. Carlucci had been asked what President Reagan was doing, with the summit meeting of Central American presidents then one week away, to help prevent the democratic presidents from giving in to pressures to sign a false political settlement and to reassure the democratic presidents that U.S. Central America policy remained intact in the wake of the Iran-contra affair. My friend said that Carlucci gave no indication that he knew about the Central American summit or had examined the regional politics. Instead, his answer had focused on Washington politics: support for the Nicaraguan resistance was growing in Congress, he explained, and the administration was seeking a bipartisan approach. "What do you think?" my friend asked me.

"That doesn't sound good." I said. "But at least your question has alerted Carlucci about the coming Central America summit. I'm glad he's been warned, I hope now he does something.''

On Sunday morning, August 2, an item in the back pages of *The Washington Post* caught my eye: Habib and Abrams had just visited Central America together, and a "dramatic breakthrough" might be made at the coming Central America summit. The next day, I called Kemp and told him that this story worried me.

"Jack, this could be the same old pattern—the State Department falling for or pushing a defective political settlement which the congressional Democrats can then use as the pretext for not voting more aid to the Nicaraguan freedom fighters when this year's funding expires on September 30."

"I'll ask around," Kemp said. "You do the same, and let's compare what we find out."

I called Arnaud de Borchgrave at the *Washington Times* and told him of my concerns. Mark Klugman, a brilliant writer, was assigned to do an editorial, published on Tuesday, August 4, which urged Frank Carlucci by name to take the lead to help avoid the defective Arias treaty and suggested that President Reagan immediately cable the Central American presidents to clarify his view that unless the Arias plan were improved, it was a defective treaty and would fail.

That morning—Tuesday, August 4—Kemp called me: "Constantine, please come right over. I have a document in my hand that I think will open the way to defeat for our friends in Central America. I'll order a sandwich for us both, and let's discuss what to do."

When I arrived Kemp handed me a single sheet of paper and said, "I hear Jim Wright wrote most of this, though State agrees. Reagan is supposed to sign this with Jim Wright tomorrow. Then Bob Dole and Bob Michel will stand with the president on one side while Jim Wright and Bob Byrd stand on the other. All the resistance leadership will also be present, and there will be a press conference in the Rose Garden to announce the Reagan-Wright 'peace plan.' "

I read the document. Its only good feature was that it explicitly endorsed the Sandinista obligation to live up to their "pledges made to the OAS—free speech, free press, religious liberty, and a regularly established system of free, orderly election." Nevertheless, I told Kemp: "The overall tone and timing of this document moves the administration in the wrong direction. Instead of agreeing to delay the freedom fighter vote until after September 30, Reagan should be following your advice and going for an up-or-down vote on more money *now*. I'll bet Shultz and Howard Baker pushed this, and that there has been no NSC meeting to discuss it. Most likely no one has told Reagan that the Central America summit is happening the day after he makes this announcement. The four friendly Central American leaders will *perceive* this as a decision by Reagan—their anchor of stability in all these years—to give up on the Nicaraguan freedom fighters. In my opinion, unless you or Weinberger can persuade the president not to sign this document, it will likely lead to the Arias plan being signed by all five Central American governments. And the Arias plan is a trap."

Kemp said, "I agree." And he immediately had his staff place an urgent call to the president. David Hoppe, Kemp's astute and knowledgeable top aide, came in and said, "Jack, all six leaders of the Nicaraguan resistance are going to be downstairs with the Republican Study Committee in a few minutes. So far this morning they've met with Secretary Shultz and the congressional leadership, but no one has shown them a copy of the Reagan-Wright plan or told them about it. Apparently the idea is to have them appear with the president and the bipartisan congressional leadership tomorrow and give them a copy of the Reagan-Wright plan when they leave—after it's too late for them to protest." We were both stunned at this deceptive treatment of our friends.

Kemp immediately issued a public statement and had it distributed to the White House and about two hundred journalists who had come to Capitol Hill for a press conference with the contra leaders.

> This is the time for the Administration to request more and immediate aid for the Nicaraguan armed resistance.
>
> The $210 million a year will shorten the war and help bring democracy to Nicaragua more quickly as promised to the OAS in 1979.
>
> I support President Reagan's policy that a genuine political settlement in Nicaragua means that on the day there is a real democratic government there, the military aspects of the agreement also enter into force.
>
> Anything else is a false settlement and I am disturbed to read that Ambassador Habib and the State Department seem to be pushing toward a false settlement. (Tuesday, August 4, 1987)

Then Kemp tried to talk several Republican congressional leaders out of backing the proposal. He phoned some and visited others in their offices, explaining that it would likely push our Central American friends into making the mistake of signing the Arias plan at their August 6–7 summit meeting. In the middle of these conversations Kemp and the other congressmen had to go to the House floor to vote, so I found myself continuing a conversation with one Republican congressman in the little subway cars that run between the House office buildings and the Capitol.

Quite understandably, these Republican congressional leaders—who looked at the plan from an entirely domestic political point of view—seemed not even to know that the Central America summit was scheduled. They respected Kemp and listened carefully, but by early afternoon, Tuesday, August 4, they seemed to feel that the administration had made a firm decision and they could not stop it.

Secretary of Defense Weinberger had known nothing about any of this proposal until Monday evening August 3. He and Under Secretary Ikle felt it was a major mistake. Weinberger immediately requested an appointment with Reagan. On Tuesday afternoon he met with Reagan and Shultz and did his best to persuade the president this would be a mistake. No success—events were moving forward. That evening the resistance leadership argued against the plan, but the administration officials they met with said, "It's too late to stop this now."

I could hardly believe it! The central message of the Tower Commission report in February and of the just concluded Iran-contra hearings had been the need for a fair NSC decision-making process to give the president a chance to know the views of his key foreign policy advisers on major decisions. This was a major foreign policy decision, and there obviously had been no meeting of the National Security Council. *Shultz had done it again!* He had excluded Weinberger and the rest of the foreign policy cabinet. My guess is that he and Howard Baker had probably presented this to Reagan as mostly a decision about congressional political tactics in order to *win* the vote on aid for the Nicaraguan freedom fighters—again putting the State Department's tactical preference in the wrappings of Reagan's objectives. This was the *eighth end run* on Central America—and this time Shultz succeeded.

Where were Carlucci and the NSC staff? Carlucci and Weinberger, as I knew from personal experience going back to 1973, worked well together and respected each other. As it turned out, Carlucci was on a trip to Europe discussing Persian Gulf issues with our NATO allies.

The next day, August 5, the Reagan-Wright plan was announced *before* the president met with the leaders of the Nicaraguan resistance. Perhaps someone wanted to make sure that they would not have any chance to try to voice their objections?

I felt deeply saddened by this mistake and believed it would mark the beginning of the unraveling of Reagan's successful prodemocracy policy in Central America. That evening several Democratic congressional leaders appeared on various television news programs and made it clear how badly the administration had bargained. No, they said, they had not agreed to *vote for aid* to the Nicaraguan resistance right after September 30 if the Reagan-Wright plan did not work by then. They had merely agreed to permit a vote to occur sometime after that date.

As Kemp (and I) had judged, Reagan's agreement with Wright was *perceived* by our friends in Central America as abandoning the Nicaraguan armed resistance. Duarte later told Kemp that he "could not sleep all night after learning about the Reagan-Wright plan." On August 7 all the Central American countries signed the Arias plan.

Some days later Reagan correctly described it as "fatally flawed." The reason? Because the Arias plan provided that in the next months there would be a total termination of outside support to the armed resistance opposing the communist Sandinistas in return for which the Nicaraguan regime would promise to hold democratic elections in 1990.

Besides that, the verification group set up to monitor compliance would consist of fifteen members: the secretary generals of the UN and the OAS, the eight Contadora countries, and the five Central American countries. At best this would mean the verification group would be eleven to four against the Central American democracies.

Immediately, Speaker Wright unilaterally withdrew from his August 5 agreement with the president and instead endorsed the Arias plan. He said as long as that "peace process" continued, he could not imagine Congress voting any more military aid to the contras. That was the trap! The Sandinistas and Mexico and Arias could stretch an inconclusive "peace process" into months, even years, while the contras withered for lack of aid while Soviet bloc weapons continued arriving in Nicaragua.

From news reports I had the impression that President Reagan was startled by the adoption of the Arias plan. For his part the Democratic leader of the House explained that he had known the summit meeting was coming and felt his proposal to Reagan would help bring about the Arias plan. In fact, on August 5 Congressman Wright appeared on the *MacNeil-Lehrer NewsHour* and said that he had discussed the outlines of his plan with the Nicaraguan ambassador to the United States on July 25. When I read that Ambassador Habib had resigned as special envoy to Central America on August 14, I took this as a sign that the Reagan administration would try to reverse the damage.

In early September, Kemp, along with a number of political leaders, visited Central America and met with the four democratic presidents and many others. Virtually all were deeply concerned by events since August

7. Duarte told Kemp that the Sandinistas had stepped up their supply of weapons to the communist guerrillas in his country. Kemp returned and wrote the president a letter proposing a five-step plan to help rescue his policy. The *Washington Times* endorsed the Kemp plan and wrote:

> The core of Rep. Jack Kemp's plan to preserve the Nicaraguan freedom fighters, outlined in his Sept. 25 letter to Mr. Reagan, is for the president to shift the focus of the issue both here and in Central America from the unfinished, inadequate plan of Aug. 7 to the existing negotiated settlement of 1979 which removed Somoza and requires Nicaragua to implement genuine democracy. . . .
>
> Mr. Kemp urges the president to send letters to the presidents of Central America's four democracies (as he did in September 1984) warning them to stop the rush to capitulate because U.S. policy is to support the resistance until the Sandinistas fully implement the eight-year-old agreement. Mr. Reagan should make clear to Costa Rica, El Salvador, Guatemala and Honduras that if they enact the new plan (which is clearly a formula for disaster), they must bear the full consequences and should not expect increased U.S. aid *or rescue by U.S. troops* from the future communist aggression that their plan will unleash. [October 2, 1987; emphasis added]

The Arias plan provided for two dates to review compliance: November 5, 1987, and January 4, 1988. During October President Arias was awarded the Nobel Peace Prize (reminding some of the award for the disastrous 1973 Vietnam "peace treaty") and the presidents of El Salvador and Honduras visited Washington, D.C. They made clear that communist Nicaragua was not complying with the terms. Although the Sandinistas had taken a few steps toward political liberalization, the secret police were still in control. Nicaragua released some hundreds of political prisoners, but thousands still remained. Covert Sandinista aid to communist guerrillas and terrorists continued as it had since 1979.

On November 5 Kemp held a press conference on Capitol Hill attended by about thirty journalists. He summarized the Sandinistas' failure to comply with the Arias plan during its first ninety days as required and said:

> The OAS, whose foreign ministers are meeting here in Washington next Monday and Tuesday, should censure Nicaragua for its noncompliance with the Arias plan. I urge the democratic Central American presidents to return to the 1979 OAS plan for peace and democracy in Nicaragua.

He proposed other actions that the administration should take and then made a dramatic comment: "I have read that Speaker James Wright has been meeting to discuss pending legislation with the communist ambassador of Nicaragua. If true, this is deplorable and totally contrary to our traditions, and I request a full investigation by the House of Speaker Wright's negotiating contacts with the Sandinista regime."

The following week the Nicaraguan dictator visited Washington to speak at the OAS foreign ministers' meeting. Ortega had just returned from Moscow, where he was accorded all the honors due a fellow communist head of state as the Soviet leadership marked its seventieth year in power. Ortega had announced his willingness to talk to the contras through an intermediary. But he wanted direct negotiation with the Reagan administration but continued to refuse direct negotiations with the leaders of the armed resistance, whom the communists always call "bandits." The administration would not meet with Ortega, but Jim Wright did. Even the liberal *Washington Post* criticized Wright, and *The New Republic* wrote a strong editorial, "Wright is Wrong":

> What he is doing, in effect, is supporting the Sandinistas' position in delicate negotiations . . . he's huddling with Ortega at the Capitol, hammering out the Sandinista cease-fire offer. . . .
>
> In effect, we now have two policies: an administration policy, which is allied with the contras, and a congressional policy, which has allied itself with the Sandinistas. The Democrats have long argued that they are not so allied. Speaker Wright is sorely testing that proposition. (December 7, 1987)

It seemed to me that the stratagem of the Democratic-controlled Congress during 1988 would be to continue using the Arias plan as a pretext for refusing renewed military aid to the Nicaraguan resistance. The "peace process" could be defined as continuing month after month, with additional meetings and discussions, while the Soviet-supplied Sandinista armed forces continued their drive to hunt down and kill the armed resistance. With food, ammunition, and medicine getting scarcer with each month of delay during 1988, more of the resistance would have to leave Nicaragua or be defeated.

On January 15, 1988 a Central American summit meeting convened to review compliance with the Arias plan. The four democratic presidents agreed to require "total compliance without excuses from Nicaragua," rejected any further extension of the plan's deadlines, and disbanded the verification commission, which Duarte called "disrespectful and biased."

Even though the Arias plan had failed, the Democratic majority in the House voted on February 3, and March 3, 1988, to reject Reagan's request for aid to the contras. On March 12, 1988, the Sandinistas launched a "triumph or death" military attack into Honduras. Reagan sent 3,500 U.S. troops for two weeks to back up Honduras. Then it was reported that Speaker Wright urged contra backers to sign a one-sided truce with the Sandinistas on March 23, 1988, as the price of the subsequent approval of nonmilitary aid. The contras were now in mortal danger as a result of communist cunning, the false peace treaty, and the misjudgments of Democratic congressional leaders. But I still felt that the administration could win military aid if it made a major political effort. Until then, each passing month would increase the danger of communist victory in all of Central America and, then, in Mexico.

THE MISGUIDED DEMOCRATS IN THE CONGRESS

The picture would be incomplete without considering the role of the isolationist Democrats in opposing Reagan's policy in Central America. That role has been one of hardly seeing evil—except in the Reagan administration.

In 1979 the Carter administration, with the full support and participation of Democratic leaders in Congress, helped bring the Sandinista regime to power in Nicaragua. At the time most of these Democrats ignored evidence that the new coalition was communist-dominated. Sometimes the evidence was denied. When it became overwhelmingly clear, it was either disregarded as irrelevant, or the Reagan administration was accused of "driving the Sandinistas into the arms of the Cubans (and Soviets)."

Likewise these isolationist Democrats have been reluctant to support counteraction based on the evidence that, since 1979, the Sandinistas have been committing aggression through armed subversion against neighboring countries. Nor have they really tried to hold the Sandinistas to their 1979 pledges to the OAS, including the pledge to establish genuine democracy.

From 1981 to 1984, they opposed providing the levels of aid needed to help El Salvador avoid a communist takeover, even though at the last minute the Carter administration did initiate military aid, which helped prevent a communist victory there in January 1981. In September 1981, Congress imposed stringent political conditions on U.S. aid to El

Salvador—which have been imposed on aid to most communist countries, for example.

This opposition to Reagan's pro-democratic Central America policy has been all the more regrettable since so many of these same Democratic congressmen had totally misjudged the tragic consequences of communist victory in southeast Asia. For example, Representative Obey (D., Wisc.) spoke to the Congress in 1970 using the same ideas he would later apply in Central America:

> And we further believe that when it becomes unmistakably clear that America intends to end its involvement in Vietnam, all contending political factions in South Vietnam will have incentive to make the accommodations necessary for negotiating a political compromise. (Gregorsky, p. 16)*

The now famous Congressman Boland said in 1971 about southeast Asia:

> A negotiated political settlement is the only way—quite literally, the only way—to stop the bloodshed. (Gregorsky, p. 16)

And Senator Christopher Dodd (D., Ct.), one of the most active and energetic opponents of Reagan's effort to help the people of Central America defend themselves, said about Cambodia only weeks before the communist victory in March 1975:

> The greatest gift our country can give to the Cambodian people is not only guns but peace. And the best way to accomplish that goal is by ending military aid now. (Gregorsky, p. 20)

In fact, history showed that the defective Vietnam "peace treaty" of 1973 was a communist deception that overturned their defeat in the long guerrilla war by opening the way to congressional reduction of military aid in 1974–5 and ended with a communist victory by conventional invasion. This "peace" was *followed* by the death of two to three million civilians under communist occupation in Vietnam, Cambodia, and Laos.

By late 1975 Senator Dodd had seen the victorious Cambodian communists force more than two million men, women, and children—the entire population of the capital city—to leave their homes and endure forced labor, starvation, and sudden execution in the concentration camp that included the whole country. In late 1975 did that tragedy bring then

* Frank Gregorsky, *What's Wrong With the Democrats' Foreign Policy*, Washington, D.C., 1984.

Representative Dodd to the realization that the United States should help the pro-Western liberation movement in Angola that was facing thousands of newly arrived Cuban troops and Soviet weapons? No. On December 19, 1975, Dodd denounced equally "the Ford administration, the Soviet Union, and the South African and Cuban regimes" and urged that the United States *cut off* its help to the pro-Western groups (Gregorsky, p. 20).

Year after year the isolationist Democrats in Congress opposed the Reagan administration's proposal for aid to the Nicaraguan armed resistance. They have tried to have it both ways: expressing support for peace in Central America while refusing to give the needed aid to the Nicaraguan resistance that could make peace a reality by bringing real democracy to Nicaragua. Under political pressure they have sometimes voted aid to the contras, but more often they have tried to avoid the responsibility of a straight vote to cut off that aid while simultaneously trying to avoid actually giving it. In this they have sometimes been helped by the political ineptitude of the administration, which, as we have seen, has sometimes offered premature and self-defeating "compromises" instead of seeking a clear "yes" or "no" decision from the Congress.

The most famous of Congress's obstructive devices, of course, have been several Boland amendments, which prohibited military aid to the contras by the Defense Department and intelligence agencies, including the CIA. Though it has become the Democrats' habit to talk as if the Boland amendments were simple statutes, in fact they were not. They were ambiguous and highly political riders on appropriations bills. Their constitutionality has been questioned by some legal experts. But that is only one difficulty with them.

As appropriations riders, they lack statutory force: no penalty was attached to violating them, so it is doubtful that their violation is criminal. They prohibited action only by specific agencies; I agree with the Minority Report that they did not apply to the NSC staff, contrary to the flat assertions of many Democrats and pundits. If Congress had wanted to prohibit the entire executive branch from aiding the armed resistance, it could easily have said so. It did not. Nor did it prohibit private citizens from giving aid to the contras, though it could easily have said that, too. Nor did Congess prohibit requests to foreign governments to provide aid: moves to do so were voted down.

Yet by a kind of "loose construction," some have tried to interpret the Boland amendments as having done all these things. This interpretation is not plausible to me.

Increasingly, the isolationist Democrats in Congress have worked as lobbyists abroad against their own president. Since late 1981 it seemed to me that these congressional Democrats agreed with some State Department officials that the Nicaraguan armed resistance should only be used as a bargaining lever to obtain a treaty with Nicaragua, under the terms of which Nicaragua could remain communist and forgo its pledge of democracy, provided only that it promised to halt its aggression against its neighbors. In this there was a parallelism of interest, and sometimes active coordination, between some congressional Democrats and State officials on the one hand, and Mexico on the other. Such an arrangement would have phased out the armed resistance without the Democrats having to vote on the matter.

After contra aid was defeated in March 1986, House Speaker Tip O'Neill led delegations of his fellow Democrats to South America where they lobbied against the administration's policy. Other Democrats attended a meeting of the Contadora countries for this purpose. In April the Philip Habib letter to three Democratic congressmen (described in chapter 11) in tandem with Mexican activism nearly led to the signing of a defective peace treaty in June, which would have resulted in the defeat of contra aid in the House. Then, in 1987–88, Congressman Jim Wright himself, O'Neill's successor as Speaker, seemed to pursue his own unilateral diplomacy (when does private diplomacy violate a legal statute with penalties—the Logan Act?).

Equally, could the actions of many Democratic congressmen in 1986–87 be seen as direct violations of the Burton amendment (which has the same status as an appropriations rider as the Boland amendment)? The Burton amendment specifies that it shall be the policy of the United States to seek a political settlement that carries out the 1979 Nicaraguan OAS promises of real democracy.

I had watched all these events from outside the administration with a mounting sense of irony. The damage done to American foreign policy by the Iran-contra matter had been exposed to the public, and the congressional Democrats and the media seemed to assume that this exposure would restore internal order to the foreign policy decision-making process within the executive branch. I was not so sure. From where I sat it looked as if George Shultz's State Department was still up to its old tricks and Reagan did not realize it.

For example, on Afghanistan there has been strong bipartisan congressional support for Reagan's policy that aid to the resistance must continue until all Soviet troops are out and an independent Afghan government exists. But the State Department had been backing a defective settlement and then on February 11, 1988 *The New York Times* reported that "an American commitment in 1985 to end military aid to the Afghan guerrillas at the beginning of a Soviet troop withdrawal was made without the knowledge or approval of President Reagan." The much-talked-about "lesson" of the Iran-contra affair that there must be a fair NSC decision-making process still did not seem to be applied.

13

THE PEOPLE AND THE INSTITUTIONS

For five years I worked with the people who figured in all these events. Their names have become well known, but to me they are neither celebrities nor characters in a political soap opera. They are familiar, flesh-and-blood human beings.

I got to know them all, and though the conduct of some of these individuals was sometimes far from ideal, all of them *believed* their actions were in the best interests of their country and their president. None intended to damage the president or his administration.

But good intentions are not enough. Citizens have a right to measure the performance of public officials by the actual results of their actions. In foreign policy, competence means having the foresight and judgment to choose actions that accomplish the intended results. This requires careful assessment of the likely impact any contemplated U.S. move or policy will have on foreign governments, both friendly and hostile, and on our domestic politics as well.

In my view, the difference between the two key groups of foreign policy participants—Casey, Kirkpatrick, Weinberger, and Clark; and McFarlane, Poindexter, Shultz, and North—is not that one was good and the other evil, but that one was competent and one was not.

We all come to know the people we work with little by little, day by day. Few of us can choose our colleagues when we are employees. And in so many organizations people can have offices right next door to one another—lawyers, managers, technicians, craftsmen—have a nodding

335

acquaintance, and yet know very little about each other's activities, personalities or true characters. My approach to people has always been to expect normal and reasonable behavior. And I think that this positive presumption is sensible and, fortunately, is (mostly) borne out by experience. Few working people in any setting ask themselves whether their associates are committing improper or illegal acts.

My intense and interesting five years with the Reagan administration did permit me to work with all the key individuals I will now discuss in their roles as public officials. I worked with them on enough tough issues to develop an understanding of the way they approached and performed their work. In addition, the revelations around the Iran-contra matter provided a great deal of new factual information about some of these individuals, especially McFarlane, Poindexter, and North.

As I think about these three career military officers, I am struck by their mixed record and impact. All three served our country for many years in the profession we rely on every day for the defense of our freedom. All three served with honor and risked their lives to fulfill their duties. All three have an intense feeling of devotion and loyalty to our country—as do all of the people in this story.

When I proposed the Grenada rescue and restoration of democracy, McFarlane and Poindexter could easily have deferred action. In his first day as NSC adviser McFarlane could have told me something like "Let's wait before discussing possible action, let's see how things work out." Instead, after the bloody events of October 19, 1983, in Grenada, he and Poindexter showed real leadership. McFarlane, I am told, was a driving force in early 1983 behind Reagan's excellent proposal for the Strategic Defense Initiative. In October 1985 McFarlane and Poindexter were willing to recommend military action to capture the *Achille Lauro* hijackers. In April 1986 Poindexter took the lead to bring about the military counterattack against Libya for its aggression through terrorism. Reagan made the correct decision in all these cases—but he got good advice from McFarlane and Poindexter (as well as others in the cabinet).

All these actions were risky. All could have been passed by if McFarlane and Poindexter had wanted simply to avoid taking risks. But a common thread in these important decisions that were recommended to the president is that they were tactical *military* operations to accomplish legitimate purposes.

How, then, was it that these same men also went so wrong? A retired military officer, in perhaps the most heartrending criticism of the Iran arms deal I have read, asked: How could McFarlane, Poindexter, and

North—all career military officers—have initiated and participated in selling military weapons to the hostile Iranian government, which *they knew* had a major responsibility for killing 241 marines in Beirut? And how was it that McFarlane and Poindexter, who had demonstrated physical courage, often seemed to lack the moral courage to properly perform the NSC job for their president and risk the displeasure of Shultz and his powerful allies in the Reagan White House?

ROBERT C. MCFARLANE

In his three days of dramatic testimony in May of 1987, and in a return engagement one day in July, McFarlane told the Senate-House Investigating Committee that he was responsible for the actions of Lieutenant Colonel Oliver North. He told the committee members that in November of 1986, when the crisis was beginning to unravel, he had told North, "Ollie, look. You have acted under instructions at all times . . . and I'll back you up." (*Washington Post,* May 14, 1987, p. A16.) However, after North had testified, McFarlane returned to rebut major aspects of North's testimony and told Congress that he did *not* know or authorize *everything* that North had done.

McFarlane was the official who'd had authority over Poindexter and North during the crucial period when the first decisions were being made. As I've said, the NSC system worked reasonably well on behalf of the president under Bill Clark; only when McFarlane took over did the process begin to tilt toward Shultz, and only then was Ollie North permitted freer and freer reign.

McFarlane, a 1959 Annapolis graduate, served one combat tour of duty as a marine officer in Vietnam. Later the marines sent him to Geneva, Switzerland, where he studied international relations for a year. In 1971 he joined Henry Kissinger's NSC staff as a White House fellow and stayed at the NSC as assistant first to Kissinger and then to Brent Scowcroft. On the White House staff from 1971 to 1977, he had a ringside seat not only for the drama of Watergate, but also for the foreign policy of the Nixon-Ford years.

McFarlane witnessed a number of foreign policy failures: a SALT I accord and ABM treaty the Soviets immediately began violating; the Soviet-encouraged Egyptian surprise attack on Israel in 1973, a violation of the "norms of international conduct" signed at the U.S.-Soviet summit in Moscow but a year earlier; the communists' massive military invasion of South Vietnam, which violated the 1973 "peace treaty"; and the use of Soviet weapons and thousands of Cuban troops to bring communist movements to power in Angola and Mozambique.

McFarlane also saw what happened when some White House aides lied to cover up improper actions—the eventual resignation of a president who had been elected by a large margin.

I was in a good position to observe McFarlane closely from his earliest days in the Reagan administration. Certainly he had ambition: in late 1984 North told me that McFarlane was thinking about running for president someday. If true, perhaps McFarlane saw the top job at the State Department as the next rung to the top.

The well-informed columnist William Safire described McFarlane's rise:

> Al Haig welcomed him at State . . . where . . . McFarlane soon cultivated William Clark . . . and through him Michael Deaver. When Mr. Allen came under fire at the NSC, Mr. Deaver urged the President to bring in Mr. Clark and Mr. McFarlane; [later] Deaver . . . helped slot his friend 'Bud' into the sensitive spot at NSC. (*New York Times,* November 17, 1986)

As I reflect on the years with McFarlane, there is one fundamental paradox: as National Security Council adviser he could be occasionally strong and enormously weak.

It seemed to me that McFarlane was repeatedly unwilling to take risks in order to stand up for the authority and policy of the president. As National Security Council adviser this was his most important duty. But when he witnessed how Bill Clark, an old and valued friend of President Reagan, was maneuvered into resigning, he seemed to become afraid to stand up to Shultz and Shultz's White House allies Deaver and Jim Baker. I believe that is why McFarlane refused to help Senator Stone, and I believe that is why McFarlane had to be pushed into holding the June and July 1984 NSC meetings, at which the president found out about Shultz's unilateral moves and put a stop to them. This also led McFarlane, in October of 1984, into cooperating with Shultz in what appeared to me a scheme to preempt President Reagan.

After McFarlane's emotional resignation, he wanted to participate and took the very great physical risk of flying to Iran in May of 1986. Why? He says that part of the reason was that he hoped the success of the mission could mark the beginning of his return to power. Safire put it this way:

> The rejected McFarlane saw he could gain the credit given concep-
> tualizers: what he needed to break out of the apparatchik mold was
> a secret mission to the forbidden city of the 80s. Tehran. (*New York
> Times*, November 17, 1986)

McFarlane's own published article comparing the Iran opening with that of China under Nixon suggests this objective.

And why did he get involved in writing the inaccurate chronology of the Iran initiative once it had become public? To protect the president? The actual result was anything but protective; it misled and embarrassed President Reagan even further.

McFarlane's suicide attempt, which occurred in early 1987, was a deeply sad episode. He said publicly that he attempted suicide because he felt he'd let the president down and because now he would never have a chance to work in the government again.

Only weeks after this attempt McFarlane gave two interviews. In these he revealed a few more personal details that might have bearing on his actions. He spoke of his congressman father having taught him never to complain, never to ask for help in finishing a job. (When I read that I thought of Bob Kimmitt's remark that McFarlane felt he could do the NSC job all by himself.) McFarlane also said—and this may well indicate a basic insecurity—that Ronald Reagan seemed to prefer rich, self-made men like George Shultz and Don Regan to someone like himself.

Yet by May of 1987, in spite of all he had seen and suffered, it seemed to me that McFarlane was back to thinking how he could use his Iran-contra testimony to his best advantage. To me this was illustrated by his prepared opening statement to the investigating committee.

First, he told the Congress that he understood why they were confused about Central America policy—because the Reagan administration had not clearly defined its policy until the Kissinger Commission reported in January 1984. McFarlane said that before then there had been no interagency process to address this issue. This was nonsense.

McFarlane *himself* had chaired extensive interagency meetings in 1981. There had been NSC-level discussions in 1982 and an interagency review of Central American strategy in June 1983 in which both McFarlane and North had participated. Again, it was McFarlane himself who had ordered the review of Central American strategy from November 1983 to the NSC meeting of January 1984. Was McFarlane's statement designed to appease the Democrats in Congress and flatter Henry Kissinger?

McFarlane's opening statement also contended that there had been no interagency decision-making process in 1981 because Secretary Haig's proposal for managing foreign policy had been shelved at the White House. In fact there *was* an interagency process that the State Department chaired and dominated at the subcabinet level from 1981 on. Did McFarlane make this statement to flatter Haig, a possible presidential contender in 1988?

McFarlane's testimony was replete with self-serving statements. One of the most outrageous was his effort to point the finger of blame for North's conduct at William Casey, who had died on May 6, 1987— only days before his testimony. Asked whether he suspected North "was taking instructions not from the National Security Adviser but from the DCI [director of central intelligence, William Casey]," McFarlane responded, "Yes, sir . . . I became aware in the fall of 1985 that Ollie had more contact with the director . . . a relationship that surprised me." When asked "Did you come to believe that perhaps Mr. Casey was giving him instructions in how to conduct this particular operation with respect to either Nicaragua or Iran?" McFarlane replied, "I think so" (excerpts from *The Washington Post*, May 14, 1987, p. A16).

In three days of testimony the *only fact* McFarlane cited for this headline-making allegation was an offhand anecdote in which North had told McFarlane that Casey had allegedly said he might contribute a million dollars of his own money to the contras.

For those of us who worked at the NSC, McFarlane's finger pointing had no credibility. A number of senior NSC staff people had contacts with Bill Casey, as well as the other members of the foreign policy cabinet. It was a normal part of the job. Since North was assigned by McFarlane to manage NSC activities on behalf of the contras, as well as worldwide counterterrorism and the Iran operation—all topics with a high degree of input from the intelligence organizations—it was perfectly natural for North to talk with Casey, and McFarlane *had* to know that.

McFarlane met *weekly* with Director Casey. If he had any questions about whether or not Casey was giving orders to any NSC staff member, all he had to do was raise the issue and indicate this was not to be done. What's more, although I had worked directly for Casey for two years immediately before coming to the National Security Council and saw him frequently, I can testify that in my three years at the NSC Casey *never* gave me an order. He was very careful to fully respect the managerial authority of McFarlane and Poindexter over the NSC staff.

In August 1985, while I was out of the country with my family, there were a series of allegations in the U.S. media that North was managing an operation to supply weapons to the contras. This led to formal requests from Congress for McFarlane to answer the allegations. After their meeting with McFarlane in early September 1985, one press report quoted the chairman of the Senate Select Intelligence Committee as saying McFarlane agreed that any effort to "solicit or help raise private funds for the Nicaraguan rebels would violate the so-called Boland amendment" (*New York Times,* September 6, 1985). The same news report said McFarlane denied any such violations, but it went on to say:

> Administration officials have acknowledged that a ranking member of the NSC, Lt. Col. Oliver North, helped raise private funds for the rebels and had been involved in some rebel activities during the time the Boland Amendment was in effect. (*Ibid.*)

Given McFarlane's view—as he testified in July 1987, a "political judgment," *not* a legal conclusion—that the Boland amendment prohibited such actions, and given the many press reports, I believe it was a major dereliction of McFarlane's leadership responsibility not to have found out in detail what North was doing. I believe McFarlane's testimony that he did not authorize those of North's actions that went "over the line." I believed in 1985 that the allegations in the press were inaccurate. But given McFarlane's own conception of the political situation with Congress and his view of what North could and could not do (which I never once heard him express in the senior staff meetings until my departure from them on July 9, 1985), it was incumbent on McFarlane to get the facts—and not just by asking North.

Having heard North testify for six days that McFarlane and Poindexter had authorized everything he had done, McFarlane asked the committee for permission to testify again. He then said, on July 14, 1987, that he had not known about or authorized North's activities to conduct a clandestine operation to supply the resistance; that he did not know North had hired General Secord to set up a private airlift operation; that he had told North not to alter some NSC documents in 1985; that he had told North not to solicit funds from private citizens and did not know of North's relationship with the Spitz Channel fund-raising operation. The essence of McFarlane's rebuttal of North's testimony was this statement:

The contras had to continue in some fashion to buy beans, bullets, Band-Aids and the hardware of war. Now the line is crossed when instead of their doing that Colonel North does that . . . (going beyond coordination) to serve as liaison for them in the chartering of aircraft, the hiring of third parties to sell arms, things like that, went over the line from advice to an operational role, and that was not authorized. (McFarlane's testimony in *New York Times*, July 15, 1987)

By this statement McFarlane pointed to the dividing line between what he thought North was doing to help the resistance during the Boland times: coordination, politcal encouragement, serving as their link to the U.S. government, and helping direct foreign and private benefactors who wanted to help the contra leaders. This is what I thought North was doing, and this is what most of his associates in the rest of the government testified they thought North was doing for "his account."

The difference between McFarlane and the rest of North's colleagues in the U.S. government is that North worked for him. He had the means to find out what North was doing in as much detail as he wanted.

By the summer of 1985, when I had been "moved up" out of Latin America, McFarlane had enough reasons to ask questions about North's actions.

My successor as the senior NSC staff person for Latin America was a career foreign service officer whom McFarlane had hand-picked. He could have been asked to do a thorough analysis. Setting aside North's record and simple common sense, the reason McFarlane should have been more careful is that several NSC staff members had the courage to talk to McFarlane about the potential dangers of North's well-intentioned activisim. They realized this was risky—and they knew both McFarlane and Poindexter seemed to think North could do no wrong. They understood their warnings about North—though intended to help the Reagan policy succeed—were likely to be viewed as deriving from personal jealousy or disputes. Nevertheless, the NSC staffers talked straight to McFarlane. He ignored them.

We now know that McFarlane misinformed both the president and the Congress about Oliver North's activities on behalf of the contras when the first allegations about North were published in the media in August 1985. McFarlane's written denials to the committee were complete and explicit. In his testimony to the Senate-House Investigating Committee, Assistant Secretary of State Elliott Abrams said repeatedly that because he had believed these assurances from McFarlane to the Congress, the press allegations about North did not overly concern him. Likewise, the attorney for the Intelligence Oversight Board testified that he relied heavily on McFarlane's assurances to Congress in deciding that North was not involved in such activities.

Although I had been "moved up" by this time and was not following Latin America in the same detail as before, I did read some of the August 1985 press reports when I got back from my vacation at the end of that same month. McFarlane's letters of assurance to the committee also reassured me, and I didn't give the press allegations any further thought.

In May 1986, when North told McFarlane about the diversion of funds to the contras, did McFarlane try to persuade Poindexter or anyone else that this was a mistake? No. He kept silent. In November 1986, when everything was unraveling, did McFarlane recognize his mistake? Did he act to encourage North to make certain that President Reagan knew the full truth of who did what in the Iran-Nicaragua matter? No. When North told McFarlane in late November 1986 that he was going back to his office for a "shredding party," by McFarlane's own testimony he said and did nothing to persuade North to make certain the president got all the facts.

At just about the time McFarlane was urging Reagan to approve the Israeli sale of U.S.-supplied weapons to Iran, a Heritage Foundation report written by a naval officer described Iran in these words:

> Iran has been waging a nontraditional war against the U.S. that has all but driven it from Lebanon. . . . Khomeini's regime has bombed the American Embassy, Marine headquarters, and the embassy annex in Beirut. . . . Iran trains, equips, and directs the local Lebanese Shi'ite extremists. To all of this there has been no U.S. response. . . .
>
> Iran controls these terrorists (in Lebanon) and wields them as weapons. Declared a Hezballah leader, 'Khomeini is our big chief. He gives the orders to our chiefs, who give them to us.' . . .
>
> Violence against American targets has not been confined to Lebanon. . . . December 1983 bombing of the U.S. Embassy in Kuwait . . . in December 1984 . . . hijacked a Kuwaiti airliner, then tortured and murdered two of the American passengers on board. The evidence strongly suggests that the hijackers were receiving their orders from Tehran, as they had been in an early November (1984) attempt to blow up the U.S. embassy in Rome. . . .
>
> Late this January (1985) Iranian Prime Minister Mir Hussein Moussavi believed . . . to direct Iran's overseas terrorist activities paid a three-day visit to Nicaragua. It was Moussavi's third meeting with Nicaraguan leader Daniel Ortega. (Report 452; September 3, 1985)

Obviously this published information was only a small part of what McFarlane had available to him about violent aggression by Iran. Year after year McFarlane, in my view, had done virtually nothing to help the Reagan administration develop a counterstrategy against this form of indirect warfare. Then in the summer of 1985 McFarlane responded to proposals for an opening to the Iranian regime. Reagan was ill and recovering from cancer surgery when, McFarlane testified, he first obtained approval for weapons sales, and then the next cabinet-level discussions on record are December 6, 1985, and January 6, 1986—after McFarlane had resigned. While talking about a "strategic initiative" toward Iran in his article, McFarlane as NSC adviser apparently failed to use full meetings of the National Security Council with the president to consider in a careful way with open debate how this might be done—or whether some reprisals against Iranian aggression might be more in the national interest.

The questions that needed to be explored for the president through full discussion in one or more NSC meetings included the impact on counterterrorism policy of selling weapons to Iran; the impact on Iran's likelihood of winning its war with Iraq (a *major disaster* for the moderate Persian Gulf oil states and therefore for NATO and Japan), because U.S. weapons sales would open up other suppliers and would increase the morale of the Iranian side; the quality of information about the Iranian factions; whether the sale of weapons was the right first step toward "Iranian moderates" and alternative ways of exploring an opening to them.

The NSC consultant who was involved in the initial contacts with Israel has written that McFarlane quickly dropped the broader strategic aspects of the idea and began to focus on weapons for hostages. When the consultant objected he found himself "cut out." The ad hoc, day-by-day improvisational approach, which I had seen so often in McFarlane, was followed even in this high-risk operation with a hostile, powerful foreign government. That incompetence is one of the reasons the operation failed. One result is that in 1987 the U.S. deployed more than twenty U.S. naval warships to escort fuel tankers in the Persian Gulf.

I believe that in 1984 and 1985 the president could have won the vote in Congress to obtain military aid for the Nicaraguan resistance. Three things were required, and McFarlane failed to do any of them. First, a systematic effort to build a winning coalition in Congress. This had to begin in January of each year and had to involve a determination to win an up-or-down vote. Instead McFarlane was always expending enormous time and energy negotiating compromises that he judged "likely to get through" but which were self-defeating. Second, McFarlane had to take the risk of opposing Shultz in 1984 by urging a contra vote in May or June, and in 1985 by seeking a national television speech by the president shortly before the vote in the House. Third, McFarlane had to stop the State Department from conducting its own foreign policy in Central America. Had McFarlane done these things, I am certain that Reagan would have backed him fully as would Casey, Weinberger, and Kirkpatrick. But he seemed unwilling to take the risks required by the difficult NSC job.

As a manager of staff McFarlane left a great deal to be desired. He undercut his own hard work by an unwillingness to *really work with* most of his senior staff. To be fair, McFarlane did *try* to run a tight ship. There were senior staff meetings every morning at seven-thirty, and there was a highly controlled system of assigning the hundreds of actions that came to the NSC staff each week to a principal staff member for action. Virtually all staff-written NSC communications to other agencies were sent out only over the NSC adviser's signature, or they took the form of presidential memos. All media contact, public speaking, and travel required the explicit approval of the NSC adviser. Like Clark before him and Poindexter after him, McFarlane followed orderly administrative procedures.

But McFarlane's essential duty was to see that the NSC staff served as the president's eyes and ears in foreign policy, enabling him to have a comprehensive vision, to resist the pressures and wiles of the separate departments and agencies, to make all major decisions with full knowledge of the options and likely consequences and to assure that presidential decisions were implemented. In this McFarlane failed.

JOHN POINDEXTER

In 1981 the navy detailed Admiral John Poindexter to serve as military assistant to President Reagan's NSC adviser. Undoubtedly the navy believed it was sending one of its best and brightest officers to this important assignment. Clearly John Poindexter is an intelligent man: he holds a Ph.D. in nuclear physics, and in 1958 he graduated first in his class at the Naval Academy.

The navy had made use of his training and skills by assigning him duties involving high-technology weapons and electronics systems. He was commander of a destroyer squadron. Then in 1971 Poindexter moved into years of work on policy issues: as a special assistant to three secretaries of the navy: John Chafee (now senator), John Warner (also a U.S. senator), and William Middendorf. From 1976 to 1978 he was the top assistant to the chief of naval operations and a senior officer for naval training until joining the NSC staff.

He had a lot in common with his predecessor Robert McFarlane. Both were military men and got along well. They had many of the same strengths and some of the same shortcomings. Perhaps it's only natural that they would both feel comfortable with the same types of people, those who *seemed* low-key, unassertive, and obedient. They seemed uncomfortable with independent-minded experts who urged them to act on behalf of the president's objectives in ways they feared might upset their relations with Shultz, Jim Baker, Michael Deaver, Don Regan, or any other powerful administration personalities.

In my judgment Poindexter fully shares with McFarlane the responsibility for all the times they decided *not* to fully inform the president about major issues and for the presidentially unauthorized actions involving NSC staff in efforts to provide direct military help to the contras. However, Poindexter is responsible, by his own testimony, for the improper and politically disastrous decision to divert Iran military sales funds to the Nicaraguan freedom fighters. I believe Poindexter meant to "protect" the president by not asking or informing him. But in fact he usurped his authority.

During my time at the NSC, I made a number of unsuccessful attempts to persuade Poindexter that the president had to know about the planned, unauthorized actions of the State Department on Central American negotiations. His responses were never different from McFarlane's. After December 1985, when he became national security adviser, Poindexter merely continued the methods that, it seemed to me, he, McFarlane, and Shultz had used so often in the past to give the president only a partial, selected picture of the views of the foreign policy cabinet on a major issue.

The following seems to me another example. Early in 1987 the White House declassified (and made public) the January 17, 1986, NSC memorandum to the president that recommended he sign an intelligence finding approving the direct sale of weapons to Iran, because of a claimed strategic opening to that country. This would be a major new foreign policy decision. Up until then it was Israel that had supplied weapons to Iran with the United States agreeing to replenish Israeli stockpiles.

The way this important decision was reached reveals several significant things about Poindexter. At the bottom of the decision memo (drafted by North) Poindexter wrote: "Orally briefed to President, present were Vice President, Don Regan, Don Fortier. . . ."

First, this major decision should have been discussed in a full NSC meeting, where the president could have heard Shultz and Weinberger argue against the recommended action. The January 6 full NSC meeting had given Reagan (and Bush) a chance to hear Weinberger's and Shultz's objections to any military dealings with Iran. But the January 17 informal meeting did not and it involved the new issue of direct military shipments to Iran. Thus Poindexter seemed to be employing a Shultz technique—the use of informal Oval Office discussions—*against* Shultz. Perhaps Poindexter felt he could do this because by then he had established a solid relationship with Don Regan.

Second, the decision memo itself is misleading. Most of it seems to discuss a strategic opening to Iran. But the content of the recommended covert action finding the president is asked to sign, and the operative paragraphs of the memo, are really about exchanging weapons for hostages.

To me this memo smacks of something written to make the president believe there was a broad strategic purpose, while in fact the real action focused on the more narrow purpose of weapons for hostages. In his speech of March 19, 1987, President Reagan described himself as having believed in the strategic purpose and as having misled himself on the arms for hostages aspect. It seems to me that Poindexter and North, with their memo, clearly contributed to this misperception.

Poindexter and McFarlane were both remote people to begin with, and in their high-pressure jobs they became increasingly distant from nearly all the NSC staff. Both preferred to communicate in writing through the prof computer system rather than deal with anyone face to face. Poindexter liked modern office technology, and ironically, it was these notes, passed among McFarlane, Poindexter, and North and preserved in the computer system, that the Tower Commission and the congressional investigators have used to document the facts of their conduct.

For example, on May 15, 1986, Poindexter sent North a "prof" message that revealed his willingness to mislead both William Casey and the general public: "I am afraid you are letting your operational role become too public. *From now on, I don't want you to talk to anybody else, including Casey,* except me about any of your operational roles. In fact, you need to quietly generate a cover story that I have insisted that you stop" (Tower, p. 467; emphasis added). Soon after, North began telling friendly congressmen and journalists that Poindexter intended to send him back to the marines. The result was the launching of a major campaign of support for North from Congress and the conservative media. Many of the people who tried to help North then are wondering now if they were just manipulated as part of this "cover story" (Tower, p. 467).

Equally revealing was Poindexter's note to North congratulating him for his skill in misinforming a congressional committee. After North reported this, Poindexter wrote back, "Well done" (Tower, p. 468).

Why did McFarlane and Poindexter never really talk with most of the senior NSC staff? Why, in May of 1985, did five of us have to search for a way of having *ten minutes* of private discussion every few weeks and ponder how we could encourage McFarlane and Poindexter to think ahead on some of the big international issues?

McFarlane and Poindexter's managerial approach was illustrated by their manipulation of their staff by deciding who would be "cut out" on particular issues, then using the system for distributing actions and incoming data and cables to enforce their decisions. This was a classic bureaucratic technique. McFarlane and Poindexter picked an inner clique of people they felt comfortable with, which meant, as we have now learned, that the senior NSC staffer for the Middle East apparently knew virtually nothing of the Iran initiative.

By seeming to deal with nearly all foreign policy issues one day at a time, McFarlane and Poindexter failed to use the skills of the senior NSC staff or the rest of the government to help the Reagan administration look ahead systematically or devise practical strategies for advancing U.S. interests and avoiding festering problems that had not yet become visible crises (such as Panama). *Never* in three years did I see McFarlane or Poindexter initiate this type of discussion with the senior staff.

They seemed equally incapable of understanding the international strategy of the Soviet bloc and its partners in key regions, especially when this strategy involved the use of political means and paramilitary forces rather than direct military threats. For example, despite his having seen the tragic sequel to the defective Vietnam peace treaty, McFarlane was willing to go along with Shultz and the State Department in bringing about a defective treaty for Central America. Why? Either McFarlane and Poindexter could not understand the political dynamics in Central America and the consequences of such a treaty, or they had decided that if the State Department peace treaty did not work out, then the United

States could simply invade Nicaragua and "clean things up" through military action.

During his May 1987 congressional testimony, McFarlane said he had never really believed the "contra" approach could work. He revealed that he hadn't really agreed with Reagan's policy. Instead he testified that the United States should either have a diplomatic settlement or use "much stronger" means. Only one journalist picked up what I thought McFarlane seemed to be saying that if Shultz's "peace treaty" failed, then the United States should invade. Again, the result of incompetent State Department diplomacy that would cost many more lives than had McFarlane wholeheartedly backed Reagan's correct "middle policy" of helping the people of Nicaragua *liberate themselves* from communism.

With regard to Central America, Poindexter was *both* weak and reckless—weak by giving in to Shultz and State; reckless for giving North free rein. It seems to me he was willing to go along with Shultz for careerist reasons and because, like McFarlane, he thought that if the peace treaty failed, there could be a U.S. military invasion. In the meantime Poindexter could remain true to his national security concerns by letting North direct Iran military sales funds to the contras.

These actions, aside from being contradictory and unauthorized by the president, also revealed that basically Poindexter did not understand American politics. The first question he should have asked himself about North's activities was, given the enormous political opposition by most of the Democratic Congress, what would be the political effect on the president and on future political support for the contras if these NSC activities were to become known?

An equally important reason Poindexter should never have authorized the diversion is the simple rule that two major and sensitive operations should never be connected. As the Iran-contra minority report said, "The decision to mix two intelligence operations increased the risk of pursuing either one with predictably disastrous consequences" (Minority Report, p. 447). Since Poindexter knew this rule, and since he had no way of being certain that some of the Iranians involved in the weapons sales were not friendly to Nicaragua, the Soviet Union, or other communist countries, it was a major, foreseeable risk.

In spite of all this, Poindexter failed to supervise North. He failed to require North to provide any sensible accounting of the millions of dollars that he had authorized for diversion to the resistance, and he failed—as North did—to check up to make sure the money got to the resistance. Once the House passed aid to the Nicaraguan resistance in June 1986,

Poindexter should have immediately ordered North to totally separate himself from any further operational control over the private resupply network. It had been set up, it was functioning, it had funds. There was never a need for North to manage it directly and continue exposing the policy, the president, and the country to the risks that entailed. This seems not even to have occurred to Poindexter.

Nor is there evidence of any significant Poindexter leadership in other difficult policy areas. Not on emerging crises in Panama and Haiti, where in 1985–86 I urged comprehensive action proposals be brought to the president in an NSC meeting. Not on a strategy to counter subversive aggression and terrorism, not on effective preparation for the Iceland summit in October 1986, which State seemed to dominate. The positive exception was the military counterstrike against Libya in April 1986—a well-done, tactical military operation. Like McFarlane, Poindexter was best in this area and worst at international strategy.

OLIVER NORTH

As the American people saw on television in July 1987, Oliver North is highly intelligent, possesses great energy, and is patriotic, personable, and persuasive.

I fully understand the positive impression North made, because that is just how I and many of his co-workers initially felt about him—and that certainly is the way his superiors, McFarlane and Poindexter, felt. (How do they really feel now, I wonder?) Earlier, I have discussed how—with one exception—it usually took many, many months for me and others at the NSC who worked *directly* with North to understand that in addition to his good qualities and intentions, he had serious shortcomings. We fully agreed on the need to support armed resistance in Nicaragua until democracy was achieved there. We assumed that Ollie's important work as the government's liaison with the resistance forces was proper and constructive. North might point foreign or private benefactors of the armed resistance in the right direction, but the reason I believe McFarlane's testimony on this is that apparently none of us working in Washington guessed that Ollie would take a direct management role— even those of us who had come to know his faults as well as his abilities.

The congressional investigating committee's Iran-contra report issued on November 18, 1987, provides the most complete documentation of what actually happened—it uses and refers to NSC memos, the prof notes, documents from the entire government, and the testimony of the participants. As I interpret all this evidence, the other publicly released information and use my own knowledge of the people and the NSC process, this is my understanding of North's role and of the diversion.

McFarlane testified that as early as February 1984 he began thinking about the need for third-country support (Report, p. 38). On March 27 McFarlane and Casey met to discuss approaching third countries for contra assistance. The report then makes clear this was "McFarlane's plan" and that Casey was agreeing with it (Report, p. 38).

In May 1984 McFarlane approached a foreign country that then offered to "provide a contribution of one million per month" (Report, p. 39). McFarlane told Poindexter and then testified that he asked North to arrange the transfer of the funds and "be in touch with contra leaders and *find out* where the bank account was kept. . . ." North gave McFarlane the information, and McFarlane gave this to the donor country's ambassador "by handing him an index card with the account number on it" (Report, p. 39).

North, however, recalls it differently. He testified that McFarlane asked him, in North's words, "to *establish* the initial resistance account offshore to which money was sent from a foreign government." North testified that with those funds in 1984 a decision was made to establish a "covert operation" to get supplies to the contras (Report, p. 40). Whom to believe?

The report describes a June 25, 1984, NSC meeting (which I attended) and says:

> Director Casey urged the President to seek third-country aid. Secretary Shultz responded that Chief of Staff James Baker (absent) had told him that if the U.S. government acted as a conduit for third-country funding . . . *that would be an "impeachable offense."* Casey responded that it was permissible if the plan called for direct contributions from third countries to the contras. [emphasis added; Report, p. 39]

Casey's interpretation of the law was also sustained by the majority and minority reports of the Iran-contra committee. The majority report said:

> The constitutional plan does not prohibit a president from asking a foreign state or anyone else to contribute funds to a third party. But it does prohibit such solicitation where *the United States exercises control* over their receipt and expenditure. [emphasis added]

This defines the constitutionally permitted executive branch actions. Before and after the Boland amendment, the president or any of his designees could ask third countries to provide aid. But no U.S. government official could exercise control over those funds. The report says that North was advised of this discussion at the NSC meeting (he did not attend), and "his notes recorded phrases such as 'impeachable offense' " (Report, p. 40).

The report goes on to say that the *next day* (June 26, 1984) Casey met with Attorney General Smith along with Justice Department and CIA legal staff to discuss the " 'legal limits' of funding options" (Report, p. 40). And the attorney general "saw no legal concern if the U.S. government discussed this matter with other nations so long as it was made clear they would be using their own funds to support the contras" (Report, p. 40).

To me, this prompt legal consultation is exactly what I would have expected Casey to do. It illustrates his strong concern about remaining within the law.

The report concludes that in the summer of 1984 North approached retired General Secord about setting up a supply operation to help the contras. The report documents that in September and October 1984 North made two proposals to McFarlane that North should take action to obtain donors for equipment needed by the contras. McFarlane *wrote*, "I don't think this is legal," and another time, "Check with CIA legal counsel promptly to confirm this is legal" (Report, p. 41).

According to the report, the first step North took to manage some of these third-country funds for the contras was in late 1984 or early 1985 when *"North decided* to use the money sent directly to Calero from country two to support other resistance leaders" (Report, p. 46). North testified that he asked for and received about $100,000 in cash from the contra accounts so that he could personally begin providing monthly support payments to selected resistance leaders" (Report, p. 46). Poindexter testified that at some point he knew about these funds and was concerned that "any time you handle cash there are perception problems that can develop . . . so I told Col. North he should get rid of the money by returning it" (Report, p. 47). In fact, according to the report, *North disobeyed this order* and kept on making payments during 1985 and 1986 (Report, p. 47).

In July 1987, with Casey having died in May, North testified that the idea for this cash fund came from Casey. This seems to me highly implausible in view of Casey's obvious determination to avoid illegal actions. And I believe Casey would have viewed it as a trivial reason to take the political risk of having an NSC staffer disbursing cash directly— merely so that Ollie, rather than Calero, could gain whatever influence came with being the one who provided these monthly payments.

In April 1985 came North's "Easter peace initiative." It backfired, and the House rejected aid to the resistance. During May and June a public-spirited private citizen tried to help provide money and weapons; he came to North and Calero with prices about 40 percent lower than Secord's (the report concludes that Secord's operation had a markup of about 38 percent) (Report, p. 51). Although North was cordial to the private citizen and seemed helpful, the report documents that North tried to persuade Calero not to buy the cheaper weapons. The report then states: "This was the last shipment Calero was to order from . . . any arms dealer other than Secord. . . . Thereafter money raised by North and Secord was given directly to Secord, who then provided the contras with arms. Calero testified he was 'never given a reason' why his 'authority to have cash directly sent . . . to make those purchases in the future was taken away' " (Report, p. 51).

The report indicates this is when North became a co-manager of the funds in the Secord foreign bank accounts. If so, this was North's second step in direct control of funds not appropriated by the U.S. Congress.

The report goes on to state that in the fall of 1985 North asked Secord to develop the air resupply system for the contras (Report, p. 504). In mid-November 1985 North at McFarlane's request became involved in trying to help Israel with its shipment of weapons to Iran. North brought Secord in to obtain his help.

On November 14 North and the Israeli counterterrorism coordinator, Nir, met to discuss a variety of future U.S.-Israeli covert operations that could "require at least a million dollars a month." They met again five days later (Report cited in *Washington Post*, Nov. 19, 1987, p. A28). The report indicates that the Israeli government provided $1,000,000 to pay the transportation costs of weapons for Iran, but only $200,000 was needed. As for the remaining $800,000, the report says that on November 20, 1985:

> North directed the Enterprise (Secord) to retain the money and spend it for the contras. *The diversion had begun.* [emphasis added; Report, p. 7]

McFarlane testified that he did not authorize *any* of these actions by North, and McFarlane was the NSC adviser until December 5, 1985. I believe the evidence supports McFarlane's testimony that he did not authorize these actions by North.

Next, the report concludes:

> North realized that the sale of missiles to Iran could be used to support the contras. He told Israeli Defense Ministry officials on December 6, 1985 . . . that he planned to generate profits on future arms sales for activities in Nicaragua. (Report, p. 7)

On December 7, 1985, the president heard his top advisers debate the issue: reportedly Poindexter and Casey agreed with the idea of approving Israeli military sales to Iran, while Shultz and Weinberger were opposed. McFarlane, after meeting with Iranians and Israelis in London, changed sides and returned to Washington, D.C., *opposed* to continuing the sales (Report, p. 7).

In early January 1986 the Israeli counterterrorism chief came to Washington to meet with North. At the same time the draft report on Bush's task force on counterterrorism was urging that a counterterrorism coordinator be named for the U.S. government. And it was quite obvious to us on the inside that Poindexter was going to name North to that position.

The evidence is clear that North was the most persistent and active supporter of continuing the weapons sales to Iran. The report tells us that on January 6, 1986, Reagan agreed and signed a finding authorizing more shipments of weapons by Israel (with the United States to replenish those types). But the *CIA general counsel* was concerned that this could violate the Arms Export Control Act. Therefore, another presidential finding was written to authorize direct sales from the United States to Iran. North also prepared the decision memo and the final draft of this finding, and this was signed by Reagan on January 17, 1986 (Report, p. 7).

The report then offers this judgment:

> Although North had become skeptical that the sales would lead to the release of all the hostages or a new relationship with Iran, he believed that the prospect of generating funds for the contras was an "attractive incentive" for continuing the arms sales. No matter how many promises the Iranians failed to keep . . . the arms sales continued to generate funds for the Enterprise and North and his superior, Poindexter, were consistent advocates for their continuation. (Report, p. 7)

At this point there is an interesting contrast between the majority and the minority reports. The majority report infers that the ability to use the

Iran military sales proceeds for the contras was part of the motivation for the decisions by the president. The dissenting minority is emphatic in rejecting this:

> The committees have no evidence that would give them any reason to believe that anyone other than North even considered the contras in connection with the Iran sales before the January finding (i.e., the January 17 presidential decision). *Poindexter* specifically testified that he *first heard of the idea* when North asked him to authorize it in *February* (1986). [emphasis added; Minority Report, p. 440]

My sense of the people involved and my reading of the evidence lead me to believe Poindexter on this issue. If my guess is correct, this would mean that North undertook the diversion in November 1985 without authorization from any superior. Further, I agree with the minority report: the evidence suggests that inside the Administration, until he told Poindexter in February 1986, *only North* was thinking of this connection to the contras.

This in turn leads me to agree with the judgment of the majority report that a reason North pushed so hard to lead his president into the arms sales to Iran was because he wanted to get some of the money to the contras and also because *he* (not anyone else in the administration) wanted to have access to money banked in the Secord Enterprise for the covert operations he hoped to do jointly with Nir, his new associate from Israel when Poindexter named him to the counterterrorism job.

These judgments also lead me not to believe North's testimony that CIA Director Casey proposed, endorsed, and approved the idea of such a privately funded, "off the shelf" covert operations capability. I will discuss this later.

This chronology of events conforms to the personality and operating approach of the North I came to know close up—the North who was determined to "box them in," to "make the right things happen" . . . the North who was skilled at manipulating or misrepresenting one senior official to get what he wanted from another . . . the North who wanted to be in charge and might well welcome the chance to control and direct his own private sector group that could not compete with him within the government.

In fact, this analysis of the evidence is important because only with that as background is it possible to make some judgments about the key conflicts in testimony between North and virtually all the other major witnesses: McFarlane, Poindexter, Meese, Shultz.

McFarlane testified on July 14, 1987, to refute North's Iran-contra testimony. He said categorically that he had not authorized North to become directly involved in the management of funds and operational support to the contras. McFarlane testified that he assumed North would remain in liaison with the contras to keep their spirits up and provide a link to the U.S. government, but that he also assumed the contras would make their own arrangements to use the funds from foreign donors to meet their needs.

I believe McFarlane on this for several reasons. First, once the Boland prohibitions were established, it would be *politically* self-defeating for an NSC official to be directly involved in managing and controlling their funds. Second, this would be the commonsense and most efficient approach for the contras. Why would the contras need or want a marine officer or anyone else in the Old Executive Office Building controlling access to their funds? This would be especially true when they could buy supplies 38 percent cheaper through persons other than Secord. Third, North was a thorough bureaucrat. If this had been an authorized "covert operation," he would likely have prepared an action memo for decision by McFarlane both as a matter of procedure and to be sure he was designated the official in charge. Among the million documents it examined, the Iran-contra committees mention no such memorandum from North.

Another example of conflicting testimony between McFarlane and North concerned an effort North made in 1985 to get a donation from a third country. North testified McFarlane had authorized his actions (Report, p. 63). But McFarlane testified he told North there should be "absolutely no participation from you or any other staff member in any kind of approach to this country" (Report, p. 63). North had asked one of our NSC colleagues to help him and had told him it was authorized by McFarlane and was legal. That NSC staff member testified that when he later asked, McFarlane told him, "This is not possible, this cannot be done" (Report, p. 63). Nevertheless, the report states, North went ahead and made his own approach to this foreign government in the fall of 1985—during the time Congress had approved $27 million in nonmilitary aid.

I remember the grin that crossed North's face as he told the committees and the American people how he had kept on shredding documents while the attorney general's investigators were in his office. "They were working on their project, and I was working on mine," he said. But William Bradford Reynolds, one of the two officials, an assistant attorney general and pillar of the conservative movement, said this was untrue. North's deputy, U.S. Marine Lieutenant Colonel Robert Earle, filed a sworn deposition stating that North had not been shredding documents while the Justice Department investigators were in his office suite.

It seems to me that, tragically, the more authority North was given by McFarlane and Poindexter, the more his flaws came to dominate his good side. Ollie seemed to begin by exaggerating his exploits and his closeness to the powerful. Then he began to deceive in a far more serious way, misleading his colleagues and superiors about important facts, about views of other officials, and about his own actions. For example, the Tower Commission report shows that North wrote Poindexter saying that Elliott Abrams agreed that he, North, should telephone the president of Costa Rica. Later North wrote to Poindexter, "I recognize that I was well beyond my charter in dealing with a head of state this way and making threats . . . but under the circumstances—and with Elliott's concurrence—it seemed like the only thing we could do." Poindexter illustrated his own bad judgment by responding to North, "You did the right thing, but let's try to keep it quiet" (Tower, p. 473). Both Elliott Abrams and the U.S. ambassador to Costa Rica told the Tower Commission North had not been authorized to make such a call, *and they doubted he had done so.*

Some of the media coverage about North's background, written since he attained national prominence, contained information that none of us at the NSC had known. The *Washington Times* first broke the story that in 1974, after one month in command of a marine training battalion in Okinawa, North was relieved of duty and sent to Bethesda Naval Hospital for three weeks to be treated for emotional distress. The paper reported that a superior officer found North "babbling incoherently and running around naked, waving a 45 caliber pistol," saying "he didn't have anything to live for and was going to shoot himself." This episode was deleted from his military record, and North reportedly did not mention it in 1981 when he filled out his security forms for the NSC position.

North has testified twice under oath at public trials in support of friends. It has been reported that in both trials the transcript of his sworn testimony shows that he misstated and exaggerated some of his prior military duties. One article suggested that in a 1985 trial North compromised secrecy by bragging about his exploits and telling the court he had "just returned from overseas, where we are trying to effect the recovery of five Americans who are missing in Beirut" (*The New Republic*, February 16, 1987).

In July 1987 news reports said former religious broadcaster and 1988 presidential aspirant Pat Robertson revealed that some months earlier North had said hello to him at National Airport and had asked for his prayers because he was leaving on a trip to rescue U.S. hostages in Lebanon. Not long after, Robertson was interviewing Reagan and mentioned that he had "run into one of his people who was trying to get the hostages out." According to the story, Reagan replied quietly but firmly, "We don't want to talk about that."

For those of us who had watched Ollie court the powerful and wealthy with his tales of noble endeavors in the cause of freedom, these reports provided examples of self-promoting actions that in fact could have compromised the security of an authorized operation and thereby also could have harmed the hostages. After this story was published, North reportedly denied the encounter ever happened. Whom to believe? From my experience with North, I would believe Pat Robertson, who fortunately had kept the matter secret until the Iran-contra issue surfaced.

Much of North's ability to involve well-intentioned citizen activists derived from his claims of frequent one-on-one personal contact with the president. Of course, with the approval of McFarlane and Poindexter, North was sometimes able to back up this illusion, because they would arrange meetings with the president for private citizens chosen by North. I believe the president was told and believed that he was meeting with patriotic individuals who were acting lawfully by providing their own funds to support or to help obtain aid for the contras.

North cultivated the image and reputation of a "can-do guy," someone able to get things done. Clearly there is no question about his enormous energy, his long hours of work, and his ability to make things happen. But good intentions and activism are not enough to achieve positive results in foreign policy.

Like McFarlane and Poindexter, North always seemed impatient with, and insensitive to, the need for a competent, well-thought-out *political* strategy. North was moving about in so many directions on so many details of projects that he often could not focus in a thoughtful way on how to obtain the overall desired result. His desire for taking credit precluded effective teamwork unless it was required of him by his superiors.

On a directly operational level, North often did not get results. This is dramatically illustrated by his failing to assure that a proper $10 million donation from a third country actually reached the contras' Swiss bank account in 1986. North was apparently too harried that day to provide the correct account number (or to follow up to be sure the funds had arrived), thereby losing *three times the amount of money* that his entire diversion had provided for the contras. Further, in April 1986, while North was writing Poindexter that the contras lacked food, medicine, and boots, he apparently *overlooked* the fact that his partners in the diversion had *$8 million* parked in their Swiss bank accounts. It seems that North in effect "misplaced" about $20 million through mismanagement. The committee's investigation "revealed that *of the $16.1 million profit* from the sales of arms to Iran, only *about $3.8 million* went to support the contras (the amount representing 'the diversion')" [emphasis added; Report, p. 9].

It was a mistake for North to pressure the State Department– administered nonmilitary aid program in the autumn of 1985 to hire individuals and aircraft that were also participating in the secret military resupply operation. I and others had advised North that the State Department program had to be scrupulously well run and able to document everything it did because the Democrats in Congress would try to use any irregularity as a reason to deny future aid. And they did just that. Still, North risked discovery of his effort by mixing the two operations. It is also strange to me that North would want the contras to pay 38 percent more for their weapons—why?

There was a capable White House staff responsible for communicating the president's policies and maintaining liaison with citizens and leaders throughout the country. Because President Reagan publicly and frequently made clear that he hoped to persuade Congress to provide funding for the Nicaraguan resistance, this White House staff made Central America a high-priority issue. Ambassador Whittlesey and later Patrick Buchanan tried to build effective teamwork on behalf of the president's policies among government agencies. I participated in their efforts, and so, at first, did North. But then we saw much less of Ollie and didn't know why. Very dedicated and capable Reaganites like Robert Reilly, however, noticed that sometimes when they were managing public events or meetings involving the president, Ollie North would suddenly swoop in and "take over."

Many private citizens who led organizations that supported President Reagan's Central America policy found they had a hard time raising funds to get their messages out. Several of us were puzzled by this. Weren't there enough supporters of the president who understood the immense danger of a communist Central America and Mexico? Didn't they understand the need to help organizations that were trying to inform the American people and Congress? Did these people fail to see the immense efforts of private American citizens who journeyed to Nicaragua to express sympathy with the communist regime and those who were active in lobbying against Reagan's policy?

Well, only after the Iran-contra investigations did I and Bob Reilly and others from the White House who worked on these issues learn the answers. Yes, there were well-meaning, patriotic Americans who donated about $10 million in support of President Reagan's policies. It turns out that Oliver North worked closely with a group of private fund-raisers who had great success during 1985 and 1986. Unfortunately the report informs us that "of *the $10 million that was raised, only* approximately *$4.5 million* was funneled to or spent on behalf of the contras . . . the rest was retained . . . for salaries, fees, and expenses. . . ." (Report, p. 85.) Here too North's intended purposes were not met in two ways. The private fund-raisers kept far too much of the money for themselves, and of the more than $1 million ostensibly spent to communicate the president's policy, those of us working on this issue in Washington noticed virtually no impact. One of the reasons we were surprised to learn of this fund-raising network is that we had noticed no effects whatsoever.

Of course North's greatest error in judgment, concurred with by Poindexter, opened the way to the disastrous 1987–88 reversal of Reagan's 1986 success in obtaining a congressional majority for military aid to the contras. And it seriously damaged the Reagan presidency. That error was to have become *directly* involved in the management of a private operation supplying military aid for the contras after Congress prohibited Defense, CIA, "or any other agencies . . . involved in intelligence activities" from doing this. While I agree with the minority report's view that this restriction did not apply to the White House or NSC staff, simple *political common sense* suggests that if members of the NSC did what Ollie North did, and it became known (which has to be assumed in Washington), there would be a political uproar that could surely endanger future congressional funding.

In my judgment *this entire unauthorized operation was unnecessary.* I believe it would never been approved by President Reagan if Poindexter had given him the chance to make a decision. It was unnecessary because the contras needed only the relatively modest amount of $30–$50 million annually to maintain themselves until Congress undid its mistake in cutting them off. There are about sixty countries in the world that are friendly to us and depend on our strength for their security. Effective briefings could have helped them understand that *their own security interests* would be threatened if the United States had to contend with pro-Soviet dictatorships from Panama to our two-thousand-mile open southern border. Since the U.S. Congress cannot legislate for foreign governments, if they decide to help the contras, that would be entirely proper—as the Iran-contra committees explicitly agreed.

In my discussions with Ollie on alternative strategies in Central America, I had always insisted that the president had to have a clear understanding of what was involved, what sorts of risks lay behind different preliminary actions. North disagreed and said: "No, we have to make the right things happen and make sure that the president goes the way we want."

I am sure McFarlane and Poindexter believed North thought highly of them. There is the prof note from McFarlane in early 1986 in which he compliments North and says if the American people only knew about his contributions, they would make him "Secretary of State." Interestingly, after McFarlane had traveled with North to Iran in May 1986 and seen him operate firsthand, he seemed to change his mind, at least for a while. It is reported that during this trip to Iran, after McFarlane had refused to accept only one or two hostages for the weapons they had brought on their airplane, North got up at 4:00 A.M. and *secretly reopened negotiations with the Iranians*. When McFarlane woke up and found out, he ordered the group to leave immediately. It was also reported that North apparently decided to tell the Iranians that President Reagan wanted them to win the war, a statement that was totally contrary to U.S. policy and interests.

After this trip, McFarlane sent Poindexter a prof note saying that Ollie needed rest, should leave the NSC staff, and possibly spend some time on "disability leave," recuperating at the Bethesda Naval Hospital, where he'd gone to recover from his emotional crisis in 1974.

While McFarlane apparently caught Ollie that time, it was a rare exception. Ollie knew how to project just the right combination of military obedience and go-for-it initiative with his superior officers McFarlane and Poindexter. Ollie knew how to say "Yes, sir" to them with just the right dash of crisp sincerity. He didn't disagree with them as Chris Lehman, Roger Robinson, or I would; we felt we were treating McFarlane and Poindexter with respect by having an honest discussion with them.

No, it seemed to me that Ollie simply manipulated them as best he could and ignored them when necessary. Then, to colleagues like me, he would fulminate about that "stinking wimp McFarlane—he's always giving in to Shultz." He would complain bitterly about Poindexter's remoteness and ridicule Poindexter for bringing all of his "navy 'yes-men' buddies" to the NSC. Everybody lets off steam at times, but I was always startled by the vehemence and cunning with which Ollie attacked colleagues whom, for the moment, he found to be a problem.

North gave special attention to courting Vice President Bush. In retrospect, that is why I believe North wanted to take my place on the vice president's December 1983 trip to Argentina and Central America. North cultivated good relations with Donald Gregg, Bush's national security adviser. Gregg, a former CIA employee, had been on the Carter NSC and claimed to have worked with Poindexter during the Carter years.

In July 1986, when Vice President Bush was in Israel, he received truly startling news from a senior Israeli official. Contrary to what had been told President Reagan and himself, the United States and Israel were not dealing with moderates in Iran, but rather with the most radical factions because "they can deliver the hostages." Did Vice President Bush take this new information to the president and to his foreign policy cabinet? The press reported that he told his chief of staff to send the memorandum of this significant conversation to none other than Oliver North.

In my opinion McFarlane and Poindexter at times lost sight of the difference between honesty and dishonesty. Despite good intentions, they appeared to put their desire to avoid conflict with Shultz and his White House allies ahead of their obligation to assure that the president was fully in command of foreign policy. In so doing they lost sight of what was best not just for Mr. Reagan, but for the American people. And surely they were the wrong people to be supervising someone like Oliver North.

North himself had an amazing knack for telling people what would enhance his own status in their eyes. This served him well in the short run, when there was nobody to contradict him. The largely skeptical Democratic majority of the Iran-contra investigating committee, he might guess, might well be eager to believe the worst about the late William Casey.

And in fact the committee's final majority report incorporated, with no further substantiation, North's allegations that Casey knew and approved—in North's presence alone—the diversion of funds to the contras. Never mind the implausibility of Casey's supporting a dangerous and unnecessary act that North himself knew had been regarded as a potentially "impeachable offense." Never mind that the committee already knew about North's many fabrications about his personal meetings with the president. This time the congressional majority seemed to believe what it served their (partisan?) purposes to say: that the late Bill Casey was Ollie North writ large. That North could pull off another self-serving claim in such circumstances is an ironic tribute to his resourcefulness.

To me the tragedy of Oliver North is that with proper leadership and guidance, his good qualities would have predominated and he would have helped rather than damaged his president and his country.

WILLIAM CASEY

> I think I should mention that when Mr. Casey was chairman of the SEC he was an outstanding chairman. . . . And he provided a work environment which was really almost unique, where he encouraged people or inspired people. And while I think that everybody that could possibly work for someone like that would be grateful to do it one time, when the second chance came, I think you have to be doubly grateful. And I must say the second time was probably even better than the first. But he is a wonderful man and I want you to know that.

> JUDGE STANLEY SPORKIN
> TESTIMONY BEFORE THE IRAN-
> CONTRA HEARING, 6/26/87

I can but add that I totally agree with Judge Sporkin's assessment. I was very favorably impressed from the first time I met Casey in the spring of 1981. My five years of working with him only confirmed and enhanced that first impression.

As a young lawyer Casey had joined the Office of Strategic Services (OSS), the predecessor of the CIA. Before World War II ended, he was managing networks of agents penetrating Nazi lines. Then and during his entire life, Bill Casey has understood the dangers posed to freedom in this century by both fascist and communist totalitarianism. What's more, he had a quick, active mind, with good solid judgment about geopolitical realities and trends.

It is in the nature of the profession that the intelligence community's successes are unknown, but shortcomings or failures become highly visible. When Casey took over as director of CIA in 1981, the institution had been rocked by years of congressional investigations, public criticism, internal shake-ups, and new procedures for congressional oversight. There had been five CIA directors in the 1970s alone. President Reagan and others recognized that shortcomings in the intelligence community had contributed to the free world's inability to halt some major communist gains during those years. And, there was a consensus on the need to rebuild the intelligence organizations.

For six years Casey provided the leadership to do that. This included improving the quality and quantity of analytical products. Here Casey emphasized that where there were different judgments about major issues, these should be brought out clearly for the policymaker rather than hedged through the kind of guarded, ambiguous language he called "mush." Casey said publicly that during his tenure the size and budget of the intelligence organizations had increased significantly. It was evident to me that Casey helped to enhance the sense of purpose and commitment of intelligence personnel at all levels.

However, it was in his role as a member of the foreign policy cabinet that I saw Casey perform with high distinction time and again during my three years at the NSC. He truly believed the president should govern in foreign policy. I have recounted *some* of the times Bill Casey prevented serious foreign policy setbacks because he was willing to take the issue to the president. In doing so, he acted with moral courage. He did not hesitate for fear that George Shultz and his White House allies might seek or bring about his removal. I believe Casey recognized the risk but simply decided that he had the duty to alert the president whatever the consequences to himself.

Yet no matter how many times Shultz was caught in what seemed to me a sneaky maneuver, Casey continued to work with him as a colleague. He did not react in a personal way, nor, to my knowledge, did he counterplot against Shultz. Casey felt that Schultz should have his say before the president, and that the NSC meeting was the best setting for a good debate.

What connection did Casey have with the NSC operation to obtain military support to the contras from October 1984 to October 1986, when Congress had declared that this could not be done by Defense, CIA, or agencies "involved in intelligence activities"? My guess (and here I am speculating, because Casey never discussed these NSC activities with me) is that Casey agreed with the advisory legal opinion of the Intelligence Oversight Board and with a commonsense reading of the law that the White House and NSC staffs were not covered by this restriction. After all, Casey was serving as director of the CIA, which meant he supervised all the agencies "involved in intelligence activities." He did not supervise the NSC staff, which was part of the executive office of the president and received its appropriated funds by congressional processes and from accounts entirely separate from those of the intelligence organizations.

Apparently Casey knew McFarlane and Poindexter had authorized North to serve as the point of contact for American citizens and others who might want to make legal contributions to help the contras. President Reagan frequently and publicly asserted that American citizens have long exercised the right to provide lawful assistance to foreign political groups with whom they agreed. Since North was in touch with leaders of the Nicaraguan armed resistance, it would be natural to refer potential donors to him. This function is, I believe, the reason Casey referred possible private donors to North.

Such referrals also illustrated Casey's determination to obey the law by keeping CIA or any intelligence organizations away from this activity. The Tower Commission report points out that "as soon as the congressional restrictions were put into effect, CIA Headquarters sent instructions to its field stations '. . . to cease and desist with actions which can be construed as providing any type of support' " (Tower, p. 451). In June 1987 the House Intelligence Committee released to the public secret testimony Casey had given on November 21, 1986 (before Meese's discovery of the diversion). Casey had said forthrightly: "The NSC has been guiding and active in the private provision of weapons to the contras down there. . . . I don't know all the details. I have kept away from the details because I was barred [by the Boland amendment passed by Congress] from doing anything. . . . It came to McFarlane, and he began to develop it" (*Washington Post*, November 18, 1987).

I believe such *freely volunteered* information *before* this question had become controversial illustrates Casey's view that it was perfectly proper for the NSC staff to be doing what he believed they were doing, pointing private donors in the right direction. My guess is that Casey did not know about Ollie North's various banking activities or about the unauthorized diversion of monies from the Iran weapons sale to the contras.

Had Casey known about the use of "residuals" to finance contra arms purchases, it is highly unlikely he would have brought this up. He probably learned about it later in November 1986, right after Attorney General Meese did.

And when Meese discovered the diversion and asked North who knew about it, North did *not* name Casey, I believe, because Casey was still able to defend himself. North knew that McFarlane had not authorized his initial diversion, and that McFarlane would likely tell that to Meese. If North had wanted to claim authority from a higher official, he most likely would have made his allegation about Casey to Meese. But it was only after Casey's death on May 6, 1987, that North pointed the finger of blame at Casey. (Since North liked to boast about even fictitious connections with important people and revealed sensitive information to enhance this impression, it is probably significant that he is not known to have suggested to *anyone* that Casey supported his operations until Casey was dead.)

Do I believe North's allegation that Casey directed him to establish a future ''off-the-shelf, stand-alone'' covert action capability with funds diverted from the Iran military sale?

Casey's respect for the Constitution and the authority of the president makes it highly unlikely that he would have agreed to an extralegal covert action organization. Casey also was too savvy and realistic about American politics to endorse such an idea. He would know there was some probability this would be exposed either through a leak by participants or as a result of discovery by a hostile foreign government. Casey would think ahead *politically* (as North might not) and reckon that the exposure of such an operation might well produce a ground swell of opposition to *any* covert action. And Casey knew that to defend our freedom the United States urgently needs a range of methods between diplomacy and the use of our troops.

Aside from North's proven and self-admitted record of misstatements, there is other important evidence against his allegations. In my judgment the select committee's report makes clear that it was North and the Israeli counterterrorism official Nir who first began talking about joint covert operations. The minority report was correct to have criticized the majority report for

> swallowing North's testimony that Director Casey *intended to create* a privately funded, off-the-shelf, covert operation capability . . . this despite the fact that two people close to Casey . . . Deputy Director of Central Intelligence John M. McMahon and Deputy Director for Operations Clair George both denied Casey would ever have countenanced such an idea. ''My experience with Bill Casey was

absolute," said George. "He would never have approved it."
[emphasis added; Minority Report, p. 441]

Having had five years' association with Casey, I share that judgment. In fact, it is important to note that the majority report offered this explicit qualification about its own judgment in believing North's allegation:

> The Committees are mindful, however, of the fact that the evidence concerning Casey's role comes mainly from North; that this evidence, albeit under oath, was used by North to exculpate himself, and that Casey could not respond. (Report, p. 20)

The Majority report said "the evidence . . . comes mainly from North," but I found *nothing else* cited to support this conclusion! There is also documentary evidence *against* North's allegation. The Tower report documented that Poindexter sent a prof note in May 1986 telling North not to tell anyone about his operational activities, "including Casey." Then, in June 1986, after the House vote was won and the CIA was planning to resume its aid to the resistance, North wanted the CIA to pay several million dollars to purchase the privately owned air resupply equipment from Secord. But the CIA wanted no connection with any private operation (probably concerned about the political consequences of a future misunderstanding by some in Congress). North *wrote* Poindexter:

> That seems to be the direction they are heading, apparently based on NSC guidance. *If you have already given Casey instructions* to this effect, *I would very much like to talk to you* about it in hopes that we can reclaim the issue. [emphasis added; Report, p. 73]

This *note* does not depict an Oliver North who is buddy-buddy with William Casey in a secret operation only they know about. Rather, it shows clearly that it is *Poindexter* who would be giving Casey instructions. And it is not *North* who will talk to Casey: he is asking *Poindexter* to do so. This is what my experience with all three men would lead me to expect.

But the report says, "North *testified* that the idea to sell the Enterprises' assets to the CIA was Director Casey's" (Report, p. 73). Here is a vivid case where North's own memo of June 1986 contradicts directly his 1987 testimony before the investigating committees. If this had been Casey's idea, there would obviously have been no need for North to try to persuade Poindexter to have Casey buy the assets of the Secord resupply operation.

There's also another important example of documentary evidence. The Majority report states that at the May 16, 1986, NSC meeting, Casey gave the president the "bad news" that only $2 million remained of the nonmilitary congressionally approved funds for the resistance (Report, p. 70). *That same day* North wrote Poindexter that $5 million from the Iran arms sales had come in; this meant that "the resistance support organization now has more than six million available for immediate disbursement" (Report, p. 70). If Casey had known about those funds, he would have had no reason to tell the president the "bad news" that so little remained. He would not have misinformed the president.

Rather than Casey, it was McFarlane who in a March 1986 prof note to North mused about himself and North acting jointly from McFarlane's research institute office, "building clandestine capabilities so much in demand here and there." Then in 1987 McFarlane, returning before the Congress under oath without immunity, said: "Colonel North testified that he and Director Casey had agreed upon a full-service operation to support the contras using nonappropriated funds. I never heard of any such full-service operation from either Director Casey or Colonel North, and I certainly never concurred in one." None of the other witnesses in any way provided any information to back up North's accusation.

It should be remembered that Casey was prudent, and took the initiative in seeking the Justice Department's opinion as to the legality of third-country direct aid to the contras in 1984. And in 1986 the record shows that he consulted and followed the advice of the CIA General Counsel on Military Sales to Iran.

Stanley Sporkin's June 1987 testimony illustrated Casey's concern for the law that the president be correctly informed by his advisers. In writing the first draft of the intelligence finding by which the president would authorize the sale of weapons to Iran in January 1986, *North had omitted* any mention of the U.S. hostages to be ransomed. When Sporkin, then CIA's legal counsel, asked North why this was not in the document, North replied (according to Sporkin's testimony), "Either the Secretary of State or the Department of State did not want it in" (*Washington Post,* June 25, 1987, p. A12). This was most likely a typical North subterfuge since it seemed to be North who did not want to alert the president to the arms for hostages deal that was being presented to him as a "strategic opening."

Sporkin further testified that he had insisted it did not "seem right," so he and North put their respective arguments to Casey—who agreed with

Sporkin. In the end Casey made sure the document given to the president *did* mention the hostages.

Meese testified that Casey was not involved in the diversion. He said when Casey learned about it on November 25, 1986, he urged that all facts about the diversion be made public (Report, p. 646). *Time* magazine interviewed Casey only days before his incapacitating illness in December 1986. Among Casey's statements were the following:

> I don't know everything the NSC did. The NSC was operating this thing; we were in a support mode [referring to the Iranian sales]. I don't know anything about diversion of funds. What you've got to understand is we were barred from being involved with the contras, and we kept away from that. (*Time,* December 22, 1986)

Finally, I know from personal experience that Casey is unlikely to have given orders to an NSC staff member—he was very concerned about respecting the lines of management authority. I had worked for Casey two years at CIA and saw him frequently during my three years at the White House. Never once did he give me an order after I left CIA. Against this evidence, we have only one unsupported posthumous allegation that Casey suddenly deviated from his demonstrated concern for acting within the law.

As an activist Casey was inevitably drawn to individuals (like North) who were also activists. I believe it is possible to be an activist while behaving in a way that is legal, ethical, and effective. I call this *prudent activism*, and it requires thinking matters through before recommending and taking significant actions. (Naturally, this is how I see myself.) But some activists tend to be impatient with having to weigh alternate courses of action and consider how they may be countered or perceived. They tend to view such questions as an irrelevant intrusion, a sign of timidity, or, worse, a lack of commitment. I believe that because of his political wisdom, Casey was a prudent activist. But he, like so many others, may have been partly taken in by Oliver North. There were those who knew and tried to warn Casey about North's dark side. It is not clear whether he heeded that advice.

I should say a few words about the portrait of Casey in Bob Woodward's book *Veil*. On many of the issues and people it discusses, my knowledge is limited to that of the newspaper reader. But Woodward writes a lot about Reagan administration policy in Central America. Sometimes he's right, at times he's somewhat correct, and quite often, I believe, he's wrong. For example, he is incorrect in writing that the CIA concluded in 1981 that there was no connection between the Soviet Union and international terrorism. As Deputy CIA Director Robert Gates wrote in November 1987, analysts differed about the *extent* of Soviet involvement, but there was and is solid evidence of a years-long pattern of direct and indirect Soviet support to terrorist groups, including those in Latin America (*Washington Post,* November 29, 1987).

For some weeks in the spring of 1987 Woodward had telephoned my home seeking an appointment. I had never met him and was hesitant to talk with him. It seemed to me that a journalist who reportedly had revealed so many national security secrets was not a person likely to give Casey or his organization a fair hearing. But my wife, Nancy, argued: "Woodward's book is likely to be negative about Casey. You worked closely with him and saw Casey over five years. You know how important to the country his leadership and good judgment have been. You ought to meet Woodward and try to tell him about Casey's overall contributions—and if you don't, there won't be many others who will."

I finally called Woodward back. He was cordial as I listed my conditions: "I will not discuss any covert activities or classified information. None in any way. I have never done so during my time of government service and will not do so now."

He replied something like, "I understand that. I know you're not a leaker. I just want to talk with you in broad terms about Bill Casey."

I continued, "And I would like to tape-record our conversation, and I would like my wife, Nancy, to join us."

"Sure," Woodward said. "Let's all have lunch at my house."

Some days later we met at his Georgetown home. Woodward is extremely personable and persuasive. He served a delicious lunch, and we both had our tape recorders playing. After about half an hour of conversation, Woodward had asked virtually no questions about Casey. I steered the conversation to Casey. Briefly I summarized the four areas of his contribution: improved analysis; prudent but vigorous action to help our friends; enhancement of morale; and excellent judgment on the key geopolitical issues.

Later, Woodward asked me, "Isn't it true that Nicaragua virtually stopped providing military support to the guerrillas in El Salvador in 1981?"

I replied: "No, this support has continued right to the present minute, and our government has released declassified reports on this every year since 1981."

Woodward challenged this, and I gave him examples of the declassified evidence. He held to his opinion on this matter and obviously ignored the contrary evidence he got from me (and available from the well-documented government reports). And when I read his book, that was my feeling about many issues I knew about.

Concerning what Woodward wrote about me personally: some is correct, some is not. He is totally wrong in alleging: "Menges suggested that the captured Cuban prisoners not be released. He urged that the Cubans be made to suffer" (*Veil,* p. 299). Quite the contrary, I was deeply concerned that all the captured persons be treated humanely, and that the multinational force assure there be no revenge or violent acts committed against any former members of the Grenadan dictatorship or its foreign supporters. Where did Woodward get this false statement about me? *And why didn't he ask me about it or about many of the things he wrote about me?*

One of the most amusing observations was his description of my "radio announcer's voice." How could Woodward publish that after having met with me? Where did he get this idea? One of my friends may have solved the mystery. I have a telephone answering machine with a prerecorded message done by a person with a "radio announcer's voice." Woodward might have written this physical description of me after hearing my answering machine during the weeks before I had agreed to meet with him. It seems he then simply left the description in the text. I use these personal examples because they illustrate that Woodward's account has to be read with a great deal of caution and skepticism. When it comes to the closing scene of his alleged sickbed conversation with Casey, I believe Mrs. Sophia Casey—that her tragically ill husband could not have replied with full understanding and clarity to the question about whether he knew about the diversion to the contras.

GEORGE SHULTZ

> In almost every area . . . these noble objectives, which Ronald
> Reagan has espoused throughout his political life, bear little
> resemblance to the policies being carried out by his State
> Department. Instead, his policies and goals often are being
> betrayed by the foreign policy establishment.

That was the conclusion of a January 1986 Heritage Foundation report entitled "Rhetoric Vs. Reality: How the State Department Betrays the

Reagan Vision.'' It is a view with which I wholeheartedly agree. And I believe a major reason is George Shultz.

Taken in, again and again, by the dominant State Department faction, George Shultz tried, in my opinion, to steer the president and his foreign policy cabinet in order to make sure events would turn out his way. After the president's 1983 rejection of his Central American initiatives, for example, Shultz attempted to maneuver them by the next year. Apparently he was helped in his attempts by Michael Deaver, who made sure Shultz got an hour alone with the president once or twice a week when both were in town. Donald Regan told Congress (July 30, 1987) that during the two years he was chief of staff, Shultz met privately with the president ninety-nine times. My view is that Shultz tried to use these informal meetings to substitute for the NSC, and that this started the breakdown of the NSC process, a breakdown that ultimately led to the Iran-Nicaragua crisis.

When Shultz first took office, however, it was by no means clear that he would take this ultimately destructive route. In the early days, George Shultz sounded like the ultimate team player.

When I traveled with him to Central America, South America, and the Caribbean, he could not have been a more hardworking, courteous, and considerate leader. He made a point, in each country, of meeting with the ambassador and the entire embassy staff and telling them what a great job they were doing.

At these gatherings the secretary would regale people with a story about himself, telling of his experiences, which included the academic world (Ph.D. in industrial economics, professor at MIT and the University of Chicago), government (former secretary of labor, secretary of the treasury), business, and now government service once again. And he would always end by saying how impressed he was by the quality of the career civil service employees.

In June 1982 Shultz accepted President Reagan's invitation to succeed Haig as secretary of state. Right from the start the dominant foreign service group in the State Department hoped that Shultz would be the kind of secretary of state they could influence strongly. Reportedly he knew little about foreign policy—the major international issues, the detailed history of the post–World War II period, and, specifically, Soviet actions and strategies, not to mention the internal politics of major foreign countries—hostile and friendly.

The key jobs at the State Department are the five regional assistant secretaries, the under secretary for political affairs, the two people who control the flow of paper and individuals into the secretary's office, and the under secretary for management, who presides over promotions and assignments. Career foreign service officers held virtually all of the top positions, and on most issues they seemed quickly to bring Shultz around to the State Department point of view. In the fall of 1982 it was reported that Shultz would hold a series of "issue seminars," with experts on major international issues such as U.S.-Soviet relations, arms control, and Central America. It was evident to those of us who had worked in foreign policy that Shultz was not getting a representative cross section of expert opinion. Many of the most knowledgeable people in the administration, who also happened to be Reagan supporters, such as Jeane Kirkpatrick, were not asked to participate. In fact, it seemed to many of us that the career foreign service officers quickly constructed an impenetrable wall around Shultz to keep him from having any real discussions with Reagan appointees. Within weeks, it seemed, State had persuaded Shultz on most of the major foreign policy issues.

Consider the following examples as I see them:

Strategic arms reduction and SDI—The State Department position is to trade away any real development or deployment of SDI for some type of reduction in offensive strategic weapons. This is not Reagan's view, and it makes no sense for two reasons: first, because it is logical to bargain for mutual, reciprocal cuts in offensive weapons on their own terms; second, because strategic defensive systems threaten no lives and provide both sides with an incentive to cut offensive weapons because they provide security against a first strike. In October 1985, a month before the first U.S.-Soviet summit, Shultz told the Soviets in advance that he had persuaded President Reagan to agree to a "narrow interpretation" of the ABM treaty that would limit SDI to laboratory testing. (At the time, Assistant Secretary of Defense Richard Perle said this unilateral concession was the equivalent of testing new submarines on dry land.) In July 1986 Shultz persuaded Reagan to send Gorbachev a letter offering a seven-and-one-half-year delay in the deployment of SDI, again a unilateral concession *in advance* of the negotiations.

Counterstrategy against terrorism—Despite strong rhetoric, Shultz and the State Department have failed for years to move beyond anything more than an episodic and defensive approach.

Central America—Enders, who decided the State approach in the summer of 1981, was able to persuade Shultz to follow the State Department formula. Evidence of this includes Shultz's January 1983 proposal to the president (rejected); his June/July 1984 four-point plan (twice rejected); his attempted October 1984 treaty (rejected); the "Habib letter" push for a treaty in the spring of 1986 (rejected). While he was energetic in countering the president, Shultz failed to assure that the State Department did its job effectively and used diplomacy, information, and persuasion to build increasing support in Europe and Latin America for the democratic forces of Central America. And once Kirkpatrick, Clark, Casey, and I were gone, Shultz persuaded the president in August 1987 to sign the Reagan-Wright plan, which triggered the destructive Arias plan.

Angola and Mozambique—While Reagan's speeches committed his administration to helping pro-Western freedom fighters, for five years the Shultz State Department pursued the same failed policy of providing and encouraging Western economic aid to Angola and Mozambique, hoping to "wean" these communist dictatorships away from the Soviet bloc.

Certainly Shultz and State Department officials had every right to their own points of view on these foreign policy issues and every right to try to persuade President Reagan to follow their proposals. But I believe they should not lull the president with tough-sounding speeches and then continually work against his policy decisions. I believe Shultz, sometimes with the acquiescence of McFarlane and Poindexter, did this time and time again on Central America.

Having heard Shultz speak in many NSC meetings, I was surprised by what seemed to me to be the misleading way he made his case to the president. He always presented his proposals in the most general way, virtually never mentioning the potential risks that might result from actions by our adversaries to take advantage of, or violate, the agreements he was proposing. So he seemed never to consider the need to prepare for counteractions, just in case.

Moreover, Shultz rarely seemed to consider whether the vulnerabilities and deep fears of friendly countries—directly affected by his proposed diplomatic initiatives—would lead *them* into problems.

My guess, based on Shultz's manner in trying to persuade Ronald Reagan during NSC meetings, is that he used the same misleading and one-sided approach in their private discussions. That is probably how in late May 1984 Shultz (with McFarlane going along) got Reagan to endorse the sudden opening of bilateral negotiations with Nicaragua.* Then Shultz most likely hoped to use this general endorsement of

---

* In April 1988, at a moment of great peril for the Nicaraguan democratic opposition (unarmed and armed), the press reports that Shultz is sending a special envoy to explore renewed, secret bilateral negotiations with the Sandinistas—another mistake!

"negotiations" as sufficient presidential authority for State's totally new four-point plan.

Sometimes it seemed the Shultz State Department would defy common sense in order to avoid "problems" with the Soviet Union that might interfere with the planned summits of 1985 and 1986. In October 1985 a Ukrainian sailor escaped from his Soviet ship in New Orleans, Louisiana, and requested political asylum. The State Department seemed to fear that granting his request might cause complications for the decided November 1985 summit. With Shultz's concurrence, State concluded that this refugee, Miroslav Medvid, wished to return to the Soviet Union, even though his alleged statement to that effect was given only after Medvid had been forcibly returned to Soviet control, handcuffed, kicking, and screaming.

In August 1986 the United States arrested an alleged Soviet spy working at the United Nations who did not have diplomatic immunity and announced the intention to put him on trial. On August 30, in an obvious setup, an American journalist, Nicholas Daniloff, was arrested by the KGB in Moscow and charged with espionage. Suddenly Moscow had a hostage for their accused spy under arrest in the United States. Within a few days, and while President Reagan was on vacation at his ranch in California, a story leaked, most probably from the State Department, that perhaps there could be an exchange of Daniloff for the accused Soviet spy. This leak immediately produced protests against such an idea. With great courage, speaking through his wife from a KGB prison cell, Daniloff rejected the idea of such an exchange; numerous Republican congressional leaders protested; and leaders in the media were also opposed to setting this type of precedent.

Knowing President Reagan's general approach, my guess is that when he was briefed, he probably ordered there should be no exchange, even if it interfered with the second U.S.-Soviet summit then planned for November 1986. Shultz then made a tough speech at Harvard University, thundering that there would be no trade of the U.S. journalist for the accused Soviet spy.

Meanwhile the State Department, through Under Secretary Armacost, announced it would continue holding presummit meetings with the Soviet Union, but that at each it would express "grave concern" about the detention of Daniloff. Later in September 1986, Shultz and the Soviet foreign minister had many hours of meetings while both were in New York for the opening of the United Nations General Assembly. Some days later the accused Soviet spy was turned over to Soviet embassy officials, and Daniloff was released from the KGB prison in custody of the

U.S. ambassador in Moscow. A Soviet airplane left the United States with the accused Soviet spy *within hours* of the time Daniloff returned to the United States. Yet Shultz and the State Department insisted there had been "no swap."

Shortly thereafter the Soviet Union proposed a "presummit" meeting between Reagan and Gorbachev to be held in mid-October 1986 in Iceland. The Soviets presented this as an informal discussion to prepare the agenda for the negotiations at the "real" summit meeting to follow. Shultz persuaded Reagan to agree and was clearly in charge of making the preparations for this "presummit" meeting. (A sign that there was no systematic NSC process to prepare the U.S. position was that Secretary of Defense Weinberger was away from Washington in the days just before and during the Iceland meeting.)

In fact, the Soviet leadership had misled the United States. They did not intend to have an informal discussion about the agenda for a future meeting. The Soviet Union, probably assuming that Reagan's political advisers and many Republican candidates would perceive a U.S.-Soviet arms control agreement as a political asset in the November 1986 elections, immediately proposed major, dramatic (though vague) strategic arms reductions. Intense negotiations followed during the next days and nights. The Soviet leader offered deep cuts in offensive strategic weapons if President Reagan would, in effect, give up the SDI (which was essentially the position that many at the State Department had favored since Reagan announced SDI in 1983). President Reagan would not, and there was no deal. When he announced this to the media, Shultz looked absolutely crestfallen.

Watching these events from outside the administration, I had to wonder. Was the State Department so incompetent that it had failed to forewarn the president about such a dramatic Soviet move, one that was totally in keeping with their known diplomatic tactics? Or was this a more elaborate version of the "last-minute memo" whereby— once they had Reagan away from Weinberger and Casey—the State Department hoped to be able to persuade him to accept its advice and viewpoint in responding to the "surprise" Soviet proposals?

After the Iran-contra matter became public, Jeane Kirkpatrick published an insightful column on the obligations of the president's cabinet and staff in such situations:

> The decisions a president makes are not personal decisions. They are corporate decisions for his entire administration. And they are made with the counsel of the president's top advisors, who act as participants in collective policy-making. Cabinet members who bask

in the president's popularity and exercise his powers share collective responsibility for those decisions, whether the president has accepted their personal recommendations or not.

Individual members of the administration can avoid responsibility for decisions only by resigning at the time the decisions are made. Don Regan is not just responsible for cleaning up after the parade. He shares responsibility for the parade itself. George Shultz cannot avoid responsibility for all decisions that do not reflect his personal views. (*Washington Post,* November 30, 1986, p. C8)

I agree with these judgments. I was among those who were surprised by the public conduct of Secretary Shultz in the immediate aftermath of the disturbing revelations. In regard to the substance, I agree with Shultz and Weinberger—who argued against the weapons for hostages deal with Iran. I also believe Shultz was correct in pressing for truthful disclosure by the administration.

However, once a cabinet member decides not to resign because of his deep political or moral objection to a president's decision, he becomes "co-responsible." Shultz seemed in the first weeks of the crisis to focus on protecting his own interests.

First there were leaks, seemingly from the State Department, which sought to create the impression that Shultz *knew virtually nothing,* and later that Shultz had been on the "correct side" and was blameless. After some days of these leaks, former NSC adviser McFarlane spoke up and said he had kept Shultz fully informed, with frequent briefings about the weapons-for-hostage moves since they had begun in 1985. On June 25, 1987, Assistant Attorney General Cooper told the Senate-House investigating committee that McFarlane had also told him he had "informed Shultz of the arms-for-hostage deal as it was unfolding" (*Washington Post,* June 26, 1987, p. A16).

It seems to me that sometimes Shultz's behavior toward this president has illustrated the problem defined by former Secretary of State Dean Rusk (1961–69): "Every president has to make sure that his secretary of state understands who is the president and who is the secretary of state."

I perceived that the pattern of scheming and deception among colleagues at the subcabinet level began in the State Department during the first year of the Reagan administration. When Shultz arrived in the summer of 1982, he had a chance to make a fresh start. He could have brought into the policy jobs at State experts who shared the foreign policy views of the elected president. Shultz did not do this. He could have insisted the State Department chairmanship of the interagency committees be scrupulously fair. Shultz did not do that, either. He could have made clear that a presidential decision had to be obeyed and that no major unilateral initiatives could be taken without the approval of the president. Instead, I witnessed Shultz doing the opposite.

In my opinion, as Oliver North and John Poindexter observed State doing this *for several years*, they decided to do the same—which shows how the breakdown of the fair decision-making process can snowball until it seriously damages a president.

During the Iran-contra hearings, Shultz was lionized by many in contrast with McFarlane, Poindexter, and North—the "rogue operators." What nobody seemed to realize was how much he had in common with them. When Ollie spoke to me of boxing the president in so he would *have* to do the "right thing," he could have been describing George Shultz's modus operandi. They knew best, and Ronald Reagan would simply have to be brought—and maneuvered, if necessary—into line.

CASPAR WEINBERGER

During the late 1960s, when I was living in California, the local television news would carry interviews with Governor Reagan's articulate and intelligent finance director Caspar Weinberger. Later President Nixon brought this same man to Washington, first as chairman of the Federal Trade Commission, then as deputy to George Shultz at the Office of Management Budget, next as director, and then from 1973 to 1975 as secretary of health, education and welfare.

Given the professional and personal relationship Weinberger had with Ronald Reagan, it was no surprise when he accepted the call to become the Reagan administration's first secretary of defense (1981–87).

Weinberger had to deal with three main challenges. First, there was the threat posed by the Soviet bloc's ever-expanding strategic and conventional arsenal. Second, after two years of a pro-defense consensus, Weinberger faced prolonged and complex political negotiations about the Pentagon budget with Congress every year. Third, Weinberger had to duel constantly with his former colleague in government and business, George Shultz. The State Department has been pursuing its version of arms control with the Soviet Union for years, and Weinberger had to be constantly alert to assure that the president was not maneuvered into approving State proposals that the Defense Department judged to be a serious mistake. With McFarlane and Poindexter often tilting toward

Shultz, there was a need for Weinberger to use his personal access to the president on a few dramatic occasions. For example, before the November 1985 summit in Geneva, Weinberger delivered a personal letter about the arms control proposals to the president, perhaps because McFarlane had been unwilling to call an NSC meeting to review the final U.S. position for the summit. This became public when his letter was leaked (most likely by an opponent of Weinberger's at the State Department).

It is my experience that like Casey, Weinberger did not respond to State Department scheming with his own manipulation of the decision-making process. Rather, he tried to make the NSC system work. When Central America and other similar issues needed to reach the president, Weinberger was always willing to join Casey, Kirkpatrick, and Clark in telling the president. On a number of occasions Weinberger wrote McFarlane or the president proposing an NSC meeting be convened to discuss a major issue. At NSC meetings Weinberger was incisive and precise in making his case. I felt President Reagan was always impressed by Weinberger's eloquence, by his command of information, and by his strategic vision.

JEANE KIRKPATRICK

In 1963 Jeane Kirkpatrick coauthored *The Strategy of Deception,* her first book on foreign policy. Even today that volume offers one of the best analyses of the Soviet method of indirect warfare against the free world. In the years since, Kirkpatrick's understanding of this grave threat and what must be done to counter it has deepened.

A professor at Georgetown University and a resident scholar at the American Enterprise Institute for many years, Jeane Kirkpatrick was active in the Senator Henry Jackson centrist wing of the Democratic party. In 1981 she was among the "neoconservatives" who joined the Reagan administration because they felt deeply that the United States needed a more effective foreign policy.

As a forceful writer and speaker and a creative student of international politics, Kirkpatrick was in her element as President Reagan's ambassador to the United Nations. American political values and interests needed to be asserted at the UN, and Ambassador Kirkpatrick performed brilliantly. The media were fascinated by her eloquence and her command of foreign policy issues.

Secretary of State Haig should have perceived this and treated her as a valuable colleague. Instead, Haig and the State Department establishment seemed to treat her as an alien force—to be kept in New York, away from major foreign policy issues if at all possible. There were the usual backstabbing and anonymous detractions leaked to the Washington media. When George Shultz took over, this same treatment continued. It seemed to me that Shultz rarely worked closely with Kirkpatrick, though he seemed to feel less threatened by her than had Haig.

Kirkpatrick could hardly have enjoyed her petty treatment by some in the State Department, but she did not let this affect her morale or her energetic pursuit of her responsibilities. President Reagan had invited her to serve as a member of the National Security Council, and in all the NSC meetings I saw, Kirkpatrick spoke up with clarity, with cogent arguments, and with a civil but uncompromising directness. Of course, this was another reason Shultz did not want NSC meetings. In my experience it was always Casey, Weinberger, and Kirkpatrick who displayed great command of the facts, in contrast with Shultz's general and vague presentations.

Jeane Kirkpatrick also played an invisible but important role as the result of cordial relations with Bill Clark, Casey, and Weinberger; her wide-ranging foreign policy knowledge served to give all these cabinet members a broader perspective on current foreign policy issues. They liked to talk with Kirkpatrick and valued her judgment. At the same time Kirkpatrick's natural curiosity and her UN contacts with ambassadors from all over the world gave her up-to-date information on the thinking and actions of countries both hostile and friendly.

McFarlane showed his misunderstanding of these important relationships during his May 1987 congressional testimony. While revealing that he had never believed the contra strategy could work in Nicaragua, he admitted he had been unwilling to tell the president so because he was afraid that "Casey, Kirkpatrick, and Weinberger would call me a 'commie' or something."

That was a ridiculous statement. I have never heard any of the three refer to any American citizen that way. Quite the contrary, no matter how often Shultz and McFarlane seemed to manipulate the foreign policy process, these three and Bill Clark continued to work within the system, serving the president according to the rules. They did not leak to the press about the many times they "won" and Shultz "lost." They did not boast to pundits that once again the president had rejected Shultz's proposals. And they did not plant damaging stories about their bureaucratic opponents. Jeane Kirkpatrick served honorably and with great effect.

GEORGE BUSH

One could hardly design a more ideal preparation for a future president than the professional experience of George Bush. A World War II naval aviator who fought bravely, Bush is the son of a well-to-do Connecticut Republican senator. As an adult George Bush left home, settled in Texas with his bride, and attained financial success in the oil business. Next Bush was elected to Congress, lost a bid for the Senate, served as Republican party national chairman during the difficult Watergate years, and then became, in succession, ambassador to the UN, ambassador to China, and CIA director.

Although I did not work closely with Vice President Bush, I saw quite a bit of him in meetings over the years. Since I had once considered supporting Bush for the 1980 presidential race, I naturally expected that over the years of the Reagan administration he would become the natural Republican choice in 1988.

My experiences led me to conclude that Bush is unfailingly considerate and an honorable, well-intentioned man. But I found it surprising that a potential future president seemed so unconcerned with the maintenance of President Reagan's authority and a fair decision-making process. When Ambassador Winsor and I alerted him to Shultz's four-point Central America plan in June 1984 and urged that he press for an NSC meeting, Bush apparently did nothing. In December 1984, during the "Battle of the Ambassadors" when the president was being seriously misinformed, Bush seemed to do nothing. At the fateful Oval Office meeting on Iran in January 1986, I would have expected Regan or Bush to stop Poindexter, saying something like "This Iran decision is very big. I know Shultz and Weinberger disagree and think the president should have the chance to hear a full debate." But neither spoke up.

I was disappointed when, in Ecuador, Bush never raised the president's Central America policy with several influential Latin American presidents who might well have been swung from their foreign ministers' endorsement of the false treaty drafted by Mexico (with behind-the-scenes help from Cuba and Nicaragua). Again Bush did nothing. When the vice president had six months as chairman of the "task force to combat terrorism," he staffed it entirely with career government employees and produced a bland report that had little impact. Is George Bush most comfortable following the recommendations of accommodationist elements in the government bureaucracy? Bush knew me, but not very well, and that may well explain why he would not take my advice against that of Shultz, McFarlane, and Poindexter.

Bush has far better instincts, judgments, and experience on key foreign policy issues than do the 1988 group of Democratic presidential candidates. During Grenada, Bush was superb; and I believe that with a competent staff of experts from outside the career services, his own sensible instincts could lead to an effective foreign policy.

RONALD REAGAN

Although not without blemish, the Reagan record in foreign policy so far has been a major improvement over U.S. performance in the previous decade. An American program to encourage democracy abroad without the coercion of friendly governments has been institutionalized during the Reagan years, and more than 250 million people live in countries that have—also during the Reagan years—made a peaceful transition from dictatorship to democracy. No new pro-Soviet regimes have come to power. Grenada was liberated and is democratic. More than four hundred thousand resistance fighters are trying to replace seven pro-Soviet dictatorships, though none has yet succeeded. The strategic defense initiative has been launched; military strength has been improved; the political pressures for "any" U.S.-Soviet arms control and unilateral "freezes" have been resisted, and a reciprocal, realistic strategic arms reduction agreement might be possible. During the Reagan years, there have been no serious *direct* political or military confrontations with the Soviet Union, in part because the Reagan administration has acted prudently to help friendly countries and movements meet their own goals of resisting Soviet indirect aggression, instead of making the mistake of doing nothing or believing that only U.S. combat forces or U.S. military threats can be effective.

These are important achievements. They point the path toward a long-term, politically sustainable foreign policy that can maintain both freedom and peace.

But President Reagan has not lived up to his potential in foreign policy. There have not yet been any decisive, positive historical improvements anywhere in the balance between the free world and the Soviet empire and its allies. The outlook is very uncertain in Central America. If the Sandinistas defeat the freedom fighters, the most likely result will be a communist Central America, which will then threaten a communist takeover of Mexico and Panama. This would sharply alter the world balance of power against us, and could increase the risk of major war.

In Afghanistan the anti-Soviet resistance still fights bravely, but the Soviets continue their military occupation, and the killing goes on (an estimated one million have died since 1979; four of sixteen million Afghans are now refugees abroad). There, the pro-Western resistance *could* win, but it can also be defeated, either through continued Soviet military attack—including increased military pressure and attacks that could coerce Pakistan into denying the use of its territory to the Afghan resistance—or by the ruse of a defective political settlement into which the State Department might well mislead President Reagan in 1988. A consolidated, communist Afghanistan, along with the whole pro-Soviet terrorist apparatus in the Middle East, would then likely become the launching pad for increased Soviet efforts to destabilize and dismember Pakistan and bring pro-Soviet groups to power in one or more Persian Gulf oil states, including Saudi Arabia.

There is a dark cloud over the future of 100 million people in southern Africa. Victory for the pro-Western resistance, UNITA in Angola and RENAMO in Mozambique, remains feasible. This would improve the lives of the people in those countries immeasurably. It could also help promote multiracial democracy in South Africa and Namibia by sharply reducing the threat posed by procommunist antiapartheid groups (such as the ANC) and reactionary white racist elements.

Furthermore, the Reagan administration has failed to think through and carry out a systematic counterstrategy against subversive aggression and terrorism. There have been some important defensive steps, and there have been some intelligence improvements. The administration publicly claimed that in 1985–86 improved intelligence had prevented or caused the termination of about 125 planned terrorist attacks.

The April 1986 military counterstrike against terrorist-supported aggression from the Qaddafi regime was an important tactical success, but that same Libyan regime continues in power and reportedly remains active in supporting anti-Western terrorism while being more careful to use added concealment and more intermediaries. Compounding the absence of a counterstrategy was the apparent appeasement of the terrorist hijackers of the TWA airplane in June 1985, followed by

McFarlane's success in August 1985 in persuading President Reagan to approve the use of ransom to free American hostages held by pro-Iranian terrorist groups. These facts—the omissions and the actions—all mean that in early 1988, despite the strong rhetoric of Reagan, Shultz, and others, the terrorist threat seems to be as severe and as pervasive as it was in 1981.

I believe the accomplishments of Reagan's foreign policy have derived from *his* good strategic judgment and that of Casey, Kirkpatrick, Weinberger and Bill Clark along with their help in preventing Shultz and the State Department from making serious mistakes.

Why, then, does Shultz remain? Why did Ronald Reagan continue to trust McFarlane and Poindexter even when events might have shown him that they were not keeping him fully informed? Why does Reagan not ask how come virtually all the Reagan appointees in foreign policy have left or been pushed out? Why doesn't Reagan understand that "people are policy," and that he also needs a loyal, competent first- and second-echelon staff to assume *his* foreign policy agenda is implemented?

A cartoon in June 1987 showed two executives sitting in armchairs at their social club, one saying to the other: "It's awful that so many people around the President did these things—who in the world hired those people?"

That highlights what may be President Reagan's most serious flaw: his occasional inability to distinguish those who are honest, competent, and share his political values from those who lack these attributes. Everyone who hires people makes mistakes, and there are no infallible predictors of how a given individual will perform in a new job. But Reagan's method of choosing his top appointees seems to have changed little from 1981 to 1987. He tends to rely mostly on the judgments of those currently around him rather than on his own direct discussions with candidates for cabinet positions.

In 1982 Reagan reportedly asked Shultz to serve as secretary of state in a telephone conversation while Shultz was in Europe. If so, could the matter not have waited for a few days for Shultz to return and for President Reagan to probe his views in depth on the key foreign policy issues? In 1987 there are no reports that Reagan personally assessed the skills and foreign policy perspectives of either his first nominee to succeed Casey as director of the Central Intelligence Agency or his second, FBI Director Webster, who moved into a quite different area of professional work.

Nor does Ronald Reagan seem willing to hold his appointees to account: for example, when Shultz frequently seemed to maneuver against his decisions on Central America, southern Africa, Afghanistan, strategic arms control, and SDI. Partly, this unwillingness to require accountability was explained by McFarlane's and Poindexter's failure to give President Reagan a clear and concise factual picture of what Shultz was doing. It may also have been an unintended by-product of the "gentlemanly" reluctance of Casey, Weinberger, Kirkpatrick, and Clark to go after Shultz once they had again succeeded in helping Reagan undo or prevent another of State's wily bureaucratic stratagems.

Someone who worked directly for Reagan in the California days gave me two insights. He said: "A movie star works hard to learn his part, and then comes onto the set. The actor does his best but doesn't think about who the people are behind the scenes running the cameras, setting the lights, and he doesn't get involved in all the squabbles of these technical guilds or of the supporting cast. He assumes that if he does his best, the others will do the same, and the film will be fine." I found this perceptive and thought-provoking.

Reagan's friend continued: "When Ronald Reagan has good people around him, things will go well. Otherwise, things can go badly, because he is so trusting that he won't notice until a major problem has become visible to the entire public."

During my three years at the White House, I saw a great deal of President Reagan—at small Oval Office meetings, at many NSC meetings, at meetings with visitors in the Cabinet Room, at meetings with members of Congress, and at innumerable speaking events, usually at the White House.

I arrived at the NSC not knowing how much truth there was in the media image of a "detached" president. I learned that Ronald Reagan is indeed the good-natured, good-humored man he seems to be. I learned that he cares deeply about the foreign policy goals he espouses, and that he is an honest man who means what he says and says what he means. The reason I could work so confidently for his Central America policy is that time and again I witnessed with my own eyes and ears how he participated in the NSC discussions and how he definitively rejected the State Department's misguided proposals.

Ronald Reagan is by no means a weak president. Yet it would be misleading to say that he is a strong one. Perhaps the central paradox of the man can be suggested by one biographer's phrase: "passively decisive."

Presented with clear options, Reagan chooses. And in my judgment, he usually chooses rightly. That is why it was so especially vital that he be presented with all the options through the NSC process.

But it is not in his nature to assert himself in pursuit of his own policy. He waits until an issue has been presented to him; *then* he decides. And how it is presented makes the difference. If he can listen to a full discussion, he will usually make the right choice; if only one course is shown to him, that is the one he may well take. Some of his aides realized this early and took full advantage of it.

Reagan's passive side is connected with his trusting nature. He implicitly relies on those around him to keep him fully informed of the courses available to him, and he seldom looks beneath or beyond what they tell him. This, of course, makes him vulnerable to manipulation and outright deceit.

Part of Reagan's charm lies in his thorough lack of guile. Shakespeare describes a character "whose nature is so far from doing harms that he suspects none." Reagan makes the mistake of assuming that those around him are as generous, and as far above contriving, as he is. Such innocence is winning and morally laudable, but it is not always an asset at court. A healthy dash of skepticism may be a necessity for a president. It is fine to be as harmless as the dove, but it helps to be as wise as the serpent.

This innocence is at the core of Reagan's much discussed "management style." He is not lazy; for a man his age, he can work extremely hard. But there are certain things he must delegate and other things he prefers to delegate. He delegates easily because he trusts easily, and his trust is not always distributed wisely—to his and the nation's cost.

Throughout this book I have described occasions in which the president was deceived or otherwise maneuvered into compromising his own basic policies. The question arises, how many times can he be excused for allowing himself to be deceived? The saying is familiar: "If you fool me once, it's your fault. If you fool me twice, it's my fault." Reagan has been deceived more than twice.

No doubt he should have known better. He should have been a shrewder judge of character. He should have done his own cross-checking even on his closest advisers. My own wife, Nancy, whose "people radar" is so much better than mine, thinks I let the president off the hook too leniently. One person's "trust" is another's "gullibility."

Yet having said all that, I feel obliged to point out that *any president* depends on the expert advisers who have far more time to assess complex situations and assimilate information than he does. It is not always clear, even months after the event, when he has been deliberately misled. Nobody is busier than a president of the United States, and foreign policy is only one of many areas where he is under pressure to make frequent judgments and decisions about matters with which he cannot possibly be fully intimate.

And here I need to stress the other half of the phrase "passively *decisive*." I saw how authoritatively and intelligently Ronald Reagan acted when he was reasonably well informed. I was in a much better position than he to see when he was being misled about the area of my own speciality, yet it often took *me* a long time to perceive it. After all, he was not being guided by amateurs. These were men who knew how to cover their tracks and to prevent people with different views from gaining access to the president. In retrospect the pattern seems terribly clear. It was not always so at the time. Sometimes I too was initially unable to see or reluctant to believe what was being done by the State Department, nor did I suspect what Poindexter had authorized.

If President Ragan keeps his administration to his course in foreign policy, then I believe he will be judged one of America's best presidents. But history will judge him harshly if the State Department succeeds in persuading Reagan: to delay SDI for many years; to go along with the congressional Democratic leaders in watching the Nicarguan resistance defeated; to support a settlement in Afghanistan which fails to *guarantee* and *achieve* an independent non-communist government; and, to continue an ambiguous policy in Angola and help the communist regime of Mozambique which contributes to prolonging those internal wars instead of helping the resistance movements win and bring real peace. These foreign policy mistakes in 1988 would bring enormously greater dangers, including the possibilities of a communist Central America, Mexico, and Panama; a sharp increase in the danger that pro-Soviet groups will succeed in destabilizing one or more of the Persian Gulf oil states, and the greatly increased risk that South Africa will fail to end apartheid peacefully and will ultimately be taken over by a pro-Soviet regime. And just as the American people held President Carter—not Secretary of State Vance or the State Department—accountable for the consequences of his foreign policy misjudgments, so too would they hold President Reagan, not Secretary of State Shultz, to account.

On April 12, 1988, thanks to Paul Weyrich, I had the chance to share several of these concerns with President Reagan in a White House meeting which also included Chief of Staff Howard Baker, Secretary of Defense Frank Carlucci, NSC adviser Colin Powell, and private citizens

Peter Flaherty, General Daniel Graham, Henry Kriegel, Daniel McMichael, and William Pascoe.

The Iran-Nicaragua crisis has made visible that part of the problem connected with some NSC staff.

After the Tower Commission report came out in February 1987, I believed President Reagan would understand how serious the problems had become at the NSC. But I felt my August 1985 letter was still relevant, because it documented the *equally damaging* actions of Shultz and the State Department which I believed could pose an even greater future risk since Bill Casey was absent from the cabinet. So I called one of the president's close friends, someone whom I had asked to give my letter to the president in May 1986. At that time, after reading the letter, he had told me simply, "I can't get in the middle of an internal executive branch matter like this."

Now, some ten months later, in early March 1987, I reached him on the telephone and said, "You will recall my August 1985 letter to 'your friend' which you read in May 1986. I think that the Iran-contra mess makes it all the more important that 'your friend' read this letter now, because Shultz and the State Department are likely to become even more aggressively manipulative in the future."

In a warm and cordial voice he replied, "I agree with you. He *should* read your letter, and the sooner the better. Unfortunately, I can't take it to him now. I've just participated in removing Donald Regan, and if I gave the president your letter, it would look as though I were going after Shultz."

I interjected, "But my letter doesn't really 'go after' Shultz. It simply states the facts. The top man needs to know what has really been happening. And, as I told you almost two years ago, we *still* need a counterterrorism strategy."

The president's friend continued, "I agree with you about that, too. Yes, the letter should reach the president, and the person who can get it to him is_____. Call him, use my name, and I'll call him, too."

Within a day or two I was meeting with the person he had suggested, a well-known supporter of President Reagan and member of Congress. He and his top assistant heard my arguments for the continued relevance of the letter, then promised to give it to President Reagan personally within the next days—"as soon as an opportunity comes up."

Two months later, after having been confronted with this letter by Mark Belnick of the Iran investigating team, the word I received from this member of Congress was that the letter still had not been given to the president.

In the autumn of 1987, after the negative effects of the Arias plan for Central America were visible, one of the president's friends called me: "I am sorry I did not give your letter to the president last year. Things are going as badly as you tried to warn him. Please send me a copy of your letter and I'll send it using the personal code." Some days later he told me he had indeed sent my letter but had received no reaction: "I hope they're not opening the coded mail too," he concluded. I appreciated his effort.

Now to the Iran-contra question. Do I believe President Reagan knew about the activities of North and Poindexter in diverting funds from the Iran weapons sale to the contras? In the group meetings I attended with President Reagan wherein the contra issue was discussed, never once did I detect from him even the hint of a word or gesture that implied his staff should "do whatever is necessary—proper or not" to help the contras. McFarlane, in his May 1987 congressional appearance, testified that President Reagan had not been asked, nor had he given his authorization to the NSC staff, to divert funds to the contras from the sale to Iran or to become directly involved in the management of the nongovernment military supply operation. In July 1987 Poindexter testified that he had not told the president about this to give him "plausible deniability."

Having worked three years at the NSC, I believe President Reagan and am virtually certain that he neither knew about nor approved the diversion of Iran military sale funds to the Nicaraguan resistance.

THE FOREIGN POLICY INSTITUTIONS

The Constitution designates the president as chief executive: all members of the cabinet are appointed by him and can be removed by him. Approximately three hundred senior officials in foreign policy may also be chosen by him from outside or inside the career services. The more than four million civilian and military career employees of the executive branch all have taken an oath of office to support the Constitution, and that means to carry out the decisions made by the president. Any who disagree for serious ethical or political reasons have the right to resign, as Attorney General Elliot Richardson did during the Nixon administration and as Secretary of State Vance did in the Carter administration.

The post–World War II era has produced a major change in the challenges facing the United States and the requirements for effective foreign policy. Before World War II, the United States had mainly been concerned to remain neutral and maintain normal diplomatic relations with all governments to facilitate travel and commerce. After World War II American foreign policy faced unprecedented tasks: helping to build democratic institutions in defeated Germany, Japan, and the newly liberated countries; promoting a return of economic growth in devastated Europe and Asia; deterring open aggression by the four million–plus standing army that Stalin refused to dismantle (as the United States reduced its twelve-million-strong armed forces to three hundred thousand by the end of 1946); and helping friendly governments in Europe, the Middle East, Asia, and Latin America resist the deceptive, indirect war of subversive aggression, launched by the USSR against Greece and Iran in 1944 and continued since then with an ever-widening array of methods and accomplices.

Initially the United States tried to face this new postwar world by relying on the State Department and the United Nations system. The intelligence service and virtually all of the standing army were dismantled. This is when the Truman administration learned that foreign policy in the modern era was far more than just diplomacy and commerce.

After two years of major setbacks—the communist takeovers of Eastern Europe and North Korea, with Soviet-aided communists waging war in Greece, the Philippines, and Vietnam and on the brink of success in China—the president and Congress starting in 1947 created the new institutions needed to meet the post–World War II challenge: political assistance to prodemocratic, friendly groups within foreign countries; foreign economic aid; the CIA to inform, warn, and act secretly when ordered; and, after the communist invasion of South Korea in 1950, a large standing army, including a strategic attack force capable of retaliating to destroy any aggressor's homeland with nuclear weapons.

How could *any* single individual—the president—really carry out his constitutional duty to be in charge of all these new, large foreign policy agencies, especially when much of their activity takes place abroad, is unknown to the public, and occurs in the context of stealthy, cunning, hostile actions by powerful and unfriendly governments?

To help the president, Congress passed the National Security Act of 1947, which created the National Security Council, consisting of the president, vice president, secretary of state, and secretary of defense. The president may invite others to participate in the National Security Council. Among the regular participants during Reagan's first years have been the director of the Central Intelligence Agency, the chairman of the

Joint Chiefs of Staff, the attorney general, the secretary of the treasury, and the U.S. ambassador to the United Nations. The duties of the NSC were spelled out in the 1947 law:

> The function of the Council shall be to advise the President with respect to the integration of domestic, foreign, and military policies relating to the national security so as to enable the military services and the other departments and agencies of the Government to cooperate more effectively in matters involving the national security. (Tower, p. 7)

From the start the NSC had a small staff with President Eisenhower creating the position in 1953 that has come to be known as the National Security adviser. This NSC adviser and staff, in the words of the Tower Commission, are supposed to provide "advice from the President's vantage point unalloyed by institutional responsibilities and biases. Unlike the Secretaries of State or Defense, who have substantial organizations for which they are responsible, the President is the National Security Advisor's only constituency" (Tower, p. 10).

The NSC staff was intended to be the president's eyes and ears, assuring that he really knew what his own foreign policy agencies were doing, that he made the key decisions, and that these were actually carried out. This personal staff to the president exists to help him coordinate the diplomatic, economic, and security aspects of foreign policy. And it was also intended to help the president assess the domestic political aspects of foreign policy. Were certain foreign policy initiatives feasible and supportable in the domestic political arena? How might the president increase domestic support for foreign policy decisions required in the national interest?

For many in the Congress of 1947, history would suggest that the most likely risk resulting from these new foreign policy institutions to the authority of any president is posed by the standing armed forces—either unauthorized action abroad or coercion of the president at home. To avoid this, there has been a strict tradition of civilian control, both at the Department of Defense and through the independent ability of the president to monitor the actions of the military through reports of other agencies, the press, and, his NSC staff.

Would a president have this assurance of control over the military if at the Department of Defense thirty-eight of forty top policy jobs were held by on-duty career military officers—and if, at the same time, his senior NSC staff for all regions of the world were career military officers? It is interesting to note that in the spring of 1986, career foreign service officers held about thirty-eight of forty presidentially appointed *policy* jobs at State and occupied most of the senior NSC policy jobs. (Career military personnel occupied most other top NSC staff positions.)

A second obvious concern in 1947 was that a secret intelligence organization could manipulate events abroad (or at home) to acquire ever-increasing control over foreign policy. Any president needed the help of his NSC staff to oversee this huge bureaucratic complex as well. In the 1970s Congress decided it needed a more formal intelligence oversight process, and this has been implemented.

In 1947 the diplomatic service, the long-established and traditional foreign policy institution possessing neither weapons nor secret agents, had not been widely seen to constitute an institution that could or would usurp the authority of the president. Yet today it is the Department of State through the presidentially appointed ambassadors who report to the secretary of state that actually has day-to-day *management control* of the diplomatic, military, intelligence, and other U.S. personnel serving in about 150 U.S. embassies abroad. On average, 70 percent of U.S. ambassadors are career foreign service officers. And the remaining politically appointed ambassadors serve abroad surrounded by foreign service officers who considerably shape what they read, whom they meet with, and how they perceive events. A politically appointed ambassador is lucky to pick his personal secretary and, under Shultz's management, must pick his deputy from among foreign service officers offered to him by the State Department. Although the military and intelligence personnel serving abroad can and do report to their own agencies, the ambassador can usually monitor all their written reports. And it is rare for anyone to challenge the ambassador's viewpoints on major issues.

The real institutional surprise of the postwar era is illustrated by my experience in the Reagan administration—that in foreign policy it is elements within the State Department that most often have decided to ignore, undermine, challenge, and countermand the president. During the Reagan administration, with rare exception—among which must be included the unauthorized actions of North and Poindexter—it has not been the military or intelligence organizations that have conducted their own foreign policy. Instead this has been done—almost as an accepted matter of professional conduct (with apparently no thought to the threat this poses to the integrity of our institutions)—by some key officials of the State Department, whenever they decided they knew the national interest better than the temporary occupant of the presidency.

Had I known about any military or intelligence operation contrary to the policies and orders of President Reagan—even if I personally agreed with the intended purposes—I would have been just as energetic and persistent in bringing these before the president—in a full NSC meeting if possible, but to the president in any case. My guess is that the reason North and Poindexter made sure that I did not catch a whiff of the unauthorized contra supply operation is that they feared I would insist a large issue like this be brought to the president in an NSC meeting for his decision.

There was an enormous uproar about the unauthorized decision by Poindexter and North—but their actions were pointed in the direction of the president's policy intentions. One can picture the scandal if it came to light that with this knowledge and involvement of their top officials, our military and intelligence services had been conducting the sort of rogue foreign policy I have just described hypothetically. Part of the scandal would lie in the risks such operations posed to our national interests. But even more shocking would be the sheer arrogant impropriety of govern-ment institutions that were disobeying the president.

But while allegations of even minor rogue actions by the CIA and solitary military men are the stuff of newspaper exposé and popular books, the State Department's subtler and quieter manipulations have received little notice in recent years. They do not shock us. But they should.

Somehow, for an activist minority of public officials over too many years, making and implementing foreign policy has become a contest of competing ambitions, marked by vanity and personalities, where decep-tion and manipulation are acceptable methods. For too many of the men in the foreign policy process, their oaths of obedience to the president seem to have become mere empty formalities. One-upmanship has become a way of life; a kind of tradition of deception has come into being. The participants not only want to win, but also, as a sort of added refinement, to win while "putting one over" on their colleagues and superiors, as if it were all part of a huge sport.

But it is no game. The stakes in foreign policy are too high for millions, even billions, of human beings—an elementary fact that can get completely forgotten in the preoccupations of executive branch infighting. Imagine if a team of doctors were to carry their personal rivalries and professional competition into the operating room. What if the surgeon doing the triple bypass noticed that the anesthesiologist was inadvertently allowing the patient's blood level to fall dangerously low—but refrained from saying anything because he wanted him to "look bad?" The "patients" in foreign policy are the countries of the free world, and far too many have been needlessly lost through incompetence.

Yet the actions of the dominant faction in the State Department that I observed, year after year, constituted the substitution of their own foreign policy for that of President Reagan. And the principal defenses for any president against either this kind of insubordination are the foreign policy cabinet, the vice president, *and* the NSC adviser and his staff.

One of the ways of gauging a president's power, and his place in history, is to rate his ability to achieve intended results, as opposed to simply his nominal authority over the executive branch. Nearly half a century ago President Franklin D. Roosevelt said: "The Treasury is so large . . . and ingrained in its practices that I find it impossible to get the actions and results I want . . . but the Treasury is not to be compared with the State Department. You should go through the experience of trying to get any changes in the thinking, policy, and action of the career diplomats, and then you'd know what a real problem was."

And at the beginning of this book I quoted President Harry Truman's scathing criticism of "foreign service officers," "admirals," and "civil servants" who tried to take charge of foreign policy rather than carry out his decisions.

More recently, after he'd been Richard Nixon's national security adviser for several years, Henry Kissinger said:

> The outsider believes a Presidential order is consistently followed out. Nonsense. I have to spend considerable time seeing that it is carried out, and in the spirit the President intended. Inevitably, in the nature of bureaucracy, departments become pressure groups for a point of view. If the President decides against them, they are convinced some evil influence worked on the President: if only he knew all the facts, he would have decided their way.

In the future as in the past, major decisions about foreign policy will usually involve conflicts among the president's key advisers. This is inevitable, because of different judgments about the likely effects of decisions, because there is usually limited information and much uncertainty about the actions of foreign governments, and because of differences in temperament, life experience, and institutional tendencies among any president's top advisers.

Conflict of this type is neither good nor bad, it is simply a fact of life. Every new president should expect this, realizing that only his decisions will resolve such disputes. The question for future presidents and for the citizens of America is: Will the foreign policy decision-making process be fair and collegial, giving each member of the foreign policy cabinet a chance to make his case to the president and hear that made by his colleagues? Or will it be a process that becomes ever more devious and manipulative? Then, once the president has made a decision, will it be carried out in good faith by the career agencies—including the Department of State?

I believe that common sense and the record of the post-World War II years strongly suggest that the answers to these questions depend on a combination of the personality of the president, the caliber of the people he chooses, *and* the extent to which the NSC staff works in an honest and forthright way to assure that he governs in foreign policy. President Reagan's personality favored free and open discussion. He was comfortable leading and participating in highly intense NSC debates. His sense of humor and even temperament set a good example by not letting the intensity of any debate or differences in judgment about policy become a cause for personal hostility and alienation. It also seemed to me that Casey, Kirkpatrick, Weinberger, and Clark were able to distinguish between disagreeing and becoming disagreeable. In my experience, neither McFarlane, Poindexter, nor Shultz was able to do this. Shultz clearly was not, as demonstrated by his angry and petty behavior toward some cabinet colleagues and even White House staff members such as some of the president's speech writers and myself.

With William P. Clark as national security adviser (January 1982 to October 1983), the foreign policy system worked reasonably well. And I am convinced that had Clark remained as NSC adviser, the conduct of Shultz, McFarlane, and Poindexter would never have become a continuing problem for administration foreign policy. McFarlane and Poindexter gradually but steadily moved away from correctly carrying out their responsibilities to the president. That was a major theme in my letter of August 1985, but the president only discovered it after the Iran/Nicaraguan scandal became public in late 1986.

A false dichotomy has been established in much of the discussion of foreign policy-making between a "State Department–dominated" or an "NSC-dominated" system. Neither approach is correct: this is *not* the inevitable choice facing a president, whom the Constitution and the people hold responsible for the conduct of foreign policy.

The practical realities of the foreign policy challenges American presidents face *require* that the diplomatic, economic, military, and intelligence institutions of the United States work toward the same purposes abroad. This necessitates that the president be in direct charge and that virtually all major issues be explored and discussed in a setting at *both* the *subcabinet* and *cabinet* level, where officials can bring their agencies' information, skills, and perspectives to be shared and debated. This is not an idealistic vision, but a practical imperative.

Every president must find a way to make the inevitable conflict among his advisers a constructive opportunity to produce a fair, open, and candid debate with full information so that he can make the best-possible decision. Given the imperfections of human nature, every president will face some degree of special pleading and manipulation as advisers try to push him in their preferred direction. And most of the difficult, hard-fought foreign policy decisions are taken in secret. So any president is heavily dependent for the real exercise of his authority on a decision-making process that is generally fair and honest.

There are four types of challenges that every president will face. Here's a scorecard for the way they were handled from 1983 to 1986.

Type one. Sudden foreign event, containing both risk and opportunity, but will the United States act? Example: Grenada, 1983.

Grenada was an illustration of the NSC system working just the way it should work. The internal communist coup created a risk and an opportunity; proposals flowed from the subcabinet, were debated, and then referred up to the NSC members and the president. The debate that followed was open and honest, and all the relevant cabinet members got a chance to participate, and, for once, absolute secrecy prevailed. Aware that speed was essential, the president acted decisively. The operation was a success: all the U.S. citizens were rescued, and a communist dictatorship was succeeded by a constitutional democracy.

Type two. The president has a stated policy, but part of the bureaucracy is going against it. Example: Central America, 1984–86.

Initially, McFarlane made the right move in acting to prevent the State Department's unauthorized, unilateral initiatives of December 1983, but then, apparently intimidated by Shultz's power, McFarlane refused to press the idea of the subcabinet interagency groups performing their proper function. Under pressure he agreed, but only reluctantly, to hold an NSC meeting so the president could review—and reject—State's secret initiatives of June and July 1984. Then, in October of that same year, McFarlane and Poindexter joined forces with Shultz, in a *major* effort to bring about a treaty that was contrary to the president's decision. McFarlane refused to call an NSC meeting, and only the timely intercession of Casey, Weinberger, and Kirkpatrick—who managed to get the president's ear—stopped the State Department's pressure campaign to have the false treaty signed. I believe that by his actions McFarlane had completely abdicated the NSC adviser's most important function, assuring that the president makes the major decisions.

Type three. The administration has a set policy, but some elements, as the result of new circumstances, want the president to consider changing it. Example: Angola, 1985.

When Congress repealed the Clark amendment in the summer of 1985, Republican senators told the president and wrote Shultz to suggest that this was an excellent opportunity to initiate a new, pro-Western strategy. As NSC adviser, McFarlane should have been willing to present this issue to the president in an NSC meeting, but once again, rather than challenge Shultz, McFarlane did nothing. It took Bill Casey to get an NSC meeting with the president on the issue, and the result was a change in the U.S. policy.

Type four. A serious, continuing threat that occasionally flares up into a crisis, which the bureaucracies tend to handle reactively, requires strategic planning for cooperative preventive actions by all foreign policy agencies. Example: Counterstrategy against subversive aggression and terrorism.

This is an almost classic example of the kind of international threat that caused Congress to establish the NSC in 1947, because it is one that requires the systematic, secret coordination of diplomatic, economic, intelligence, and military resources in order to accomplish strategic objectives. Nonetheless, neither McFarlane nor Poindexter ever seemed to give the whole problem serious attention. They dealt with parts of the problem in a piecemeal fashion by pushing the agencies to take defensive measures such as improving security at our installations abroad and producing better intelligence; but time and time again they reacted to each new terrorist episode as it hit, with no systematic effort to try and prevent it—or the next one—by helping friendly countries act to reduce violence from these terrorist groups.

What is to be learned from these cases and from the Iran-contra matter? Let me quote a person who is not only a foreign policy scholar, but who also had four years of top-level experience in the Reagan administration, Ambassador Jeane Kirkpatrick.

The lesson for this and future presidents surely is the importance of formal decision-making. Such a process ensures that the essential questions have been clearly stated, that the president has heard the views of his principal advisers, and that there is a written record of his decisions to guide subordinates. While it cannot protect the president against bad advice or mistaken judgments, a formalized process can guard him against hasty decisions, inadequately defined options, and against misunderstandings about what has and has not been authorized.

The national security council adviser and his staff have the *duty* to see to it that he governs in foreign policy and that he does so with full and timely information. Neither in theory nor in practice is it right for the Department of State to fill this role. It is an operating agency, and its job is to implement the president's decisions, not to make those decisions for him. What's more, as part of the way our system works, State will inevitably and naturally have disagreements over policy with other government agencies—especially with the Department of Defense on arms control issues—and the president has to be aware of this "partisanship" when he studies the State Department's position and its relationship to that of other elements of the executive branch.

All of this means that the function of the NSC is *vital*. Without an honest and independent NSC adviser, future presidents could lose much of their constitutional authority in foreign policy. The American voters, who elect the president, do not intend to give that power to the permanent bureaucracy. They want the president to have it and to exercise it. And they are right.

The substance of foreign policy, vital though it is, is not the only thing at stake. If we are to be a democracy in the true sense, it is imperative that future presidents be fully in command of foreign policy. The job cannot be usurped by a McFarlane, a Poindexter, a North: by now all agree on that. But it must not be usurped, either, by a George Shultz. If on some issues he really does know better than the president, it is up to him to *persuade* the president.

The president of the United States bears the most awesome responsibilities in the world. It is hard enough to reconcile the duty of preserving freedom and peace for billions of people with the petty rivalries of office politics, too. We must end the pervasive attitude that deception and manipulation—even of the president himself—are just "part of the process."

The National Security Council and its staff was created to prevent precisely the kind of rogue operations that have harmed the Reagan presidency. Those operations erupted into public view with the Iran-contra scandal. But in other, subtler forms, they had been going on for years, as I have described them in this book. It is bad enough that some tried to sidestep the NSC process; worse was that a few in the NSC staff itself became participants in intrigues that violated their very *raison d'être*.

The Reagan administration has paid a heavy price. The nation may yet pay a heavier one unless there is a new ethical commitment by the leaders and institutions involved with foreign policy to work fairly and assure the authority of the president.

The world is too dangerous, the risks to our freedom too great, for some elements of the U.S. government to systematically undermine the president and pursue their own policy goals—as I saw the Department of State do for five years. When the people of the United States vote and elect their president, they have the right to expect that he will actually govern—not preside—and have real power to determine U.S. foreign policy, in cooperation with a Congress exercising its constitutional responsibilities. The American people do not want to give up this authority to unelected and unseen elements of the foreign policy bureaucracy.

You might ask, If most career employees working on foreign policy try to do a good job, why does a president need to bring in his own first- and second-echelon policy officials? The answer is simple. Career government employees have a wide range of political views, although the Department of State tends to be predominantly liberal Democratic and the career military predominantly conservative. The effect of a president failing to bring in his own policy team is to transpose the decision of the American people into a series of conflicts among factions within the bureaucracy that also have competing political views and institutional interests. A politically appointed subcabinet in foreign policy can have the legitimacy and shared values to bring a reasonable level of harmony into the inevitable competition among the foreign policy bureaucracies. But, as we saw in the Reagan administration, when foreign service officers fill most or all of the presidentially appointed key policy jobs in the Department of State and the NSC, and when most of the subcabinet are career officials, the tendency is for the Department of State to dominate and enforce its foreign policy views.

Future presidents, whether they are Republicans or Democrats, will really govern in foreign policy and master the perennial institutional challenges to their authority only if they have an independent, competent NSC staff and only if they bring into the top presidentially appointed foreign policy positions about three hundred individuals who are honest and competent in their fields and who want to see their president succeed. In this country of more than 240 million people, both major political parties have the reservoirs of talented men and women who can be brought in by a new president to serve in those comparatively few politically appointed policy-level jobs that Congress has provided to help the president govern in foreign policy.

If President Reagan had done this, I believe that many of the destructive battles inside the executive branch would have been avoided, and there would have been much more progress in expanding freedom, assuring our security, and reducing the risks of war. I hope that my fellow citizens who have read these true stories of life inside the NSC will urge future presidents to bring in good people and assure a fair decision-making process—our future freedom and peace depend on the competence of our nation's foreign policy.

BIBLIOGRAPHY

I. *Selected Writings by Constantine C. Menges*

BOOKS, CHAPTERS, AND MONOGRAPHS:

"Castro: Nearly Thirty Years of Revolutionary Warfare," in *Cuba: The International Dimension.* Washington, D.C.: Center for Strategic and International Studies, 1988.

"The Record of the United States and the Soviet Union in Post–World War II International Politics," in William R. Kinter, ed., *Arms Control: The American Dilemma.* Washington, D.C.: The Washington Institute, 1987.

"The Foreign Policy of Mexico," in *The Future of Mexico.* New York: The Hudson Institute, 1981.

"Central American Revolutions: A New Dimension of Political Warfare," in *The 1980s: Decade of Confrontation?* Washington D.C.: National Defense University, 1981.

"The United States and Latin America in the 1980s," in Prosser Gifford, ed., *The National Interests of the United States in Foreign Policy.* Washington, D.C.: Woodrow Wilson International Center for Scholars, December 1980/February 1981.

Spain: The Struggle for Democracy Today. Beverly Hills and London: Stage Press, 1978.

Politics and Agrarian Reform Bureaucracies in Chile. Santa Monica, California: RAND paper, 1968.

Chile's Landowners Association and Agrarian Reform Politics. Santa Monica, California: RAND paper, 1968.

The Central Bank of Colombia as a Political Institution, 1968.

Between the Public and Private Sector in Colombia, 1968.

Military Aspects of International Relations in the Developing Areas. Santa Monica, California: RAND paper, 1966.

"A Free Press in a Democratic State?" With Otto Kirchheimer, in A. Weston, ed., *Politics in Europe.* New York: Harcourt Brace, 1965.

401

ARTICLES:

"The Arias Plan: The Evidence Is In." *National Review,* April 15, 1988.

"The Afghan Trap." *National Review,* April 1, 1988.

"Mexico Hanging in the Balance." *Washington Times,* March 9, 1988.

"How Democracies Keep Secrets." *Public Opinion,* January/February 1988.

"Where We Succeeded, Where We Failed: Lessons from Reagan Officials for
      the Next Conservative Presidency." *Policy Review,* No. 43 (Winter
      1988), pp. 51–53.

"What Next on Arias?" *Washington Times,* November 9, 1987.

"Central America's Future: Communism or Democracy?" *Global Affairs,*
      Summer 1987.

"Detente's Dark History." *Wall Street Journal,* January 9, 1987.

"The President and the NSC." *Wall Street Journal,* December 2, 1986.

"Mexican Actions in Central America: Time for a Positive Change." Washing-
      ton, D.C.: Fund for an American Renaissance, August 1986.

"The Wall 25 Years Later: Troops, Tanks, and Barbed Wire. *Washington
      Times,* August 13, 1986.

"South Africa: Encouraging a Peaceful Transition to Multi-Racial, Democracy."
      Washington Post, July 20, 1986.

Commentary on "The Alternative Futures of Latin America." *AEI Foreign
      Policy and Defense Review,* Vol. 5, No. 3, Winter 1985.

"With Adequate Aid, Democracy Is Possible." *USA Today,* January 9, 1984.

"Central America and its Enemies." *Commentary,* August 1981.

"Mexico's Central America Strategy." *Christian Science Monitor,* July 13,
      1981.

"Central America and the United States." *School of Advanced International
      Studies Review,* Summer 1981.

"Nicaragua: An Army to Dwarf Central America." *Washington Star,* May 22,
      1981.

"European Allies' Latin Connection." *Miami Herald,* March 2, 1981.

"Coping with Radical Destabilization in the Middle East and Central America/
      Mexico: Trends, Causes, and Alternatives." *Conflict,* Vol. 3, No. 1,
      1981.

"Ideologies Battle for El Salvador." *San Diego Union,* June 29, 1980.

"Radicalism Abroad." *New York Times,* June 11, 1980.

"Iran: The Turning Point." *New Republic,* December 15, 1979.

"Bridges to Democracy in Chile." *Worldview,* December 1979.

"Spying: The Invisible War. Soviet Union and United States Make Widespread
      Use of Advanced Technology." *Los Angeles Times,* September 21,
      1979.

"Mexico: The Iran Next Door?" *San Diego Union,* August 5, 1979.

"Time to Support Genuine Democracy in Nicaragua." *San Diego Union,* July
      29, 1979.

"SALT II—It Neither Cuts nor Controls Weapons, so the U.S. Must Develop an Anti-Missile System." *Los Angeles Times*, July 10, 1979.

"Democracy for Latins." *New York Times*, June 29, 1979.

"Echoes of Cuba in Nicaragua." *Chicago Tribune*, June 29, 1979.

"Remembering the Resistance in Czechoslovakia—1968." *Worldview*, December 1978.

"The Political Use of Soviet Strategic Power." *San Diego Union*, October 29, 1978.

"SALT II: Truth or Consequences." *New Leader*, September 25, 1978.

"Stopping a Soviet Oil Takeover." *Christian Science Monitor*, August 14, 1978.

"Sharing the Democratic Experience with Spain." *Christian Science Monitor*, February 27, 1978.

"Resistance in Czechoslovakia: An Underground in the Open." *Trans-Action*, December 1968.

"Public Policy and Organized Business in Chile." *Journal of International Affairs*, Vol. XX, No. 2, June 1966.

II. *U.S. Government Reports on the Iran-Contra Issue*

The Tower Commission Report: The Full Text of the President's Special Review Board. New York: Random House, 1987.

U.S. House of Representatives, Select Committee to Investigate Covert Arms Transactions with Iran, and U.S. Senate, Select Committee on Secret Military Assistance to Iran and the Nicaraguan Opposition, 100th Congress, 1st Sess., *Report of the Congressional Committees Investigating the Iran-Contra Affair.* House Report No. 100-433; Senate Report No. 100-216. Washington: U.S. Government Printing Office, 1987.

III. *Selected U.S. Government Reports on Central America*

"Nicaraguan Biographies: A Resource Book." U.S. Department of State, Special Report No. 174, January 1988.

National Security Strategy of the United States. The White House, January 1988.

"The Soviet Space Challenge." U.S. Department of Defense, November 1987.

"The Sandinista Military Build-up: An Update." U.S. Department of State and U.S. Department of Defense, October 1987.

"Nicragua's Interior Ministry: Instrument of Political Consolidation." U.S. Department of State, August 1987.

"What Latin American Leaders Say About the Situation in Central America." U.S. Department of State, Publication 9526, March 1987.

"Libyan Activities in the Western Hemisphere." U.S. Department of State, August 1986.

"Sandinista Prisons: A Tool of Intimidation." U.S. Department of State, Publication 9492, August 1986.

"The Challenge to Democracy in Central America." U.S. Department of State and U.S. Department of Defense, June 1986.

"Prospects for the Containment of Nicaragua's Communist Government." U.S. Department of Defense, May 1986.

"In Their Own Words: Testimony of Nicaraguan Exiles." U.S. Department of State, March 1986.

"Inside the Sandinista Regime: A Special Investigator's Perspective." U.S. Department of State, February 1986.

"Lessons of Grenada." U.S. Department of State, February 1986.

" 'The 72-Hour Document': The Sandinista Blueprint for Constructing Communism in Nicaragua." U.S. Department of State, February 1986.

"Revolution Beyond Our Borders: Sandinista Intervention in Central America." U.S. Department of State, Special Report 132, September 1985.

"The Sandinistas and Middle Eastern Radicals." U.S. Department of State, August 1985.

"The Sandinista Military Build-up." U.S. Department of State and U.S. Department of Defense. Department of State Publication 9432, Inter-American Series 119, May 1985.

"The Soviet-Cuban Connection in Central America and the Caribbean." U.S. Department of State and U.S. Department of Defense, March 1985.

"Democracy in Latin America and the Caribbean." U.S. Department of State, Current Policy No. 605, August 1984.

"Background Paper: Nicaragua's Military Buildup and Support for Central American Subversion." U.S. Department of State and U.S. Department of Defense, July 18, 1984.

"Nicraguan Repression of Labor Unions." White House Digest, August 24, 1983.

"The PLO in Central America," White House Digest, July 24, 1983.

"Soviet/Cuban Threat and Buildup in the Caribbean," White House Digest, July 6, 1983.

"Background Paper: Central America." U.S. Department of State and U.S. Department of Defense, May 27, 1983.

"Cuba's Renewed Support for Violence in Latin America." U.S. Department of State, Special Report No. 90, December 14, 1981.

"Communist Interference in El Salvador." U.S. Department of State, Special Report No. 80, February 23, 1981.

INDEX

ABC, 76, 312
Abrams, Elliott, 281, 320
  Arias plan and, 324
  contra aid and, 278, 283–85, 287–89
  Iran-contra affair and, 342–43
  Menges's suggestions to, 278–80
  nomination of, 211–13
  North and, 357
Achille Lauro hijacking, 195, 266, 270, 336
"Actions to Win the Freedom Fighter
  Vote" (Menges), 290–91
Afghanistan, 42, 81
  communist coup in, 25–26
  Soviet withdrawal from, 16–17, 334
  U.S. aid to resistance in, 333–34, 383
AFL–CIO, 45–46, 65, 81, 87, 99
Allen, Richard, 43, 46, 49, 255, 338
Allende, Salvador, 35, 84
Alvor Agreement, 232
Amber in the Amberdines, Operation, 64
American Bar Association, 222, 265
American Enterprise Institute (AEI), 16,
  311, 379
American Institute for Free Labor Devel-
  opment, 65
Ames, Robert, 257
Angola, 75, 81, 231–42, 245, 338, 383
  ban on covert aid to, 231–32, 234,
    235–38, 248, 397
  pro-Western strategy for, 237–41
  Shultz and, 237, 239, 241–42, 245,
    374, 397
  U.S. aid to, 236, 239, 241–42, 248–49,
    332
Anti-Ballistic Missile (ABM) treaty, 246,
  337, 373
Aquino, Benigno, 261
Aquino, Corazon, 292
Ardito Barletta, Nicholas, 152
Argentina, 111–12
  British conflict with, 199
Arias Sanchez, Oscar, 294, 300
  Central American peace plan of, 311,
    319–30, 374, 389

Armacost, Michael, 26, 260–61, 292, 303,
  320, 375
"Arms Control in Latin America"
  (Menges), 33
Arms Export Control Act, 354

Baker, Howard, 83, 387–88
  Arias plan and, 319, 324, 326
Baker, James, 51, 61–62, 71, 95, 182,
  185, 198, 201, 338, 346
  Central American policy and, 116, 155–
    156
  contra aid and, 120–21, 207, 351
Baldrige, Malcolm, 119–20
Barnes, Michael, 206, 284, 295
Bay of Pigs invasion, 218
Belize, 199
Belnick, Mark, 19–20, 388–89
Berlin blockade, 30
Betancur Cuartas, Belisario, 134, 138–39,
  204
Bish, Milan, 65, 76
Bishop, Maurice, 58–60, 65–67, 85
Blackwell, Morton, 268
Boehm, Ken, 315
Boland amendments, 209, 278, 332, 341–
  342, 352, 356
Bolivia, 131, 138–39
Borchgrave, Alexandra de, 316
Borchgrave, Arnaud de, 316, 322, 324
Bosworth, Steven, 107
Bouterse, Desi, 65–66
"Box Called Contadora, A" (Evans and
  Novak), 301
Brzezinski, Zbigniew, 31, 37, 207
  Salvadoran policy and, 43, 45
Buchanan, Pat, 207, 267, 291, 359
Burghardt, Raymond, 213, 219
  Central American policy and, 122–124,
    141, 158, 160, 175, 192, 217, 300
  contra aid and, 200, 203, 205, 282–83,
    285–86, 294–95
Burton, Dan, 241, 295–96, 298
Burton amendment, 333